THE GUINNESS BOOK OF RUGBY FACTS & FEATS

THE GUINNESS BOOK OF
RUGBY
FACTS & FEATS

GUINNESS SUPERLATIVES LIMITED
2 CECIL COURT, LONDON ROAD, ENFIELD, MIDDLESEX

ACKNOWLEDGMENTS

The production of this second edition of *The Guinness Book of Rugby Facts and Feats* would not have been possible without the continued assistance of many correspondents throughout the world, most of whom realise the value of the book to followers of the game in every country in the world. I offer all my profound thanks not only for information already submitted but for any additional material which would prove useful in further editions.

TERRY GODWIN

Title page illustration **Ireland v France 1983—the forwards battle for possession at a maul. Ireland won the match 22–16 (Geo. Herringshaw).**

Editor Alex E Reid
Design and layout David Roberts and Eddie Botchway

Published in Great Britain by
Guinness Superlatives Ltd,
2 Cecil Court, London Road,
Enfield, Middlesex EN2 6DJ.

British Library Cataloguing in Publication Data

Godwin, Terry
The Guinness book of rugby facts and feats.—
2nd ed.
1. Rugby football—History
I. Title
796.33'3'09 GV944.85

ISBN 0-85112-264-7

Colour separation by Technik Litho Plates Ltd, Chesham, Bucks.

Typeset by Fakenham Photosetting Ltd, Fakenham, Norfolk.

Printed and bound in Great Britain by Butler & Tanner Ltd, Frome, Somerset.

CONTENTS

Introduction	**7**
The International Board Countries	**9**
Cyril Lowe—Boy's Own Hero	**84**
Rugby Around The World	**104**
Did You Know?	**186**
World Records	**209**
John Burgum—Referee For All Seasons	**215**
Tours, Lions, Barbarians	**216**
Rhymney RFC	**228**
Milestones—A Chronology of World Rugby	**236**
Index	**245**

INTRODUCTION

Since the publication of the first edition of *The Guinness Book of Rugby Facts and Feats* in 1981, the game of rugby football has continued to expand world-wide. There are now over 120 countries playing the game, and although there have been casualties, notably the disbandment of Malta, rugby arguably now is in the world's top four of organised sports, in company with football, basketball and athletics. Put another way, rugby football is now indisputably the world's No. 1 totally amateur sport.

The development of the game naturally has been of particular interest to rugby's governing body, the International Board. It was their commendable intention to stage a World Congress in London in 1984, when all rugby-playing countries were to have been represented. Unfortunately, that plan has had to be postponed until 1985 or 1986, by which time the Board will be better prepared for the project, largely because by then they hope to have established a permanent Secretariat at Twickenham. Of course, it is the Board's aim to confirm itself as the governing body, the law makers and so on: at the same time they recognise that their role inevitably has to change now that the game has become so large. A more professional administrative set-up is only part of the transformation envisaged.

Clearly, all this is an enormous challenge for the members of the International Board, and developments will be keenly awaited throughout the world. From a personal point of view, it was an enormous pleasure to be able to assist the Board in their request for detailed information about the spread of the game. I shall be similarly gratified to assist any country in passing on information to the Board in the process of updating statistics, particularly those with regard to the number of players and clubs.

A mere glance through the following pages will confirm to many that much in the game has already changed, records have gone and new stamping-grounds have been established by small and large rugby playing countries. The arrival of a professional rugby tournament has caused much interest and concern—and there have been other causes for concern, major and minor, for many countries. In 1983, however, the game had its saddest moments in the deaths of three of the game's most outstanding personalities—Cyril Lowe, Carwyn James and Wavell Wakefield. It would be hard to imagine a trio who have done more for the game or have contributed so effectively off and on the field. I have given Cyril Lowe's career appropriate space within these pages; for Carwyn James, a personal friend and advisor, and for Lord Wakefield, one can only add that rugby football was the better for their contributions and the worse for their passing.

TERRY GODWIN
Penrhiw, Dihewyd, Dyfed, Wales
1 September 1983

THE INTERNATIONAL BOARD COUNTRIES

AUSTRALIA

Foundation	1949
Headquarters	Rugby Union House, Crane Place, Sydney N.S.W. 27777
Main stadium	Sydney Cricket Ground (capacity 49 000)
Colours	Gold and green jerseys
Number of clubs	250
Number of players	10 000
Season	April–November
Temperatures	45° F (7° C) to 65° F (18° C)—Sydney
Population	14 248 600

Oldest club
Sydney University, formed 1864

Sydney Premiership
1981 Randwick 1982 Randwick

Brisbane Grand Final
1981 Brothers 1982 Brothers

Inter-state
1980 Queensland 24 NSW 7
1981 Queensland 26 NSW 15, NSW 7 Queensland 6
1982 Queensland 23 NSW 16

Bledisloe Cup results (since 1931)
Australia won 12, New Zealand 39, drawn 3

State Championship
1980 Final: Queensland 24 NSW 7

Centenary Match
1982 Queensland 41 NSW 7

Representative Matches
Queensland 15 NSW 10, Queensland 17 Canterbury 12, NSW 20 Counties 12, Taranaki 10 NSW 9

Tour statistics

Most points on tour
500 British Isles/France 1947–8

Individual
154 Paul McLean, British Isles 1975–6

Most tries
23 C J Russell, British Isles 1908–9

Most tour tries
115 British Isles, France (35 matches) 1947–8

Most points in any tour match
23 John Hindmarsh v Glamorgan, Neath 1975

Most tries in a tour match
6 Jim Boyce v Wairarapa, Masterton 1962

Individual points
28 Phil Hawthorne, British Isles/France, 1966–7

Most tries in an international
4 G Cornelsen, v New Zealand, 1978

Most points in an international
21 Paul McLean, Australia v Scotland, 1982 (3 conversions, 5 penalties)

Leading cap winners
39 Peter Johnson, Greg Davis
37 John Thornett
32 John Hipwell

Paul McLean, Australia's record holder with 162 points in 22 internationals against International Board countries 1974–82. McLean scored 257 points in all international matches. (Geo. Herringshaw.)

Most capped players by position

Full Back	19	Arthur McGill (NSW) 1968–72
Wing	22	John Cole (NSW) 1968–74
Centre	21	Geoff Shaw (NSW) 1969–79
Fly half	21	Phil Hawthorne (NSW) 1962–67
Scrum half	34	John Hipwell (NSW) 1968–78
Prop	24	Bob Prosser (NSW) 1967–72
Hooker	39	Peter Johnson (NSW) 1959–71
Lock	20	Garrick Fay (NSW) 1971–79
Flanker	39	Greg Davis (NSW) 1963–72
No. 8	20	Mark Loane (Queensland) 1973–81

Crowd

48 698 Australia's biggest ever Test attendance, v New Zealand, Sydney, 1980

Most tries in an international

6 v Scotland, Sydney 1970 (23–3)

Most points in internationals

163 P E McLean 1974–82 (21 appearances)

Most tries conceded

8 v South Africa, Johannesburg 1961 (3–28)

Most tries in internationals

17 Colin Windon 1946–52 (15 appearances, but not including 5 matches against Fiji and Maoris)

Hong Kong Sevens

1983 W 42–0 Japan, W 44–0 Indonesia, W 38–0 Malaysia, W 26–0 Solomon Islands, W 12–6 Tonga, W 16–0 Western Samoa. *Final*: W 14–4 Fiji.

Non-international defeats in Australia

AUSTRALIAN CAPITAL TERRITORY		
Beat Wales	21–20	1978
NEW SOUTH WALES		
Beat New Zealand	25–3	1893
Beat New Zealand	27–8	1897
Beat New Zealand	14–0	1907
Beat British Isles	6–3	1908
Beat New Zealand	14–8	1922
Beat New Zealand	8–6	1922
Beat New Zealand	18–16	1924
Beat New Zealand	26–20	1926
Beat British Isles	28–3	1930
Beat South Africa	17–6	1937
Beat New Zealand	12–9	1938
Beat British Lions	17–12	1950
Beat British Lions	18–14	1959
Beat South Africa	12–3	1965
Beat Ireland	21–9	1967
Beat Scotland	28–14	1970
Beat New Zealand	9–3	1980
NEW SOUTH WALES COUNTRY		
Beat England	14–13	1975
QUEENSLAND		
Beat British Isles	11–3	1899
Beat Scotland	16–13	1970
Beat British Lions	15–11	1971
Beat New Zealand	9–3	1980
Beat Scotland	18–7	1982
SYDNEY		
Beat British Isles	8–5	1899
Beat Ireland	30–8	1967
Beat England	14–10	1975
Beat Wales	18–16	1978
Beat Ireland	16–12	1979
Beat France	16–14	1981
Beat Scotland	22–13	1982
WESTERN DISTRICTS		
Beat British Isles	15–10	1908

Mark Loane, Australia's most capped No. 8, who made 20 appearances between 1973–81. (Geo. Herringshaw.)

Trans-Tasman Cup
1981 New South Wales 30 Auckland 17

1982 Tour to New Zealand

W 16–15	Taranaki	New Plymouth
W 26–10	Manawatu	Palmerston North
W 13–12	Hawke's Bay	Napier
W 21–0	Southland	Invercargill
W 29–22	South Canterbury	Timaru
L 16–23	New Zealand	Christchurch
W 65–10	Buller	Westport
W 29–12	Otago	Dunedin
W 19–16	New Zealand	Wellington
W 23–3	Waikato	Hamilton
L 16–40	Bay of Plenty	Rotorua
L 9–15	Counties	Pukekohe
L 16–12	North Auckland	Whangarei
L 18–33	New Zealand	Auckland

Tour summary:
P 14 W 10 L 4 F 316 A 223

Incoming Tour 1982
Scotland
Queensland Country
W 44–16
Queensland
L 7–18
Sydney
L 13–22
Victoria
W 38–3
NSW
W 31–7
NSW Country
W 44–3
Australia
W 12–7
Australian Capital
Terr.
W 22–4
Australia
L 9–33

Greg Cornelsen, who became Australian holder of the record most tries in an international when he scored four against New Zealand in Auckland in 1978. (Geo. Herringshaw.)

International statistics

Opposition	*Highest score*	*Winning points margin*	*Most points conceded*	*Biggest points margin defeat*
England	30 (30–21) 1975	12 (23–11) 1967	23 (6–23) 1976	17 (3–20) 1973 (6–23) 1976
Scotland	33 (33–9) 1982	24 (33–9) 1982	24 (15–24) 1981	9 (15–24) 1981
Ireland	20 (20–10) 1976	13 (16–3) 1947	27 (12–27) 1979	15 (12–27) 1979
Wales	19 (19–17) 1978	10 (18–8) 1978	28 (3–28) 1975	25 (3–28) 1975
France	24 (24–14) 1981	10 (24–14) 1981	34 (6–34) 1976	28 (6–34) 1976
New Zealand	30 (30–16) 1978	16 (26–10) 1980	38 (13–38) 1936 (3–38) 1972	35 (3–38) 1972
South Africa	21 (21–6) 1933	15 (21–6) 1933	30 (11–30) 1969	25 (3–28) 1961
British Lions	8 (8–11) 1966	1 (6–5) 1930	31 (0–31) 1966	31 (0–31) 1966

'Where's that ball?' England players Barry Nelmes (left) and Roger Uttley try to work out a ploy by a NSW Country XV during the 1975 England tour of Australia. The ruse involved one player hiding the ball beneath his jersey, the others imitating the subterfuge and then the whole lot fanning out so that the defenders had no idea which player to tackle. (Colorsport.)

International results

			W	D	L
Argentina	1979	Buenos Aires			13–24
	1979	Buenos Aires	17–12		
Fiji	1952	Sydney	15–9		
	1952	Sydney			15–17
	1954	Brisbane	22–19		
	1954	Sydney			16–18
	1961	Brisbane	24–6		
	1961	Sydney	20–14		
	1961	Melbourne		3–3	
	1976	Sydney	22–6		
	1976	Brisbane	21–9		
	1976	Sydney	27–15		
	1980	Suva	22–9		

			W	D	L
Italy	1973	Aquila	59–21		
	1976	Milan	16–15		
Japan	1975	Sydney	37–7		
	1975	Brisbane	50–25		
Tonga	1973	Sydney	30–12		
	1973	Brisbane			11–16
United States	1976	Annaheim	24–12		

ENGLAND

Foundation	1871
Headquarters	RFU Twickenham, Middlesex
Main stadium	Twickenham (capacity 75 000)
Colours	White jerseys and shorts
Number of clubs	1702
Number of players	300 000
Season	September–April
Temperatures	30°F (−1°C) to 58°F (14°C)
Population	46 349 400

Foundation of English Clubs

Order of foundation		*Year*
6	Bath	1865
40	Bedford	1886
11	Birkenhead Park	1871
49	Birmingham	1911
2	Blackheath	1858
8	Bradford	1866
43	Bristol	1888
37	Broughton Park	1882
29	Camborne	1878
13	Cambridge University	1872
21	Coventry	1874
14	Exeter	1872
50	Fylde	1919
16	Gloucester	1873
25	Gosforth	1877
17	Halifax	1873
7	Harlequins	1866
12	Harrogate	1871
31	Hartlepool Rovers	1879
30	Headingley	1878
48	Huddersfield	1909
46	Hull and East Riding	1901
35	Leicester	1880
1	Liverpool	1857
44	London Irish	1898
27	London Scottish	1878
39	London Welsh	1885
3	Manchester	1860
51	Metropolitan Police	1923
15	Middlesbrough	1872
28	Morley	1878
18	Moseley	1873
20	New Brighton	1873
34	Northampton	1880
24	Northern	1876
26	Nottingham	1877
32	Nuneaton	1879
53	Orrell	1927
10	Oxford University	1869
23	Plymouth Albion	1876
4	Richmond	1861
33	Rosslyn Park	1879
52	Roundhay	1924
19	Rugby	1873
42	St Ives	1887
5	Sale	1861
22	Saracens	1876
47	Sheffield	1902
45	Wakefield	1901
9	Wasps	1867
38	Waterloo	1883
36	West Hartlepool	1881
41	Wilmslow	1886

NB Guy's Hospital, founded 1843, were the first closed club.

A larger than life Peter West, television rugby commentator, during a test run of the Rugby Football Union's new video screen at Twickenham before the England v Scotland match in March 1983. (Colorsport.)

County Championship

1st System

1889 Yorkshire, having remained undefeated, were declared Champions by the Rugby Union.
1890 Yorkshire, again undefeated, were declared Champions.

2nd System

	Champions	Group winners
1891	Lancashire	Gloucestershire, Surrey, Yorkshire
1892	Yorkshire	Kent, Lancashire, Midlands
1893	Yorkshire	Cumberland, Devon, Middlesex
1894	Yorkshire	Gloucestershire, Lancashire, Midlands
1895	Yorkshire	Cumberland, Devon, Midlands

3rd System

	Champions	Runners Up	Venue
1896	Yorkshire	Surrey	Richmond
1897	Kent	Cumberland	Carlisle
1898	Northumberland	Midlands	Coventry
1899	Devon	Northumberland	Newcastle
1900	Durham	Devon	Exeter
1901	Devon	Durham	West Hartlepool
1902	Durham	Gloucestershire	Gloucester
1903	Durham	Kent	West Hartlepool
1904	Kent	Durham	Blackheath
1905	Durham	Middlesex	West Hartlepool
1906	Devon	Durham	Exeter
1907	Devon Durham	Joint Champions	West Hartlepool & Exeter
1908	Cornwall	Durham	Redruth
1909	Durham	Cornwall	West Hartlepool
1910	Gloucestershire	Yorkshire	Gloucester
1911	Devon	Yorkshire	Headingley
1912	Devon	Northumberland	Devonport
1913	Gloucestershire	Cumberland	Carlisle
1914	Midlands	Durham	Leicester
1915–19	Suspended owing to First World War		
1920	Gloucestershire	Yorkshire	Bradford

4th System

	Winners		Runners Up	Venue
1921	Gloucestershire	31–4	Leicestershire	Gloucester
1922	Gloucestershire	19–0	North Midlands	Birmingham
1923	Somerset	8–6	Leicestershire	Bridgwater
1924	Cumberland	14–3	Kent	Carlisle
1925	Leicestershire	14–6	Gloucestershire	Bristol
1926	Yorkshire	15–14	Hampshire	Bradford
1927	Kent	22–12	Leicestershire	Blackheath
1928	Yorkshire	12–8	Cornwall	Bradford
1929	Middlesex drew with Lancashire			Twickenham
	Middlesex	9–8	Lancashire	Blundellsands
1930	Gloucestershire	13–7	Lancashire	Blundellsands
1931	Gloucestershire	10–9	Warwickshire	Gloucester
1932	Gloucestershire	9–3	Durham	Blaydon
1933	Hampshire	18–7	Lancashire	Boscombe
1934	East Midlands	10–0	Gloucestershire	Northampton
1935	Lancashire	14–0	Somerset	Bath
1936	Hampshire	13–6	Northumberland	Gosforth
1937	Gloucestershire	5–0	East Midlands	Bristol
1938	Lancashire	24–12	Surrey	Blundellsands
1939	Warwickshire	8–3	Somerset	Weston-super-Mare
1940–6	Suspended owing to Second World War			
1947	Lancashire*	14–3	Gloucestershire	Gloucester
1948	Lancashire	5–0	Eastern Counties	Cambridge
1949	Lancashire	9–3	Gloucestershire	Blundellsands
1950	Cheshire	5–0	East Midlands	Birkenhead Park
1951	East Midlands	10–0	Middlesex	Northampton

1952	Middlesex	9–6	Lancashire	Twickenham
1953	Yorkshire	11–3	East Midlands	Bradford
1954	Middlesex	24–6	Lancashire	Blundellsands
1955	Lancashire	14–8	Middlesex	Twickenham
1956	Middlesex	13–9	Devon	Twickenham
1957	Devon	12–3	Yorkshire	Plymouth
1958	Warwickshire	16–8	Cornwall	Coventry
1959	Warwickshire	14–9	Gloucestershire	Bristol
1960	Warwickshire	9–6	Surrey	Coventry
1961	Cheshire	0–0	Devon	Plymouth
	Cheshire	5–3	Devon	Birkenhead Park
1962	Warwickshire	11–6	Hampshire	Twickenham
1963	Warwickshire	13–10	Yorkshire	Coventry
1964	Warwickshire	8–6	Lancashire	Coventry
1965	Warwickshire	15–9	Durham	Hartlepool
1966	Middlesex	6–0	Lancashire	Blundellsands
1967†	Durham	14–14	Surrey	Twickenham
	Durham	0–0	Surrey	Durham
1968	Middlesex	9–6	Warwickshire	Twickenham
1969	Lancashire	11–9	Cornwall	Redruth
1970	Staffordshire	11–9	Gloucestershire	Burton-on-Trent
1971	Surrey	14–3	Gloucestershire	Gloucester
1972	Gloucestershire	11–6	Warwickshire	Coventry
1973	Lancashire	17–12	Gloucestershire	Blundellsands
1974	Gloucestershire	22–12	Lancashire	Blundellsands
1975	Gloucestershire	13–9	Eastern Counties	Gloucester
1976	Gloucestershire	24–9	Middlesex	Richmond
1977	Lancashire	17–6	Middlesex	Blundellsands
1978	North Midlands	10–7	Gloucestershire	Moseley
1979	Middlesex	19–6	Northumberland	Twickenham
1980	Lancashire	21–15	Gloucestershire	Vale of Lune
1981	Northumberland	15–6	Gloucestershire	Gloucester
1982	North Midlands	3–7	Lancashire	Moseley
1983	Gloucestershire	19–7	Yorkshire	Bristol

* After 8–8 draw at Blundellsands
† Title shared

Billy Beaumont displays the OBE he was awarded for his services to rugby football. Beaumont, who captained England a record 21 times, ended his career (see below) after being injured playing for Lancashire against North Midlands in the County Championship final at Moseley in 1982. (Colorsport.)

County Championship Records

Most points in a season
253 Lancashire 1979–80

Most tries in a season
42 Lancashire 1979–80

Most county career points
462 Peter Butler (Gloucestershire)

County Cup Winners

Bedfordshire 1983 Bedford Athletic

Berkshire 1970 Reading, 1971–2 REME Arborfield, 1973 RCMS Shrivenham, 1974–7 Maidenhead, 1978 Abbey, 1979 Newbury, 1980 Abbey, 1981 Newbury, 1982 Maidenhead, 1983 Maidenhead

Buckinghamshire 1969 Aylesbury, 1970 Aylesbury, 1971 Marlow, 1972 Aylesbury, 1973 Aylesbury, 1974 Marlow, 1975 Marlow, 1976 Marlow, 1977 High Wycombe, 1978 Marlow, 1979 High Wycombe, 1980 High Wycombe, 1981 High Wycombe, 1982 High Wycombe, 1983 High Wycombe

Cambridgeshire 1982 Shelford, 1983 Shelford

Cheshire 1878 Birkenhead Park, 1879 Birkenhead Park, 1880 New Brighton, 1881 Birkenhead Park (competition lapsed), 1970 Sale, 1971 Caldy, 1972 Wilmslow, 1973 Sale, 1974 Sale, 1975 Sale, 1976 Sale, 1977 Sale, 1978 Sale, 1979 Sale, 1980 Sale, 1981 Sale, 1982 Sale, 1983 Alsager

Cornwall 1967 Penryn, 1968 St Ives, 1969 Penryn, 1970 St Ives, 1971 Penryn, 1972 Penryn, 1973 Falmouth, 1974 Penryn, 1975 Penzance & Newlyn, 1976 Falmouth, 1977 Camborne, 1978 Camborne, 1979 Redruth, 1980 Redruth, 1981 St Ives, 1982 St Ives, 1983 Launceston

Cumbria 1978 Aspatria, 1979 Wigton, 1980 Aspatria, 1981 Aspatria, 1982 Aspatria, 1983 Aspatria

Derbyshire 1982 Chesterfield, 1983 Chesterfield

Devon 1969 St Luke's College, 1970 St Luke's College, 1971 Exeter, 1972 Exeter, 1973 Exeter, 1974 Plymouth Albion, 1975 St Luke's College, 1976 Exeter, 1977 Plymouth Albion, 1978 Exeter, 1979 Torquay Athletic, 1980 Exeter, 1981 Exeter University, 1982 Exeter, 1983 Devon & Cornwall Police

Dorset & Wiltshire 1971 Devizes, 1972 Salisbury, 1973 Devizes, 1974 Salisbury, 1975 Wimborne, 1976 Salisbury, 1977 Salisbury, 1978 Salisbury, 1979 Bournemouth, 1980 Bournemouth, 1981 Bournemouth, 1982 Wimborne, 1983 Bournemouth

Durham 1976 Hartlepool Rovers, 1977 Hartlepool Rovers, 1978 Hartlepool Rovers, 1979 Hartlepool Rovers, 1980 Hartlepool Rovers, 1981 Hartlepool Rovers, 1982 West Hartlepool, 1983 West Hartlepool

Eastern Counties 1978 Ipswich, 1979 Norwich, 1980 Southend, 1981 Thurrock, 1982 Norwich, 1983 Norwich

East Midlands 1978 Peterborough, 1979 Kettering, 1980 Kettering, 1981 Kettering, 1982 Kettering, 1983 Bedford Athletic

Essex 1979 Woodford, 1980 Southend, 1981 Thurrock, 1982 Thurrock, 1983 Southend

Gloucestershire 1970 Lydney, 1971 Matson, 1972 Clifton, 1973 Lydney, 1974 Gordon League, 1975 Gordon League, 1976 Lydney, 1977 Matson, 1978 Matson, 1979 Stroud, 1980 Stroud, 1981 Matson, 1982 Lydney, 1983 Lydney

Hampshire 1970 United Services Portsmouth, 1971 United Services Portsmouth, 1972 Aldershot Services, 1973 Bournemouth, 1974 Havant, 1975 Winchester, 1976 United Services Portsmouth, 1977 Havant, 1978 Havant, 1979 Havant, 1980 Havant, 1981 United Services Portsmouth, 1982 United Services Portsmouth, 1983 United Services Portsmouth

Hertfordshire 1979 Fullerians, 1980 Fullerians, 1981 Hertford, 1982 Hertford, 1983 Tabard

Kent 1980 Blackheath, 1981 Blackheath, 1982 Blackheath, 1983 Blackheath

Lancashire 1971 Orrell, 1972 Orrell, 1973 Waterloo, 1974 Orrell, 1975 Widnes, 1976 Liverpool, 1977 Orrell, 1978 Liverpool, 1979 Waterloo, 1981 Waterloo, 1982 Orrell, 1983 Waterloo

Leicestershire 1971 Hinckley, 1972 Hinckley, 1973 Wigston, 1974 Westleigh, 1975 Westleigh, 1976 Hinckley, 1977 Loughborough Students, 1978 Hinckley, 1979 Hinckley, 1980 Westleigh, 1981 Westleigh, 1982 Hinckley, 1983 Vipers

Lincolnshire 1982 Stamford, 1983 Lincoln

Middlesex 1972 Saracens, 1973 Metropolitan Police, 1974 Wasps, 1975 Wasps, 1976 Saracens, 1977 Wasps, 1978 Wasps, 1979 Wasps, 1980 Saracens, 1981 Metropolitan Police, 1982 Wasps, 1983 Harlequins

North Midlands 1980 Camp Hill, 1981 Stourbridge, 1982 Bromsgrove, 1983 Stourbridge

Northumberland 1970 Northern, 1971 Gosforth, 1972 Gosforth, 1973 Gosforth, 1974 Gosforth, 1975 Gosforth, 1976 Gosforth, 1977 Gosforth, 1978 Gosforth, 1979 Gosforth, 1980 Gosforth, 1981 Gosforth, 1982 Gosforth, 1983 Alnwick

Norfolk 1982 Norwich, 1983 Norwich

Nottinghamshire 1982 Newark, 1983 Newark

Nottinghamshire, Lincs & Derbyshire 1972 Old Baileans, 1973 Scunthorpe, 1974 Old Baileans, 1975 Chesterfield, 1976 Moderns, 1977 Paviors, 1978 Chesterfield, 1979 Chesterfield, 1980 Derby, 1981 Stamford, 1982 Stamford, 1983 Nottingham

Oxfordshire 1980 Oxford, 1981 Oxford, 1982 Oxford, 1983 Henley

Somerset 1970 Bath, 1971 Bath, 1972 Bridgwater & Albion, 1973 Bath, 1974 Bath, 1975 Bath, 1976 Bridgwater & Albion, 1977 Avon & Somerset Police, 1978 Weston-super-Mare, 1979 Midsomer Norton, 1980 Midsomer Norton, 1981 Weston-super-Mare, 1982 Keynsham, 1983 Bath

Staffordshire 1980 Walsall, 1981 Walsall, 1982 Lichfield, 1983 Walsall

Suffolk 1982 Sudbury, 1983 Sudbury

Surrey 1970 Guildford & Godalming, 1971 Guildford & Godalming, 1972 Camberley, 1973 Streatham-Croydon, 1974 Streatham-Croydon, 1975 Esher, 1976 Esher, 1977 Esher, 1978 Esher, 1979 Guildford & Godalming, 1980 Guildford & Godalming, 1981 London Irish, 1982 London Irish, 1983 KCS Old Boys

Andy Ripley, England's most capped No. 8 forward, who made 24 appearances between 1972–6. (Geo. Herringshaw.)

Sussex 1979 Crawley, 1980 Crawley, 1981 Lewes, 1982 East Grinstead, 1983 Worthing

Warwickshire 1971 Solihull, 1972 Solihull, 1973 Solihull, 1974 Newbold on Avon, 1975 Solihull, 1976 Solihull, 1977 Newbold on Avon, 1978 Coventry Welsh, 1979 Coventry Welsh, 1980 Coventry Welsh, 1981 Bedworth, 1982 Stoke Old Boys, 1983 Solihull

Yorkshire 1979 Roundhay, 1980 Roundhay, 1981 Harrogate, 1982 Wakefield, 1983 Headingley

John Player Cup

1972 Gloucester 17 Moseley 6 **1973** Coventry 27 Bristol 15 **1974** Coventry 26 London Scottish 6 **1975** Bedford 28 Rosslyn Park 12 **1976** Gosforth 23 Rosslyn Park 14 **1977** Gosforth

In an era when the principal job for hookers was to win their own ball and the second was to take the opposition's, Bristol's John Pullin (above) had few peers. Pullin captained England 13 times in a record 42 appearances between 1966–76. (Geo. Herringshaw.)

27 Waterloo 11 **1978** Gloucester 6 Leicester 3 **1979** Leicester 15 Moseley 12 **1980** Leicester 21 London Irish 9 **1981** Leicester 22 Gosforth 15 **1982** Gloucester 12 Moseley 12 (title shared) **1983** Bristol 28 Leicester 22

John Player Cup records
Highest attendance 37 000, 1983.
Most points in final 15, Alan Pearn (Bristol), 1973; Dusty Hare (Leicester), 1980.
Most tries 8 in 1975 final (5 to Bedford, also a record).
Record score Bournemouth 6 Bedford 66 (first round 1975).
No tries record
London Irish did not concede a try in 1980, a record for the competition.

1983 Competition
Quarter finals: Coventry 19 Nottingham 9, Leicester 18 Harlequins 4, London Welsh 6 London Scottish 15, West Hartlepool 14 Bristol 16. *Semi-finals*: Coventry 3 Bristol 22, London Scottish 9 Leicester 30.

Alistair Hignell, who scored a record 19 points for Cambridge in the 1975 University match, was also a highly talented cricketer with Gloucestershire. Hignell was capped 14 times for England. (Geo. Herringshaw.)

The University Match

1871–72 Oxford (1G 1T) beat Cambridge (no score) at Oxford
1872–73 Cambridge (1G 2T) beat Oxford (no score) at Cambridge
1873–74 Cambridge (1T) drew with Oxford (1T) at The Oval
1874–75 Cambridge (no score) drew with Oxford (2T) at The Oval (**NB** team had to score a goal to win)
1875–76 Oxford (1T) beat Cambridge (no score) at The Oval
1876–77 Cambridge (1G 2T) beat Oxford (no score) at The Oval
1877–78 Oxford (2T) beat Cambridge (no score) at The Oval
1878–79 Cambridge (no score) drew with Oxford (no score) at The Oval
1879–80 Cambridge (1G 1DG) beat Oxford (1DG) at The Oval
1880–81 Cambridge (1T) drew with Oxford (1T) at Blackheath
1881–82 Oxford (2G 1T) beat Cambridge (1G) at Blackheath
1882–83 Oxford (1T) beat Cambridge (no score) at Blackheath
1883–84 Oxford (3G 4T) beat Cambridge (1G) at Blackheath
1884–85 Oxford (3G 1T) beat Cambridge (1T) at Blackheath
1885–86 Cambridge (2T) beat Oxford (no score) at Blackheath
1886–87 Cambridge (3T) beat Oxford (no score) at Blackheath
1887–88 Cambridge (1DG 2T) beat Oxford (no score) at Queens Club
1888–89 Cambridge (1G 2T) beat Oxford (no score) at Queens Club
1889–90 Oxford (1G 1T) beat Cambridge (no score) at Queens Club
1890–91 Oxford (1G) drew with Cambridge (1G) at Queens Club
1891–92 Cambridge (2T) beat Oxford (no score) at Queens Club
1892–93 Cambridge (no score) drew with Oxford (no score) at Queens Club
1893–94 Oxford (1T) beat Cambridge (no score) at Queens Club
1894–95 Oxford (1G) drew with Cambridge (1G) at Queens Club
1895–96 Cambridge (1G) beat Oxford (no score) at Queens Club
1896–97 Oxford (1G 1DG) beat Cambridge (1G 1T) at Queens Club
1897–98 Oxford (2T) beat Cambridge (no score) at Queens Club
1898–99 Cambridge (1G 2T) beat Oxford (no score) at Queens Club
1899–1900 Cambridge (2G 4T) beat Oxford (no score) at Queens Club
1900–01 Oxford (2G) beat Cambridge (1G 1T) at Queens Club
1901–02 Oxford (1G 1T) beat Cambridge (no score) at Queens Club
1902–03 Oxford (1G 1T) drew with Cambridge (1G 1T) at Queens Club
1903–04 Oxford (3G 1T) beat Cambridge (2G 1T) at Queens Club
1904–05 Cambridge (3G) beat Oxford (2G) at Queens Club
1905–06 Cambridge 15 (3G) Oxford 13 (2G 1T) at Queens Club
1906–07 Oxford 12 (4T) Cambridge 8 (1G 1T) at Queens Club
1907–08 Oxford 17 (1G 4T) Cambridge 0 at Queens Club
1908–09 Oxford 5 (1G) Cambridge 5 (1G) at Queens Club
1909–10 Oxford 35 (4G 5T) Cambridge 3 (1T) at Queens Club
1910–11 Oxford 23 (4G 1T) Cambridge 18 (3G 1T) at Queens Club
1911–12 Oxford 19 (2G 3T) Cambridge 0 at Queens Club
1912–13 Cambridge 10 (2G) Oxford 3 (1T) at Queens Club
1913–14 Cambridge 13 (1DG 3T) Oxford 3 (1T) at Queens Club
1914–18 No matches due to War
1919–20 Cambridge 7 (1DG 1PG) Oxford 5 (1G) at Queens Club
1920–21 Oxford 17 (1G 4T) Cambridge 14 (1G 3T) at Queens Club
1921–22 Oxford 11 (1G 2T) Cambridge 5 (1G) at Twickenham
1922–23 Cambridge 21 (3G 2T) Oxford 8 (1G 1T) at Twickenham
1923–24 Oxford 21 (3G 2T) Cambridge 14 (1G 1PG 2T) at Twickenham
1924–25 Oxford 11 (1G 2T) Cambridge 6 (2T) at Twickenham
1925–26 Cambridge 33 (3G 6T) Oxford 3 (1T) at Twickenham
1926–27 Cambridge 30 (3G 5T) Oxford 5 (1G) at Twickenham
1927–28 Cambridge 22 (2G 2PG 2T) Oxford 14 (1G 3T) at Twickenham
1928–29 Cambridge 14 (1G 3T) Oxford 10 (1DG 1PG 1T) at Twickenham
1929–30 Oxford 9 (1G 1DG) Cambridge 0 at Twickenham
1930–31 Oxford 3 (1PG) Cambridge 3 (1T) at Twickenham
1931–32 Oxford 10 (1DG 2T) Cambridge 3 (1T) at Twickenham
1932–33 Oxford 8 (1G 1T) Cambridge 3 (1T) at Twickenham
1933–34 Oxford 5 (1G) Cambridge 3 (1T) at Twickenham
1934–35 Cambridge 29 (2G 1DG 1PG 4T) Oxford 4 (1DG) at Twickenham
1935–36 Cambridge 0 Oxford 0 at Twickenham
1936–37 Cambridge 6 (2T) Oxford 5 (1G) at Twickenham
1937–38 Oxford 17 (1G 4T) Cambridge 4 (1DG) at Twickenham
1938–39 Cambridge 8 (1G 1PG) Oxford 6 (2PG) at Twickenham
*1939–40 Oxford 15 (1G 1DG 2T) Cambridge 3 (1T) at Cambridge
*1940–41 Cambridge 11 (1G 2T) Oxford 9 (1G 1DG) at Oxford
Cambridge 13 (2G 1T) Oxford 0 at Cambridge
*1941–42 Cambridge 9 (1PG 2T) Oxford 6 (1PG 1T) at Cambridge
Cambridge 17 (1G 2PG 2T) Oxford 8 (1G 1T) at Oxford

* Wartime series

*1942–43 Cambridge 9 (1G 1DG) Oxford 0 at Oxford
Cambridge 14 (1G 3T) Oxford 13 (2G 1T) at Oxford
Cambridge 16 (2G 2T) Oxford 3 (1T) at Cambridge
*1943–44 Cambridge 13 (2G 1T) Oxford 4 (1DG) at Cambridge
Oxford 6 (2T) Cambridge 5 (1G) at Oxford
*1944–45 Oxford 3 (1T) Cambridge 3 (1T) at Oxford
Cambridge 16 (2G 2T) Oxford 4 (1DG) at Cambridge
1945–46 Cambridge 11 (1G 2T) Oxford 8 (1G 1PG) at Twickenham
1946–47 Oxford 15 (1G 1DG 2T) Cambridge 5 (1G) at Twickenham
1947–48 Cambridge 6 (2PG) Oxford 0 at Twickenham
1948–49 Oxford 14 (1G 1DG 2T) Cambridge 8 (1G 1PG) at Twickenham
1949–50 Oxford 3 (1T) Cambridge 0 at Twickenham
1950–51 Oxford 8 (1G 1PG) Cambridge 0 at Twickenham
1951–52 Oxford 13 (2G 1T) Cambridge 0 at Twickenham
1952–53 Cambridge 6 (1PG 1T) Oxford 5 (1G) at Twickenham
1953–54 Oxford 6 (1PG 1T) Cambridge 6 (2PG) at Twickenham
1954–55 Cambridge 3 (1PG) Oxford 0 at Twickenham
1955–56 Oxford 9 (1PG 2T) Cambridge 5 (1G) at Twickenham
1956–57 Cambridge 14 (1G 1DG 1PG 1T) Oxford 9 (2PG 1T) at Twickenham
1957–58 Oxford 3 (1T) Cambridge 0 at Twickenham
1958–59 Cambridge 17 (1G 1PG 3T) Oxford 6 (1PG 1T) at Twickenham
1959–60 Oxford 9 (3PG) Cambridge 3 (1PG) at Twickenham
1960–61 Cambridge 13 (2G 1T) Oxford 0 at Twickenham
1961–62 Cambridge 9 (1DG 2T) Oxford 3 (1DG) at Twickenham
1962–63 Cambridge 14 (1G 1DG 1PG 1T) Oxford 0 at Twickenham
1963–64 Cambridge 19 (2G 1PG 2T) Oxford 11 (1G 1DG 1PG) at Twickenham
1964–65 Oxford 19 (2G 1PG 2T) Cambridge 6 (1PG 1GM) at Twickenham
1965–66 Oxford 5 (1G) Cambridge 5 (1G) at Twickenham
1966–67 Oxford 8 (1G 1T) Cambridge 6 (1DG 1T) at Twickenham
1967–68 Cambridge 6 (1T 1PG) Oxford 0 at Twickenham
1968–69 Cambridge 9 (1T 1PG 1DG) Oxford 6 (2T) at Twickenham
1969–70 Oxford 9 (3PG) Cambridge 6 (2PG) at Twickenham
1970–71 Oxford 14 (1G 1DG 2T) Cambridge 3 (1PG) at Twickenham
1971–72 Oxford 21 (3PG 3T) Cambridge 3 (1PG) at Twickenham
1972–73 Cambridge 16 (1G 1PG 1DG 1T) Oxford 6 (2PG) at Twickenham
1973–74 Cambridge 14 (1DG 1PG 2T) Oxford 12 (1G 2PG) at Twickenham
1974–75 Cambridge 16 (1G 2PG 1T) Oxford 15 (5PG) at Twickenham
1975–76 Cambridge 34 (2G 5PG 1DG 1T) Oxford 12 (3PG 1DG) at Twickenham
1976–77 Cambridge 15 (1G 3PG) Oxford 0 at Twickenham
1977–78 Oxford 16 (4PG 1T) Cambridge 10 (2PG 1T) at Twickenham
1978–79 Cambridge 25 (2G 1T 3PG) Oxford 7 (1PG 1T) at Twickenham
1979–80 Oxford 9 (2PG 1DG) Cambridge 3 (1PG) at Twickenham
1980–81 Cambridge 13 (1T 3PG) Oxford 9 (3PG) at Twickenham
1981–82 Cambridge 9 (3PG) Oxford 6 (2PG) at Twickenham
1982–83 Cambridge 20 (2T 3PG 1DG) Oxford 13 (1G 1T 1PG) at Twickenham

University Match details (to end 1982)
Played 101 Oxford 43
Cambridge 45 Drawn 13

University Match records
Peter Enevoldson, the Oxford captain, won a record fifth dark blue when he appeared against Cambridge in the 99th University Match at Twickenham on 10 December 1980. The all-time blues record is held by Harry Fuller of Cambridge who played six times between 1878 and 1883. Another Cambridge player, John Greenwood, won five blues between 1910 and 1919.

Most appearances in winning side
4 Sir Carl Aarvold, Cambridge 1926–9

Most wins in sequence
5 Cambridge 1972–6

Most individual points
19 Alistair Hignell, Cambridge 1975
17 John Robbie, Cambridge 1978

Oxford's most points
35 1909 (35–3). Biggest winning margin, same match

Cambridge's most points
34 1975 (34–12). Biggest winning margin, 33–3, 1925

Highest aggregate points
46 Cambridge 34–12, 1975

Universities Athletic Union
1969 Durham, 1971 Bristol, 1974, 1975 Loughborough, 1976 UWIST, 1977 Loughborough. Finals since:

1978 Loughborough 17 Bristol 0
1979 Loughborough 18 Exeter 12
1980 UWIST 9 Exeter 0
1981 Durham 6 Loughborough 3
1982 Durham 7 Exeter 6
1983 Durham 9 Exeter 9 (Durham won by virtue of scoring the only try)

British Colleges Cup
1974 Carnegie, 1975 Madeley, 1976–7 Cardiff, 1978 St Paul's Cheltenham, 1979 South Glamorgan Institute, 1980 South Glamorgan Institute, 1981 Jordanhill, 1982 South Glamorgan Institute, 1983 Crewe & Alsager

Internationals
English Colleges 7 Scottish Colleges 17 (Centaurs RFC)
English Colleges 18 Welsh Colleges 27 (Cheltenham)
British Police 26 British Colleges 3

British Polytechnics Cup
1974 Leeds, 1979 Bristol, 1980–83 Polytechnic of Wales

The Hospitals' Cup

1875 Guy's (1G 1TD) beat St George's (2TD)
1876 St George's (5TD) beat University College (1TD)
1877 Guy's (6TD) beat St Thomas's (1TD)
1878 St Thomas's (3TD) beat University College (1TD)
1879 Guy's (2G 3T 3TD) beat St Bartholomew's (2TD)
1880 St George's (2TD) beat St Bartholomew's (1TD)
1881 St Bartholomew's (2G 6T 9TD) beat London (1TD)
1882 St George's (1G 1T 6TD) beat St Bartholomew's (1G 2TD)
1883 St Bartholomew's (3T 5TD) beat St George's (1TD)
1884 London (2G 2TD) beat St Bartholomew's (1G 1TD)
1885 London (2T) beat University College (3TD)
1886 Guy's (2T 6TD) beat University College (2TD)
1887 Middlesex (3T) beat St Thomas's (1TD)
1888 St Thomas's (2T 1TD) beat St Mary's (no score)
1889 St Thomas's (13G 6T 5TD) beat Middlesex (1T 1TD)
1890 St Thomas's (3T) beat St Bartholomew's (2TD)
1891 Competition not held
1892 St Thomas's (2G 8T) beat St Bartholomew's (no score)
1893 St Thomas's (1G 2T) beat Guy's (1G)
1894 St Thomas's (1G 10T) beat University College (1T)
1895 St Thomas's (3G 3T) beat St George's (no score)
1896 St Thomas's (3T) beat St George's (1G)
1897 St Thomas's (1T) beat Guy's (no score)
1898 Guy's (1G 3T) beat St Thomas's (1DG)
1899 Guy's (3T) beat London (no score)
1900 St Mary's (2T) beat London (no score)
1901 Guy's (3G 2T) beat London (1T)
1902 Guy's (1G 4T) beat St Mary's (no score)
1903 Guy's (1G 2T) beat London (no score)
1904 London (1G 1DG) beat Guy's (no score)
1905 Guy's (3T) beat London (no score)
1906 London 13 (2G 1T) Guy's 0
1907 Guy's 7 (1DG 1T) London 0
1908 London 11 (1G 2T) Guy's 3 (1T)
1909 Guy's 21 (7T) Middlesex 3 (1T)
1910 Guy's 8 (1G 1T) London 5 (1G)
1911 Guy's 8 (1G 1T) London 0
1912 Guy's 6 (2T) London 0
1913 Guy's 3 (1T) London 0
1914 London 16 (2G 2T) St Bartholomew's 0
1915–19 No competition, due to War
1920 Guy's 6 (2T) St Bartholomew's 0
1921 Guy's 3 (1T) St Bartholomew's 0
1922 Guy's 42 (6G 4T) London 3 (1PG)
1923 Guy's 3 (1T) St Bartholomew's 0
1924 St Bartholomew's 11 (1G 1PG 1T) King's College 3 (1T)
1925 Guy's 7 (1DG 1T) London 0
1926 St Thomas's 5 (1G) Guy's 0
1927 Guy's 10 (2G) King's College 0
1928 St Bartholomew's 11 (1G 1PG 1T) London 3 (1T)
1929 Guy's 3 (1T) London 0
1930 Guy's 23 (4G 1T) St Bartholomew's 9 (1PG 2T)
1931 St Bartholomew's 8 (1G 1T) St Mary's 0
1932 Guy's 13 (1DG 1PG 1GM 1T) St Mary's 7 (1DG 1T)
1933 Guy's 7 (1DG 1T) St Bartholomew's 0
1934 St Mary's 32 (4G 1PG 3T) St Thomas's 7 (1DG 1T)
1935 St Mary's 14 (1G 2PG 1T) King's College 3 (1T)
1936 St Mary's 19 (2G 3T) St Thomas's 8 (1G 1T)
1937 St Mary's 11 (1G 1PG 1T) Guy's 4 (1DG)
1938 St Mary's 18 (3G 1T) Guy's 0
1939 St Mary's 5 (1G) St Thomas's 3 (1T)
1940–45 No competition owing to War.
1946 St Mary's 18 (3G 1T) Guy's 8 (1G 1PG)
1947 Competition not played owing to severe winter.
1948 Guy's 8 (1G 1T) St Mary's 3 (1PG)
1949 St Mary's 6 (2T) Guy's 5 (1G)
1950 St Thomas's 8 (1G 1T) London 6 (1DG 1PG)
1951 St Mary's 9 (2PG 1T) London 8 (1G 1PG)
1952 St Mary's 14 (1G 3T) St Thomas's 9 (3T)
1953 St Mary's 14 (1G 1PG 2T) London 6 (2PG)
1954 St Thomas's 3 (1DG) St Mary's 0
1955 London 9 (1PG 2T) Guy's 3 (1T)
1956 St Mary's 16 (2G 1DG 1T) Guy's 0 (after 3–3 draw)
1957 London 5 (1G) St Bartholomew's 3 (1PG) (after 9–9 draw)
1958 St Thomas's 6 (2PG) Guy's 3 (1PG)
1959 St Mary's 6 (2T) St Bartholomew's 0 (after 6–6 draw)
1960 St Thomas's 8 (1G 1T) London 0
1961 Guy's 9 (2PG 1T) St Thomas's 6 (1PG 1T)
1962 St Thomas's 10 (2G) St Mary's 0
1963 St Mary's 6 (1PG 1T) St Thomas's 0
1964 St Thomas's 5 (1G) St Mary's 3 (1T)
1965 London 3 (1DG) St Mary's 0
1966 Guy's 3 (1T) St Thomas's 0 (after 0–0 draw)
1967 St Mary's 3 (1T) London 0 (after 3–3 draw)
1968 London 6 (1PG 1DG) Guy's 3 (1DG)
1969 St Bartholomew's 11 (1G 1PG 1DG) Guy's 3 (1T)
1970 St Bartholomew's 15 (2PG 1DG 2T) Guy's 0
1971 Guy's 14 (1G 1PG 2T) St Mary's 3 (1T)
1972 St Mary's 20 (4PG 2T) St Bartholomew's 9 (1G 1PG)
1973 St Mary's 20 (1G 1PG 1DG 2T) Westminster 12 (1G 1PG 1DG)
1974 Westminster 7 (1PG 1T) Guy's 6 (1PG 1DG)
1975 Westminster 12 (4PG) St Mary's 3 (1PG)

1976 St Bartholomew's 12 (1T 1G 1PG) London 0
1977 St Bartholomew's 12 (1G 2PG) St Mary's 6 (1G)
1978 St Mary's 30 (3T 2G 1PG 1DG) London 12 (1G 1PG 1DG) (after 3–3 draw)
1979 St Mary's 49 (5G 4T 1PG) Westminster 0
1980 St Mary's 23 (2T 2G 1PG) Westminster 3 (1PG)
1981 St Mary's 9 London 0
1982 Westminster 16 St Mary's 6
1983 St Mary's 10 Westminster 0

Hospitals' Cup Record

St Mary's 49–0 in 1979 was highest-ever margin in final

Middlesex Sevens

1926: Harlequins 25 St Mary's Hospital 3 (Harlequins: J C Gibbs R H Hamilton-Wickes V G Davies J R B Worton J S Chick W F Browne W W Wakefield)
1927: Harlequins 28 Blackheath 6 (Harlequins: R H Hamilton-Wickes H C Pattison H C C Laird H B Style W W Wakefield W F Browne J S Chick)
1928: Harlequins 19 Blackheath 8 (Harlequins: J C Gibbs J S R Reeves V G Davies H C C Laird W W Wakefield C K T Faithful W F Browne)
1929: Harlequins 16 Rosslyn Park 9 (Harlequins: J C Hardy J E Rylands V G Davies C C McCreight H L Price W W Wakefield W F Browne)
1930: London Welsh 6 Blackheath 0 (London Welsh: E L Francis W T Lewis A H Jones W C Powell R Jones W A V Thomas M H Evans)
1931: London Welsh 19 Harlequins 5 (London Welsh: B H Morgan R Thomas A H Jones W C Powell R Jones W A V Thomas M H Evans)
1932: Blackheath 18 Harlequins 10 (Blackheath: C D Aarvold A B Chorlton J A Tallent F W Simpson T W Gibbs B H Black C B Bailey)
1933: Harlequins 23 Wasps 0 (Harlequins: J C Gibbs H A Style J R Cole G J Dean P E Dunkley F D Russell-Roberts C Thompson)
1934: Barbarians 6 Richmond 3 (aet) (Barbarians: B T V Cowey R A Gerrard K C Fyfe H Lind J Graham J Beattie J A Waters)
1935: Harlequins 10 London Welsh 3 (Harlequins: A G Butler G E C Hudson J R Cole G J Dean P W P Brook P E Dunkley E Hamilton-Hill)
1936: Sale 18 Blackheath 6 (Sale: W Wooller K C Fyfe E C Davey G C Norden G D Shaw R U Reynolds J Mycock)
1937: London Scottish 19 OMT 3 (London Scottish: J Park R W Dunn H Lind A H B Adair D A Thom G B Horsburgh A W B Buchanan)
1938: Metropolitan Police 13 London Scottish 3 (Metropolitan Police: T Cranfield H S Webber C A Pridmore A C Jones W E Coles L J Davies A M Wynne)
1939: Cardiff 11 London Scottish 6 (Cardiff: G L Porter G Hale W Wooller W R Davies L Spence W E N Davies S Davies)
1940: St Mary's Hospital 14 OCTU Sandhurst 10 (St Mary's: R W Morrison C M Squire J Graham-Jones H D Cockburn C A Young G S Jacklind G J Reynolds)
1941: Cambridge University 6 Welsh Guards 0 (Cambridge: E R Knapp R E Crighton G T Wright E Anderson R P Sinclair R P Masters D G Bratherton)
1942: St Mary's Hospital 8 RAF 6 (St Mary's: F M McRae N O Bennett T A Kemp H D Cockburn A W Young C J Hodson D J B Johnston)
1943: St Mary's Hospital 8 Middlesex Hospital 3 (St Mary's: N O Bennett R W Watson T A Kemp V Morris A W Young G Robbins D J B Johnston)
1944: St Mary's Hospital 15 RAF Jurby 5 (St Mary's: R W Watson N O Bennett N M Hall V Morris D J B Johnston G Robbins L D Bromley)
1945: Nottingham 6 St Mary's Hospital 3 (Nottingham: D A Barker R S Miller J Heaton R F Clarke H E F Heath P J Kilkelly A G Mould)
1946: St Mary's Hospital 13 Cardiff 3 (St Mary's: P R G Graham N O Bennett N M Hall E K Scott W Whittingham G Robbins M B Devine)
1947: Rosslyn Park 12 Richmond 6 (Rosslyn Park: J C M Wilkinson J M Reichwald B Boobbyer J H Burgess N J Carver E Kverndal R Crouch)
1948: Wasps 14 Harlequins 5 (Wasps: B Young J E Woodward P H Till M C Morgan H J Costley D W Malcolm J MacGillivray)
1949: Heriot's FP 16 London Scottish 6 (Heriot's FP: A M Mason F C Cheshire T Gray R E Smith E Munro A S Dunbar D W Deas)
1950: Rosslyn Park 16 Heriot's FP 0 (Rosslyn Park: J V Smith J M Reichwald G C Phipps B E Cox N E Williams R F Dorey R Crouch)
1951: Richmond 13 Wasps 10 (Richmond: M F Bye H Tranter N M Hall G N Peters N C S Barling N A H Creese M Walker. Wasps: J E Woodward J Marker G A Phillips M C Morgan D W Malcolm M U Hughes R E Syrett)
1952: Wasps 12 St Thomas's Hospital 10 (Wasps: A L Stalder J Marker G A Phillips P W Sykes D W Malcolm M U Hughes R E Syrett. St Thomas's: J Bootham R W Ross-Russell W E N Maeckleberghe J Mynott M Yates W J D Bradfield A H Diamond)
1953: Richmond 10 London Welsh 3 (Richmond: V R Tindall T R Beatson J M Williams N M Hall N C S Barling G C Hoyer-Millar J H Henderson. London Welsh: G Griffiths A C Lewis C James H Evans B V Meredith R Cooper T J Griffiths)
1954: Rosslyn Park 16 London Scottish 0 (Rosslyn Park: D Diamond G Palmer C E Winn T C Pearson F R Dorey S F Read J C Kail. London Scottish: J S Swan D W C Smith M K Elgie J W Smith E E Tattersall L B Sandeman B E Thomson)
1955: Richmond 5 St Luke's College 0 (Richmond: B M Gray J M Williams D W Holman N M Hall G J B Edgecombe W M Patterson R P Boggon. St Luke's: K Stocksbury M Greenhow B E Jones D B Rees D A Thomas J B Thomas D R Main)
1956: London Welsh 24 Emmanuel College Cambridge 10 (London Welsh: C G Jones C Bosley C James H Evans R H Davies G Thomas J Leleu. Emmanuel College: P J Watson M E Wates G McClung P Grant W Downey N C Raffle W Wiggans)
1957: St Luke's College 18 London Welsh 5 (St Luke's: K J Bartlett G G Luke B E Jones J Tasker W Williams D R Main B Sparks. London Welsh: C G Jones C Bosley C James H Evans H J Mainwaring B V Meredith J Leleu)
1958: Blackheath 16 Saracens 3 (Blackheath: D L Gudgeon J C Watts A C J Sharp P J Davies J B Williamson D G Wells C L J Bailey. Saracens: B H G Wright L A Williams D J Frazer B Mead V S J Harding L J R de Luca P Beck)
1959: Loughborough Colleges 3 London Welsh 0 (aet) (Loughborough: G Williams A A Bailey L Tatham A Rees D Hackett A Pask D P M Williams. London Welsh: P. Donovan K Chilton M Smith A O'Connor J B Thomas B I Jones J Leleu)
1960: London Scottish 16 London Welsh 5 (London Scottish: I P Reid J A P Shackleton K J F Scotland I H P Laughland R I Marshall D B Hayburn D G Trow. London Welsh: A Jones K Chilton P Donovan R Richards D R Main E J Jones D I Jones)

1961: London Scottish 20 Stewart's College FP 6 (London Scottish: K J F Scotland R H Thomson J A P Shackleton I H P Laughland D G Trow D B Hayburn R I Marshall. Stewart's College: M J Pringle N A D Sinclair G Sharp G M Robertson J C M Sharp A G Sinclair J Douglas)
1962: London Scottish 18 Rosslyn Park 6 (London Scottish: R H Thomson J A P Shackleton I H P Laughland J A T Rodd A C W Boyle R I Marshall W R A Watherston. Rosslyn Park: J M Ranson P M W Stafford D J J Allanson T C Wintle A R Tanner M Williams G W Hines)
1963: London Scottish 15 Hawick 11 (London Scottish: R H Thomson J A P Shackleton I H P Laughland J A T Rodd A C W Boyle R I Marshall W R A Watherston. Hawick: D Jackson G D Stevenson A R Broatch R G Turnbull T O Grant H F McLeod D Grant)
1964: Loughborough Colleges 18 London Scottish 16 (Loughborough: R Tennick N Barker D Hill P Scurfield J Mantle T G R Davies R Sleigh. London Scottish: D A Hamilton J A P Shackleton I H P Laughland J A T Rodd J C Brash D B Hayburn M J Walsh)
1965: London Scottish 15 Loughborough Colleges 8 (London Scottish: S Wilson J A P Shackleton I H P Laughland J A T Rodd J C Brash J G R Percival W R A Watherston. Loughborough: T G R Davies D R Davies C Macfadyean A Dobbins D Rollitt N Barker T Tennick)
1966: Loughborough Colleges 29 Northampton 10 (Loughborough: R Sleigh T G R Davies G B Davies B S Walker G McDonald T G Williams J Taylor. Northampton: R Kottler G R Allen J Cooley D Jenkins P J Larter N Barker J M Parsons)

Mike Biggar, of London Scottish, breaks clear in the clash against Stewart's-Melville in 1983 Middlesex Sevens at Twickenham. (Colorsport.)

1967: Harlequins 14 Richmond 11 (Harlequins: R H Lloyd T Rutter R Hiller R Lewis M Mason P Orr CM Payne. Richmond: H Waller J Browntree I Moffatt T P Bedford E Preece L G Cormack B Stoneman)
1968: London Welsh 16 Richmond 3 (London Welsh: C T Gibbons N B Thomas S J Dawes G W James T G Evans G Patterson A J Gray. Richmond: A Blake H G Waller R P K Whitcomb N G C Wilson E Preece W G Hadman L G Cormack)
1969: St Luke's College 21 Edinburgh Wanderers 16 (St Luke's: P Knight A Porter J Warren R Codd I Morgan R Williams J Vaughan. Edinburgh Wanderers: J Perrins R H Lamb W M Campbell P Thompson J Douglas D R Anderson T J Ellesmere)
1970: Loughborough Colleges 26 Edinburgh Wanderers 11 (Loughborough: K J Fielding J L Regan A Robinson S C Winship S T Williams J D Gray D A Sellar. Edinburgh Wanderers: J Perrins R Parsons R H Lamb D Tweedie J Douglas R R Anderson T J Ellesmere)
1971: London Welsh 18 Harlequins 9 (London Welsh: T Davies K Hughes C T Gibbons W G Hullin I C Jones A M Phillips A J Gray. Harlequins: T Rutter R H Lloyd D Coley J Gronow N O Martin J Stockdill M Mason)
1972: London Welsh 22 Public School Wanderers 18 (London Welsh: T G R Davies S J Dawes T Davies W G Hullin J P R Williams A M Phillips I C Jones. Public

School Wanderers: J J Williams V Jenkins I Lewis R J Dyer A T J Hodge J Billington S G Hannath)
1973: London Welsh 24 Public School Wanderers 22 (London Welsh: A Richards A J Gray S J Dawes W G Hullin J Vaughan J Taylor J P R Williams. Public School Wanderers: K J Fielding A R Irvine I Robertson N C Starmer-Smith S G Hannath R M Wilkinson N Barker)
1974: Richmond 34 London Welsh 16 (Richmond: P S Maxwell N R Boult P H D Lavery N G C Wilson A L Bucknall P Hearn W G Hadman. London Welsh: R Ellis-Jones T G R Davies G W James W G Hullin J Vaughan A M Phillips J Taylor)
1975: Richmond 24 Loughborough Colleges 8 (Richmond: P S Maxwell N R Boult P H D Lavery T O'Hanlon W G Hadman P Hearn A L Bucknall. Loughborough: C W Lambert I Ray P Ubee A Armstrong W Cuthley S Oliver N Gillingham)
1976: Loughborough Colleges 21 Harlequins 20 (Loughborough: K Williams M Knight J Glynn G Gilbert K Douglas R Black N Gillingham. Harlequins: C W Lambert D A Cooke K M Bushell S Winship N O Martin P B Tikoisuva A C Alexander)
1977: Richmond 26 Gosforth 16 (Richmond: J P A Janion T O'Hanlon A Mort I R Shackleton (sub: A Mansfield) N Dobson N Vinter C Yeomans. Gosforth: S Archer K Britten R Breakey M Young T Roberts C White D Robinson)
1978: Harlequins 40 Rosslyn Park 12 (Harlequins: G Wood D A Cooke G Gilbert C St J Lamden A C Alexander K Douglas C W Lambert. Rosslyn Park: G Lloyd R Fisher N Anderson I George D Starling P J Warfield A G Ripley)
1979: Richmond 24 London Scottish 10 (Richmond: B Preston I R Shackleton I Ray T O'Hanlon M Mallett P Williams R Pearson. London Scottish: T McNab R Gordon R Wilson A J M Lawson (sub D Robertson) M Biggar G McQuater A F McHarg)
1980: Richmond 34 Rosslyn Park 18 (Richmond: C W Lambert I Ray N J Preston T O'Hanlon N Dobson N Vinter C Yeomans. Rosslyn Park: N Anderson P J Warfield R Sainter S Tiddy S Henderson B Bazell A G Ripley)
1981: Rosslyn Park 16 London Welsh 14 (Rosslyn Park: P Bate J Gill R Fisher N Anderson S Henderson B Bazell A G Ripley. London Welsh: C F W Rees N Rees D Rees I George (sub A Clements) E Lewis T Jones K Bowring)
1982: Stewart's Melville FP 34 Richmond 12 (Stewart's Melville: J. Mackenzie A Blackwood D Wylie D W Morgan F Calder A Brewster. Richmond: N J Preston M Humberstone I Ray D Mayle J Fenton N Vinter B Crawsham)
1983: Richmond 20 London Welsh 13 (Richmond: J Dyson N J Preston (Capt) I Ray T O Hanlon P Williams J Fenton B Crawshaw. London Welsh: C F W Rees J Hurley D Slater I George E Lewis T Jones K Bowring (Capt))

Unlucky finalist
Norman Barker, a hooker, played in three finals for different sides (Loughborough 1965, Northampton 1966 and Public School Wanderers 1973) and was on the losing side each time. In 1964 Barker played for Loughborough when they won, 18–16 against London Scottish

Most wins
10 Richmond

Most finals
16 London Welsh
15 Richmond

Most points in final
40 Harlequins (40–12 v Rosslyn Park 1978)

Most points by losing finalist
22 Public School Wanderers (22–24 v London Welsh 1973)

Rosslyn Park Schools Sevens
1983 Open winner: Millfield. Festival: Ampleforth. Junior Festival: St Mary's, Liverpool. Prep Schools: Caldicot

Inter-Services Champions

1920	Navy	1946	Army	1966	Navy
1921	Navy	1947	RAF	1967	Army
1922	Navy	1948	Triple tie	1968	Army
1923	RAF	1949	Army/RAF	1969	Army
1924	Triple tie	1950	Army	1970	Navy
1925	Army/RAF	1951	Navy	1971	RAF
1926	Army	1952	Army	1972	Army
1927	Navy	1953	Army	1973	Navy
1928	Army	1954	Triple tie	1974	Navy
1929	Army	1955	RAF	1975	Triple tie
1930	Army	1956	Triple tie	1976	Army
1931	Navy	1957	Army	1977	Navy
1932	Army	1958	RAF	1978	Triple tie
1933	Army	1959	RAF	1979	RAF
1934	Army	1960	Army	1980	Army
1935	Triple tie	1961	Navy	1981	Navy
1936	Army	1962	RAF	1982	RAF
1937	Army	1963	Army	1983	Army
1938	Navy	1964	Army		
1939	Navy	1965	Army		

The Army have won the Tournament outright 25 times, Royal Navy 15, and RAF 9.

Non-International Touring Defeats in England

Cambridge University		
Beat Australia	13–3	Cambridge 1957–58
Combined Midlands & East Midlands		
Beat Australia	16–5	Leicester 1908
East Midlands		
Beat Australia	11–8	Leicester 1975
Lancashire & Cheshire		
Beat Australia	9–8	Blundellsands 1947–48
Leicester & East Midlands		
Beat South Africa	30–21	Leicester 1931–32
London Counties		
Beat South Africa	10–8	Twickenham 1912
Beat Australia	14–8	Twickenham 1947–48
Beat South Africa	11–9	Twickenham 1951–52
Beat Australia	14–9	Twickenham 1966–67

Midland Counties
Beat Australia 8–3 Coventry 1957–58

Midland Counties West
Beat New Zealand 16–8 Moseley 1972–73

Midland Division
Beat Australia 16–10 Leicester 1981

North East Counties
Beat Australia 17–14 Newcastle 1966–67

Northern Counties
Beat Australia 16–13 Gosforth 1973

North West Counties
Beat Australia 6–3 Blundellsands 1957–58
Beat New Zealand 16–14 Workington 1972–73

Northern Division
Beat New Zealand 21–9 Otley 1979

Oxford University
Beat Australia 12–6 Oxford 1957–58
Beat South Africa 6–3 Oxford 1969–70

South & South West Counties
Beat Australia 14–5 Bath 1973

South West Counties
Beat Australia 9–0 Camborne 1966–67

Western Counties
Beat Australia 9–8 Bristol 1957–58

West Midlands
Beat Australia 17–9 Coventry 1966–67

Most capped player
43 Tony Neary 1971–80

Most capped players by position

Full back	19	Bob Hiller 1968–72
Wing	29	Peter Squires 1973–79
		Mike Slemen 1976–82
Centre	28	Jeff Butterfield 1953–59
Stand off	22	W J A Davies 1913–23
Scrum half	26	Steve Smith 1973–83
Prop	31	Fran Cotton 1971–81
Hooker	42	John Pullin 1966–76
Lock	32	Bill Beaumont 1975–81
Flanker	43	Tony Neary 1971–80
No. 8	24	Andy Ripley 1972–76

Most points on tour
48 Neil Bennett in Australia 1975

Most points in a tour match
36 Neil Bennett v Western Australia 1975

Stalwarts of England rugby—the highly accomplished Bob Hiller (top), holder of a record 19 caps at full-back, Fran Cotton (centre), most capped prop-forward with 31 appearances, and Tony Neary, England's most capped player with 43 internationals to his credit. They played together in the same England side for a first time, against Scotland at Twickenham on 20 March 1971, and on two other occasions before Hiller was dropped in favour of Peter Knight in 1972. (Geo. Herringshaw.)

England's Records Against Other Countries

Opposition	*Highest score*	*Biggest winning margin*	*Most points conceded*	*Biggest losing margin*
Scotland	30 (30–18) 1980	20 (26–6) 1977	28 (19–28) 1931	20 (6–26) 1971
Ireland	36 (36–14) 1938	22 (36–14) 1938	26 (21–26) 1974	22 (0–22) 1947
Wales	25 (25–0) 1896	25 (25–0) 1896	34 (21–34) 1967	25 (0–25) 1905
France	41 (41–13) 1907	37 (37–0) 1911	37 (12–37) 1972	25 (12–37) 1972
New Zealand	16 (16–10) 1973	13 (13–0) 1936	23 (11–23) 1967	15 (0–15) 1905
South Africa	18 (18–9) 1972	9 (18–9) 1972	9 (3–9) 1913 (18–9) 1972	7 (0–7) 1932
Australia	23 (23–6) 1976	17 (20–3) 1973 (23–6) 1976	30 (21–30) 1975	12 (11–23) 1967

Most tries in a tour match
4 Alan Morley v Western Australia 1975
Peter Preece v New South Wales 1975

Most points in internationals
164 Dusty Hare 1974–83 (18 matches)

Most points in an international
22 D Lambert v France 1911

Most tries in internationals
18 Cyril Lowe 1913–23 (25 matches)

Most tries in an international
5 D Lambert v France 1907

Most points in championship season
38 Roger Hosen 1966–67 (4 matches)

Most tries in championship season
8 Cyril Lowe 1913–14 (4 matches)

Mike Davis and (left) Don Gatherer, two of England's premier figures on the coaching front during the late Seventies and early Eighties. Davis was also an outstanding lock-forward for England, winning 16 caps. (Colorsport.)

John Scott (No. 8) aggressively contends for the ball at the end of a line-out against France at Twickenham on 15 January 1983. Awaiting the outcome is the blond-haired Jean-Pierre Rives (No. 6), the French captain. (Geo. Herringshaw.)

Most points by England in championships
82 1913–14

Most tries in championships
20 1913–14

Most tries in an international
9 v France (35–8) 1906
v France (41–13) 1907
v France (39–13) 1914

Most tries against
8 by Wales (6–28) 1922

England Students Tour to Japan 1982
W 71–0 Kyushu Provinces, W 51–14 Kansai Provinces, W 43–0 All Japan, W 19–9 New Zealand Universities, W 99–0 Japan B, W 40–0 Hong Kong

Other Overseas Tours

	P	W	D	L	F	A
1910 Argentina	6	6	0	0	213	31
1927 Argentina	9	9	0	0	295	9
1936 Argentina	10	10	0	0	399	12
1967 Canada	5	5	0	0	164	9
1971 Far East	7	7	0	0	228	52
1979 Japan, Tonga, Fiji	7	7	0	0	270	93
1981 Argentina	7	6	1	0	193	100

Non-International Board Matches

			W	D	L
Argentina	1978	Twickenham		13–13	
	1981	Buenos Aires		19–19	
	1981	Buenos Aires	12–6		
Canada	1967	Vancouver	29–0		
Fiji	1973	Suva	13–12		
	1979	Suva	19–7		
Hong Kong	1971	Hong Kong	26–0		
Japan	1971	Osaka	27–19		
	1971	Tokyo	6–3		
	1979	Osaka	21–19		
	1979	Tokyo	38–18		
Singapore	1971	Singapore	39–9		
Sri Lanka	1971	Colombo	40–11		
	1971	Colombo	34–6		
Tonga	1979	Nuku' Alofa	37–17		
USA	1977	Twickenham	37–11		

Incoming tour 1982

Fiji
L 4–19 Northern Division
L 6–36 South and South-West
L 16–25 Midland Division
L 12–30 Cambridge University
L 9–26 English Students
L 19–60 England XV

Fiji also played 4 matches in Scotland, losing all 4

Outgoing tour 1982

England under 23s to Italy

W	15–0	Italian Under 23s	Treviso
W	21–10	Italy B	Mantua
L	7–12	Italy	Padua

B International 1982
Ireland 6 England 10 (Ravenhill, Belfast)

FRANCE

Foundation	1920
Headquarters	FFR 7 Cité D'Antin, Paris 9E
Main stadium	Parc des Princes, Paris (capacity 50 000)
Colours	Blue jerseys, white shorts
Number of clubs	1732
Number of players	185 000
Season	September–June
Temperatures	40°F (4°C) to 73°F (23°C)
Population	53 324 000

French Club Championship finals

1892 Racing Club de France 4 Stade Français 3. 1893 Stade Français 7 Racing Club de France 3. 1894 Stade Français 18 Inter-Nos 0. 1895 Stade Français 16 Paris Olympique 0. 1896 Paris Olympique 12 Stade Français 0. 1897 Stade Français won group. 1898 Stade Français won group. 1899 Stade Bordelais UC 5 Stade Français 3. 1900 Racing Club de France 37 Stade Bordelais UC 3. 1901 Stade Français beat Stade Bordelais UC on disqualification. 1902 Racing Club de France 6 Stade Bordelais UC 0. 1903 Stade Français 16 Stade Toulousain 8. 1904 Stade Bordelais UC 3 Stade Français 0. 1905 Stade Bordelais UC 12 Stade Français 3. 1906 Stade Bordelais UC 9 Stade Français 0. 1907 Stade Bordelais UC 14 Stade Français 3. 1908 Stade Français 16 Stade Bordelais UC 3. 1909 Stade Bordelais UC 17 Stade Toulousain 0. 1910 FC Lyon 13 Stade Bordelais UC 8. 1911 Stade Bordelais UC 14 SCUF 0. 1912 Stade Toulousain 8 Racing Club de France 6. 1913 Bayonne 31 SCUF 8. 1914 Perpignan 8 Tarbes 7. 1920 Tarbes 8 Racing Club de France 3. 1921 Perpignan 5 Stade Toulousain 0. 1922 Stade Toulousain 6 Bayonne 0. 1923 Stade Toulousain 3 Bayonne 0. 1924 Stade Toulousain 3 Perpignan 0. 1925 Perpignan 5 Carcassonne 0. 1926 Stade Toulousain 11 Perpignan 0. 1927 Stade Toulousain 19 Stade Français 9. 1928 Pau 6 Quillan 4. 1929 Quillan 11 Lezignan 8. 1930 Agen 4 Quillan 0. 1931 Toulon 6 Lyon OU 3. 1932 Lyon OU 9 Narbonne 3. 1933 Lyon OU 10 Narbonne 3. 1934 Bayonne 13 Biarritz 8. 1935 Biarritz 3 Perpignan 0. 1936 Narbonne 6 Montferrand 3. 1937 Vienne 13 Montferrand 7. 1938 Perpignan 11 Biarritz 6. 1939 Biarritz 6 Perpignan 0. 1943 Bayonne 3 Agen 0. 1944 Perpignan 20 Bayonne 5. 1945 Agen 7 Lourdes 3. 1946 Pau 11 Lourdes 0. 1947 Stade Toulousain 10 Agen 3. 1948 Lourdes 11 Toulon 3. 1949 Castres 14 Mont de Marsan 3. 1950 Castres 11 Racing Club de France 8. 1951 Carmaux 14 Tarbes 12. 1952 Lourdes 20 Perpignan 11. 1953 Lourdes 21 Mont de Marsan 16. 1954 Grenoble 5 Cognac 3. 1955 Perpignan 11 Lourdes 6. 1956 Lourdes 20 Dax 0. 1957 Lourdes 16 Racing Club de France 13. 1958 Lourdes 25 Mazamet 8. 1959 Racing Club de France 8 Mont de Marsan 3. 1960 Lourdes 14 Beziers 11. 1961 Beziers 6 Dax 3. 1962 Agen 14 Beziers 11. 1963 Mont de Marsan 9 Dax 6. 1964 Pau 14 Beziers 0. 1965 Agen 15 Brive 8. 1966 Agen 9 Dax 8. 1967 Montauban 11 Begles 3. 1968 Lourdes 9 Toulon 9 (Lourdes won on tries). 1969 Begles 11 Stade Toulousain 9. 1970 La Voulte 3 Montferrand 0. 1971 Beziers 15 Toulon 9. 1972 Beziers 9 Brive 0. 1973 Tarbes 18 Dax 12. 1974 Beziers 16 Narbonne 14. 1975 Beziers 13 Brive 12. 1976 Agen 13 Beziers 10. 1977 Beziers 12 Perpignan 4. 1978 Beziers 31 Montferrand 9. 1979 Narbonne 10 Bagneres 0. 1980 Beziers 10 Stade Toulousain 6. 1981 Beziers 22 Bagneres 13. 1982 Agen 18 Bayonne 9. 1983 Beziers 14 Nice 6

France's record against other countries

Opposition	*Highest score*	*Biggest winning margin*	*Most points conceded*	*Biggest losing margin*
Australia	34 (34–6) 1976	28 (34–6) 1976	24 (24–14) 1981	10 (24–14) 1981
England	37 (37–12) 1972	25 (37–12) 1972	41 (13–41) 1907	37 (0–37) 1911
Scotland	23 (23–3) 1977	20 (23–3) 1977	31 (3–31) 1912	28 (3–31) 1912
Ireland	27 (27–6) 1964	23 (26–3) 1976	25 (5–25) 1911 (6–25) 1975	24 (0–24) 1913
Wales	22 (22–13) 1965	10 (16–6) 1958	49 (14–49) 1910	42 (5–47) 1909
New Zealand	24 (24–19) 1979	7 (13–6) 1973	38 (8–38) 1906	30 (8–38) 1906
South Africa	25 (25–38) 1975	5 (19–14) 1967	38 (5–38) 1913 (25–38) 1975	33 (5–38) 1913

Club Championship records

Most points
731 Beziers, 1978

Most tries
125 Beziers, 1977

Most individual points
55 Jean Pierre Romeu (Montferrand), 1978

Record total attendance
339 245 in 1972

Record score
Beziers 100 Montchanin 0 (also record 21 tries), 16 December 1979 (Michel Fabre scored 11 tries, world record for a first-class club match)

Record attendance at final
45 000 Beziers–Narbonne (Parc des Princes, Paris, 1974)

Club record score
Racing Club de France 140, St Medard 0 (Racing also scored 27 tries), 1979

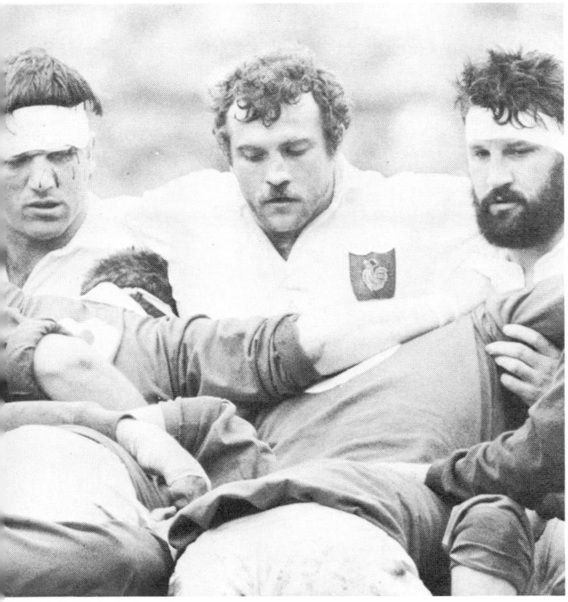

Les Formidables—The French front row of Robert Paparemborde, Bernard Herrero and Pierre Dospital, hesitate before going down against Ireland at Lansdowne Road 19 February 1983. (Geo. Herringshaw.)

Jean-Pierre Rives, the French captain, takes a last look at the Welsh defensive line-up before packing down at a scrummage in the Championship match at Cardiff on 6 February 1982. Wales won 22–12. (Geo. Herringshaw.)

Individual records

Most capped player
52 Roland Bertranne 1971–81

Most capped players by position

Full back	30	Michel Vannier 1953–61
Wing	28	Jean Dupuy 1956–64
		Christian Darrouy 1957–67
Centre	39	Roland Bertranne 1971–81
Stand off	23	Pierre Albaladejo 1954–64
Scrum half	33	Gerard Dufau 1948–57
Prop	42	Robert Paparemborde 1975–83
Hooker	25	Alain Paco 1974–80
Lock	30	Elié Cester 1966–74
Flanker	39	Michel Crauste 1958–66
No. 8	26	Guy Basquet 1947–52

Serge Blanco, the multi-talented French full-back, who scored 36 points in the 1983 International Championship, a record haul for a Frenchman. (Colorsport.)

Most points in internationals
139 J-P Romeu 1973–7 (22 matches)

Most points in an international
17 Guy Camberabero v Australia 1967

Most tries in internationals
14 Christian Darrouy 1957–67 (28 matches)

Most tries in an international
3 Michel Crauste v England 1962
Christian Darrouy v Ireland 1963

Most points in championship season
36 Serge Blanco 1983

Most tries in championship season
5 Patrick Esteve 1983 (4 matches)
4 Michel Crauste 1961–2 (4 matches)
Christian Darrouy 1964–5 (3 matches)

Most points on tour
71 J-P Romeu South Africa 1975 (7 matches)

Most points in a tour match
19 J L Dehez v S W Districts, South Africa 1967

Most tries in a tour match
4 Roland Bertranne v Western Transvaal 1971
Michel Bruel v Australian Capital Territory 1981

Team records

Most points in championship season
82 1975–6

Most tries
13 1975–6

Most tries in an international
6 v Ireland (27–6) 1964
v England (35–13) 1970
v England (37–12) 1972
v England (30–9) 1976
v Australia (34–6) 1976

Most tries against
11 by Wales (5–47) 1909

France to Australia and New Zealand

		P	W	D	L	F	A
1961	New Zealand	13	6	0	7	150	149
1961	Australia	2	2	0	0	30	20
1968	New Zealand	12	8	0	4	154	120
1968	Australia	2	1	1	0	41	22
1972	Australia	9	8	1	0	254	122
1979	New Zealand	9	6	0	3	168	116
1981	Australia	9	6	0	3	189	112

France to South Africa

	P	W	D	L	F	A
1958	10	5	2	3	137	124
1964	6	5	0	1	117	55
1967	13	8	1	4	209	161
1971	9	7	1	1	228	92
1975	11	6	1	4	282	190
1980	4	3	0	1	90	95

Other overseas tours

		P	W	D	L	F	A
1976	USA	3	3	0	0	120	33
1977	Argentina	7	6	1	0	192	53
1978	Canada and Far East	7	7	0	0	310	72

Most points on tour
282 South Africa 1975

Incoming tour 1982

Argentina

W	38–15	French Selection	Clermont-Ferrand
L	15–25	French Selection	Valence
L	9–27	French Army	Aurillac
W	22–8	French Barbarians	Dax
L	12–25	France	Toulouse
W	12–9	French Selection	Angoulême
L	6–13	France	Paris

Tour summary: P 7 W 3 L 4 F 114 A 122

1983 Crawshay's Welsh XV
W 30–22 Oloron, W 24–10 Aire sur Adour

France 'B' 1982
W 16–15 Wales B Pontypool

1983
W 26–12 Scotland B Dundee

Other match 1982
French Selection 19 French Police 3 (Tarbes)

New Zealand to France 1981

W	15–13	French Selection	Strasbourg
W	18–10	French Selection	Clermont-Ferrand
L	16–18	French Selection	Grenoble
W	28–18	French Barbarians	Bayonne
D	6–6	French Selection	Perpignan
W	13–9	France	Toulouse
W	17–13	French Selection	La Rochelle
W	18–6	France	Paris

Tour summary: P 8 W 6 D 1 L 1 F 131 A 93

Non-International touring defeats in France

South West France

Beat New Zealand	11–8	Bordeaux	1954
Beat Australia	11–9	Bordeaux	1967
Beat South Africa	11–3	Bordeaux	1968

Regional XVs

Beat Australia	16–9	Limoges	1971
Beat Australia	7–6	Strasbourg	1971
Beat South Africa	7–4	Angouleme	1974
Beat Australia	15–13	Narbonne	1976
Beat Australia	10–6	Clermont-Ferrand	1976
Beat Australia	16–7	Tarbes	1976
Beat Australia	25–7	Bourg-en-Bresse	1976

International results

			W	D	L
Argentina	1949	Buenos Aires	5–0		
	1949	Buenos Aires	12–3		
	1954	Buenos Aires	22–8		
	1954	Buenos Aires	30–3		
	1960	Buenos Aires	37–3		
	1960	Buenos Aires	12–3		
	1960	Buenos Aires	29–6		
	1974	Buenos Aires	20–15		
	1974	Buenos Aires	31–27		
	1975	Lyon	29–6		
	1975	Paris	36–21		
	1977	Buenos Aires	26–3		
	1977	Buenos Aires		18–18	
	1982	Toulouse	25–12		
	1982	Paris	13–6		
Canada	1978	Calgary	24–9		
	1979	Paris	34–15		
Czechoslovakia	1957	Toulouse	28–3		
	1957	Moscow	38–19		
	1957	Liberec	30–3		
	1966	Prague	36–12		
	1968	Prague	19–6		

			W	D	L
	1969	Besançon	34–14		
	1970	Prague	53–6		
	1972	Colmar	68–3		
	1974	Bourg-en-Bresse	28–3		
	1977	Hagondange	63–0		
Fed. Rep. Germany	1982	Heidelberg	53–15		
	1983	Bourg-en-Bresse	84–0		
Fiji	1964	Paris	21–3		
	1979	Suva	13–4		
Italy	1935	Rome	44–6		
	1937	Paris	43–5		
	1948	Rovigo	39–6		
	1949	Marsiglia	27–0		
	1952	Milan	17–8		
	1953	Lyon	22–8		
	1954	Rome	39–12		
	1965	Grenoble	24–0		
	1955	Barcelona	16–8		
	1956	Padua	16–3		
	1957	Agen	38–6		
	1958	Naples	11–3		
	1959	Nantes	22–0		
	1960	Treviso	26–0		
	1961	Chambery	17–0		
	1962	Breschia	6–3		
	1963	Grenoble	14–12		
	1964	Parma	12–3		
	1965	Pau	21–0		
	1966	Naples	21–0		
	1967	Toulon	60–13		
	1969	Catonia	22–8		
	1971	Nice	37–13		
	1975	Rome	16–9		
	1976	Milan	23–11		
	1977	Grenoble	10–3		
	1978	Aquila	31–9		
	1979	Padua	15–9		
	1981	Rovigo	17–9		
	1982	Carcassone	25–19		
	1983	Rovigo		6–6	
Netherlands	1975	Hilversum	26–18		
	1976	Lille	71–6		
Japan	1973	Bordeaux	30–18		
	1978	Tokyo	55–16		
	1980	Paris	23–3		
Morocco	1972	Casablanca	72–3		
	1973	Marmande	73–6		
	1974	La Rochelle	54–3		
	1977	Casablanca	69–0		
	1980	Casablanca	33–4		
	1983	Casablanca	16–9		
Poland	1969	Warsaw	67–0		
	1977	Warsaw	26–9		
	1977	Albi	35–24		
	1977	Czestochova	26–9		
	1980	Lodz	42–0		
	1981	Bully	49–6		
Romania	1919	Paris	48–5		
	1924	Paris	59–3		
	1936	Berlin	26–5		

			W	D	L
	1937	Paris	27–11		
	1938	Bucharest	11–8		
	1957	Bucharest	18–15		
	1957	Bordeaux	39–0		
	1960	Bucharest			5–11
	1961	Bayonne		5–5	
	1962	Bucharest			0–3
	1963	Toulouse		6–6	
	1964	Bucharest	9–6		
	1965	Lyon	8–3		
	1966	Bucharest	9–3		
	1967	Nantes	11–3		
	1968	Bucharest			14–15
	1969	Tarbes	14–9		
	1970	Bucharest	14–3		
	1971	Béziers	31–12		
	1972	Constanta	15–6		
	1973	Valencia	7–6		
	1974	Bucharest			10–15
	1975	Bordeaux	36–12		
	1976	Bucharest			12–15
	1977	Clermont Ferrand	9–6		
	1978	Bucharest	9–6		
	1979	Montauban	30–12		
	1980	Bucharest			0–15
	1981	Narbonne	17–9		
	1982	Bucharest			9–13
Soviet Union	1978	Toulouse	29–7		
	1980	Moscow			7–18
	1981	Angoulême	23–10		
	1982	Moscow		10–10	
	1982	Mérignac			6–12
Spain	1927	Madrid	66–6		
	1928	Bordeaux	53–6		
	1954	Barna	45–26		
	1955	Limoges	50–6		
	1965	Valencia	42–3		
	1965	Barna	45–3		
	1967	Valencia	42–3		
	1970	Madrid	58–6		
	1973	Barna	30–23		
	1974	Madrid	15–7		
	1975	Mauleon	46–3		
	1976	Madrid	36–0		
	1977	Hendaye	28–21		
	1978	Madrid	20–3		
	1979	Oloron	92–0		
	1981	Barcelona	40–19		
USA	1920	Paris	14–5		
	1924	Paris			3–17
	1976	Chicago	33–14		
Yugoslavia	1979	Split	86–6		

Distribution of a reputed 5000 forged tickets caused the Irish Rugby Union a major headache at the Ireland v France game at Lansdowne Road on 19 February 1983. The consequent overcrowding and seat duplication was solved by at least some of the spectators, who found vantage points on the roof of the Lansdowne Clubhouse, which adjoins the main stadium. (Geo. Herringshaw.)

IRELAND

Foundation	1879
Headquarters	IRFU, 62 Lansdowne Road, Dublin 4
Main stadium	Lansdowne Road, Dublin (capacity 58 000)
Colours	Green jerseys
Number of clubs	210
Number of players	10 000
Season	September–May
Temperatures	32°F (0°C) to 60°F (16°C)
Population	4 760 000 (combined)

Irish Senior Cup winners

Leinster: 1882 Trinity. 1883 Trinity. 1884 Trinity. 1885 Wanderers. 1886 Trinity. 1887 Trinity. 1888 Wanderers. 1889 Bective Rangers. 1890 Trinity. 1891 Lansdowne. 1892 Bective Rangers. 1893 Trinity. 1894 Wanderers. 1895 Trinity. 1896 Trinity. 1897 Trinity. 1898 Trinity. 1899 Monkstown. 1900 Trinity. 1901 Lansdowne. 1902 Monkstown. 1903 Lansdowne. 1904 Lansdowne. 1905 Trinity. 1906 Wanderers. 1907 Trinity. 1908 Trinity. 1909 Old Wesley. 1910 Bective Rangers. 1911 Wanderers. 1912 Trinity. 1913 Trinity. 1914 Bective Rangers. 1915–19 no matches. 1920 Trinity. 1921 Trinity. 1922 Lansdowne. 1923 Bective Rangers. 1924 University College. 1925 Bective Rangers. 1926 Trinity. 1927 Lansdowne. 1928 Lansdowne. 1929 Lansdowne. 1930 Lansdowne. 1931 Lansdowne. 1932 Bective Rangers. 1933 Lansdowne. 1934 Bective Rangers. 1935 Bective Rangers. 1936 Clontarf. 1937 Blackrock College. 1938 University College. 1939 Blackrock College. 1940 Old Belvedere. 1941 Old Belvedere. 1942 Old Belvedere. 1943 Old Belvedere. 1944 Old Belvedere. 1945 Old Belvedere. 1946 Old Belvedere. 1947 Wanderers. 1948 University College. 1949 Lansdowne. 1950 Lansdowne. 1951 Old Belvedere. 1952 Old Belvedere. 1953 Lansdowne. 1954 Wanderers. 1955 Bective Rangers. 1956 Bective Rangers. 1957 Blackrock College. 1958 St Mary's College. 1959 Wanderers. 1960 Trinity. 1961 Blackrock College. 1962 Bective Rangers. 1963 University College. 1964 University College. 1965 Lansdowne. 1966 Terenure College. 1967 Terenure College. 1968 Old Belvedere. 1969 St Mary's

Neither Tom Kiernan, the coach, nor Ciaran Fitzgerald, the captain, look over-impressed with Ollie Campbell's findings during a walkabout before the match against England at Lansdowne Road on 19 March 1983. (Geo. Herringshaw.)

College. 1970 University College. 1971 St Mary's College. 1972 Lansdowne. 1973 Wanderers. 1974 St Mary's College. 1975 Blackrock College. 1977 University College. 1978 Wanderers. 1979 Lansdowne. 1980 Lansdowne. 1981 Lansdowne. 1982 Wanderers. 1983 Blackrock College.

Ulster: 1885 NIFC. 1886 Queen's University. 1887 Queen's University. 1888 Lisburn. 1889 Albion. 1890 Queen's University. 1891 Queen's University. 1892 Queen's University. 1893 NIFC. 1894 NIFC. 1895 NIFC. 1896 NIFC. 1897 NIFC. 1898 NIFC. 1899 NIFC. 1900 Queen's University. 1901 NIFC. 1902 NIFC. 1903 Queen's University. 1904 Malone. 1905 Malone. 1906 Collegians. 1907 Malone. 1908 NIFC. 1909 Queen's University. 1910 Collegians. 1911 Knock. 1912 Queen's University. 1913 Collegians. 1914–19 no matches. 1920 NIFC. 1921 Queen's University. 1922 Instonians. 1923 Instonians. 1924 Queen's University. 1925 Queen's University. 1926 Collegians. 1927 Instonians. 1928 Instonians. 1929 Instonians. 1930 NIFC. 1931 Instonians. 1932 Queen's University. 1933 Queen's University. 1934 Instonians. 1935 NIFC. 1936 Queen's University. 1937 Queen's University. 1938 Instonians. 1939 NIFC. 1940–45 no matches. 1946 Instonians. 1947 Queen's University. 1948 Instonians. 1949 Instonians. 1950 Instonians. 1951 Queen's University. 1952 Collegians. 1953 CIYMS. 1954 Instonians. 1955 NIFC. 1956 Instonians. 1957 Instonians. 1958 Instonians. 1959 Queen's University. 1960 Queen's University. 1961 Collegians. 1962 Collegians. 1963 Ballymena. 1964 Dungannon. 1965 Instonians. 1966 CIYMS. 1967 CIYMS. 1968 Dungannon. 1969 NIFC. 1970 Ballymena. 1971 Malone. 1972 CIYMS. 1973 NIFC. 1974 CIYMS. 1975 Ballymena. 1977 Ballymena. 1978 CIYMS. 1979 Instonians. 1980 Bangor. 1981 Queen's University. 1982 Bangor. 1983 Collegians.

Munster: 1886 Bandon. 1887 Queen's College. 1888 Queen's College. 1889 Garryowen. 1890 Garryowen. 1891 Garryowen. 1892 Garryowen. 1893 Garryowen. 1894 Garryowen. 1895 Garryowen. 1896 Garryowen. 1897 Queen's College. 1898 Garryowen. 1899 Garryowen. 1900 Queen's College. 1901 Queen's College. 1902 Garryowen. 1903 Garryowen. 1904 Garryowen. 1905 Cork Constitution. 1906 Cork Constitution. 1907 Cork Constitution. 1908 Garryowen. 1909 Garryowen. 1910 Cork Constitution. 1911 Garryowen. 1912 University College Cork. 1913 University College Cork. 1914 Garryowen. 1915–19 no matches. 1920 Garryowen. 1921 Dolphin. 1922 Cork Constitution. 1923 Cork Constitution. 1924 Garryowen. 1925 Garryowen. 1926 Garryowen. 1927 Bohemians. 1928 Young Munster. 1929 Cork Constitution. 1930 Young Munster. 1931 Dolphin. 1932 Garryowen. 1933 Cork Constitution. 1934 Garryowen. 1935 University College Cork. 1936 University College Cork. 1937 University College Cork. 1938 Young Munster. 1939 University College Cork. 1940 Garryowen. 1941 University College Cork. 1942 Cork Constitution. 1943 Cork Constitution. 1944 Dolphin. 1945 Dolphin. 1946 Cork Constitution. 1947 Garryowen. 1948 Dolphin. 1949 Sunday's Well. 1950 University College Cork. 1951 University College Cork. 1952 Garryowen. 1953 Sunday's Well. 1954 Garryowen. 1955 University College Cork. 1956 Dolphin. 1957 Cork Constitution. 1958 Bohemians. 1959 Bohemians. 1960 Shannon. 1961 Cork Constitution. 1962 Bohemians. 1963 Cork Constitution. 1964 Cork Constitution. 1965 University College Cork. 1966 Highfield. 1967 Cork Constitution. 1968 Highfield. 1969 Garryowen. 1970 Cork Constitution. 1971 Garryowen. 1972 Cork Constitution. 1973 Cork Constitution. 1974

Garryowen. 1975 Garryowen. 1977 Shannon. 1978 Shannon. 1979 Garryowen. 1980 Young Munster. 1981 University College Cork. 1982 Shannon. 1983 Cork Constitution.

Connacht: 1896 Galway Town. 1897 Queen's College Galway. 1898 Galway Grammar School. 1899 Queen's College Galway. 1900–02 no matches. 1903 Queen's College Galway. 1904 Queen's College Galway. 1905 Queen's College Galway. 1906 Galway Town. 1907 Queen's College Galway. 1908 Queen's College Galway. 1909 University College Galway. 1910 University College Galway. 1911 Galway Town. 1912 University College Galway. 1913 Galway Town. 1914 Sligo Town. 1915–21 no matches. 1922 Galway Town. 1923 University College Galway. 1924 University College Galway. 1925 University College Galway. 1926 Galwegians. 1927 Galwegians. 1928 Galwegians. 1929 Galwegians. 1930 University College Galway. 1931 Loughrea. 1932 University College Galway. 1933 Corinthians. 1934 Corinthians. 1935 University College Galway. 1936 University College Galway. 1937 University College Galway. 1938 Galwegians. 1939 University College Galway. 1940 University College Galway. 1941 Corinthians. 1942 University College Galway. 1943 Galwegians. 1944 University College Galway. 1945 University College Galway. 1946 University College Galway. 1947 Corinthians. 1948 Ballinsloe. 1949 Corinthians. 1950 Ballinsloe. 1951 Ballina. 1952 Galwegians. 1953 University College Galway. 1954 Corinthians. 1955 Athlone. 1956 Galwegians. 1957 Galwegians. 1958 Galwegians. 1959 Galwegians. 1960 Galwegians. 1961 University College Galway. 1962 University College Galway. 1963 Galwegians. 1964 University College Galway. 1965 Galwegians. 1966 University College Galway. 1967 University College Galway. 1968 Galwegians. 1969 Galwegians. 1970 University College Galway. 1971 Galwegians. 1972 Corinthians. 1973 Galwegians. 1974 University College Galway. 1975 Galwegians. 1977 Athlone. 1978 Corinthians. 1979 Ballina. 1980 Galwegians. 1981 Galwegians. 1982 Corinthians. 1983 Galwegians.

Inter-provincial matches

1981 Leinster 20 Connacht 10—Ulster 18 Munster 16—Munster 21 Connacht 18—Leinster 19 Ulster 6—Ulster 6 Connacht 3—Munster 15 Leinster 15.
Champions: Leinster

1982 Leinster 6 Munster 9—Ulster 22 Connacht 21—Munster 9 Connacht 7—Ulster 9 Leinster 15—Connacht 7 Leinster 13—Munster 10 Ulster 19.
Joint champions: Leinster, Ulster, Munster

1983 Connacht 7 Leinster 13—Munster 10 Ulster 19—Munster 9 Connacht 7—Ulster 9 Leinster 15—Leinster 6 Munster 9—Ulster 22 Connacht 21.
Joint champions: Ulster, Leinster, Munster

Foundation of Irish rugby clubs

Order of foundation		*Year*
31	Academy (formerly Belfast Royal)	1975
24	Ballymena	1922
14	Bangor	1886
10	Bective Rangers	1881
11	Blackrock College	1882
25	Bohemians	1922
26	CIYMS	1922
9	Clontarf	1876
15	Collegians	1890
18	Cork Constitution	1892
21	Dolphin	1902
7	Dungannon	1873
27	Galwegians	1922
13	Garryowen	1884
23	Instonians	1919
6	Lansdowne	1872
17	Malone	1892
12	Monkstown	1883
2	NIFC	1859
29	Old Belvedere	1930
16	Old Wesley	1891
19	Palmerston	1899
3	Queen's University Belfast	1869
20	St Mary's College	1900
28	Sunday's Well	1924
30	Terenure College	1941
1	Trinity College Dublin	1854
5	University College Cork	1872
22	University College Dublin	1910
8	University College Galway	1874
4	Wanderers	1870

Individual records

Most capped player

69 Mike Gibson 1964–79

Most capped players by position

Full back	54	Tom Kiernan 1960–73
Wing	25	Tom Grace 1972–78
		Alan Duggan 1964–72

Ireland's master craftsman—Mike Gibson, seen here in Barbarian colours, had the ability to play anywhere in the backs. He won a record 40 caps in the centre, 25 at outside-half and four on the wing—his 69 appearances making him not only Ireland's but the world's most capped player. (Geo. Herringshaw.)

Centre	40	Mike Gibson 1964–79
Stand off	46	Jackie Kyle 1947–58
Scrum half	27	Mark Sugden 1925–31
Prop	40	Ray McLoughlin 1962–75
Hooker	45	Ken Kennedy 1965–75
Lock	63	Willie John McBride 1962–75
Flanker	60	Fergus Slattery 1970–83
No. 8	35	Willie Duggan 1975–83

Most points in internationals
158 Tom Kiernan 1960–73 (54 matches)

Most points in an international
21 Ollie Campbell v Scotland 1982

Most tries in internationals
11 Alan Duggan 1964–72 (25 matches)

Most tries in an international
3 Jerry Quinn v France 1913
Eddie O'D Davy v Scotland 1930
Sean Byrne v Scotland 1953

Most points in championship season
52 Ollie Campbell 1983 (4 matches)

Most tries in championship season
5 Jack Arigho 1927–8 (3 matches)

Most points on tour
60 Ollie Campbell in Australia 1979 (5 matches)

Most points in tour match
19 Tony Ward v Australian Capital Territory 1979
Ollie Campbell v Australia 1979

Most tries in tour match
3 Alan Duggan v Victoria 1967
Fergus Slattery v South African President's XV 1981
Mike Kiernan v Gold Cup XV 1981

Team records

Most points in Championship season
71 1983

Ireland's record against other countries

Opposition	*Highest score*	*Biggest winning margin*	*Most points conceded*	*Biggest losing margin*
England	26 (26–21) 1974	22 (22–0) 1947	36 (14–36) 1938	22 (14–36) 1938
Scotland	26 (26–8) 1953	21 (21–0) 1950	29 (14–29) 1913	19 (0–19) 1920
Wales	21 (21–24) 1979 (21–7) 1980	16 (19–3) 1925	34 (9–34) 1975	29 (0–29) 1907
France	25 (25–5) 1911 (25–6) 1975	24 (24–0) 1913	27 (6–27) 1964	23 (3–26) 1976
New Zealand	10 (10–10) 1973	—	17 (9–17) 1935	15 (0–15) 1905
South Africa	15 (15–23) 1981	3 (9–6) 1965	38 (0–38) 1912	38 (0–38) 1912
Australia	27 (27–12) 1979	15 (27–12) 1979	20 (10–20) 1976	13 (3–16) 1947

Most tries
12 1927–8 & 1952–3

Most tries in an international
6 v France (24–0) 1913
v Scotland (26–8) 1953

Most tries against
10 by South Africa (0–38) 1912

The brilliant attacking skills of Tony Ward have been frugally employed by Ireland—largely because of the selectors' preference for a scoring machine called Ollie Campbell. Ward shares one distinction with Campbell—they both scored a record 19 points in a tour match. (Geo. Herringshaw.)

Fergus Slattery, who became the world's third most capped player in 1983. His 64 appearances in a 14-year period from 1972 has been bettered only by his two countrymen, Mike Gibson and Willie-John McBride. (Geo. Herringshaw.)

Non-international touring defeats

Combined Provinces		
Beat South Africa	8–3	Belfast 1964–5
Beat Australia	9–3	Belfast 1968
Combined Universities		
Beat South Africa	12–10	Dublin 1964–5
Munster		
Beat Australia	11–8	Limerick 1966–7
Beat New Zealand	12–0	Limerick 1978
Beat Australia	15–6	Cork 1981

Other international results

			W	D	L
Argentina	1952	Buenos Aires		3–3	
	1952	Buenos Aires	6–0		
	1969	Buenos Aires	16–9		
	1969	Buenos Aires	6–3		
	1970	—			3–8
	1970	—			3–6
	1976	Dublin	21–8		
Fiji	1976	Suva	8–0		

Other tours

	P	W	D	L	F	A
1953 Argentina	8	5	2	1	126	43

B International 1982

Ireland 6 England 10 (Ravenhill, Belfast)

Ireland to South Africa 1981

L 15–18	South African Gazelles	Pretoria
W 46–7	South African Mining XV	Potchetstroom
W 54–3	President's Trophy XV	East London
L 16–17	SA Country District 'B'	Wellington
L 15–23	South Africa	Cape Town
W 51–10	Gold Cup XV	Oudtshoorn
L 10–12	South Africa	Durban

Moss Keane sets off on a typical rampaging run, against Scotland in the 1982 Championship match (Colorsport) while (below) John Scott, the England No. 8, seems to be employing technique more associated with Robin Cousins as he leaps for a line-out ball against Ireland at Lansdowne Road on 19 March 1983. (Geo. Herringshaw.)

NEW ZEALAND

Foundation 1892
Headquarters c/o Secretary, Huddart Parker Building, Post Office Square (PO Box 2172), Wellington
Main stadia Auckland (capacity 58 000), Wellington (45 000), Dunedin (35 000), Christchurch (52 500)
Colours All black
Number of clubs 1000
Number of players 170 000
Season April–November
Temperatures 32°F (0°C) to 55°F (13°C)
Population 3 107 100

Number of provincial unions
26 (Canterbury, founded 1879, is oldest)

Ranfurly Shield
1980 Waikato
1981 Wellington
1982 Canterbury

Most successful defences of Ranfurly Shield
25, by Auckland, who won the Shield by beating North Auckland 6–3 in 1960 and held it for three years before losing 3–8 to Wellington. Since its inception, when Wellington challenged Auckland in 1904, the Ranfurly Shield has been won by Auckland on 10 occasions

Inter-Island
1975 South Island
1976 South Island
1977 South Island
1978 North Island
1979 North Island
1980 North Island won 13–9
1981 North Island
1982 South Island

National Championship
1976 Bay of Plenty. 1977 Canterbury. 1978 Wellington. 1979 Counties. 1980 Manawatu. 1981 Wellington. 1982 Auckland

National Sevens
1975 Marlborough. 1976 Marlborough. 1977 Manawatu. 1978 Manawatu. 1979 Manawatu. 1980 Auckland. 1981 Taranaki. 1982 Taranaki. 1983 Auckland

Bryan Williams, New Zealand's most capped wing threequarter, who played 36 times between 1970–8. He also won two caps as a centre. His 66 tries for the All Blacks in all matches is a record. (Geo. Herringshaw.)

Individual records

Most tries in provincial rugby
20 Bernie Fraser (Wellington) 1981

Most capped player
55 Colin Meads 1957–71

Most caps by position

Full back	31	Don Clarke 1956–64
Wing	36	Bryan Williams 1970–78
Centre	34	Bruce Robertson 1972–81
Stand off	14	Doug Bruce 1976–79
Scrum half	29	Sid Going 1967–77
Prop	32	Wilson Whineray 1957–65
Hooker	27	Tane Norton 1971–77
Lock	48	Colin Meads 1957–71
Flanker	36	Kel Tremain 1959–68
		Ian Kirkpatrick 1967–77
No. 8	24	Brian Lochore 1963–71

New Zealand's record against other countries

Opposition	*Highest score*	*Biggest winning margin*	*Most points conceded*	*Biggest losing margin*
England	23 (23–11) 1967	15 (15–0) 1905	16 (10–16) 1973	13 (0–13) 1935
Scotland	40 (40–15) 1981	25 (40–15) 1981	15 (40–15) 1981	—
Ireland	17 (17–9) 1935	15 (15–0) 1905	10 (10–10) 1973	—
Wales	33 (33–12) 1969	21 (33–12) 1969	16 (19–16) 1972	5 (8–13) 1953
France	38 (38–8) 1906	30 (38–8) 1906	24 (18–24) 1980	7 (6–13) 1973
South Africa	25 (25–22) 1981	17 (20–3) 1965	24 (12–24) 1981	17 (0–17) 1928
Australia	38 (38–13) 1936 (38–3) 1972	35 (38–3) 1972	30 (16–30) 1978	16 (10–26) 1980
British Lions	24 (24–11) 1966	17 (20–3) 1966	17 (18–17) 1959	10 (3–13) 1971

Graham Mourie (above), who in 61 matches for New Zealand, was on the losing side only six times. Sid Going (right) arguably was one of the great All Black scrum-halves, who in 87 appearances compensated for what might be charitably described as his erratic passing, with powerful surges from scrum and line-out, and an unmatched competitiveness. (Geo. Herringshaw.)

Most points in internationals
207 Don Clarke 1956–64 (31 matches)

Most points in an international
26 Allan Hewson v Australia 1982

Most tries in internationals
19 Stewart Wilson 1977–83 (29 matches)

Most tries in an international
4 Duncan McGregor v England 1905

Most points on tour
230 Billy Wallace British Isles/France 1905–6 (25 matches)

Most tries on tour
42 Jimmy Hunter British Isles/France 1905–6 (23 matches)

Most points in tour match
41 Joe Karam v South Australia 1974

Most tries in tour match
8 Rod Heeps v Northern New South Wales 1962

Team records

Most tries in an international
13 v All-America 1913

Most tries against
5 South Africa (6–17) 1937
 Australia (16–30) 1978

Most points on tour
868 British Isles/France 1905–6 (33 matches)

Most tries on tour
215 British Isles/France 1905–6 (33 matches)

Tours to British Isles and France

		P	W	D	L	F	A
1888–89	British Isles	74	49	5	20	394	188
1905–06	British Isles	32	31	0	1	830	39
1905–06	France	1	1	0	0	38	8
1924–25	British Isles	28	28	0	0	654	98
1924–25	France	2	2	0	0	67	14
1926–27	England/Wales	16	8	2	6	126	113
1926–27	France	15	14	0	1	333	81
1935–36	British Isles	28	24	1	3	431	180
1953–54	British Isles	29	25	2	2	438	115
1953–54	France	2	0	0	2	8	14
1963–64	British Isles	30	28	1	1	508	137
1963–64	France	4	4	0	0	60	16
1967	British Isles	11	10	1	0	207	78
1967	France	4	4	0	0	87	51
1972–73	British Isles	26	20	2	4	521	227
1972–73	France	4	3	0	1	47	27
1974	Ireland/UK	8	7	1	0	127	50
1977	France	8	7	0	1	199	77*
1978	British Isles	18	17	0	1	364	147
1979	England/Scotland/Italy	11	10	0	1	192	95
1980	Wales	5	5	0	0	101	25
1981	France/Romania	10	8	1	1	170	108

Tours to South Africa

	P	W	D	L	F	A
1928	22	16	1	5	339	144
1949	24	14	3	7	230	146
1960	26	20	2	4	441	164
1970	24	21	0	3	687	228
1976	24	18	0	6	610	291

Additional tours

		P	W	D	L	F	A
1976	Argentina	8	8	0	0	257	69
1980	Australia/Fiji	16	12	1	3	507	126

Incoming tour

1982 Australia

W	16–15	Taranaki	New Plymouth
W	26–10	Manawatu	Palmerston North
W	13–12	Hawke's Bay	Napier
W	21–0	Southland	Invercargill
W	29–21	South Canterbury	Timaru
L	16–23	New Zealand	Christchurch
W	65–10	Buller	Westport
W	29–12	Otago	Dunedin
W	19–16	New Zealand	Wellington
W	23–3	Waikato	Hamilton
L	16–40	Bay of Plenty	Rotorua
L	9–15	Counties	Pukekohe
W	16–12	North Auckland	Whangarei
L	18–33	New Zealand	Auckland

Tour summary: P 14 W 10 L 4 F 316 A 222

Record receipts
350 000 dollars New Zealand v Australia Eden Park, Auckland 1982

Joe Karam, the Wellington full-back, set the New Zealand record for most points in a tour match when he scored 41 against South Australia at Adelaide in 1974. (Colorsport.)

Outgoing Tours 1982

Maoris in Wales

W 17–10	Cardiff	Cardiff
D 10–10	Maesteg	Maesteg
L 12–15	Swansea	Swansea
W 18–9	Monmouthshire	Newport
L 9–16	Llanelli	Llanelli
W 34–6	Aberavon	Aberavon
L 19–25	Wales XV	Cardiff

Tour summary: P 7 W 3 D 1 L 3 F 119 A 91

Maoris in Spain

W 62–13	Spanish B	Barcelona
W 66–3	Spain	Madrid

Tour summary: P 2 W 2 F 128 A 16

Wellington in British Isles

L 14–29	Ulster	Belfast
L 10–12	Leinster	Dublin
L 19–20	Swansea	Swansea
W 31–3	Morley XV	Leeds
L 6–24	South of Scotland	Galashiels
W 31–3	Brixham XV	Brixham

Tour summary: P 6 W 2 L 4 F 111 A 91

Hong Kong Sevens

1983 W 18–0 South Korea, W 26–0 American Eagles, W 22–0 Bahrain, W 48–0 Singapore, L 0–4 Western Samoa

Matches against non-International Board countries

			W	D	L
Argentina	1976	Buenos Aires	21–9		
	1976	Buenos Aires	26–6		
	1979	Dunedin	18–9		
	1979	Wellington	15–6		
Canada	1980	Burnaby	43–10		
Fiji	1980	Suva	33–6		
	1980	Auckland	33–0		
	1980	Suva	30–6		
Italy	1977	Rome	17–9		
	1978	Rome	18–12		
USA	1980	San Francisco	53–6		

Non-International touring defeats in New Zealand

Auckland			
beat	British Isles	4–0	1888
	British Isles	13–0	1904
	Australia	15–13	1913
	British Isles	19–6	1930
	Australia	8–5	1936
	Australia	11–6	1964
	South Africa	15–14	1965
	Ireland	13–10	1976
	British Isles	13–12	1983
Bay of Plenty			
beat	Australia	40–16	1982
Canterbury			
beat	Anglo-Welsh Team	13–8	1908
	South Africa	6–4	1921
	British Isles	14–8	1930
	Australia	16–13	1931
	Australia	19–18	1936
	Australia	20–11	1946
	South Africa	9–6	1956
	British Isles	20–14	1959
	Australia	5–3	1962
	England	19–12	1973
	Scotland	20–9	1975
	Ireland	18–4	1976
	British Isles	22–20	1983
Canterbury–South Canterbury			
beat	Australia	6–3	1905
Combined Marlborough–Buller–Nelson–West Coast XV			
beat	Australia	12–3	1905
Combined Nelson–West Coast–Buller–Golden Bay XV			
beat	Australia	14–5	1931
Counties			
beat	Australia	15–9	1982
Hanan Shield Districts			
beat	Australia	21–9	1946
Hawke's Bay			
beat	Australia	20–14	1936
	Australia	14–11	1955
	Australia	8–6	1958
	England	20–5	1963
	Australia	15–14	1972
King Country–Wanganui			
beat	British Isles	12–6	1966
Manawatu			
beat	Australia	12–6	1958
	Australia	20–10	1978
Maoris			
beat	British Isles	8–6	1904
	Australia	20–0	1946
	France	5–3	1961
Marlborough			
beat	France	24–19	1968
Mid-Canterbury			
beat	Australia	16–10	1964

The 1980 New Zealand team which toured Wales was among the most popular ever All Black sides—and a good one too for they won all five matches. (All Sport.)

New Zealand Universities

beat	South Africa	22–15	1956
	British Isles	21–9	1977

North Auckland

beat	Australia	32–19	1946
	Australia	9–8	1958
	France	8–6	1961

North Otago

beat	Australia	14–13	1962

Otago

beat	Anglo-Welsh Team	9–6	1908
	British Isles	23–9	1950
	British Isles	26–8	1959
	England	14–9	1963
	British Isles	17–9	1966
	Australia	26–0	1972
	Scotland	19–15	1975
	Australia	10–8	1978

Seddon Shield Districts

beat	Australia	14–5	1931

South Canterbury

beat	France	17–14	1961

South Canterbury–North Otago

beat	Australia	21–9	1946

Southland

beat	Australia	13–8	1913
	Australia	14–8	1931
	Australia	14–6	1936
	Australia	8–6	1946
	British Isles	11–0	1950
	Australia	24–9	1952
	Australia	26–8	1958
	Australia	16–11	1962
	British Isles	14–8	1966
	Australia	10–7	1978
	France	12–11	1979

Taranaki

beat	British Isles	1–0	1888
	Anglo-Welsh Team	5–0	1908
	Australia	11–10	1931
	England	6–3	1973

Thames Valley

beat	Australia	16–14	1962

Waikato

beat	South Africa	14–10	1956
	France	22–3	1961
	Australia	26–24	1972
	France	18–15	1979

Wairarapa–Bush

beat	Australia	19–13	1936

Wanganui

beat	Australia	11–6	1913

Wellington

beat	Australia	23–7	1905
	Anglo-Welsh Team	19–13	1908
	British Isles	12–8	1930
	Australia	15–8	1931
	South Africa	23–6	1965
	British Isles	20–6	1966
	England	25–16	1973
	Scotland	19–15	1981

Wellington–Wairarapa–Horowhena

beat	Australia	23–7	1905

West Coast–Buller

beat	Australia	17–15	1949
	Australia	15–10	1972

SCOTLAND

Foundation	1873
Headquarters	Murrayfield, Edinburgh 12
Main stadium	Murrayfield (capacity 85 000)
Colours	Dark blue jerseys, white shorts
Number of clubs	116
Number of players	25 000
Season	September–April
Temperatures	30°F (−1°C) to 55°F (13°C)
Population	5 179 000

Schweppes Club Championship
Division I: 1974–8 Hawick. 1979 Heriot's FP. 1980 Gala. 1981 Gala. 1982 Hawick. 1983 Gala (runners-up Hawick)
Division II: 1979 Melrose. 1980 Gordonians. 1981 Selkirk. 1982 Kilmarnock. 1983 Ayr (runners-up Haddington)
Division III: 1979 Royal High. 1980 Glasgow Acads. 1981 Haddington. 1982 Ayr. 1983 Aberdeen GSFP (runners-up Portobello)
Division IV: 1979 Musselburgh. 1980 Stirling County. 1981 Dalziel HSFP. 1982 Broughton. 1983 Greenock Wanderers (runners-up Cambuslang)
Division V: 1983 Grangemouth (runners-up Currie)
Division VI: 1983 Lenzie (runners-up Lismore)
Division VII: 1983 Linlithgow (runners-up Uddingston)

Border League champions
1979 Hawick. 1980 Gala. 1981 Gala. 1982 Hawick. 1983 Hawick

Inter-District champions
1979 South. 1980 Edinburgh. 1981 South. 1982 Edinburgh. 1983 South

Individual records

Drop goal record
5 David Shiel (Melrose) (25–11 v Langholm 11 September 1982)

Most points
507 Colin Flannigan (Kelso) 1982–3

The men behind the mike—Bill McLaren, a lucid commentator who has mastered the delicate balance of informing the uninitiated without enraging the experts, and Gareth Edwards, who joined the BBC TV Rugby team after retiring from the game. (Geo. Herringshaw.)

First substitute in international rugby
Ian McCrae (Gordonians) for Gordon Connell, Scotland v France 1969

International championship—most points
77 1925

International championship—most tries
17 1925

Most tries in an international
8 Wales (35–10) 1925

Most tries against
9 South Africa (0–44) 1951

Most tries in internationals
24 Ian Smith (32 matches) 1924–33

Most tries in an international
4 W A Stewart v Ireland 1913, Ian Smith v France 1925

Most international points
273 Andy Irvine, 1972–83

Most points in an international
17 Andy Irvine v Australia, Murrayfield, 1981

Most championship points in season
35 Andy Irvine, 1980

Most capped players
51 Andy Irvine, Jim Renwick

Most caps by position

Full-back	46	Andy Irvine 1973–83
Wing	33	Arthur Smith 1955–62
Centre	49	Jim Renwick 1972–83
Stand off	21	John Rutherford 1979–83
Scrum half	25	J B Nelson 1925–31
Prop	50	Sandy Carmichael 1967–78
Hooker	32	Frank Laidlaw 1965–71
Lock	42	Alistair McHarg 1968–79
Flanker	29	W I D Elliot 1947–54
No. 8	22	Jim Telfer 1964–70

B international
1983 Scotland 12 France 26 (Dundee)

Andy Irvine (right) and Jim Renwick (below) who share the distinction of being Scotland's most capped players, with 51 appearances each. Irvine is also Scotland's most capped full-back (46 matches) and Renwick the most capped centre (49 matches). Irvine undoubtedly would have increased his number of appearances but for injury problems. (Geo. Herringshaw.)

Record against other countries

Opposition	*Highest score*	*Biggest winning margin*	*Most points conceded*	*Biggest losing margin*
England	28 (28–19) 1931	20 (26–6) 1971	30 (18–30) 1980	20 (6–26) 1977
Ireland	29 (29–14) 1913	19 (19–0) 1920	26 (8–26) 1953	21 (0–21) 1950
Wales	35 (35–10) 1924	25 (35–10) 1924	35 (12–35) 1972	23 (12–35) 1972
France	31 (31–3) 1912	28 (31–3) 1912	23 (3–23) 1977	20 (3–23) 1977
New Zealand	15 (15–40) 1981	—	40 (15–40) 1981	25 (15–40) 1981
South Africa	10 (10–18) 1960	6 (6–0) 1906	44 (0–44) 1951	44 (0–44) 1951
Australia	24 (24–15) 1981	9 (24–15) 1981	33 (9–33) 1982	24 (9–33) 1982

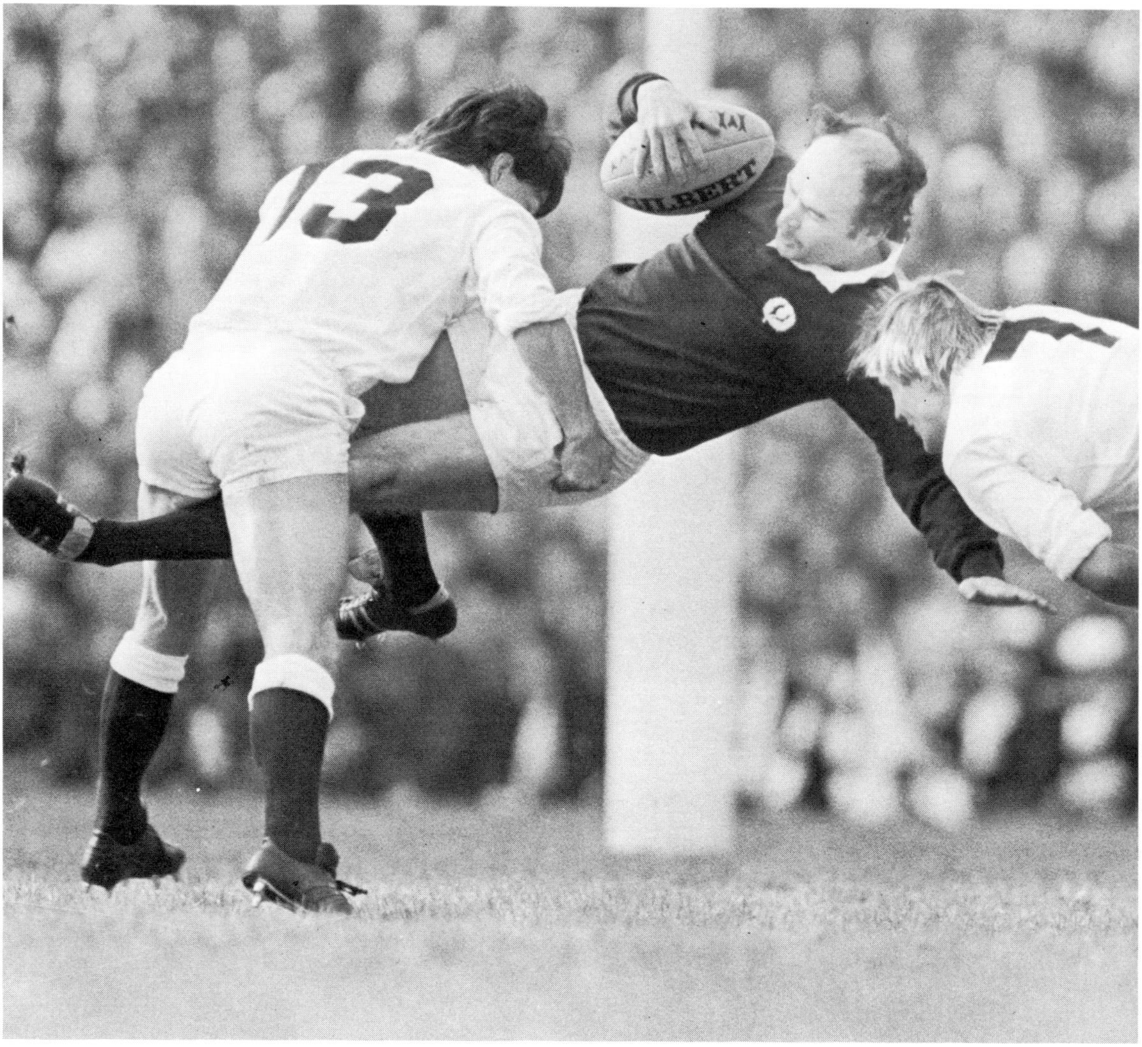

Huw Davies (No. 13) and Peter Winterbottom give Jim Renwick the treatment during the England–Scotland match at Twickenham, 5 March 1983. (Geo. Herringshaw.)

Other internationals

			W	D	L
Hong Kong	1977	Hong Kong	42–6		
Japan	1974	Murrayfield	34–9		
	1977	Tokyo	74–9		
Netherlands	1975	Hilversum	29–3		
	1978	Hilversum	19–0		
Thailand	1977	Bangkok	82–6		
Tonga	1977	Murrayfield	44–8		

Incoming tour 1982

Fiji

L 12–47 Edinburgh
L 17–23 South of Scotland
L 19–29 Anglo-Scots
L 12–32 Scotland XV

Fiji also played 6 matches in England, losing all 6

Outgoing Tours

		P	W	D	L	F	A
1964	Canada	5	5	0	0	172	16
1969	Argentina	6	5	0	1	68	46
1977	Far East	5	5	0	0	307	47
1981	New Zealand	8	5	0	3	181	125
1982	Australia	9	6	0	3	220	113

SOUTH AFRICA

Foundation 1889
Headquarters South African Rugby Board, Boundary Road, Newlands 7700
Main stadium Ellis Park, Johannesburg (capacity 75 000)
Colours Green jerseys, old gold collar, white shorts
Number of clubs 1028
Number of players 220 769 (including 159 238 schoolboys)
Season April to October
Temperatures 50°F (10°C) to 70°F (21°C)
Population 26 129 000

Currie Cup winners
1889, 1892, 1894, 1895, 1897, 1898 Western Province. 1899 Griqualand West. 1904, 1906, 1908 Western Province. 1911 Griqualand West. 1914, 1920 Western Province. 1922 Transvaal. 1925, 1927, 1929 Western Province. 1932, 1934 Western Province & Border. 1936 Western Province. 1939 Transvaal. 1946 Northern Transvaal. 1947 Western Province. 1950, 1952 Transvaal. 1954 Western Province. 1956 Northern Transvaal. 1959, 1964, 1966 Western Province. 1968, 1969 Northern Transvaal. 1970 Griqualand West. 1971 Transvaal & Northern Transvaal. 1972 Transvaal. 1973 Northern Transvaal. 1974 Northern Transvaal. 1975 Northern Transvaal. 1976 Orange Free State. 1977 Northern Transvaal. 1978 Northern Transvaal. 1979 Northern Transvaal & Western Province. 1980, 1981 Northern Transvaal. 1982 Western Province

Highest score in Currie Cup
99–9 Transvaal v Far North, Ellis Park, 7 July 1973

Number of referees 5000

Number of coaches 3000

The record attendance for a non-test touring match was 68 000 at the Northern Transvaal v British Isles at Loftus Versfeld, Pretoria, 21 June 1980. (All Sport.)

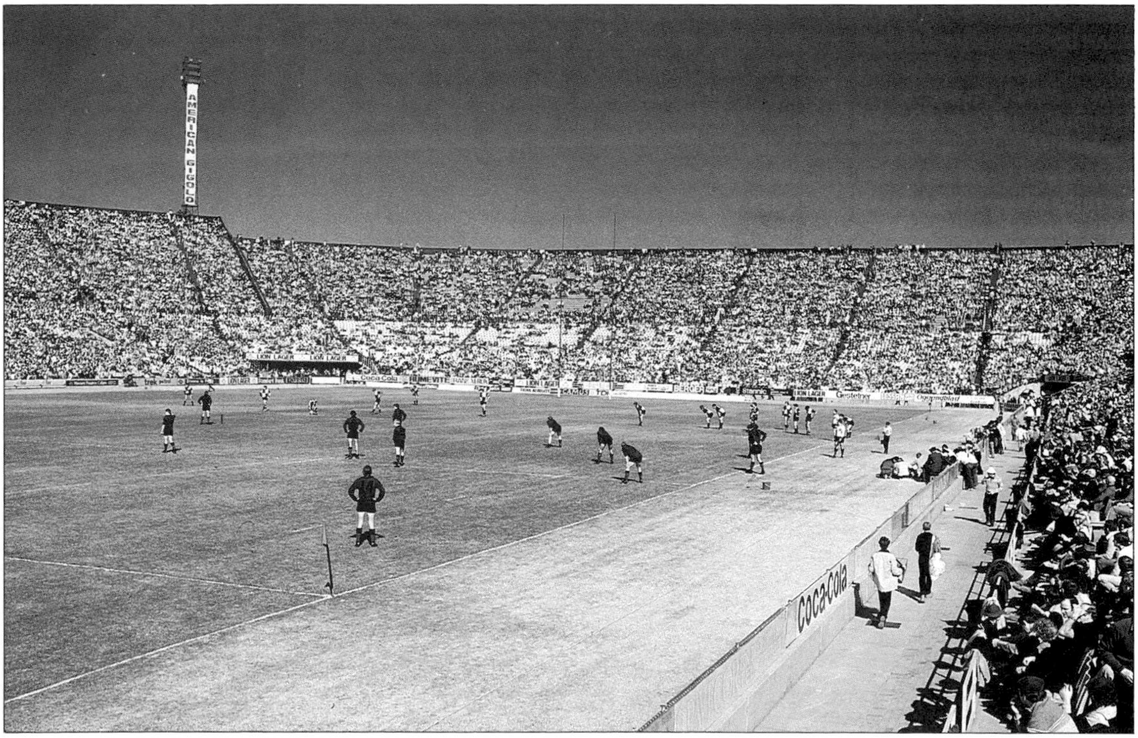

Sport Pienaar Trophy
1964 Griqualand West. 1966 Orange Free State. 1968 Griqualand West. 1969 Griqualand West. 1970 Northern Transvaal. 1971 Northern Transvaal & Transvaal. 1972 Eastern Transvaal. 1973 Orange Free State. 1974 Transvaal. 1975 (new competition) Border. 1976 South West Africa. 1977 Griqualand West. 1978 Griqualand West. 1979 South West Africa. 1980 Eastern Transvaal. 1981, 1982 South Western Districts

Gold Cup
1979 Western Province Juniors. 1980 North Western. 1981 Western Province Juniors. 1982 South Western Districts (B)–East

President's Cup
1979 North Eastern Cape. 1980 Eastern Province. 1981 Eastern Province Juniors. 1982 Eastern Province Juniors

Club championship
1983 final: Pretoria Harlequins 29 University of Pretoria 12 (Durban). Other placings: 3 Stellenbosch University, 4 Durban Collegians, 5 Brakpan, 6 Defence, 7 University of PE, 8 Alberton

Most individual points in a Currie Cup match
36 Gerald Bosch, Transvaal v Far North, 1973. (Bosch scored a try, 2 dropped goals and 13 conversions)

Most individual tries in a Currie Cup match
5 Piet Maritz, Northern Free State v S.E. Transvaal, 1982

Highest score in first class match
132–3 Orange Free State v Eastern Free State, Boerbok Park, Senekal, 31 May 1977

Most individual points in first class match
48 De Wet Ras, Orange Free State v Eastern Free State, 1977

Highest score in a first division club match
160–6 Ammosal v Defence, Kimberley Grand Challenge competition, Beeshoek, 10 August 1980. Ammosal scored 29 tries, also a record

Most individual points and tries in a first division club match
80 Jannie van der Westhuizen, Carnarvon v Williston, Carnarvon, North West Cape, 11 March 1972. Carnarvon won 88–12. Playing at centre, Van der Westhuizen scored 14 tries, 9 conversions, 1 dropped goal and 1 penalty goal

National club championship
1975 Stellenbosch University. 1976 Pretoria University. 1977 Stellenbosch University. 1978 Stellenbosch University. 1979 Stellenbosch University. 1980 Villagers. 1981 Stellenbosch University. 1982 Stellenbosch University

Longest international career
13 seasons Barrie Heatlie and Jackie Powell, 1891–1903

Biggest international victory
44–0 v Scotland, Murrayfield, 1951

Biggest international defeat
9–28 v British Isles, Pretoria, 1974

Most points on overseas tour
753 Australia and New Zealand, 1937

Most individual points
190 Gerry Brand in Australia and New Zealand, 1937

Most tries on overseas tour
161 Australia and New Zealand, 1937 (26 matches)

Most points in internationals
173 Naas Botha, 1980–2 (17 matches)

Most points in international series
43 Piet Visagie v Australia, 1969

Most points in one international
22 Gerald Bosch v France, Pretoria, 1975

Most appearances
37 Frik du Preez

Most points in all matches
304 Naas Botha (24 matches)

Record against other countries

Opposition	*Highest score*	*Biggest winning margin*	*Most points conceded*	*Biggest losing margin*
England	9 (9–3) 1913 (9–18) 1972	7 (7–0) 1932	18 (9–18) 1972	9 (9–18) 1972
Scotland	44 (44–0) 1951	44 (44–0) 1951	10 (18–10) 1960	6 (0–6) 1906
Ireland	38 (38–0) 1912	38 (38–0) 1912	15 (23–15) 1981	3 (6–9) 1965
Wales	24 (24–3) 1964	21 (24–3) 1964	6 (6–6) 1970	—
France	38 (38–5) 1913 (38–25) 1975	33 (38–5) 1913	25 (38–25) 1975	5 (14–19) 1967
New Zealand	24 (24–12) 1981	17 (17–0) 1928	25 (22–25) 1981	17 (3–20) 1965
Australia	30 (30–11) 1969	25 (28–3) 1961	21 (6–21) 1933	15 (6–21) 1933
British Lions	34 (34–14) 1962	20 (34–14) 1962	28 (9–28) 1974	19 (9–28) 1974
South America	50 (50–18) 1982	32 (50–18) 1982	21 (12–21) 1982	9 (12–21) 1982
USA	38 (38–7) 1981	31 (38–7) 1981	7 (7–38) 1981	—

Most points in one match
35 De Wet Ras v British Schools OB, Montevideo, 1980

Most tries in all matches
44 Jannie Engelbrecht (67 matches)

Most tries in one match
6 Roy Dryburgh v Queensland, Brisbane, 1956

Most capped player
38 Frik du Preez 1960–71
Jan Ellis 1965–76

Most caps by position

Full back	27	L G Wilson 1960–65
Wing	33	J P Engelbrecht 1960–69
Centre	33	J L Gainsford 1960–67
Stand off	25	P J Visagie 1967–71
Scrum half	25	D J De Villiers 1962–70
Prop	35	J F K Marais 1963–74
Hooker	18	G F Malan 1958–65
Lock	38	F C H Du Preez 1960–71
Flanker	38	J H Ellis 1965–76
No. 8	22	D Hopwood 1960–65

Test results

	P	W	D	L	F	A
British Isles	40	20	6	14	471	383
New Zealand	37	20	2	15	395	350
Australia	28	21	0	7	429	229
France	19	12	4	3	328	166
Ireland	10	8	1	1	159	73
Scotland	8	5	0	3	104	38
Wales	7	6	1	0	61	15
England	7	4	1	2	49	38
South America	6	5	0	1	156	86
World Team	1	1	0	0	45	24
USA	1	1	0	0	38	7
	164	103	15	46	2235	1409

Incoming Tour 1982

South America

W 43–4	Griqualand West	Kimberley
W 47–3	NW Cape	Upington
W 72–3	NE Cape	Cradock
W 24–9	Border	East London
W 16–10	Natal	Durban
W 37–0	N Natal	Newcastle
W 30–18	W Transvaal	Potchefstroom
W 49–12	Stellaland	Lichtenburg
L 18–50	South Africa	Pretoria

The third Test at Port Elizabeth in 1980 when South Africa beat the British Isles 12–10 to clinch the series. (All Sport.)

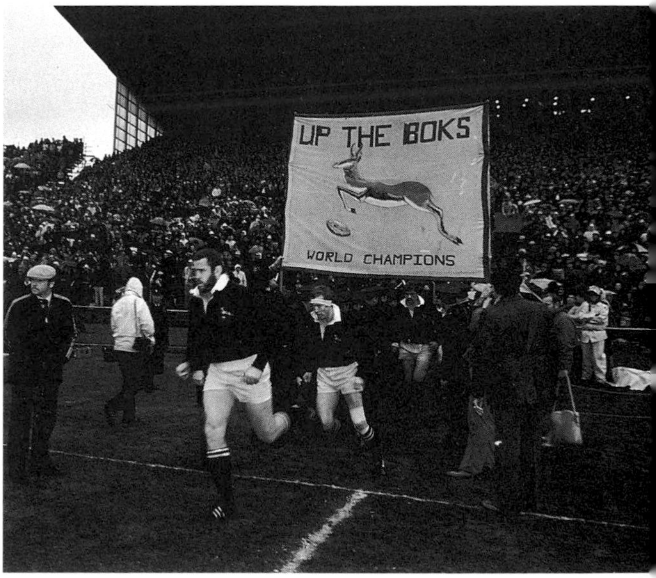

W 33–24	SA Country	Pretoria
W 18–12	N Free State	Welkom
D 18–18	E Free State	Bethlehem
W 21–12	South Africa	Bloemfontein
W 22–4	SA Country	Bloemfontein

Outgoing Tours 1981

South Africa to New Zealand & USA

W 24–6	Poverty Bay	Gisborne
Cancelled	Waikato	Hamilton
W 34–9	Taranaki	New Plymouth
W 31–19	Manawatu	Palmerston North
W 45–9	Wanganui	Wanganui
W 22–6	Southland	Invercargill
W 17–13	Otago	Dunedin
L 9–14	New Zealand	Christchurch
Cancelled	South Canterbury	Timaru
W 83–0	Nelson Bays	Nelson
D 12–12	Maoris	Napier
W 24–12	New Zealand	Wellington
W 29–24	Bay of Plenty	Rotorua
W 39–12	Auckland	Auckland
W 19–10	North Auckland	Whangarei
L 22–25	New Zealand	Auckland

Tour summary: P 14 W 11 D 1 L 2 F 410 A 191
Test summary: P 3 W 1 L 2 F 55 A 51

W 46–12	Mid-Western	Racine
W 41–0	Eastern Union	Albany
W 38–7	USA	Glenville

Tour summary: P 3 W 3 F 125 A 19
Test summary: P 1 W 1 F 38 A 7

Springbok head

The Springbok head is a trophy awarded to the first team to beat South Africa on an overseas tour. British Isles winners: 1912 Newport. 1931 East Midlands. 1951 London Counties. 1961 Barbarians. 1969 Oxford University. Australian winners: 1937 New South Wales. 1965 New South Wales. New Zealand winners: 1921 Canterbury. 1937 New Zealand. 1956 Waikato. 1965 Wellington. 1981 New Zealand. French winners: 1968 SW France. 1974 W France.

Non-test tour defeats in South Africa

Province	*Date*	*Opposition*	*Score*
Boland	1969	Australia	12–3
Border	1949	New Zealand	9–0
	1955	British Isles	14–12
Cape Colony	1910	British Isles	19–0
Combined Services	1960	New Zealand	8–3
	1969	Australia	19–3
Eastern Province	1924	British Isles	14–6
	1955	British Isles	20–0
Eastern Transvaal	1949	New Zealand	6–5
	1962	British Isles	19–16
Gazelles	1981	Ireland	18–15
Griqualand West	1903	British Isles	8–6
		British Isles	11–0
	1910	British Isles	8–0
	1910	British Isles	9–3
	1933	Australia	14–9
	1953	Australia	13–3
	1967	France	20–14
	1969	Australia	21–13
Johannesburg Reef & Country	1933	Australia	13–6
Junior Springboks	1958	France	9–5
	1963	Australia	12–5
Natal	1953	Australia	15–14
	1963	Australia	14–13
	1969	Australia	19–14
North & West Transvaal	1958	France	19–18
Northern Provinces	1933	Australia	16–8
	1938	British Isles	26–8

Morne du Plessis, the South Africa captain chaired off in triumph after the third test win over the British Isles at Port Elizabeth in 1980. (All Sport.)

Northern Transvaal	1953	Australia	27–11
	1962	British Isles	14–6
	1964	Wales	22–9
	1967	France	19–5
	1969	Australia	13–3
	1976	New Zealand	29–27
Northern Universities	1963	Australia	15–9
Orange Free State	1924	British Isles	6–3
	1953	Australia	23–13
	1953	Australia	28–3
	1960	New Zealand	9–8
	1963	Australia	14–8
	1976	New Zealand	15–10
Orange Free State Country	1924	British Isles	6–0
Pretoria	1924	British Isles	6–0
	1933	Australia	13–8
South African Country XV	1981	Ireland	17–16
South African Invitation XV	1975	France	18–3
Transvaal	1903	British Isles	12–3
	1903	British Isles	14–4
	1910	British Isles	27–8
	1910	British Isles	13–6
	1928	New Zealand	6–0
	1933	Australia	11–9
	1938	British Isles	16–9
	1953	Australia	20–14
	1968	British Isles	14–6
	1969	Australia	23–14
	1975	France	28–22
Western Province	1903	British Isles	8–4
	1910	British Isles	8–0
	1928	New Zealand	10–3
	1933	Australia	13–9
	1938	British Isles	21–11
	1963	Australia	12–6
	1964	France	20–11
	1976	New Zealand	12–11
	1980	South America	15–13
Western Province Country	1903	British Isles	13–7
Western Province Town	1903	British Isles	12–3
	1928	New Zealand	7–3
Western Province Town & Country	1924	British Isles	7–6
	1933	Australia	4–0
	1938	British Isles	11–8
Western Province Universities	1953	Australia	24–5
	1963	Australia	11–9
Western Province, SW Districts & Boland XV	1958	France	38–8
Western Transvaal	1955	British Isles	9–6
	1969	Australia	18–6
Witwatersrand	1924	British Isles	10–6

WALES

Foundation 1881
Headquarters National Stadium, Cardiff
Main stadium National Stadium, Cardiff (capacity scheduled to be 70 000)

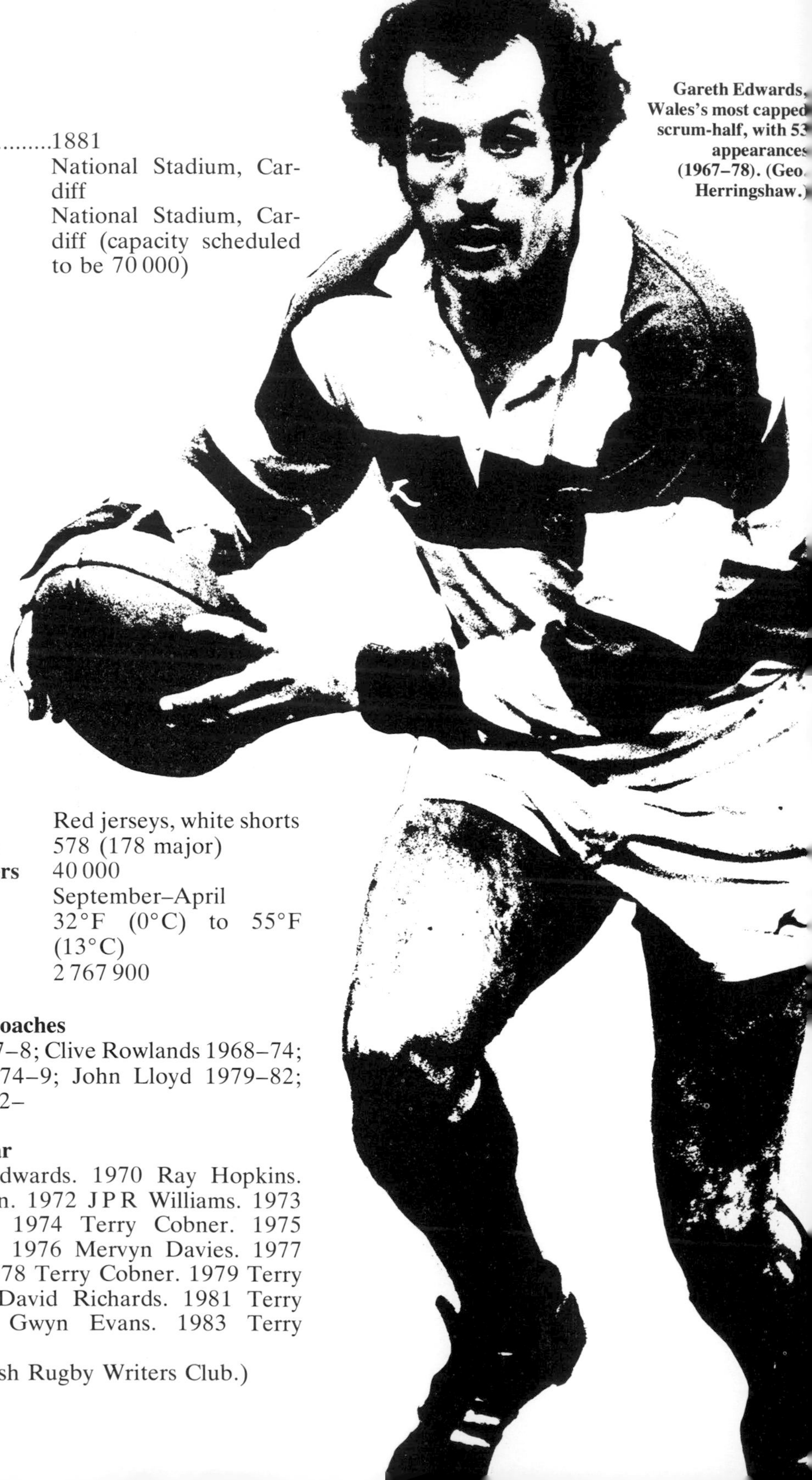

Gareth Edwards, Wales's most capped scrum-half, with 53 appearances (1967–78). (Geo. Herringshaw.)

Colours Red jerseys, white shorts
Number of clubs 578 (178 major)
Number of players 40 000
Season September–April
Temperatures 32°F (0°C) to 55°F (13°C)
Population 2 767 900

Welsh national coaches
David Nash 1967–8; Clive Rowlands 1968–74; John Dawes 1974–9; John Lloyd 1979–82; John Bevan 1982–

Player of the year
1969 Gareth Edwards. 1970 Ray Hopkins. 1971 Barry John. 1972 J P R Williams. 1973 Tommy David. 1974 Terry Cobner. 1975 Mervyn Davies. 1976 Mervyn Davies. 1977 Phil Bennett. 1978 Terry Cobner. 1979 Terry Holmes. 1980 David Richards. 1981 Terry Holmes. 1982 Gwyn Evans. 1983 Terry Holmes
(Chosen by Welsh Rugby Writers Club.)

National Sevens finals

1966 Pontypool Utd 11 UC Swansea 8. **1967** Cardiff College of Education 11 Amman Utd 10. **1968** Llanelli 13 Glynneath 8. **1969** Cardiff 11 Neath 3. **1970** Cardiff 14 Newbridge 10. **1971** Llanelli 23 Aberavon 8. **1972** Cardiff 21 Bridgend 14. **1973** Bridgend 28 Cardiff 24. **1974** Bridgend 22 Cardiff 18. **1975** Cardiff 20 Bridgend 16. **1976** Cardiff 28 Bridgend 22. **1977** Bridgend 18 Cardiff 8. **1978** Bridgend 22 Maesteg 18. **1979** Swansea 42 Llanelli 6. **1980** Swansea 16 Newport 12. **1982** South Glamorgan Institute 24, Aberavon 18

World record number of tries for club

312 Andy Hill in 454 games for Llanelli, 1965–79

Welsh Counties Cup final

1979 Glamorgan 22 Carmarthenshire 4 (Aberavon). 1980 Carmarthenshire 16 Glamorgan 15 (Kidwelly). 1981 Pembrokeshire 26 Glamorgan 6 (Neyland). 1982 Pembrokeshire 10 Monmouthshire 6. 1983 Monmouthshire 24 Glamorgan 17

Welsh Brewers' Cup final

1979 Rumney 18 Nantyglo 10 (Cardiff). 1980 Tondu 15 Rumney 10 (Cardiff). 1981 Caerleon 12 Rhydyfelin 9. 1982 Llantrisant 18 Glyncorrwg 9 (Cardiff). 1983 Baglan 13 Hedl-y-Cyw 6 (Cardiff)

Foundation of Welsh clubs

Order of foundation		*Year*
7	Aberavon	1876
13	Abertillery	1885
8	Bridgend	1878
6	Cardiff	1876
12	Cross Keys	1885
10	Ebbw Vale	1880
16	Glamorgan Wanderers	1893
2	Llanelli	1872
14	London Welsh	1885
11	Maesteg	1882
1	Neath	1871
15	Newbridge	1890
3	Newport	1874
9	Penarth	1880
18	Pontypool	1901
5	Pontypridd	1876
19	South Wales Police	1969
4	Swansea	1874
17	Tredegar	1899

Schweppes Cup final

1972 Neath 15 Llanelli 9 (12 000 attendance). **1973** Llanelli 30 Cardiff 7 (32 000). **1974** Llanelli 12 Aberavon 10 (30 000). **1975** Llanelli 15 Aberavon 6 (42 000). **1976** Llanelli 16 Swansea 4 (35 000). **1977** Newport 16 Cardiff 15 (35 000). **1978** Swansea 13 Newport 9 (39 750). **1979** Bridgend 18 Pontypridd 12 (38 000). **1980** Bridgend 15 Swansea 9 (43 000). **1981** Cardiff 14 Bridgend 6. **1982** Cardiff 12 Bridgend 12. **1983** Pontypool 18 Swansea 6. (*Quarter finals*: Bridgend 17 Neath 3, Ebbw Vale 6 Newbridge 6, Llanelli 12 Swansea 20, Pontypool 13 Cardiff 9. *Semi-finals*: Bridgend 3 Pontypool 16, Swansea 19 Newbridge 6)

Despite the restrictive grip of Richard Moriarty, John Perkins gets the ball away for Pontypool against Swansea in the 1983 Schweppes Welsh Cup final. (Colorsport.)

Phil Bennett, of Llanelli, who holds the record of scoring most points for Wales in internationals, 166, which he registered in 29 matches between 1969–78. (Geo. Herringshaw.)

Lloyd Lewis Memorial Trophy (man of the match award)

1975 Phil Bennett (Llanelli). 1976 Phil Bennett (Llanelli). 1977 Ian Barnard (Newport). 1978 David Richards (Swansea). 1979 Steve Fenwick (Bridgend). 1980 Gareth Williams (Bridgend). 1981 Bob Lakin (Cardiff). 1982 Mark Titley (Bridgend). 1983 David Bishop (Pontypool)

Highest score in WRU Cup matches

Pontypool 86 Ystralyfera 6, 1978 (1st round proper). Mountain Ash 114 Builth Wells 4, 1976 (preliminary round)

Most points in WRU Cup matches

34 Ross Edwards, Mountain Ash v Builth Wells, 1976

Most points in final

18 Phil Bennett, Llanelli v Cardiff, 1973

World's record receipts for club match

£100 000 Bridgend v Swansea, 1980 Welsh Cup final, Cardiff

Snelling Sevens

1954 Newport 6 Ebbw Vale 0 (Newport). 1955 Cardiff 8 Newport 3 (Newport). 1956 Newport 5 Penarth 3 (Swansea). 1957 Newport 11 Abertillery 8 (Swansea). 1958 Ebbw Vale 10 Newport 5 (Cardiff). 1959 Newport 6 Pontypool 3 (Newport). 1960 Llanelli 14 Penarth 10 (Cardiff). 1961 Newport 8 Pontypool 3 (Cardiff). 1962 Newport 19 Neath 3 (Swansea). 1963 Newport 6 Bridgend 3 (Cardiff). 1964 Neath 10 Cardiff 5 (Cardiff). 1965 Newport 9 Newbridge 8 (Swansea). 1966 Cardiff 23 Newport 20 (Cardiff). 1967 Newport 21 Cardiff 15 (Cardiff). 1968 Bridgend 25 Pontypool 5 (Cardiff). 1969 Cardiff 18 Llanelli 15 (Cardiff). 1970 Neath 18 Ebbw Vale 8 (Cardiff). 1971 Llanelli 31 Newport 10 (Cardiff). 1972 Cardiff 15 Bridgend 4 (Cardiff). 1973 Llanelli 52 Newbridge 6 (Cardiff). 1974 Bridgend 30 Swansea 14 (Cardiff). 1975 Bridgend 32 Cardiff 12 (Cardiff). 1976 Cardiff 18 Newport 8 (Cardiff). 1977 Cardiff 24

Newport 16 (Cardiff). 1978 Bridgend 38 Cardiff 16 (Cardiff). 1979 Llanelli 26 Ebbw Vale 16 (Cardiff). 1980 Bridgend 24 Newport 16 (Cardiff). 1981 Cardiff 20 Leicester 6 (Cardiff)

1982 Pool A: Cardiff 12 Swansea 22—Glamorgan Wanderers 14 Maesteg 16—Cardiff 20 Glamorgan Wanderers 4—Swansea 26 Maesteg 0—Cardiff 30 Maesteg 6—Swansea 18 Glamorgan Wanderers 18
Pool B: Abertillery 0 Newbridge 10—Llanelli 6 Neath 10—Abertillery 6 Llanelli 10—Newbridge 4 Neath 22—Abertillery 4 Neath 16—Newbridge 14 Llanelli 14
Pool C: Ebbw Vale 10 Pontypridd 0—Bridgend 20 Cross Keys 0—Ebbw Vale 12 Bridgend 4—Pontypridd 6 Cross Keys 18—Ebbw Vale 22 Cross Keys 0—Pontypridd 14 Bridgend 8
Pool D: Aberavon 4 Penarth 12—Newport 10 Pontypool 6—Aberavon 12 Newport 6—Penarth 12 Pontypool 4—Aberavon 36 Pontypool 6—Penarth 18 Newport 8
Semi-finals: Swansea 30 Neath 0—Ebbw Vale 30 Penarth 4. **Final**: Swansea 44 Ebbw Vale 4
Most wins: 9 Newport, 7 Cardiff, 5 Bridgend. Biggest score: 52–6 Llanelli v Newbridge, 1973. Biggest winning margin: 46 Llanelli v Newbridge (52–6 1973)
Biggest score by losing finalist: 20 Newport v Cardiff (20–23 1966)
Bill Everson Award (Player of Tournament): 1967 David Watkins (Newport) 1968 John Williams (Bridgend) 1969 Barry John (Cardiff) 1970 Dai Parker (Neath) 1971 John Thomas (Llanelli) 1972 John Davies (Cardiff) 1973 Roy Bergiers (Llanelli) 1974 Viv Jenkins (Bridgend) 1975 Stuart Lane (Cardiff) 1976 Chris Camilleri (Cardiff) 1977 John Churchill (Newport) 1978 Gareth Williams (Bridgend) 1979 Peter Morgan (Llanelli) 1980 JPR Williams (Bridgend) 1981 Gwynfor Williams (Cardiff) 1982 Jeff Herdman (Swansea)

Aberaeron Sevens

1970 Llanelli 1971 Llanelli 1972 no event 1973 Public School Wanderers 1974 Cardiff 1975 Voyagers 1976 Newport 1977 Cardiff 1978 Cardiff 1979 Pontypridd 1980 Steepholme SC 1981 Llanelli
1982 1st round: Llanelli 46 Aberaeron 0—Whitland 6 International Sportswriters 24—Neath 32 Tenby 4—Cwmllynfell 10 Aberavon 30—Steepholme SC 24 Abercynon 0—Lampeter 12 Tredegar 9—Voyagers 36 Newcastle Emlyn 6—Llandovery 6 S. Glamorgan Inst. of HE 14—Newquay Hotel 36 Trimsaran 0—Tregaron 12 Solarians 16—Old Millhillians 12 Aberystwyth 8—Llanybydder 0 Brownhill CC 32—Swansea 32 Haverfordwest 0—Narberth 6 Welsh Academicals 32—Cardigan 10 Gowerton 22—Burry Port 10 Cardiff 18

2nd round: Llanelli 14 International Sportswriters 10—Neath 8 Aberavon 16—Steepholme 28 Lampeter 0—Voyagers 12 S. Glamorgan Inst. 18—Newquay Hotel 28 Solarians 10—Old Millhillians 0 Brownhill CC 36—Swansea 18 Welsh Academicals 16—Gowerton 14 Cardiff 30

3rd round: Llanelli 19 Aberavon 12—Steepholme 18 S. Glamorgan Inst. 4—Newquay Hotel 6 Brownhill CC 10—Swansea 4 Cardiff 20

Semi-finals: Llanelli 20 Steepholme 16—Brownhill CC 20 Cardiff 4

Final: Llanelli 28 Brownhill CC 16

1983 winners: Steepholme

Man of The Match Award: 1973 Wilson Lauder (Public School Wanderers) 1974 Brynmor Williams (Cardiff) 1975 Mike Jones (Voyagers) 1976 Geoff Evans (Newport) 1977 Alan Rose (Inn on The River) 1978 Robert Dudley-Jones (Cardiff) 1979 Tommy David (Pontypridd) 1980 JPR Williams (Steepholme SC) 1981 Peter Morgan (Llanelli) 1982 Kevin Thomas (Llanelli) 1983 Mark Brown (Steepholme)

Welsh Club Champions

1947 Neath. 1948 Cardiff. 1949 Cardiff. 1950 Maesteg. 1951 Newport. 1952 Ebbw Vale. 1953 Cardiff. 1954 Ebbw Vale. 1955 Cardiff. 1956 Newport. 1957 Ebbw Vale. 1958 Cardiff. 1959 Pontypool. 1960 Ebbw Vale. 1961 Aberavon. 1962 Newport. 1963 Pontypridd. 1964 Bridgend. 1965 Newbridge. 1966 Bridgend. 1967 Neath. 1968 Llanelli. 1969 Newport. 1970 Bridgend. 1971 Bridgend. 1972 London Welsh. 1973 Pontypool. 1974 Llanelli. 1975 Pontypool. 1976 Pontypridd. 1977 Llanelli. 1978 Pontypridd. 1979 Pontypridd. 1980 Swansea. 1981 Bridgend. 1982 Cardiff. 1983 Swansea

Individual records

Most capped player
55 J P R Williams 1969–81

Most caps by position

Full back	55	J P R Williams 1969–79
Wing	44	Ken Jones 1947–57
Centre	30	Steve Fenwick 1975–80
Stand off	29	Cliff Morgan 1951–58
Scrum half	53	Gareth Edwards 1967–78
Prop	41	Graham Price 1975–83
Hooker	34	Bryn Meredith 1954–62
Lock	34	Allan Martin 1973–81
Flanker	32	Dai Morris 1967–74
No. 8	38	Mervyn Davies 1968–76

Most points in internationals
166 Phil Bennett 1969–78 (29 matches)

Most points in an international
19 Jack Bancroft v France, 1910
Keith Jarrett v England, 1967
Phil Bennett v Ireland, 1976

J P R Williams, Wales's most capped player. Williams won 54 caps at full-back and one at flank-forward in his 10-year career. (Geo. Herringshaw.)

Most tries in internationals
20 Gareth Edwards 1967–78 (53 matches)
Gerald Davies 1966–78 (46 matches)

Most tries in an international
4 Willie Llewellyn v England, 1899
Reggie Gibbs v France, 1908
Maurice Richards v England, 1969

Most championship points in a season
38 Phil Bennett 1975–6 (4 matches)
Steve Fenwick 1978–9 (4 matches)

Most championship tries in a season
6 Reggie Gibbs 1907–8
Maurice Richards 1968–9

Most points on tour
55 Steve Fenwick in Australia 1978 (7 matches)

Most points in tour match
15 Keith Jarrett v Otago, 1969

Most tries in tour match
3 Maurice Richards v Otago, 1969

Team records

Most points in championship season
102 1975–6

Most tries in championship season
21 1909–10

Most tries in an international
11 v France (47–5), 1909

Most tries against
8 Scotland (10–35) 1924

Non-international touring defeats in Wales

Bridgend

beat	Australia	12–9	1981

Cardiff

beat	South Africa	17–0	1906
	Australia	24–8	1908
	Australia	11–3	1947–48
	New Zealand	8–3	1953–54
	Australia	14–11	1957–58
	Australia	14–8	1966–67
	Australia	14–9	1975

Newport

beat	South Africa	9–3	1912
	Australia	11–0	1957–58
	New Zealand	3–0	1963–64
	South Africa	11–6	1969–70

Swansea

beat	Australia	6–0	1908
	South Africa	3–0	1912
	New Zealand	11–3	1935–36
	Australia	9–8	1966–67

Pontypool, Newbridge, Cross Keys XV

beat	Australia	12–3	1966–67

Abertillery, Ebbw Vale XV

beat	Australia	6–5	1957–58

East Wales

beat	Australia	19–11	1973

Gwent

beat	South Africa	14–8	1969–70

Llanelli

beat	Australia	8–3	1908
	Australia	11–0	1966–67
	New Zealand	9–3	1972–73

NB Pontypool beat the 'Waratahs' and the 'Maoris' in the same year, 1927

Wales B Matches

France: 1969 L 9–17 (Paris). 1970 W 13–9 (Llanelli). 1971 L 9–30 (Paris). 1972 W 35–6 (Cardiff). 1973 L 12–24 (Toulouse). 1974 W 23–20 (Cardiff). 1975 L 18–24 (Rouen). 1976 W 24–6 (Pontypool). 1977 L 3–15 (Nantes). 1978 L 18–31 (Aberavon). 1979 L 12–23 (Bourg-en-Bresse). 1980 W 12–0 (Neath). 1981 L 9–33 (Lourdes). 1982 L 15–16 (Pontypool)
Argentina: 1978 L 14–17 (Llanelli)
Australia: 1981 L 9–10 (Cardiff)
Canada: 1972 W 38–10 (Swansea). 1980 W 24–7 (Vancouver)
USA: 1980 W 24–18 (Long Beach, California)

Matches played against non-International Board countries

			W	D	L
Argentina	1968	Buenos Aires			5–9
	1968	Buenos Aires		9–9	
	1976	Cardiff	20–19		
Canada	1971	Cardiff	56–10		
	1973	Toronto	58–20		
	1980	Vancouver	24–7		
East Africa	1964	Nairobi	26–8		
Fiji	1964	Cardiff	28–22		
	1969	Suva	31–11		

Steve Fenwick, of Bridgend, who won a record 30 caps at centre for Wales, and Graham Price (below), the world's most capped prop-forward. Price played 41 times for Wales, which makes him their most capped forward, and made 12 appearances for the British Isles. (Geo. Herringshaw.)

Hong Kong	1975	Hong Kong	57–3
Japan	1973	Cardiff	62–14
	1975	Osaka	56–12
	1975	Tokyo	82–6
Romania	1979	Cardiff	13–12
Tonga	1974	Cardiff	26–7

Incoming tours 1982

Maoris

W	17–10	Cardiff	Cardiff
D	10–10	Maesteg	Maesteg
L	12–15	Swansea	Swansea
W	18–9	Monmouthshire	Newport
L	9–16	Llanelli	Llanelli
W	34–6	Aberavon	Aberavon
L	19–25	Wales XV	Cardiff

Tour summary: P 7 W 3 D 1 L 3 F 119 A 91

Wellington

L	19–20	Swansea	Swansea

Outgoing tour 1983

Wales B to Spain

W	24–3	Basque XV	Bilbao
W	32–6	Spain Under 23s	Gijon
W	83–3	Castille-Leon XV	Valladolid
W	71–0	Valencia Select XV	Valencia
W	65–16	Spain	Madrid

Tour summary: P5 W5 D0 L0 F275 A27

Other major tours

	P	W	D	L	F	A
1968 Argentina	6	3	2	1	69	46
1973 Canada	5	5	0	0	288	41
1980 North America	5	5	0	0	135	36

Mervyn Davies's 38 appearances made him Wales's most capped No. 8 forward. He is also the world record cap holder for his position with 46 caps, which includes eight matches for the British Isles. His career was ended on medical advice in 1976. (Geo. Herringshaw.)

Match Results 1871–1983

Australia v England

Played 10 Australia 6 England 4 Drawn 0
Australia 133 points England 120

			Australia				England			
Year	Venue	Results	T	C	P	D	T	C	P	D
1909	Blackheath	Australia: 9–3	3				1			
1948	Twickenham	Australia: 11–0	3	1						
1958	Twickenham	England: 9–6			1	1	2		1	
1963	Sydney	Australia: 18–9	4	3			3			
1967	Twickenham	Australia: 23–11	2	1	2	3	1	1	2	
1973	Twickenham	England: 20–3			1		3	1	2	
1975	Sydney	Australia: 16–9	1		2	2	1	1	1	
1975	Brisbane	Australia: 30–21	5	2	2		2	2	3	
1976	Twickenham	England: 23–6			2		3	1	3	
1982	Twickenham	England: 15–11	2		1		1	1	3	
		TOTALS	20	7	11	6	17	7	15	0

Australia v France

Played 13 Australia 4 France 8 Drawn 1
Australia 152 points France 217

			Australia				France			
Year	Venue	Results	T	C	P	D	T	C	P	D
1948	Paris	France: 13–6			2		3	2		
1958	Paris	France: 19–0					3	2		2
1961	Sydney	France: 15–8	1	1	1		3			2
1967	Paris	France: 20–14	2	1	1	1	1	1	4	1
1968	Sydney	Australia: 11–10	1	1	1	1	2	2		
1971	Toulouse	Australia: 13–11	2	1	1		2		1	
1971	Paris	France: 18–9			3		1	1	4	
1972	Sydney	Drawn: 14–14	2		2		3	1		
1972	Brisbane	France: 16–15			5		3	2		
1976	Bordeaux	France: 18–15			4	1	3	3		
1976	Paris	France: 34–6			2		6	2	1	1
1981	Brisbane	Australia: 17–15	3	1	1		1	1	2	1
1981	Sydney	Australia: 24–14	2	2	4		2			2
		TOTALS	13	7	27	3	33	17	12	9

Australia v Ireland

Played 9 Australia 3 Ireland 6 Drawn 0
Australia 89 points Ireland 106

			Australia				Ireland			
Year	Venue	Results	T	C	P	D	T	C	P	D
1947	Dublin	Australia: 16–3	4	2					1	
1958	Dublin	Ireland: 9–6	2				2		1	
1967	Dublin	Ireland: 15–8	1	1		1	2		1	2
1967	Sydney	Ireland: 11–5	1	1			2	1		1
1968	Dublin	Ireland: 10–3	1				2	2		

Leading Cap Winners

Australia

42 P G Johnson (New South Wales)
1959 BI (2). 1961 Fiji (3), SA (2), F. 1962 NZ (5). 1963 E, SA (4). 1964 NZ (3). 1965 SA (2). 1966 BI (2). 1966–7 W, S, E, I, F. 1967 I, NZ. 1968 NZ (2), F. 1968–9 I, S. 1970 S. 1971 SA (2). 1971–2 F (2).

41 A R Miller (New South Wales)
1952 Fiji (2), NZ (2). 1953 SA (4). 1954 Fiji (2). 1955 NZ (3). 1956 SA (2). 1957 NZ (2). 1957–8 W, E, S, F. 1958 Maoris (3). 1959 BI (2). 1961 Fiji (3), SA, F. 1962 NZ (2). 1966 BI (2). 1966–7 W, S, I, F. 1967 I, NZ.

39 G V Davis (New South Wales)
1963 E, SA (4). 1964 NZ (3). 1965 SA. 1966 BI (2). 1966–7 W, S, E, I, F. 1967 I, NZ. 1968 NZ (2), F. 1968–9 I, S. 1969 W, SA (4). 1970 S. 1971 SA (3). 1971–2 F (2). 1972 F (2), NZ (3).

37 J E Thornett (New South Wales)
1955 NZ (3). 1956 SA (2). 1957–8 W, I, S, F. 1958 Maoris (2), NZ

Leading Cap Winners continued

(2). 1959 BI (2). 1961 Fiji (2), SA (2), F. 1962 NZ (4). 1963 E, SA (4). 1964 NZ (3). 1965 SA (2). 1966 BI (2). 1966–7 F.

36 J N B Hipwell
(New South Wales)
1968 NZ (2), F. 1968–9 I, S. 1969 W, SA (4). 1970 S. 1971 SA (2). 1971–2 F (2). 1972 F (2). 1973 Tonga. 1973–4 W, E. 1974 NZ (3). 1975 E (2), Japan. 1956–6 S, W. 1978 NZ (3). 1981 F (2). 1981–2 I, W, E.

34 A A Shaw
(Queensland)
1973–4 W, E. 1975 E (2), Japan. 1975–6 S, W, E, I, USA. 1976 Fiji (3). 1976–7 F (2). 1978 W (2), NZ (3). 1979 I (2), NZ, Arg (2). 1980 Fiji, NZ (3). 1981 F (2). 1981–2 I, W, S.

31 P E McLean
(Queensland)

1974 NZ (3). 1975 Japan (2). 1975–6 S, W, E, I. 1976 Fiji (3). 1976–7 F (2). 1978 W (2), NZ. 1979 I (2), NZ, Arg (2). 1980 Fiji. 1981 F (2). 1981–2 I, W, S, E. 1982 S (2).

Match Results 1871–1983 continued

1976	Dublin	Australia: 20–10	3	1	2		1		2	
1979	Brisbane	Ireland: 27–12	1	1	2		2	2	4	1
1979	Sydney	Ireland: 9–3			1				1	2
1981	Dublin	Australia: 16–12	1		3	1			4	
		TOTALS	14	6	8	2	11	5	14	6

Australia v New Zealand

Played 74 Australia 18 New Zealand 52 Drawn 4
Australia 721 points New Zealand 1206

			Australia				New Zealand			
Year	Venue	Results	T	C	P	D	T	C	P	D
1903	Sydney	New Zealand: 22–3			1		3	1	1	2*
1905	Dunedin	New Zealand: 14–3	1				4	1		
1907	Sydney	New Zealand: 26–6			1	1*	6	4		
1907	Brisbane	New Zealand: 14–5	1	1			4	1		
1907	Sydney	Drawn: 5–5	1	1			1	1		
1910	Sydney	New Zealand: 6–0					2			
1910	Sydney	Australia: 11–0	3	1						
1910	Sydney	New Zealand: 28–13	2	2	1		8	2		
1913	Wellington	New Zealand: 30–5	1	1			8	3		
1913	Dunedin	New Zealand: 25–13	3	2			5	3		1
1913	Christchurch	Australia: 16–5	4	2			1	1		
1914	Sydney	New Zealand: 5–0					1	1		
1914	Brisbane	New Zealand: 17–0					5	1		
1914	Sydney	New Zealand: 22–7	1			1	6	2		
1929	Sydney	Australia: 9–8	1		2		1	1	1	
1929	Brisbane	Australia: 17–9	3	1	2		2		1	
1929	Sydney	Australia: 15–13	2		3		3	2		
1931	Auckland	New Zealand: 20–13	3	2			2	1	4	
1932	Sydney	Australia: 22–17	4	2	2		3	2		1
1932	Brisbane	New Zealand: 21–3	1				4	1	1	1
1932	Sydney	New Zealand: 21–13	3	2			5	3		
1934	Sydney	Australia: 25–11	4	2	3		3	1		
1934	Sydney	Drawn: 3–3	1				1			
1936	Wellington	New Zealand: 11–6	1		1		3	1		
1936	Dunedin	New Zealand: 38–13	2	2	1		9	4	1	
1938	Sydney	New Zealand: 24–9			3		4	3	2	
1938	Brisbane	New Zealand: 20–14	3	1	1		4	2		1
1938	Sydney	New Zealand: 14–6	1		1		2	1	2	
1946	Dunedin	New Zealand: 31–8	2	1			7	5		
1946	Auckland	New Zealand: 14–10	2	2			1	1	3	
1947	Brisbane	New Zealand: 13–5	1	1			3	2		
1947	Sydney	New Zealand: 27–14	1	1	3		3	3	4	
1949	Wellington	Australia: 11–6	3	1			1		1	
1949	Auckland	Australia: 16–9	3	2	1		1		1	1
1951	Sydney	New Zealand: 8–0					1	1	1	
1951	Sydney	New Zealand: 17–11	2	1	1		4	1		1
1951	Brisbane	New Zealand: 16–6			2		4	2		
1952	Christchurch	Australia: 14–9	3	1		1	2		1	
1952	Wellington	New Zealand: 15–8	1	1	1		2		2	1
1955	Wellington	New Zealand: 16–8	1	1	1		3	2	1	
1955	Dunedin	New Zealand: 8–0					1	1		1
1955	Auckland	Australia: 8–3	2	1			1			
1957	Sydney	New Zealand: 25–11	1	1	2		4	2	3	
1957	Brisbane	New Zealand: 22–9	1		2		4	2		2†
1958	Wellington	New Zealand: 25–3	1				7	2		
1958	Christchurch	Australia: 6–3	1		1		1			
1958	Auckland	New Zealand: 17–8	1	1	1		1	1	4	
1962	Brisbane	New Zealand! 20–6			2		4	1	1	1
1962	Sydney	New Zealand: 14–5	1	1			2	1	2	

Match Results 1871–1983 continued

1962	Wellington	Drawn: 9–9			3		1		2	
1962	Dunedin	New Zealand: 3–0							1	
1962	Auckland	New Zealand: 16–8	1	1	1		3	2		1
1964	Dunedin	New Zealand: 14–9	1		2		1	1	2	1
1964	Christchurch	New Zealand: 18–3	1				4	3		
1964	Wellington	Australia: 20–5	2	1	3	1	1	1		
1967	Wellington	New Zealand: 29–9	2		1		4	4	2	1
1968	Sydney	New Zealand: 27–11	1	1	2		6	3	1	
1968	Brisbane	New Zealand: 19–18	1		5		3	2	2	
1972	Wellington	New Zealand: 29–6			2		5	3		1
1972	Christchurch	New Zealand: 30–17	3	1		1	5	2	2	
1972	Auckland	New Zealand: 38–3			1		6	4	2	
1974	Sydney	New Zealand: 11–6	1	1			2		1	
1974	Brisbane	Drawn: 16–16	2	1	2		2	1	2	
1974	Sydney	New Zealand: 16–6			2		3	2		
1978	Wellington	New Zealand: 13–12	1	1	2		1		3	
1978	Christchurch	New Zealand: 22–6			1	1	3	2	1	1
1978	Auckland	Australia: 30–16	5	2	1	1	2	1	2	
1979	Sydney	Australia: 12–6			3	1			1	1
1980	Sydney	Australia: 13–9	2	1		1			3	
1980	Brisbane	New Zealand: 12–9	1	1	1		1	1	2	
1980	Sydney	Australia: 26–10	4	2	1	1	1		2	
1982	Christchurch	New Zealand: 23–16	2	1	2		4	2	1	
1982	Wellington	Australia: 19–16	2	1	3		2	1	2	
1982	Auckland	New Zealand: 33–18	1	1	3	1	2	2	5	2
		TOTALS	106	54	80	11	219	107	76	21

*Goals from mark †1 Dropped goal, 1 Goal from mark

Australia v Scotland

Played 9 Australia 3 Scotland 6 Drawn 0
Australia 113 points Scotland 97

			Australia				Scotland			
Year	Venue	Results	T	C	P	D	T	C	P	D
1947	Murrayfield	Australia: 16–7	4	2					1	1
1958	Murrayfield	Scotland: 12–8	2	1			2		2	
1966	Murrayfield	Scotland: 11–5	1	1			2	1	1	
1968	Murrayfield	Scotland: 9–3			1		1		2	
1970	Sydney	Australia: 23–3	6	1	1				1	
1975	Murrayfield	Scotland: 10–3			1		2	1		
1981	Murrayfield	Scotland: 24–15	3		1		1	1	5	1
1982	Brisbane	Scotland: 12–7	1		1		1	1	1	1
1982	Sydney	Australia: 33–9	3	3	5				3	
		TOTALS	20	8	10	0	9	4	16	3

Australia v South Africa

Played 28 Australia 7 South Africa 21 Drawn 0
Australia 229 points South Africa 429

			Australia				South Africa			
Year	Venue	Results	T	C	P	D	T	C	P	D
1933	Cape Town	South Africa: 17–3			1		4	1	1	
1933	Durban	Australia: 21–6	4	3	1		1		1	
1933	Johannesburg	South Africa: 12–3	1				2	1		1
1933	Port Elizabeth	South Africa: 11–0					2	1	1	

Leading Cap Winners continued

30 N M Shehadie (New South Wales) 1947 NZ. 1947–8 E, F. 1949 Maoris (3), NZ (2). 1950 BI (2). 1951 NZ (3). 1952 Fiji (2), NZ. 1953 SA (4). 1954 Fiji (2). 1955 NZ (3). 1956 SA (2). 1957 NZ. 1957–8 W, I.

England

43 A Neary (Broughton Park) 1971 W, I, F, S (2), Pres. XV. 1972 W, I, F, S, SA. 1973 NZ (2), W, I, F, S, A. 1974 S, I, F, W. 1975 I, F, S, W, A. 1976 A, W, S, I, F. 1977 I. 1978 F. 1979 S, I, F, W, NZ. 1980 I, F, W, S.

42 J V Pullin (Bristol)

1966 W. 1968 W, I, F, S. 1969 W, I, F, S, SA. 1970 W, I, F, S. 1971 W, I, F, S (2), Pres. XV. 1972 W, I, F, S, SA. 1973 NZ (2), W, I, F, S, A. 1974 S, I, F, W. 1975 I, W, S, A (2). 1976 F.

Leading Cap Winners continued

36 D J Duckham

(Coventry)
1969 I, F, S, W, SA. 1970 I, F, S, W. 1971 I, F, S (2), W, Pres. XV. 1972 I, F, S, W. 1973 NZ (2), W, I, F, S, A. 1974 S, I, F, W. 1975 I, F, W. 1976 A, W, S.

36 P J Wheeler

(Leicester)
1975 F, W. 1976 A, W, S, I. 1977 S, I, F, W. 1978 F, W, S, I, NZ. 1979 S, I, F, W, NZ. 1980 I, F, W, S. 1981 W, S, I, F. 1982 A, S, I, F, W. 1983 F, S, I.

34 W B Beaumont

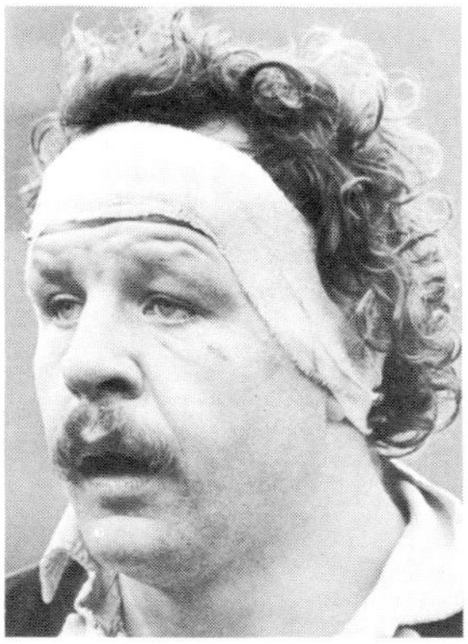

(Fylde)
1975 I, A (2). 1976 A, W, S, I, F. 1977 S, I, F, W. 1978 F, W, S, I, NZ. 1979 S, I, F, W, NZ. 1980 I, F, W, S. 1981 W, S, I, F, Arg (2). 1982 A, S.

Match Results 1871–1983 continued

1933	Bloemfontein	Australia: 15–4	3	1		1				1
1937	Sydney	South Africa: 9–5	1	1			2		1	
1937	Sydney	South Africa: 26–17	3	1	2		6	4		
1953	Johannesburg	South Africa: 25–3			1		5	2	2	
1953	Cape Town	Australia: 18–14	4	3			4	1		
1953	Durban	South Africa: 18–8	1	1	1		4	3		
1953	Port Elizabeth	South Africa: 22–9	1		2		2	2	2	2
1956	Sydney	South Africa: 9–0					2		1	
1956	Brisbane	South Africa: 9–0					2			1
1961	Johannesburg	South Africa: 28–3			1		8	2		
1961	Port Elizabeth	South Africa: 23–11	1	1	2		3	1	3	1
1963	Pretoria	South Africa: 14–3	1				2	1	2	
1963	Cape Town	Australia: 9–5	1		1	1	1	1		
1963	Johannesburg	Australia: 11–9	1	1	1	1			3	
1963	Port Elizabeth	South Africa: 22–6			1	1	3	2	3	
1965	Sydney	Australia: 18–11	2		4		2	1	1	
1965	Brisbane	Australia: 12–8			4		2	1		
1969	Johannesburg	South Africa: 30–11	1	1	2		5	3	3	
1969	Durban	South Africa: 16–9			3		3	2	1	
1969	Cape Town	South Africa: 11–3			1		2	1	1	
1969	Bloemfontein	South Africa: 19–8	1	1	1		3	2	2	
1971	Sydney	South Africa: 19–11	1	1	2		3	2	1	1
1971	Brisbane	South Africa: 14–6			1	1	3	1	1	
1971	Sydney	South Africa: 18–6	1		1		3	3	1	
		TOTALS	28	15	33	5	79	38	31	7

Australia v Wales

Played 10 Australia 3 Wales 7 Drawn 0
Australia 92 points Wales 149

			Australia				Wales			
Year	Venue	Results	T	C	P	D	T	C	P	D
1908	Cardiff	Wales: 9–6	2				2		1	
1947	Cardiff	Wales: 6–0							2	
1958	Cardiff	Wales: 9–3	1				1		1	1
1966	Cardiff	Australia: 14–11	2	1	1	1	2	1	1	
1969	Sydney	Wales: 19–16	2	2	2		3	2	2	
1973	Cardiff	Wales: 24–0					3		4	
1975	Cardiff	Wales: 28–3			1		4	3	1	1
1978	Brisbane	Australia: 18–8	1	1	4		2			
1978	Sydney	Australia: 19–17	1		3	2	2		2	1
1981	Cardiff	Wales: 18–13	2	1	1		1	1	3	1
		TOTALS	11	5	12	3	20	7	17	4

34 D P Rogers (Bedford)
1961 I, F, S. 1962 I, F, W. 1963 I, F, S, W, NZ (2), A. 1964 I, F, S, W, NZ. 1965 I, F, S, W. 1966 I, F, S, W. 1967 S, W, A, NZ. 1969 I, F, S, W.

Match Results 1871–1983 continued

England v France

Played 58 England 32 France 20 Drawn 6
England 692 points France 547

			England				France			
Year	Venue	Results	T	C	P	D	T	C	P	D
1906	Paris	England: 35–8	9	4			2	1		
1907	Richmond	England: 41–13	9	5		1	2	2	1	
1908	Paris	England: 19–0	5	2						
1909	Leicester	England: 22–0	6	2						
1910	Paris	England: 11–3	3	1			1			
1911	Twickenham	England: 37–0	7	5	2					
1912	Paris	England: 18–8	4	1		1	2	1		
1913	Twickenham	England: 20–0	6	1						
1914	Paris	England: 39–13	9	6			3	2		
1920	Twickenham	England: 8–3	1	1	1		1			
1921	Paris	England: 10–6	2	2					2	
1922	Twickenham	Drawn: 11–11	1	1	2		3	1		
1923	Paris	England: 12–3	2	1		1			1	
1924	Twickenham	England: 19–7	5	2			1			1
1925	Paris	England: 13–11	2	2		1*	3	1		
1926	Twickenham	England: 11–0	3	1						
1927	Paris	France: 3–0					1			
1928	Twickenham	England: 18–8	4	3			2	1		
1929	Paris	England: 16–6	4	2			2			
1930	Twickenham	England: 11–5	3	1			1	1		
1931	Paris	France: 14–13	3	2			2			2
1947	Twickenham	England: 6–3	2						1	
1948	Paris	France: 15–0					3	1		1
1949	Twickenham	England: 8–3	1	1		1				1
1950	Paris	France: 6–3	1				2			
1951	Twickenham	France: 11–3	1				2	1	1	
1952	Paris	England: 6–3			2		1			
1953	Twickenham	England: 11–0	3	1						
1954	Paris	France: 11–3	1				2	1		1
1955	Twickenham	France: 16–9	1		2		2	2		2
1956	Paris	France: 14–9	1		2		2	1	2	
1957	Twickenham	England: 9–5	3				1	1		
1958	Paris	England: 14–0	3	1	1					
1959	Twickenham	Drawn: 3–3			1				1	
1960	Paris	Drawn: 3–3	1						1	
1961	Twickenham	Drawn: 5–5	1	1			1	1		
1962	Paris	France: 13–0					3	2		
1963	Twickenham	England: 6–5			2		1	1		
1964	Paris	England: 6–3	1		1		1			
1965	Twickenham	England: 9–6	1		2		1		1	
1966	Paris	France: 13–0					3	2		
1967	Twickenham	France: 16–12			3	1	2	2	1	1
1968	Paris	France: 14–9			2	1	1	1	1	2
1969	Twickenham	England: 22–8	3	2	3		1	1		1
1970	Paris	France: 35–13	2	2	1		6	4	1	2
1971	Twickenham	Drawn: 14–14	1	1	3		2	1	1	1
1972	Paris	France: 37–12	1	1	2		6	5	1	
1973	Twickenham	England: 14–6	2		2		1	1		
1974	Paris	Drawn: 12–12	1	1	1	1	1	1	1	1
1975	Twickenham	France: 27–20	2		4		4	4	1	
1976	Paris	France: 30–9	1	1	1		6	3		
1977	Twickenham	France: 4–3			1		1			
1978	Paris	France: 15–6				2	2	2	1	
1979	Twickenham	England: 7–6	1		1		1	1		
1980	Paris	England: 17–13	2		1	2	2	1	1	
1981	Twickenham	France: 16–12			4		2	1		2
1982	Paris	England: 27–15	2	2	5		1	1	2	1
1983	Twickenham	France: 19–15			4	1	3	2	1	
		TOTALS	127	59	56	13	93	54	23	19

*Goal from mark

Leading Cap Winners continued

31 F E Cotton

(Loughborough, Coventry, Sale)
1971 S (2), Pres. XV. 1973 W, I, F, S, NZ, A. 1974 S, I. 1975 I, F, W. 1976 A, W, S, I, F. 1977 S, I, F, W. 1978 S, I. 1979 NZ. 1980 I, F, W, S. 1981 W.

31 W W Wakefield (Harlequins)
1920 S, I, W, F. 1921 S, I, W, F. 1922 S, I, W, F. 1923 S, I, W, F. 1924 S, I, W, F. 1925 S, I, W, F, NZ. 1926 S, I, W, F. 1927 S, F.

30 E Evans (Sale)
1948 A. 1950 W. 1951 I, F, S. 1952 W, I, F, SA. 1953 I, F, S. 1954 W, I, F, NZ. 1956 W, I, F, S. 1957 W, I, F, S. 1958 A, W, I, F, S.

France

53 R Bertranne (S Bagnerais)
1971 E, W, SA, A (2). 1972 S, I. 1973 NZ, E. 1974 I, W, E, S, SA (2). 1975 W, E, S, I, SA (2). 1976 S, I, W, E, A (2). 1977 W, E, S, I, NZ (2). 1978 E, S, I, W. 1979 I, W, E, S. 1980 W, E, S, I, SA. 1981 S, I, W, E, NZ (2).

Leading Cap Winners continued

50 B Dauga (S Montois)
1964 S, NZ, E, W, I, SA. 1965 S, E, I, W. 1966 S, I, E, W. 1967 S, E, W, I, A, SA (4), NZ. 1968 S, I, NZ (3), A, SA (2). 1969 S, I, E. 1970 S, I, W, E. 1971 S, I, E, W, SA (2), A (2). 1972 S, I, W.

44 R Paparemborde (S Paloise)
1975 SA (2). 1976 S, I, W, E, A (2). 1977 W, E, S, I, NZ (2). 1978 E, S, I, W. 1979 I, W, E, S, NZ (2). 1980 W, E, S, SA. 1981 S, I, W, E, A (2), NZ (2). 1982 W, I, A (2). 1983 E, S, I, W.

43 M Crauste (Racing Club de France)
1958 S, E, A, W, I. 1959 E, W, I. 1960 S, E, W, I. 1961 S, SA, E, W, I, NZ (3), A. 1962 S, E, W, I. 1963 S, I, E, W. 1964 S, NZ, E, W, I, SA. 1965 S, I, E, W. 1966 S, I, E, W.

42 W Spanghero (RC Narbonne)
1964 SA. 1965 E, I, S, W. 1966 E, I, S, W. 1967 A, E, S, SA (4), NZ. 1968 A, E, I, S, NZ (3), SA (2), W. 1969 I, S, W. 1971 E, SA, W. 1972 E, I, A (2). 1973 S, NZ, E, W, I.

41 J-P Rives (S Toulousain)
1975 E, S, I. 1976 S, I, W, E, A (2). 1977 W, E,

Match Results 1871–1983 continued

England v Ireland

Played 95 England 53 Ireland 34 Drawn 8
England 692 points Ireland 564

			England				Ireland			
Year	Venue	Results	T	C	P	D	T	C	P	D
1875	The Oval	England	1		2					
1876	Dublin	England	1		1					
1877	The Oval	England	2		2					
1878	Dublin	England	1		2					
1879	The Oval	England	2		3					
1880	Dublin	England	1		1		1			
1881	Manchester	England	2		2					
1882	Dublin	Drawn	2				2			
1883	Manchester	England	3		1		1			
1884	Dublin	England			1					
1885	Manchester	England	2				1			
1886	Dublin	England	1							
1887	Dublin	Ireland							2	
1890	Blackheath	England	3							
1891†	Dublin	England: 9–0	3		2					
1892	Manchester	England: 7–0	2	1						
1893	Dublin	England: 4–0	2							
1894	Blackheath	Ireland: 7–5	1	1			1			1
1895	Dublin	England: 6–3	2				1			
1896	Leeds	Ireland: 10–4				1	2	2		
1897	Dublin	Ireland: 13–9	1		2		3			1
1898	Richmond	Ireland: 9–6	1		1		2		1	
1899	Dublin	Ireland: 6–0					1		1	
1900	Richmond	England: 15–4	3	1		1				1
1901	Dublin	Ireland: 10–6	1		1		2	2		
1902	Leicester	England: 6–3	2				1			
1903	Dublin	Ireland: 6–0					1		1	
1904	Blackheath	England: 19–0	5	2						
1905	Cork	Ireland: 17–3	1				5	1		
1906	Leicester	Ireland: 16–6	2				4	2		
1907	Dublin	Ireland: 17–9	2		1		4	1		1*
1908	Richmond	England: 13–3	3	2					1	
1909	Dublin	England: 11–5	3	1			1	1		
1910	Twickenham	Drawn: 0–0								
1911	Dublin	Ireland: 3–0					1			
1912	Twickenham	England: 15–0	5							
1913	Dublin	England: 15–4	4		1					1
1914	Twickenham	England: 17–12	5	1			2	1		1
1920	Dublin	England: 14–11	4	1			2	1	1	
1921	Twickenham	England: 15–0	3	1		1				
1922	Dublin	England: 12–3	4				1			
1923	Leicester	England: 23–5	5	2		1	1	1		
1924	Belfast	England: 14–3	4	1			1			
1925	Twickenham	Drawn: 6–6	2				2			
1926	Dublin	Ireland: 19–15	3	3			4	2	1	
1927	Twickenham	England: 8–6	2	1			1		1	
1928	Dublin	England: 7–6	1			1	2			
1929	Twickenham	Ireland: 6–5	1	1			2			
1930	Dublin	Ireland: 4–3	1							1
1931	Twickenham	Ireland: 6–5	1	1			1		1	
1932	Dublin	England: 11–8	1	1	2		1	1	1	
1933	Twickenham	England: 17–6	5	1			1		1	
1934	Dublin	England: 13–3	3	2			1			
1935	Twickenham	England: 14–3	1	1	3		1			
1936	Dublin	Ireland: 6–3	1				2			
1937	Twickenham	England: 9–8	2		1		2	1		
1938	Dublin	England: 36–14	7	6	1		4	1		
1939	Twickenham	Ireland: 5–0					1	1		

Match Results 1871–1983 continued

1947	Dublin	Ireland: 22–0					5	2	1	
1948	Twickenham	Ireland: 11–10	2	2			3	1		
1949	Dublin	Ireland: 14–5	1	1			2	1	2	
1950	Twickenham	England: 3–0	1							
1951	Dublin	Ireland: 3–0							1	
1952	Twickenham	England: 3–0	1							
1953	Dublin	Drawn: 9–9	1		2		1		2	
1954	Twickenham	England: 14–3	3	1	1				1	
1955	Dublin	Drawn: 6–6	2				1		1	
1956	Twickenham	England: 20–0	3	1	3					
1957	Dublin	England: 6–0	1		1					
1958	Twickenham	England: 6–0	1		1					
1959	Dublin	England: 3–0			1					
1960	Twickenham	England: 8–5	1	1		1	1	1		
1961	Dublin	Ireland: 11–8	2	1			1	1	2	
1962	Twickenham	England: 16–0	3	2	1					
1963	Dublin	Drawn: 0–0								
1964	Twickenham	Ireland: 18–5	1	1			4	3		
1965	Dublin	Ireland: 5–0					1	1		
1966	Twickenham	Drawn: 6–6	1		1		1		1	
1967	Dublin	England: 8–3	1	1	1				1	
1968	Twickenham	Drawn: 9–9			2	1			3	
1969	Dublin	Ireland: 17–15	1		4		2	1	2	1
1970	Twickenham	England: 9–3	1			2			1	
1971	Dublin	England: 9–6			3		2			
1972	Twickenham	Ireland: 16–12	1	1	2		2	1	1	1
1973	Dublin	Ireland: 18–9	1	1	1		2	2	1	1
1974	Twickenham	Ireland: 26–21	1	1	5		4	2	1	1
1975	Dublin	Ireland: 12–9	1	1		1	2	2		
1976	Twickenham	Ireland: 13–12			4		1		2	1
1977	Dublin	England: 4–0	1							
1978	Twickenham	England: 15–9	2	2	1				2	1
1979	Dublin	Ireland: 12–7	1		1		1	1	1	1
1980	Twickenham	England: 24–9	3	3	2				3	
1981	Dublin	England: 10–6	2	1						2
1982	Twickenham	Ireland: 16–15	1	1	3		2	1	2	
1983	Dublin	Ireland: 25–15			5		2	1	5	
		TOTALS	161	53	75	10	106	39	48	16

*Goal from mark †Modern scoring values adopted

England v New Zealand

Played 12 England 2 New Zealand 10 Drawn 0
England 83 points New Zealand 145

			England				New Zealand			
Year	Venue	Results	T	C	P	D	T	C	P	D
1905	Crystal Palace	New Zealand: 15–0					5			
1925	Twickenham	New Zealand: 17–11	2	1	1		4	1	1	
1936	Twickenham	England: 13–0	3			1				
1954	Twickenham	New Zealand: 5–0					1	1		
1963	Auckland	New Zealand: 21–11	1	1	2		3	3	1	1
1963	Christchurch	New Zealand: 9–6	1		1		2			1*
1964	Twickenham	New Zealand: 14–0					2	1	2	
1967	Twickenham	New Zealand: 23–11	2	1	1		5	4		
1973	Twickenham	New Zealand: 9–0					1	1		1
1973	Auckland	England: 16–10	3	2			2	1		
1978	Twickenham	New Zealand: 16–6			1	1	2	1	2	
1979	Twickenham	New Zealand: 10–9			3		1		2	
		TOTALS	12	5	9	2	28	13	8	3

*Goal from mark

Leading Cap Winners continued

S, I. 1978 E, S, I, W. 1979 I, W, E, S, NZ (2). 1980 W, E, S, I, SA. 1981 S, I, W, E, A. 1982 W, E, S, I. 1983 E, S, I, W.

40 J-P Lux (US Tyrosse)
1967 E, I, SA (3), W. 1968 A, E, I, NZ, SA (2). 1969 E, I, S. 1970 E, I, S, W. 1971 E, I, S, W, A (2). 1972 E, I (2), S, W, A (2). 1973 S, NZ, E. 1974 I, W, E, S. 1975 W.

38 J Prat (FC Lourdais)
1947 E, I, S, W. 1948 A, E, I, S, W. 1949 E, I, S, W. 1950 E, I, S, W. 1951 E, S, W. 1952 E, I, S, SA, W. 1953 E, I, S, W. 1954 E, I, NZ, S, W. 1955 E, I, S, W.

Ireland

69 C M H Gibson (Cambridge Univ., NIFC)

Leading Cap Winners continued

1964 E, S, W, F. 1965 E, S, W, F, SA. 1966 E, S, W, F. 1967 E, S, W, F, A (2). 1968 E, S, W, A. 1969 E, S, W. 1970 E, S, W, F, SA. 1971 E, S, W, F. 1972 E, F (2). 1973 NZ, E, S, W, F. 1974 F, W, E, S, Pres. XV. 1975 E, S, F, W. 1976 A, F, W, E, S, NZ. 1977 W, E, S, F. 1978 F, W, E, NZ. 1979 S, A (2).

63 W J McBride (Ballymena)
1962 E, S, W, F. 1963 E, S, W, F, NZ. 1964 E, S, F. 1965 E, S, W, F, SA. 1966 E, S, W, F. 1967 E, S, W, F, A (2). 1968 E, S, W, F, A. 1969 E, S, W, F. 1970 E, S, W, F, SA. 1971 E, S, W, F. 1972 E, F (2). 1973 NZ, E, S, W, F. 1974 F, W, E, S, Pres. XV, NZ. 1975 E, S, F, W.

60 J F Slattery (UC

Dublin, Blackrock Coll)
1970 E, S, W, F, SA.

Match Results 1871–1983 continued

England v Scotland

Played 99 England 47 Scotland 36 Drawn 16
England 812 points Scotland 688

			England				Scotland			
Year	Venue	Results	T	C	P	D	T	C	P	D
1871	Raeburn Place	Scotland	1		1		1			
1872	The Oval	England	2		2				1	
1873	Glasgow	Drawn: no score								
1874	The Oval	England			1		1			
1875	Raeburn Place	Drawn: no score								
1876	The Oval	England	1		1					
1877	Raeburn Place	Scotland							1	
1878	The Oval	Drawn: no score								
1879	Raeburn Place	Drawn			1				1	
1880	Manchester	England	3		2				1	
1881	Raeburn Place	Drawn	1		1		1		1	
1882	Manchester	Scotland					2			
1883	Raeburn Place	England	2				1			
1884	Blackheath	England			1		1			
1886	Raeburn Place	Drawn: no score								
1887	Manchester	Drawn	1				1			
1890	Raeburn Place	England	1		1					
1891†	Richmond	Scotland: 9–3	1	1			3	3		
1892	Raeburn Place	England: 5–0	1	1						
1893	Leeds	Scotland: 8–0								2
1894	Raeburn Place	Scotland: 6–0					2			
1895	Richmond	Scotland: 6–3			1		1		1	
1896	Glasgow	Scotland: 11–0					3	1		
1897	Manchester	England: 12–3	2	1		1	1			
1898	Powderhall Edinburgh	Drawn: 3–3	1				1			
1899	Blackheath	Scotland: 5–0					1	1		
1900	Inverleith	Drawn: 0–0								
1901	Blackheath	Scotland: 18–3	1				4	3		
1902	Inverleith	England: 6–3	2				1			
1903	Richmond	Scotland: 10–6	2				2			1
1904	Inverleith	Scotland: 6–3	1				2			
1905	Richmond	Scotland: 8–0					2	1		
1906	Inverleith	England: 9–3	3				1			
1907	Blackheath	Scotland: 8–3	1				2	1		
1908	Inverleith	Scotland: 16–10	2	2			2	1		2
1909	Richmond	Scotland: 18–8	2	1			4	3		
1910	Inverleith	England: 14–5	4	1			1	1		
1911	Twickenham	England: 13–8	3	2			2	1		
1912	Inverleith	Scotland: 8–3	1				2	1		
1913	Twickenham	England: 3–0	1							
1914	Inverleith	England: 16–15	4	2			3	1		1
1920	Twickenham	England: 13–4	3	2						1
1921	Inverleith	England: 18–0	4	3						
1922	Twickenham	England: 11–5	3	1			1	1		
1923	Inverleith	England: 8–6	2	1			2			
1924	Twickenham	England: 19–0	3	3		1				
1925	Murrayfield	Scotland: 14–11	2	1	1		2	2		1
1926	Twickenham	Scotland: 17–9	3				3	2		1
1927	Murrayfield	Scotland: 21–13	2	2	1		5	1		1
1928	Twickenham	England: 6–0	2							
1929	Murrayfield	Scotland: 12–6	2				4			
1930	Twickenham	Drawn: 0–0								
1931	Murrayfield	Scotland: 28–19	4	2	1		6	5		
1932	Twickenham	England: 16–3	4	2			1			
1933	Murrayfield	Scotland: 3–0					1			
1934	Twickenham	England: 6–3	2				1			
1935	Murrayfield	Scotland: 10–7	1			1	2	2		

Match Results 1871–1983 continued

1936	Twickenham	England: 9–8	3				1	1	1	
1937	Murrayfield	England: 6–3	2						1	
1938	Twickenham	Scotland: 21–16	1		3	1	5		2	
1939	Murrayfield	England: 9–6			3		2			
1947	Twickenham	England: 24–5	4	4		1	1	1		
1948	Murrayfield	Scotland: 6–3			1		2			
1949	Twickenham	England: 19–3	5	2					1	
1950	Murrayfield	Scotland: 13–11	2	1	1		3	2		
1951	Twickenham	England: 5–3	1	1			1			
1952	Murrayfield	England: 19–3	4	2		1	1			
1953	Twickenham	England: 26–8	6	4			2	1		
1954	Murrayfield	England: 13–3	3	2			1			
1955	Twickenham	England: 9–6	2		1		1		1	
1956	Murrayfield	England: 11–6	1	1	2		1		1	
1957	Twickenham	England: 16–3	3	2	1				1	
1958	Murrayfield	Drawn: 3–3			1				1	
1959	Twickenham	Drawn: 3–3			1				1	
1960	Murrayfield	England: 21–12	3	3	1	1	1		3	
1961	Twickenham	England: 6–0	1		1					
1962	Murrayfield	Drawn: 3–3			1				1	
1963	Twickenham	England: 10–8	2	2			1	1	1	
1964	Murrayfield	Scotland: 15–6	1		1		3	3		
1965	Twickenham	Drawn: 3–3	1							1
1966	Murrayfield	Scotland: 6–3				1	1		1	
1967	Twickenham	England: 27–14	4	3	2	1	2	1	2	
1968	Murrayfield	England: 8–6	1	1	1				1	1
1969	Twickenham	England: 8–3	1	1	1				1	
1970	Murrayfield	Scotland: 14–5	1	1			2	1	2	
1971	Twickenham	Scotland: 16–15	2		3		3	2		1
1971	Murrayfield**	Scotland: 26–6			1	1	5	4	1	
1972	Murrayfield	Scotland: 23–9			3		2		4	1
1973	Twickenham	England: 20–13	4	2			2	1	1	
1974	Murrayfield	Scotland: 16–14	2		1	1	2	1	2	
1975	Twickenham	England: 7–6	1		1				2	
1976	Murrayfield	Scotland: 22–12	1	1	2		3	2	2	
1977	Twickenham	England: 26–6	4	2	2				2	
1978	Murrayfield	England: 15–0	2	2	1					
1979	Twickenham	Drawn: 7–7	1		1		1		1	
1980	Murrayfield	England: 30–18	5	2	2		2	2	2	
1981	Twickenham	England: 23–17	3	1	3		3	1	1	
1982	Murrayfield	Drawn: 9–9			3				2	1
1983	Twickenham	Scotland: 22–12			3	1	2	1	3	1
		TOTALS	159	68	63	12	132	56	51	16

**RFU centenary match †Modern scoring values adopted

England v South Africa

Played 7 England 2 South Africa 4 Drawn 1
England 38 points South Africa 49

			England				South Africa			
Year	Venue	Results	T	C	P	D	T	C	P	D
1906	Crystal Palace	Drawn: 3–3	1				1			
1913	Twickenham	South Africa: 9–3	1				1		2	
1932	Twickenham	South Africa: 7–0					1			1
1952	Twickenham	South Africa: 8–3	1				1	1	1	
1961	Twickenham	South Africa: 5–0					1	1		
1969	Twickenham	England: 11–8	2	1	1		1	1	1	
1972	Johannesburg	England: 18–9	1	1	4				3	
		TOTALS	6	2	5	0	6	3	7	1

Leading Cap Winners continued

1971 E, S, W, F. 1972 E, F (2). 1973 NZ, E, S, W, F. 1974 F, W, E, S, Pres. XV, NZ. 1975 E, S, F, W. 1976 A. 1977 S, F. 1978 S, F, W, E, NZ. 1979 F, W, E, S, A (2). 1980 E, S, F, W. 1981 F, W, E, S, SA (2), A. 1982 W, E, S, F. 1983 S, F, W, E.

54 T J Kiernan (UC Cork, Cork Constitution)
1960 E, S, W, F, SA. 1961 E, S, W, F, SA. 1962 E, W. 1963 S, W, F, NZ. 1964 E, S. 1965 E, S, W, F, SA. 1966 E, S, W, F. 1967 E, S, W, F, A (2). 1968 E, S, W, F, A. 1969 E, S, W, F. 1970 E, S, W, F, SA. 1971 F. 1972 E, F (2). 1973 NZ, E, S.

47 M I Keane (Lans-

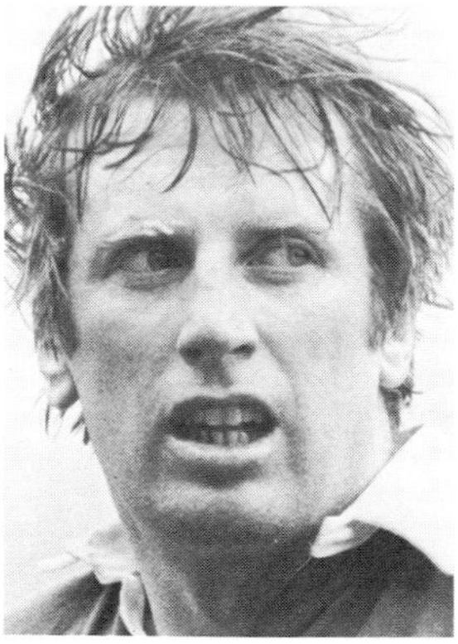

downe)
1974 F, W, E, S, Pres. XV, NZ. 1975 E, S, F, W. 1976 A, F, W, E, S, NZ. 1977 W, E, S, F. 1978 S, F, W, E, NZ.

Leading Cap Winners continued

1979 F, W, E, S, A (2). 1980 E, S, F, W. 1981 F, W, E, S. 1982 W, E, S, F. 1983 S, F, W, E.

46 J W Kyle (Queen's Belfast, NIFC)
1947 E, S, W, F, A. 1948 E, S, W, F. 1949 E, S, W, F. 1950 E, S, W, F. 1951 E, S, W, F, SA. 1952 E, S, W, F. 1953 E, S, W, F. 1954 F, NZ. 1955 E, W, F. 1956 E, S, W, F. 1957 E, S, W, F. 1958 E, S, A.

45 K W Kennedy

(Queen's Belfast, London Irish)
1965 E, S, W, F, SA. 1966 E, W, F. 1967 E, S, W, F, A (2). 1968 F, A. 1969 E, S, W, F. 1970 E, S, W, F, SA. 1971 E, S, W, F. 1972 E, F (2). 1973 NZ, E, S, W, F. 1974 F, W, E, S, Pres. XV, NZ. 1975 F, W.

Match Results 1871–1983 continued

England v Wales

Played 88 England 35 Wales 41 Drawn 12
England 664 points Wales 839

			England				Wales			
Year	Venue	Results	T	C	P	D	T	C	P	D
1881	Blackheath	England	6		7	1				
1883	Swansea	England	4		2					
1884	Leeds	England	2		1				1	
1885	Swansea	England	4		1		1		1	
1886	Blackheath	England	2			1*			1	
1887	Llanelli	Drawn: 0–0								
1890	Dewsbury	Wales					1			
1891†	Newport	England: 7–3	1		2				1	
1892	Blackheath	England: 17–0	4	3						
1893	Cardiff	Wales: 12–11	4	1			3	1	1	
1894	Birkenhead	England: 24–3	4	4		1*	1			
1895	Swansea	England: 14–6	4	1			2			
1896	Blackheath	England: 25–0	7	2						
1897	Newport	Wales: 11–0					3	1		
1898	Blackheath	England: 14–7	4	1			1			1
1899	Swansea	Wales: 26–3	1				6	4		
1900	Gloucester	Wales: 13–3	1				2	2	1	
1901	Cardiff	Wales: 13–0					3	2		
1902	Blackheath	Wales: 9–8	2	1			2		1	
1903	Swansea	Wales: 21–5	1	1			5	3		
1904	Leicester	Drawn: 14–14	3	1	1		2	2		1*
1905	Cardiff	Wales: 25–0					7	2		
1906	Richmond	Wales: 16–3	1				4	2		
1907	Swansea	Wales: 22–0					6	2		
1908	Bristol	Wales: 28–18	4	3			5	3	1	1
1909	Cardiff	Wales: 8–0					1	1	1	
1910	Twickenham	England: 11–6	2	1	1		2			
1911	Swansea	Wales: 15–11	3	1			4		1	
1912	Twickenham	England: 8–0	2	1						
1913	Cardiff	England: 12–0	2	1		1				
1914	Twickenham	England: 10–9	2	2			1	1		1
1920	Swansea	Wales: 19–5	1	1			2	1	1	2
1921	Twickenham	England: 18–3	4	1		1	1			
1922	Cardiff	Wales: 28–6	2				8	2		
1923	Twickenham	England: 7–3	1			1	1			
1924	Swansea	England: 17–9	5	1			3			
1925	Twickenham	England: 12–6	3		1		2			
1926	Cardiff	Drawn: 3–3	1				1			
1927	Twickenham	England: 11–9	1	1	1	1*	2		1	
1928	Swansea	England: 10–8	2	2			2	1		
1929	Twickenham	England: 8–3	2	1			1			
1930	Cardiff	England: 11–3	2	1	1		1			
1931	Twickenham	Drawn: 11–11	1	1	2		2	1		1*
1932	Swansea	Wales: 12–5	1	1			1	1	1	1
1933	Twickenham	Wales: 7–3	1				1			1
1934	Cardiff	England: 9–0	3							
1935	Twickenham	Drawn: 3–3			1		1			
1936	Swansea	Drawn: 0–0								
1937	Twickenham	England: 4–3				1	1			
1938	Cardiff	Wales: 14–8	2	1			2	1	2	
1939	Twickenham	England: 3–0	1							
1947	Cardiff	England: 9–6	1	1		1	2			
1948	Twickenham	Drawn: 3–3			1		1			
1949	Cardiff	Wales: 9–3				1	3			
1950	Twickenham	Wales: 11–5	1	1			2	1	1	
1951	Swansea	Wales: 23–5	1	1			5	4		
1952	Twickenham	Wales: 8–6	2				2	1		

Match Results 1871–1983 continued

1953	Cardiff	England: 8–3	1	1	1				1	
1954	Twickenham	England: 9–6	3				1		1	
1955	Cardiff	Wales: 3–0							1	
1956	Twickenham	Wales: 8–3			1		2	1		
1957	Cardiff	England: 3–0			1					
1958	Twickenham	Drawn: 3–3	1						1	
1959	Cardiff	Wales: 5–0					1	1		
1960	Twickenham	England: 14–6	2	1	2				2	
1961	Cardiff	Wales: 6–3	1				2			
1962	Twickenham	Drawn: 0–0								
1963	Cardiff	England: 13–6	2	2		1	1		1	
1964	Twickenham	Drawn: 6–6	2				2			
1965	Cardiff	Wales: 14–3			1		3	1		1
1966	Twickenham	Wales: 11–6	1		1		1	1	2	
1967	Cardiff	Wales: 34–21	3		4		5	5	2	1
1968	Twickenham	Drawn: 11–11	2	1	1		2	1		1
1969	Cardiff	Wales: 30–9			3		5	3	2	1
1970	Twickenham	Wales: 17–13	2	2	1		4	1		1
1971	Cardiff	Wales: 22–6	1		1		3	2	1	2
1972	Twickenham	Wales: 12–3			1		1	1	2	
1973	Cardiff	Wales: 25–9			2	1	5	1	1	
1974	Twickenham	England: 16–12	2	1	2		1	1	2	
1975	Cardiff	Wales: 20–4	1				3	1	2	
1976	Twickenham	Wales: 21–9			3		3	3	1	
1977	Cardiff	Wales: 14–9			3		2		2	
1978	Twickenham	Wales: 9–6			2				3	
1979	Cardiff	Wales: 27–3			1		5	2		1
1980	Twickenham	England: 9–8			3		2			
1981	Cardiff	Wales: 21–19	1		5		1	1	4	1
1982	Twickenham	England: 17–7	2		3		1			1
1983	Cardiff	Wales: Drawn 13–13	1		2	1	1		2	1
		TOTALS	136	46	66	13	166	65	49	20

*Goal from mark †Modern scoring values adopted

France v Ireland

Played 56 France 27 Ireland 25 Drawn 4
France 552 points Ireland 517

			France				Ireland			
Year	Venue	Results	T	C	P	D	T	C	P	D
1909	Dublin	Ireland: 19–8	2	1			4	2	1	
1910	Paris	Ireland: 8–3	1				2	1		
1911	Cork	Ireland: 25–5	1	1			5	3		1
1912	Paris	Ireland: 11–6	2				3	1		
1913	Cork	Ireland: 24–0					6	3		
1914	Paris	Ireland: 8–6	2				2	1		
1920	Dublin	France: 15–7	5				1			1
1921	Paris	France: 20–10	4	4			2	2		
1922	Dublin	Ireland: 8–3	1				1	1	1	
1923	Paris	France: 14–8	4	1			2	1		
1924	Dublin	Ireland: 6–0					2			
1925	Paris	Ireland: 9–3	1				2		1	
1926	Belfast	Ireland: 11–0					2	1	1	
1927	Paris	Ireland: 8–3	1				1	1	1	
1928	Belfast	Ireland: 12–8	2	1			4			
1929	Paris	Ireland: 6–0					2			
1930	Belfast	France: 5–0	1	1						
1931	Paris	France: 3–0	1							
1947	Dublin	France: 12–8	4				1	1	1	

Leading Cap Winners continued

New Zealand

55 C E Meads (King Country)
1957 A (2). 1958 A (3). 1959 BI (3). 1960 SA (4). 1961 F (3). 1962 A (4). 1963 E (2). 1963–4 I, W, E, S, F. 1964 A (3). 1965 SA (4). 1966 BI (4). 1967 A. 1967–8 E, W, F, S. 1968 A (2), F (3). 1969 W (2). 1970 SA (2). 1971 BI (4).

39 I A Kirkpatrick (Canterbury, Poverty Bay)
1967–8 F. 1968 A (2), F (3). 1969 W (2). 1970 SA (4). 1971 BI (4). 1972 A (3). 1972–3 W, S, E, I, F. 1973 E. 1974 A (3), I. 1975 S. 1976 I, SA (4). 1977 BI (4).

38 K R Tremain (Canterbury, Hawke's Bay)
1959 BI (3). 1960 SA (4). 1961 F (2). 1962 A (3). 1963 F (2). 1963–4 I, W, E, S, F. 1964 A (3). 1965 SA (4). 1966 BI (4). 1967 A. 1967–8 E, W, S. 1968 A, F (3).

38 B G Williams (Auckland)
1970 SA (4). 1971 BI (3). 1972 A (3). 1972–3 W, S, E, I, F. 1973 E. 1974 A (3), I. 1975 S. 1976 I, SA (4). 1977 BI (4), F. 1978 A (3), I, W, E, S.

34 B J Robertson (Counties)

Leading Cap Winners continued

1972 A (2). 1972–3 S, E, I, F. 1974 A (3), I. 1976 I, SA (4). 1977 BI (3), F (2). 1978 A (3), W, E, S. 1979 F (2), A. 1980 A (2), W. 1981 S (2).

36 A M Haden (Auckland)
1977 BI (4), F (2). 1978 A (3), I, W, E, S. 1979 F (2), A, S, E. 1980 A (3), W. 1981 S, SA (3), Rom, F (2). 1982 A (3). 1983 BI (4).

32 W J Whineray (Canterbury, Waikato, Auckland)
1957 A (2). 1958 A (3). 1959 BI (4). 1960 SA (4). 1961 F (3). 1962 A (5). 1963 E (2). 1963–4 I, W, E, S, F. 1965 SA (4).

31 D B Clarke (Waikato)
1956 SA (2). 1957 A (2). 1958 A (2). 1959 BI (4). 1960 SA (4). 1961 F (3). 1962 A (5). 1963 E (2). 1963–4 I, W, E, S, F. 1964 A (2).

30 Stewart Wilson (Wellington)
1977 F (2). 1978 A (3), I, W, E, S. 1979 F (2), A, S, E. 1980 A, W. 1981 S (2), SA (3), F (2). 1982 A (3). 1983 BI (4).

29 S M Going (North Auckland)
1967 A. 1967–8 F. 1968 F. 1969 W (2).

Match Results 1871–1983 continued

1948	Paris	Ireland: 13–6	2				3	2		
1949	Dublin	France: 16–9	2	2	2				3	
1950	Paris	Drawn: 3–3				1			1	
1951	Dublin	Ireland: 9–8	2	1			2		1	
1952	Paris	Ireland: 11–8	1	1	1		2	1	1	
1953	Belfast	Ireland: 16–3				1	4	2		
1954	Paris	France: 8–0	2	1						
1955	Dublin	France: 5–3	1	1					1	
1956	Paris	France: 14–8	2	1		2	1	1	1	
1957	Dublin	Ireland: 11–6			2		2	1	1	
1958	Paris	France: 11–6	1	1	1	1			2	
1959	Dublin	Ireland: 9–5	1	1			1		1	1
1960	Paris	France: 23–6	4	1		3	2			
1961	Dublin	France: 15–3	1		2	2			1	
1962	Paris	France: 11–0	3	1						
1963	Dublin	France: 24–5	4	3		2	1	1		
1964	Paris	France: 27–6	6	3		1	1			1
1965	Dublin	Drawn: 3–3	1				1			
1966	Paris	France: 11–6	2	1	1				1	1
1967	Dublin	France: 11–6	1	1		2	1		1	
1968	Paris	France: 16–6	2	2	1	1			2	
1969	Dublin	Ireland: 17–9	1		2		1	1	3	1
1970	Paris	France: 8–0	1	1		1				
1971	Dublin	Drawn: 9–9			2	1	1		2	
1972	Paris	Ireland: 14–9	1	1	1		2		2	
1972	Dublin**	Ireland: 24–14	3	1			3	3	2	
1973	Dublin	Ireland: 6–4	1						2	
1974	Paris	France: 9–0	1	1	1					
1975	Dublin	Ireland: 25–6			1	1	3	2	1	2
1976	Paris	France: 26–3	4	2	2				1	
1977	Dublin	France: 15–6	1	1	3				2	
1978	Paris	France: 10–9	1		2				3	
1979	Dublin	Drawn: 9–9	1	1	1				3	
1980	Paris	France: 19–18	2	1	2	1	1	1	3	1
1981	Dublin	France: 19–13	1		3	2	1		3	
1982	Paris	France: 22–9	2	1	4				3	
1983	Dublin	Ireland: 22–16	2	1	2		2	1	4	
		TOTALS	92	41	36	22	77	35	59	9

**Non-championship

France v New Zealand

Played 18 France 4 New Zealand 14 Drawn 0
France 153 points New Zealand 298

			France				New Zealand			
Year	Venue	Results	T	C	P	D	T	C	P	D
1906	Paris	New Zealand: 38–8	2	1			10	4		
1925	Toulouse	New Zealand: 30–6	2				8	3		
1954	Paris	France: 3–0	1							
1961	Auckland	New Zealand: 13–6				2	2	2		1
1961	Wellington	New Zealand: 5–3	1				1	1		
1961	Christchurch	New Zealand: 32–3	1				5	4	3	
1964	Paris	New Zealand: 12–3			1		2		1	1
1967	Paris	New Zealand: 21–15	1		3	1	4	3	1	
1968	Christchurch	New Zealand: 12–9			2	1	1		3	
1968	Wellington	New Zealand: 9–3			1				3	
1968	Auckland	New Zealand: 19–12	3			1	2	2	2	1
1973	Paris	France: 13–6	2	1	1				2	
1977	Toulouse	France: 18–13	1	1	3	1	1		2	1

Match Results 1871–1983 continued

1977	Paris	New Zealand: 15–3			1		1	1	2	1
1979	Christchurch	New Zealand: 23–9	1	1		1	3	1	3	
1979	Auckland	France: 24–19	4	1	1	1	2	1	3	
1981	Toulouse	New Zealand: 13–9			2	1	1		2	1
1981	Paris	New Zealand: 18–6			2		2	2	2	
		TOTALS	19	5	17	9	45	24	29	6

France v Scotland

Played 53 France 26 Scotland 25 Drawn 2
France 449 points Scotland 560

			France				Scotland			
Year	Venue	Results	T	C	P	D	T	C	P	D
1910	Inverleith	Scotland: 27–0					7	3		
1911	Paris	France: 16–15	4	2			3	1		1
1912	Inverleith	Scotland: 31–3	1				6	5	1	
1913	Paris	Scotland: 21–3	1				5	3		
1920	Paris	Scotland: 5–0					1	1		
1921	Inverleith	France: 3–0	1							
1922	Paris	Drawn: 3–3	1				1			
1923	Inverleith	Scotland: 16–3				1*	4	2		
1924	Paris	France: 12–10	4				1		1	1
1925	Inverleith	Scotland: 25–4				1	7	2		
1926	Paris	Scotland: 20–6	1		1		5	1	1	
1927	Murrayfield	Scotland: 23–6	2				4	4	1	
1928	Paris	Scotland: 15–6	2				5			
1929	Murrayfield	Scotland: 6–3	1				1		1	
1930	Paris	France: 7–3	1			1	1			
1931	Murrayfield	Scotland: 6–4				1			2	
1947	Paris	France: 8–3	2	1					1	
1948	Murrayfield	Scotland: 9–8	1	1	1		1		2	
1949	Paris	Scotland: 8–0					2	1		
1950	Murrayfield	Scotland: 8–5	1	1			2	1		
1951	Paris	France: 14–12	2	1	2		2		2	
1952	Murrayfield	France: 13–11	2	2	1		1	1	2	
1953	Paris	France: 11–5	1	1	1	1	1	1		
1954	Murrayfield	France: 3–0	1							
1955	Paris	France: 15–0	4		1					
1956	Murrayfield	Scotland: 12–0					2		2	
1957	Paris	Scotland: 6–0							1	1
1958	Murrayfield	Scotland: 11–9	1		2		2	1	1	
1959	Paris	France: 9–0	1			2				
1960	Murrayfield	France: 13–11	3	2			2	1	1	
1961	Paris	France: 11–0	1	1	1	1				
1962	Murrayfield	France: 11–3	1	1	2				1	
1963	Paris	Scotland: 11–6			1	1	1	1	1	1
1964	Murrayfield	Scotland: 10–0					2	2		
1965	Paris	France: 16–8	4	2			2	1		
1966	Murrayfield	Drawn: 3–3			1		1			
1967	Paris	Scotland: 9–8	2	1					2	1
1968	Murrayfield	France: 8–6	2	1			1		1	
1969	Paris	Scotland: 6–3			1		1		1	
1970	Murrayfield	France: 11–9	2	1		1	1		2	
1971	Paris	France: 13–8	2	2	1		1	1	1	
1972	Murrayfield	Scotland: 20–9	1	1	1		3	1	1	1
1973	Paris	France: 16–13	1		3	1	1		2	1
1974	Murrayfield	Scotland: 19–6			1	1	2	1	3	
1975	Paris	France: 10–9	1		1	1			3	
1976	Murrayfield	France: 13–6	1		3				1	1

Leading Cap Winners continued

1970 SA (2). 1971 BI (4). 1972 A (3). 1972–3 W, S, E, I, F. 1973 E. 1974 I. 1975 S. 1976 I, SA (4). 1977 BI (2).

Scotland

51 A R Irvine

(Heriot's FP)
1972 NZ. 1973 F, W, I, E, Pres. XV. 1974 W, E, I, F. 1975 I, F, W, E, NZ, A. 1976 F, W, E, I. 1977 E, I, F, W. 1978 I, F, E, NZ. 1979 W, E, I, F, NZ. 1980 I, F, W, E. 1981 F, W, E, I, NZ (2), Rom, A. 1982 E, I, F, W, A (2).

51 J M Renwick

Leading Cap Winners continued

(Hawick)
1972 E, W, F, NZ. 1973 F. 1974 W, E, I, F. 1975 I, F, W, E, NZ, A. 1976 F, W, E. 1977 I, F, W. 1978 I, F, W, E, NZ. 1979 W, E, I, F, NZ. 1980 I, F, W, E. 1981 F, W, E, I, NZ (2), Rom, A. 1982 E, I, F, W. 1983 I, F, W, E.

50 A B Carmichael (West of Scotland)
1967 I, NZ. 1968 E, I, W, F, A. 1969 E, I, W, F, SA. 1970 E, I, W, F, A. 1971 E (2), I, W, F. 1972 E, W, F, NZ. 1973 F, W, I, E, Pres. XV. 1974 W, E, I, F. 1975 I, F, W, E, NZ, A. 1976 F, W, E, I. 1977 E, I, F, W. 1978 I.

44 A F McHarg (West of Scotland, London Scottish)
1968 E, I, A. 1969 E, I, W, F. 1971 E (2), I, W, F. 1972 E, F, NZ. 1973 F, W, I, E, Pres. XV. 1974 W, E, I, F. 1975 I, F, W, E, NZ, A. 1976 F, W, E, I. 1977 E, I, F, W. 1978 I, F, W, NZ. 1979 W, E.

43 J McLauchlan (Jordanhill)
1969 E, SA. 1970 W, F. 1971 E (2), I, W, F. 1972 E, W, F, NZ. 1973 F, W, I, E, Pres. XV. 1974 W, E, I, F. 1975 I, F, W, E, NZ, A. 1976 F, W, E, I. 1977 W. 1978 I, F, W, E, NZ. 1979 W, E, I, F, NZ.

Match Results 1871–1983 continued

1977	Paris	France: 23–3	4	2	1				1	
1978	Murrayfield	France: 19–16	2	1	3		2	1	1	1
1979	Paris	France: 21–17	3		2	1	3	1	1	
1980	Murrayfield	Scotland: 22–14	2		1	1	3	1	2	
1981	Paris	France: 16–9	2	1	2		1	1	1	
1982	Murrayfield	Scotland: 16–7	1		1		1		3	1
1983	Paris	France: 19–15	2	1	3		1	1	2	
		TOTALS	72	26	38	15	93	41	48	10

*Goal from mark

France v South Africa

Played 19 France 3 South Africa 12 Drawn 4
France 166 points South Africa 328

			France				South Africa			
Year	Venue	Results	T	C	P	D	T	C	P	D
1913	Bordeaux	South Africa: 38–5	1	1			9	4	1	
1952	Paris	South Africa: 25–3				1	6	2	1	
1958	Cape Town	Drawn: 3–3				1	1			
1958	Johannesburg	France: 9–5			2	1	1	1		
1961	Paris	Drawn: 0–0								
1964	Springs	France: 8–6	1	1	1		1		1	
1967	Durban	South Africa: 26–3	1				5	4	1	
1967	Bloemfontein	South Africa: 16–3			1		3	2	1	
1967	Johannesburg	France: 19–14	2	2	1	2	2	1	2	
1967	Cape Town	Drawn: 6–6	1		1				1	1
1968	Bordeaux	South Africa: 12–9	3						4	
1968	Paris	South Africa: 16–11	1	1		2	3	2	1	
1971	Bloemfontein	South Africa: 22–9	1		2		2	2	3	1
1971	Durban	Drawn: 8–8	1	1		1	1	1		1
1974	Toulouse	South Africa: 13–4	1				1		3	
1974	Paris	South Africa: 10–8	2				1		2	
1975	Bloemfontein	South Africa: 38–25	4	3	1		5	3	4	
1975	Pretoria	South Africa: 33–18	1	1	3	1	2	2	7	
1980	Pretoria	South Africa: 37–15	1	1	3		5	4	3	
		TOTALS	21	11	15	9	48	28	35	3

France v Wales

Played 56 France 17 Wales 36 Drawn 3
France 468 points Wales 753

			France				Wales			
Year	Venue	Results	T	C	P	D	T	C	P	D
1908	Cardiff	Wales: 36–4				1	9	3	1	
1909	Paris	Wales: 47–5	1	1			11	7		
1910	Swansea	Wales: 49–14	2	1	2		10	8	1	
1911	Paris	Wales: 15–0					3	3		
1912	Newport	Wales: 14–8	2	1			4	1		
1913	Paris	Wales: 11–8	2	1			3	1		
1914	Swansea	Wales: 31–0					7	5		
1920	Paris	Wales: 6–5	1	1			2			

Match Results 1871–1983 continued

1921	Cardiff	Wales: 12–4				1	2		2	
1922	Paris	Wales: 11–3	1				3	1		
1923	Swansea	Wales: 16–8	2	1			3	2	1	
1924	Paris	Wales: 10–6	2				2			1
1925	Cardiff	Wales: 11–5	1	1			3	1		
1926	Paris	Wales: 7–5	1	1			1			1
1927	Swansea	Wales: 25–7	1			1	7	2		
1928	Paris	France: 8–3	2	1			1			
1929	Cardiff	Wales: 8–3	1				2	1		
1930	Paris	Wales: 11–0					1			2
1931	Swansea	Wales: 35–3	1				7	5		1
1947	Paris	Wales: 3–0							1	
1948	Swansea	France: 11–3	3	1					1	
1949	Paris	France: 5–3	1	1			1			
1950	Cardiff	Wales: 21–0					4	3	1	
1951	Paris	France: 8–3	1	1	1		1			
1952	Swansea	Wales: 9–5	1	1					2	1
1953	Paris	Wales: 6–3			1		2			
1954	Cardiff	Wales: 19–13	2	2	1		2	2	3	
1955	Paris	Wales: 16–11	1	1	1	1	2	2	2	
1956	Cardiff	Wales: 5–3	1				1	1		
1957	Paris	Wales: 19–13	3	2			4	2	1	
1958	Cardiff	France: 16–6	2	2		2	1		1	
1959	Paris	France: 11–3	2	1	1				1	
1960	Cardiff	France: 16–8	4	2			1	1	1	
1961	Paris	France: 8–6	2	1			2			
1962	Cardiff	Wales: 3–0							1	
1963	Paris	France: 5–3	1	1					1	
1964	Cardiff	Drawn: 11–11	1	1	2		1	1	2	
1965	Paris	France: 22–13	4	2	1	1	3	2		
1966	Cardiff	Wales: 9–8	2	1			1		2	
1967	Paris	France: 20–14	3	1	1	2	1	1	2	1
1968	Cardiff	France: 14–9	2	1	1	1	1		2	
1969	Paris	Drawn: 8–8	1	1	1		2	1		
1970	Cardiff	Wales: 11–6	2				1	1	2	
1971	Paris	Wales: 9–5	1	1			2		1	
1972	Cardiff	Wales: 20–6			2		2		4	
1973	Paris	France: 12–3			3	1				1
1974	Cardiff	Drawn: 16–16	1		3	1	1		3	1
1975	Paris	Wales: 25–10	1		2		5	1	1	
1976	Cardiff	Wales: 19–13	2	1	1		1		5	
1977	Paris	France: 16–9	2	1	2				3	
1978	Cardiff	Wales: 16–7	1			1	2	1		2
1979	Paris	France: 14–13	2		2		1		3	
1980	Cardiff	Wales: 18–9	1	1		1	4	1		
1981	Paris	France: 19–15	1		3	2	1	1	3	
1982	Cardiff	Wales: 22–12	1	1	2		1		6	
1983	Paris	France: 16–9	1		3	1	1	1	1	
		TOTALS	73	37	36	17	133	62	61	11

Ireland v New Zealand

Played 9 Ireland 0 New Zealand 8 Drawn 1
Ireland 42 points New Zealand 104

			Ireland				New Zealand			
Year	Venue	Results	T	C	P	D	T	C	P	D
1905	Dublin	New Zealand: 15–0					3	3		
1924	Dublin	New Zealand: 6–0					1		1	
1935	Dublin	New Zealand: 17–9	1		2		3	1	2	

Leading Cap Winners continued

40 H F McLeod (Hawick)
1954 E, I, W, F, NZ. 1955 E, I, W, F. 1956 E, I, W, F. 1957 E, I, W, F. 1958 E, I, W, F, A. 1959 E, I, W, F. 1960 E, I, W, F, SA. 1961 E, I, W, F, SA. 1962 E, I, W, F.

40 D M D Rollo (Howe of Fife)
1959 E. 1960 E, I, W, F, SA. 1961 E, I, W, F, SA. 1962 E, W, F. 1963 E, I, W, F. 1964 E, I, W, F, NZ. 1965 E, I, W, F, SA. 1966 E, I, W, F, A. 1967 E, W, F, NZ. 1968 I, W, F.

37 J Mac D Bannerman (Glasgow HSFP)
1921 E, I, W, F. 1922 E, I, W, F. 1923 E, I, W, F. 1924 E, I, W, F. 1925 E, I, W, F. 1926 E, I, W, F. 1927 E, I, W, F, NSW. 1928 E, I, W, F. 1929 E, I, W, F.

South Africa

38 F C H Du Preez (Northern Transvaal)
1960–1 E, S. 1961 A (2). 1962 BI (4). 1963 A. 1964 W, F. 1965 A (2), NZ (4). 1967 F. 1968 BI (4). 1968–9 F (2). 1969 A (2). 1969–70 S, I, W. 1970 NZ (4). 1971 F (2), A (3).

Leading Cap Winners continued

38 J H Ellis
(South West Africa) 1965 NZ (4). 1967 F (4). 1968 BI (4). 1968–9 F (2). 1969 A (4). 1969–70 S, I, W. 1970 NZ (4). 1971 F (2), A (3). 1972 E. 1974 BI (4), F (2). 1976 NZ.

35 J F K Marais
(Western Province) 1963 A. 1964 W, F. 1964–5 I, S. 1965 A. 1968 BI (4). 1968–9 F (2). 1969 A (4). 1969–70 S, E, I, W. 1970 NZ (4). 1971 F (2), A (3). 1974 BI (4), F (2).

33 J P Engelbrecht
(Western Province) 1960 S. 1960–1 W, E, I, S, F. 1961 A (2). 1962 BI (3). 1963 A (2). 1964 W, F. 1964–5 I, S. 1965 A (2), NZ (4). 1967 F (4). 1968 BI (2). 1968–9 F (2). 1969 A (2).

33 J L Gainsford
(Western Province) 1960 S, NZ (4). 1960–1 W, I, E, S, F. 1961 A (2). 1962 BI (4). 1963 A (4). 1964 W, F. 1964–5 I, S. 1965 A (2), NZ (4). 1967 F (3).

28 J T Claassen
(Western Transvaal) 1955 BI (4). 1956 A (2), NZ (4). 1958 F (2). 1960 S, NZ (3). 1960–1 W, I, E, S, F. 1961 I, A (2). 1962 BI (4).

Match Results 1871–1983 continued

1954	Dublin	New Zealand: 14–3			1		2	1	1	1
1963	Dublin	New Zealand: 6–5	1	1			1		1	
1973	Dublin	Drawn: 10–10	1		2		2	1		
1974	Dublin	New Zealand: 15–6			2		1	1	3	
1976	Wellington	New Zealand: 11–3			1		2		1	
1978	Dublin	New Zealand: 10–6			2		1			2
		TOTALS	3	1	10	0	16	7	9	3

Ireland v Scotland

Played 93 Ireland 43 Scotland 46 Drawn 4
Ireland 685 points Scotland 669

			Ireland				Scotland			
Year	Venue	Results	T	C	P	D	T	C	P	D
1877	Belfast	Scotland					2		6	
1879	Belfast	Scotland					1		2	
1880	Glasgow	Scotland					2		3	
1881	Belfast	Ireland	1						1	
1882	Glasgow	Scotland					2			
1883	Belfast	Scotland					1		1	
1884	Raeburn Place	Scotland	1				2		2	
1885	Raeburn Place	Scotland					2		1	
1886	Raeburn Place	Scotland					5	2		1
1887	Belfast	Scotland					3	1		1*
1888	Raeburn Place	Scotland					1	1		
1889	Belfast	Scotland								1
1890	Raeburn Place	Scotland					1			1
1891†	Belfast	Scotland: 14–0					5	3		1
1892	Raeburn Place	Scotland: 2–0					1			
1893	Belfast	Drawn: 0–0								
1894	Dublin	Ireland: 5–0	1	1						
1895	Raeburn Place	Scotland: 6–0					2			
1896	Dublin	Drawn: 0–0								
1897	Powderhall	Scotland: 8–3	1				1	1	1	
1898	Belfast	Scotland: 8–0					2	1		
1899	Inverleith	Ireland: 9–3	3						1	
1900	Dublin	Drawn: 0–0								
1901	Inverleith	Scotland: 9–5	1	1			3			
1902	Belfast	Ireland: 5–0	1	1						
1903	Inverleith	Scotland: 3–0					1			
1904	Dublin	Scotland: 19–3	1				5	2		
1905	Inverleith	Ireland: 11–5	3	1			1	1		
1906	Dublin	Scotland: 13–6	2				2	2		1*
1907	Inverleith	Scotland: 15–3			1		3	3		
1908	Dublin	Ireland: 16–11	4	2			2	1	1	
1909	Inverleith	Scotland: 9–3	1				3			
1910	Belfast	Scotland: 14–0					4	1		
1911	Inverleith	Ireland: 16–10	4	2			2			1
1912	Dublin	Ireland: 10–8	1		1	1	2	1		
1913	Inverleith	Scotland: 29–14	2	2		1	7	4		
1914	Dublin	Ireland: 6–0	2							
1920	Inverleith	Scotland: 19–0					4	2	1	
1921	Dublin	Ireland: 9–8	3				2	1		
1922	Inverleith	Scotland: 6–3	1				2			
1923	Dublin	Scotland: 13–3	1				3	2		
1924	Inverleith	Scotland: 13–8	2	1			3	2		
1925	Dublin	Scotland: 14–8	1	1	1		2	2		1
1926	Murrayfield	Ireland: 3–0	1							
1927	Dublin	Ireland: 6–0	2							
1928	Murrayfield	Ireland: 13–5	3	2			1	1		

Match Results 1871–1983 continued

1929	Dublin	Scotland: 16–7	1			1	4	2		
1930	Murrayfield	Ireland: 14–11	4	1			3	1		
1931	Dublin	Ireland: 8–5	2	1			1	1		
1932	Murrayfield	Ireland: 20–8	4	4			2	1		
1933	Dublin	Scotland: 8–6	2							2
1934	Murrayfield	Scotland: 16–9	3				3	2	1	
1935	Dublin	Ireland: 12–5	4				1	1		
1936	Murrayfield	Ireland: 10–4	2			1				1
1937	Dublin	Ireland: 11–4	3	1						1
1938	Murrayfield	Scotland: 23–14	4	1			4	2	1	1
1939	Dublin	Ireland: 12–3	2		1	1*	1			
1947	Murrayfield	Ireland: 3–0	1							
1948	Dublin	Ireland: 6–0	2							
1949	Murrayfield	Ireland: 13–3	2	2	1				1	
1950	Dublin	Ireland: 21–0	3	3	2					
1951	Murrayfield	Ireland: 6–5	1			1	1	1		
1952	Dublin	Ireland: 12–8	3		1		1	1	1	
1953	Murrayfield	Ireland: 26–8	6	4			1	1	1	
1954	Belfast	Ireland: 6–0	2							
1955	Murrayfield	Scotland: 12–3			1		1		2	1
1956	Dublin	Ireland: 14–10	4	1			2	2		
1957	Murrayfield	Ireland: 5–3	1	1					1	
1958	Dublin	Ireland: 12–6	2		2		2			
1959	Murrayfield	Ireland: 8–3	1	1	1				1	
1960	Dublin	Scotland: 6–5	1	1			1			1
1961	Murrayfield	Scotland: 16–8	2	1			3	2	1	
1962	Dublin	Scotland: 20–6	1		1		3	1	2	1
1963	Murrayfield	Scotland: 3–0							1	
1964	Dublin	Scotland: 6–3			1				2	
1965	Murrayfield	Ireland: 16–6	3	2		1			1	1
1966	Dublin	Scotland: 11–3			1		3	1		
1967	Murrayfield	Ireland: 5–3	1	1					1	
1968	Dublin	Ireland: 14–6	3	1	1				2	
1969	Murrayfield	Ireland: 16–0	4	2						
1970	Dublin	Ireland: 16–11	4	2			2	1		1
1971	Murrayfield	Ireland: 17–5	3	1	2		1	1		
1972	No match									
1973	Murrayfield	Scotland: 19–14	2		2		1		2	3
1974	Dublin	Ireland: 9–6	1	1	1				2	
1975	Murrayfield	Scotland: 20–13	2	1	1		2		2	2
1976	Dublin	Scotland: 15–6			2				4	1
1977	Murrayfield	Scotland: 21–18	1	1	3	1	3		2	1
1978	Dublin	Ireland: 12–9	1	1	2				3	
1979	Murrayfield	Drawn: 11–11	2		1		2		1	
1980	Dublin	Ireland: 22–15	2	1	3	1	2	2	1	
1981	Murrayfield	Scotland: 10–9	1	1	1		1		1	1
1982	Dublin	Ireland: 21–12			6	1	1	1	2	
1983	Murrayfield	Ireland: 15–13	1	1	3		1		2	1
		TOTALS	137	52	43	11	137	57	62	27

*Goal from mark

Ireland v South Africa

Played 10 Ireland 1 South Africa 8 Drawn 1
Ireland 73 points South Africa 159

			Ireland				South Africa			
Year	Venue	Results	T	C	P	D	T	C	P	D
1906	Belfast	South Africa: 15–12	3		1		4		1	
1912	Dublin	South Africa: 38–0					10	4		

Leading Cap Winners continued

27 F du T Roux (Western Province)
1960–1 W. 1961 A (2). 1962 BI (4). 1963 A. 1965 A (2), NZ (4). 1968 BI (2). 1968–9 F (2). 1969 A (4). 1969–70 I. 1970 NZ (4).

27 L G Wilson (Western Province)
1960 NZ (2). 1960–1 W, I, E, F. 1961 I, A (2). 1962 BI (4). 1963 A (4). 1964 W, F. 1964–5 I, S. 1965 A (2), NZ (4).

Wales

55 J P R Williams (London Welsh, Bridgend)
1969 A, E, F, I, NZ (2), S. 1970 E, F, I, S, SA. 1971 E, F, I, S. 1972 E, F, S, NZ. 1973 E, S, I, F, A. 1974 S, I, F. 1975 F, E, S, I, A. 1976 E, S, I, F. 1977 I, F, E, S. 1978 E, S, I, F, A (2), NZ. 1979 S, I, F, E. 1980 NZ. 1981 E, S.

53 G O Edwards

Leading Cap Winners continued

(Cardiff, Cardiff Coll. of Educ.)
1967 F, E, NZ. 1968 E, F, I, S. 1969 A, E, F, I, NZ (2), S. 1970 E, F, I, S, SA. 1971 E, F, I, S. 1972 E, F, S, NZ. 1973 E, S, I, F, A. 1974 S, I, F, E. 1975 F, E, S, I, A. 1976 E, S, I, F. 1977 I, F, E, S. 1978 E, S, I, F.

46 T G R Davies (Cardiff, London Welsh)
1966 A. 1967 E, F, I, S. 1968 E, S. 1969 S, I, F, NZ (2), A. 1971 E, F, I, S. 1972 E, F, S, NZ. 1973 E, S, I, F, A. 1974 S, F, E. 1975 F, E, S, I. 1976 E, S, I, F. 1977 I, F, E, S. 1978 E, S, I, A (2).

44 K J Jones (Newport)
1947 A, E, F, I, S. 1948 E, F, I, S. 1949 E, F, I, S. 1950 E, F, I, S. 1951 E, F, I, S, SA. 1952 E, F, I, S. 1953 E, F, I, NZ, S. 1954 E, F, I, S. 1955 E, F, I, S. 1956 E, F, I, S. 1957 S.

41 G Price (Pontypool)
1975 F, E, S, I, A. 1976 E, S, I, F. 1977 I, F, E, S. 1978 E, S, I, F, A (2), NZ. 1979 S, I, F, E. 1980 F, E, S, I, NZ. 1981 E, S, I, F, A. 1982 I, F, E, S. 1983 E, I, F.

38 T M Davies (London Welsh, Swansea)
1969 A, E, F, I, NZ (2),

Match Results 1871–1983 continued

1931	Dublin	South Africa: 8–3			1		2	1		
1951	Dublin	South Africa: 17–5	1	1			4	1		1
1960	Dublin	South Africa: 8–3			1		2	1		
1961	Cape Town	South Africa: 24–8	1	1	1		5	3	1	
1965	Dublin	Ireland: 9–6	1		2		1		1	
1970	Dublin	Drawn: 8–8	1	1	1		1	1	1	
1981	Cape Town	South Africa: 23–15	2	2	1		3	1	3	
1981	Durban	South Africa: 12–10	1		2				1	3
		TOTALS	10	5	10	0	32	12	8	4

Ireland v Wales

Played 85 Ireland 28 Wales 52 Drawn 5
Ireland 518 points Wales 827

			Ireland				Wales			
Year	Venue	Results	T	C	P	D	T	C	P	D
1882	Dublin	Wales					4	2		
1884	Cardiff	Wales					2			1
1887	Birkenhead	Wales	3				1			1
1888	Dublin	Ireland	2	1		1				
1889	Swansea	Ireland	2							
1890	Dublin	Drawn	1	1			1	1		
1891†	Llanelli	Wales: 6–4	1			1	1	1		1
1892	Dublin	Ireland: 9–0	3	1						
1893	Llanelli	Wales: 2–0					1			
1894	Belfast	Ireland: 3–0			1					
1895	Cardiff	Wales: 5–3	1				1	1		
1896	Dublin	Ireland: 8–4	2	1						1
1898	Limerick	Wales: 11–3			1		2	1	1	
1899	Cardiff	Ireland: 3–0	1							
1900	Belfast	Wales: 3–0					1			
1901	Swansea	Wales: 10–9	3				2	2		
1902	Dublin	Wales: 15–0					3	1		1
1903	Cardiff	Wales: 18–0					6			
1904	Belfast	Ireland: 14–12	4	1			4			
1905	Swansea	Wales: 10–3	1				2	2		
1906	Belfast	Ireland: 11–6	3	1			2			
1907	Cardiff	Wales: 29–0					6	2	1	1
1908	Belfast	Wales: 11–5	1	1			3	1		
1909	Swansea	Wales: 18–5	1	1			4	3		
1910	Dublin	Wales: 19–3	1				5			1
1911	Cardiff	Wales: 16–0					3	2	1	
1912	Belfast	Ireland: 12–5	2	1		1	1	1		
1913	Swansea	Wales: 16–13	2	2	1		3	2	1	
1914	Belfast	Wales: 11–3	1				3	1		
1920	Cardiff	Wales: 28–4				1	6	3		1
1921	Belfast	Wales: 6–0					1		1	
1922	Swansea	Wales: 11–5	1	1			3	1		
1923	Dublin	Ireland: 5–4	1	1						1
1924	Cardiff	Ireland: 13–10	3	2			2			1
1925	Belfast	Ireland: 19–3	4	2	1		1			
1926	Swansea	Wales: 11–8	2	1			3	1		
1927	Dublin	Ireland: 19–9	4	2	1		1	1		1
1928	Cardiff	Ireland: 13–10	3	2			2	2		
1929	Belfast	Drawn: 5–5	1	1			1	1		
1930	Swansea	Wales: 12–7			1	1	3		1	
1931	Belfast	Wales: 15–3	1				3	1		1
1932	Cardiff	Ireland: 12–10	4				2			1
1933	Belfast	Ireland: 10–5	1		1	1	1	1		
1934	Swansea	Wales: 13–0					3	2		

Match Results 1871–1983 continued

1935	Belfast	Ireland: 9–3	1		2				1	
1936	Cardiff	Wales: 3–0							1	
1937	Belfast	Ireland: 5–3	1	1					1	
1938	Swansea	Wales: 11–5	1	1			2	1	1	
1939	Belfast	Wales: 7–0					1			1
1947	Swansea	Wales: 6–0					1		1	
1948	Belfast	Ireland: 6–3	2				1			
1949	Swansea	Ireland: 5–0	1	1						
1950	Belfast	Wales: 6–3			1		2			
1951	Cardiff	Drawn: 3–3	1						1	
1952	Dublin	Wales: 14–3			1		3	1	1	
1953	Swansea	Wales: 5–3	1				1	1		
1954	Dublin	Wales: 12–9	1		2				3	1
1955	Cardiff	Wales: 21–3			1		4	3	1	
1956	Dublin	Ireland: 11–3	1	1	1	1			1	
1957	Cardiff	Wales: 6–5	1	1					2	
1958	Dublin	Wales: 9–6	1		1		3			
1959	Cardiff	Wales: 8–6	1		1		2	1		
1960	Dublin	Wales: 10–9	1		2		2	2		
1961	Cardiff	Wales: 9–0					1		2	
1962	Dublin	Drawn: 3–3				1			1	
1963	Cardiff	Ireland: 14–6	1	1	2	1	1			1
1964	Dublin	Wales: 15–6			2		3	3		
1965	Cardiff	Wales: 14–8	1	1	1		2	1	1	1
1966	Dublin	Ireland: 9–6	1		1	1	1		1	
1967	Cardiff	Ireland: 3–0	1							
1968	Dublin	Ireland: 9–6	1		1	1			1	1
1969	Cardiff	Wales: 24–11	1	1	2		4	3	1	1
1970	Dublin	Ireland: 14–0	2	1	1	1				
1971	Cardiff	Wales: 23–9			3		4	1	2	1
1972	No match									
1973	Cardiff	Wales: 16–12	1	1	2		2	1	2	
1974	Dublin	Drawn: 9–9			3		1	1	1	
1975	Cardiff	Wales: 32–4	1				5	3	2	
1976	Dublin	Wales: 34–9			3		4	3	4	
1977	Cardiff	Wales: 25–9			3		3	2	2	1
1978	Dublin	Wales: 20–16	1		3	1	2		4	
1979	Cardiff	Wales: 24–21	2	2	3		2	2	4	
1980	Dublin	Ireland: 21–7	3	3	1		1		1	
1981	Cardiff	Wales: 9–8	2						2	1
1982	Dublin	Ireland: 20–12	3	1	2		1	1	1	1
1983	Cardiff	Wales: 23–9	3	1	3				3	
		TOTALS	98	40	55	13	152	66	55	23

†Modern scoring values adopted

Leading Cap Winners continued

S. 1970 E, F, I, S, SA. 1971 E, F, I, S. 1972 E, F, S, NZ. 1973 E, S, I, F, A. 1974 S, I, F, E. 1975 F, E, S, I, A. 1976 E, S, I, F.

36 D Williams (Ebbw Vale)
1963 E, F, I, S. 1964 E, F, I, S, SA. 1965 E, F, I, S. 1966 A, E, I, S. 1967 E, F, NZ. 1968 E. 1969 A, E, F, I, NZ (2), S. 1970 E, I, S, SA. 1971 E, F, I, S.

35 R M Owen (Swansea)
1901 I. 1902 E, I, S. 1903 E, I, S. 1904 E, I, S. 1905 E, I, NZ, S. 1906 E, I, S, SA. 1907 E, S. 1908 A, F, I. 1909 E, F, I, S. 1910 E, F. 1911 E, F, I, S. 1912 E, S.

New Zealand v Scotland

Played 11 New Zealand 10 Scotland 0 Drawn 1
New Zealand 174 points Scotland 61

			New Zealand				Scotland			
Year	Venue	Results	T	C	P	D	T	C	P	D
1905	Inverleith	New Zealand: 12–7	4				1			1
1935	Murrayfield	New Zealand: 18–8	4	3			2	1		
1954	Murrayfield	New Zealand: 3–0			1					
1964	Murrayfield	Drawn: 0–0								
1967	Murrayfield	New Zealand: 14–3	2	1	2					1
1972	Murrayfield	New Zealand: 14–9	3	1					2	1

Match Results 1871–1983 continued

1975	Auckland	New Zealand: 24–0	4	4						
1978	Murrayfield	New Zealand: 18–9	2	2	2		1	1		1
1979	Murrayfield	New Zealand: 20–6	4	2					2	
1981	Dunedin	New Zealand: 11–4	2		1		1			
1981	Auckland	New Zealand: 40–15	7	6			1	1	2	1
		TOTALS	32	19	6	0	6	3	6	5

New Zealand v South Africa

Played 37 New Zealand 15 South Africa 20 Drawn 2
New Zealand 350 points South Africa 395

			New Zealand				South Africa			
Year	Venue	Results	T	C	P	D	T	C	P	D
1921	Dunedin	New Zealand: 13–5	3	2			1	1		
1921	Auckland	South Africa: 9–5	1	1			1	1		1
1921	Wellington	Drawn: 0–0								
1928	Durban	South Africa: 17–0					1		2	2
1928	Johannesburg	New Zealand: 7–6			1	1			1	1*
1928	Port Elizabeth	South Africa: 11–6	2				3	1		
1928	Cape Town	New Zealand: 13–5	1		2	1	1	1		
1937	Wellington	New Zealand: 13–7	1		2	1	1			1
1937	Christchurch	South Africa: 13–6	2				2	2	1	
1937	Auckland	South Africa: 17–6			2		5	1		
1949	Cape Town	South Africa: 15–11	1	1	1	1			5	
1949	Johannesburg	South Africa: 12–6			1	1	2		1	1
1949	Durban	South Africa: 9–3	1						3	
1949	Port Elizabeth	South Africa: 11–8	2	1			1	1	1	1
1956	Dunedin	New Zealand: 10–6	2	2			1		1	
1956	Wellington	South Africa: 8–3	1				2	1		
1956	Christchurch	New Zealand: 17–10	3	1	2		2	2		
1956	Auckland	New Zealand: 11–5	1	1	2		1	1		
1960	Johannesburg	South Africa: 13–0					2	2	1	
1960	Cape Town	New Zealand: 11–3	1	1	1	1	1			
1960	Bloemfontein	Drawn: 11–11	1	1	2		1	1	2	
1960	Port Elizabeth	South Africa: 8–3			1		1	1	1	
1965	Wellington	New Zealand: 6–3	2							1
1965	Dunedin	New Zealand: 13–0	3	2						
1965	Christchurch	South Africa: 19–16	3	2	1		4	2	1	
1965	Auckland	New Zealand: 20–3	5	1		1			1	
1970	Pretoria	South Africa: 17–6	1		1		2	1	2	1
1970	Cape Town	New Zealand: 9–8	2		1		1	1	1	
1970	Port Elizabeth	South Africa: 14–3			1		2	1	2	
1970	Johannesburg	South Africa: 20–17	1	1	4		2	1	4	
1976	Durban	South Africa: 16–7	1		1		2	1	1	1
1976	Bloemfontein	New Zealand: 15–9	1	1	2	1			3	
1976	Cape Town	South Africa: 15–10	1		2		1	1	2	1
1976	Johannesburg	South Africa: 15–14	2		1	1	1	1	2	1
1981	Christchurch	New Zealand: 14–9	3	1			1	1		1
1981	Wellington	South Africa: 24–12			4		1	1	5	1
1981	Auckland	New Zealand: 25–22	2	1	4	1	3	2	2	
		TOTALS	50	20	39	10	49	29	45	14

*Goal from mark

New Zealand v Wales

Played 11 New Zealand 8 Wales 3 Drawn 0
New Zealand 165 points Wales 78

Match Results 1871–1983 continued

			New Zealand				Wales			
Year	Venue	Results	T	C	P	D	T	C	P	D
1905	Cardiff	Wales: 3–0					1			
1924	Swansea	New Zealand: 19–0	4	2	1					
1935	Cardiff	Wales: 13–12	2	1		1	3	2		
1953	Cardiff	Wales: 13–8	1	1	1		2	2	1	
1963	Cardiff	New Zealand: 6–0			1	1				
1967	Cardiff	New Zealand: 13–6	2	2	1				1	1
1969	Christchurch	New Zealand: 19–0	4	2	1					
1969	Auckland	New Zealand: 33–12	3	3	5	1	2		2	
1972	Cardiff	New Zealand: 19–16	1		5		1		4	
1978	Cardiff	New Zealand: 13–12	1		3				4	
1980	Cardiff	New Zealand: 23–3	4	2	1				1	
		TOTALS	22	13	19	3	9	4	13	1

Scotland v South Africa

Played 8 Scotland 3 South Africa 5 Drawn 0
Scotland 38 points South Africa 104

			Scotland				South Africa			
Year	Venue	Results	T	C	P	D	T	C	P	D
1906	Glasgow	Scotland: 6–0	2							
1912	Inverleith	South Africa: 16–0					4	2		
1932	Murrayfield	South Africa: 6–3	1				2			
1951	Murrayfield	South Africa: 44–0					9	7		1
1960	Port Elizabeth	South Africa: 18–10	2	2			4	3		
1961	Murrayfield	South Africa: 12–5	1	1			2		2	
1965	Murrayfield	Scotland: 8–5	1	1		1	1	1		
1969	Murrayfield	Scotland: 6–3	1		1				1	
		TOTALS	8	4	1	1	22	13	3	1

Scotland v Wales

Played 87 Scotland 36 Wales 49 Drawn 2
Scotland 588 points Wales 846

			Scotland				Wales			
Year	Venue	Results	T	C	P	D	T	C	P	D
1883	Raeburn Place	Scotland	3	3			1	1		
1884	Newport	Scotland	1			1				
1885	Glasgow	Drawn: 0–0								
1886	Cardiff	Scotland	3	1						
1887	Raeburn Place	Scotland	12	4						
1888	Newport	Wales					1			
1889	Raeburn Place	Scotland	2							
1890	Cardiff	Scotland	3	1			1			
1891†	Raeburn Place	Scotland: 15–0	7	1		2				
1892	Swansea	Scotland: 7–2	2	1			1			
1893	Raeburn Place	Wales: 9–0					3		1	
1894	Newport	Wales: 7–0					1			1
1895	Raeburn Place	Scotland: 5–4	1	1						1
1896	Cardiff	Wales: 6–0					2			
1899	Inverleith	Scotland: 21–10	3			3*	2	2		
1900	Swansea	Wales: 12–3	1				4			

Match Results 1871–1983 continued

1901	Inverleith	Scotland: 18–8	4	3			2	1		
1902	Cardiff	Wales: 14–5	1	1			4	1		
1903	Inverleith	Scotland: 6–0	1		1					
1904	Swansea	Wales: 21–3	1				4	3	1	
1905	Inverleith	Wales: 6–3	1				2			
1906	Cardiff	Wales: 9–3			1		3			
1907	Inverleith	Scotland: 6–3	2						1	
1908	Swansea	Wales: 6–5	1	1			2			
1909	Inverleith	Wales: 5–3			1		1	1		
1910	Cardiff	Wales: 14–0					4	1		
1911	Inverleith	Wales: 32–10	2			1	8	2		1
1912	Swansea	Wales: 21–6	2				3	2		2
1913	Inverleith	Wales: 8–0					2	1		
1914	Cardiff	Wales: 24–5	1	1			3	2	1	2
1920	Inverleith	Scotland: 9–5	1		2		1	1		
1921	Swansea	Scotland: 14–8	3	1	1					2
1922	Inverleith	Drawn: 9–9	2		1		1	1		1
1923	Cardiff	Scotland: 11–8	3	1			1	1	1	
1924	Inverleith	Scotland: 35–10	8	4	1		2	2		
1925	Swansea	Scotland: 24–14	6	1		1	3	1	1	
1926	Murrayfield	Scotland: 8–5	1	1	1		1	1		
1927	Cardiff	Scotland: 5–0	1	1						
1928	Murrayfield	Wales: 13–0					3	2		
1929	Swansea	Wales: 14–7			1	1	4	1		
1930	Murrayfield	Scotland: 12–9	1	1	1	1	1	1		1
1931	Cardiff	Wales: 13–8	2	1			3	2		
1932	Murrayfield	Wales: 6–0					1		1	
1933	Swansea	Scotland: 11–3	2	1	1		1			
1934	Murrayfield	Wales: 13–6	1		1		3	2		
1935	Cardiff	Wales: 10–6	2				2			1
1936	Murrayfield	Wales: 13–3	1				3	2		
1937	Swansea	Scotland: 13–6	3	2			2			
1938	Murrayfield	Scotland: 8–6	1	1	1		2			
1939	Cardiff	Wales: 11–3			1		2	1	1	
1947	Murrayfield	Wales: 22–8	1	1	1		5	2	1	
1948	Cardiff	Wales: 14–0					3	1	1	
1949	Murrayfield	Scotland: 6–5	2				1	1		
1950	Swansea	Wales: 12–0					2		1	1
1951	Murrayfield	Scotland: 19–0	3	2	1	1				
1952	Cardiff	Wales: 11–0					1	1	2	
1953	Murrayfield	Wales: 12–0					3		1	
1954	Swansea	Wales: 15–3	1				4		1	
1955	Murrayfield	Scotland: 14–8	2	1	1	1	2	1		
1956	Cardiff	Wales: 9–3			1		3			
1957	Murrayfield	Scotland: 9–6	1		1	1	1		1	
1958	Cardiff	Wales: 8–3			1		2	1		
1959	Murrayfield	Scotland: 6–5	1		1		1	1		
1960	Cardiff	Wales: 8–0					1	1	1	
1961	Murrayfield	Scotland: 3–0	1							
1962	Cardiff	Scotland: 8–3	2	1						1
1963	Murrayfield	Wales: 6–0							1	1
1964	Cardiff	Wales: 11–3	1				2	1	1	
1965	Murrayfield	Wales: 14–12			2	2	2	1	2	
1966	Cardiff	Wales: 8–3			1		2	1		
1967	Murrayfield	Scotland: 11–5	2	1		1	1	1		
1968	Cardiff	Wales: 5–0					1	1		
1969	Murrayfield	Wales: 17–3			1		3	1	2	
1970	Cardiff	Wales: 18–9	1		1	1	4	3		
1971	Murrayfield	Wales: 19–18	2		4		4	2	1	
1972	Cardiff	Wales: 35–12	1	1	2		5	3	3	
1973	Murrayfield	Scotland: 10–9	2	1					3	
1974	Cardiff	Wales: 6–0					1	1		
1975	Murrayfield	Scotland: 12–10			3	1	1		2	
1976	Cardiff	Wales: 28–6	1	1			3	2	3	1
1977	Murrayfield	Wales: 18–9	1	1		1	2	2	2	
1978	Cardiff	Wales: 22–14	2		2		4		1	1
1979	Murrayfield	Wales: 19–13	1		3		2	1	3	
1980	Cardiff	Wales: 17–6	1	1			3	1	1	

Match Results 1871–1983 continued

1981	Murrayfield	Scotland: 15–6	2	2	1				2	
1982	Cardiff	Scotland: 34–18	5	4		2	1	1	4	
1983	Murrayfield	Wales: 19–15	1	1	3		2	1	3	
		TOTALS	129	51	45	21	162	67	51	17

*2 dropped goals, 1 goal from mark †Modern scoring values adopted

South Africa v Wales

Played 7 South Africa 6 Wales 0 Drawn 1
South Africa 61 points Wales 15

			South Africa				Wales			
Year	Venue	Results	T	C	P	D	T	C	P	D
1906	Swansea	South Africa: 11–0	3	1						
1912	Cardiff	South Africa: 3–0			1					
1931	Swansea	South Africa: 8–3	2	1			1			
1951	Cardiff	South Africa: 6–3	1			1	1			
1960	Cardiff	South Africa: 3–0			1					
1964	Durban	South Africa: 24–3	3	3	2	1			1	
1970	Cardiff	Drawn: 6–6	1		1		1		1	
		TOTALS	10	5	5	2	3		2	

MATCH SUMMARIES

The following are the records of the International Board Countries in matches played against each other.

Best Percentage Record

	P	W	L	D	%
New Zealand	204	141	52	11	71.81
South Africa	156	96	45	15	66.33
Wales	344	188	133	23	57.86
England	369	175	151	43	53.25
Scotland	360	152	183	25	45.69
France	273	105	148	20	42.12
Ireland	357	137	197	23	41.45
Australia	167	46	116	5	29.04

Note: South Africa is the only country with more wins than losses against each country.

Most Victories

Wales	188
England	175
Scotland	151
New Zealand	141
Ireland	137
France	105
South Africa	96
Australia	45

Fewest Defeats

South Africa	45
New Zealand	52
Australia	115
Wales	133
France	148
England	151
Scotland	182
Ireland	197

England's Record

Opposition	P	W	L	D	%
France	58	32	20	6	60.34
Ireland	95	53	34	8	60.00
Scotland	99	47	36	16	55.55
Wales	88	35	41	12	46.50
Australia	10	4	6	0	40.00
South Africa	7	2	4	1	35.71
New Zealand	12	2	10	0	16.66
	369	175	151	43	53.25

Australia's Record

Opposition	P	W	L	D	%
England	10	6	4	0	66.67
France	13	4	8	1	34.62
Ireland	9	3	6	0	33.33
Scotland	9	3	6	0	33.33
Wales	10	3	7	0	30.00
New Zealand	74	18	52	4	27.02
South Africa	28	7	21	0	25.00
British Lions	14	2	12	0	14.29
	167	46	116	5	29.04

France's Record

Opposition	P	W	L	D	%
Australia	13	8	4	1	65.37
Ireland	56	27	25	4	51.78

Scotland	53	26	25	2	50.94
England	58	20	32	6	39.65
Wales	56	17	36	3	32.23
South Africa	19	3	12	4	26.30
New Zealand	18	4	14	0	22.22
	273	105	148	20	42.12

Ireland's Record

Opposition	P	W	L	D	%
Australia	9	6	3	0	66.66
Scotland	93	43	46	4	48.38
France	56	25	27	4	48.21
England	95	34	53	8	40.00
Wales	85	28	52	5	35.35
South Africa	10	1	8	1	15.00
New Zealand	9	0	8	1	5.55
	357	137	197	23	41.45

New Zealand's Record

Opposition	P	W	L	D	%
Scotland	11	10	0	1	95.45
Ireland	9	8	0	1	94.44
England	12	10	2	0	83.33
Wales	11	8	3	0	77.78
British Lions	32	24	5	3	82.81
France	18	14	4	0	75.00
Australia	74	52	18	4	70.97
South Africa	37	15	20	2	43.24
	204	141	52	11	71.81

Scotland's Record

Opposition	P	W	L	D	%
Australia	9	6	3	0	66.66
Ireland	93	46	43	4	51.61
France	53	25	26	2	49.05
England	99	36	47	16	44.44
Wales	87	36	49	2	42.52

Geo. Herringshaw supplied pictures for this section

FIVE NATIONS CHAMPIONSHIP 1883–1983

Grand Slam winners (all 4 matches)

England 8 times: 1913, 1914, 1921, 1923, 1924, 1928, 1957, 1980.
Wales 6 times: 1908, 1909, 1911, 1950, 1952, 1971, 1976, 1978.
France 3 times: 1968, 1977, 1981.
Scotland once: 1925.
Ireland once: 1948.
Wales beat all four countries, in 1908 and 1909, before France entered the Championship.

Triple Crown winners

Wales 16 times: 1893, 1900, 1902, 1905, 1908, 1909, 1911, 1950, 1952, 1965, 1969, 1971, 1976, 1977, 1978, 1979.
England 15 times: 1883, 1884, 1892, 1913, 1914, 1921, 1923, 1924, 1928, 1934, 1937, 1954, 1957, 1960, 1980.
Scotland 8 times: 1891, 1895, 1901, 1903, 1907, 1925, 1933, 1938.
Ireland 5 times: 1894, 1899, 1948, 1949, 1982.

Winners

1883	**England**
1884	**England**
1885	**incomplete**
1886	**England**, **Scotland**
1887	**Scotland**
1888	**incomplete**
1889	**incomplete**
1890	**England**, **Scotland**
1891	**Scotland**
1892	**England**
1893	**Wales**
1894	**Ireland**
1895	**Scotland**
1896	**Ireland**
1897	**incomplete**
1898	**incomplete**
1899	**Ireland**
1900	**Wales**
1901	**Scotland**
1902	**Wales**
1903	**Scotland**
1904	**Scotland**
1905	**Wales**
1906	**Ireland**, **Wales**
1907	**Scotland**
1908	**Wales**
1909	**Wales**
1910	**England**
1911	**Wales**
1912	**England**, **Ireland**
1913	**England**
1914	**England**
1920	**England**, **Scotland**, **Wales**
1921	**England**
1922	**Wales**
1923	**England**
1924	**England**
1925	**Scotland**
1926	**Ireland**, **Scotland**
1927	**Ireland**, **Scotland**
1928	**England**
1929	**Scotland**
1930	**England**
1931	**Wales**
1932	**England**, **Ireland**, **Wales**
1933	**Scotland**
1934	**England**
1935	**Ireland**
1936	**Wales**
1937	**England**
1938	**Scotland**
1939	**England**, **Ireland**, **Wales**
1947	**England**, **Wales**
1948	**Ireland**
1949	**Ireland**
1950	**Wales**
1951	**Ireland**
1952	**Wales**
1953	**England**
1954	**England**, **France**, **Wales**
1955	**France**, **Wales**
1956	**Wales**

South Africa	8	3	5	0	37.50
New Zealand	11	0	10	1	4.55
	360	152	183	25	45.69

South Africa's Record

Opposition	P	W	L	D	%
Wales	7	6	0	1	92.86
Ireland	10	8	1	1	85.00
Australia	28	21	7	0	75.00
France	19	12	3	4	73.68
England	7	4	2	1	64.29
Scotland	8	5	3	0	62.50
British Lions	40	20	14	6	57.50
New Zealand	37	20	15	2	56.75
	156	96	45	15	66.33

Wales's Record

Opposition	P	W	L	D	%
Australia	10	7	3	0	70.00
France	56	36	17	3	66.16
Ireland	85	52	28	5	63.58
Scotland	87	47	36	2	57.47
England	88	41	35	12	53.40
New Zealand	11	3	8	0	27.27
South Africa	7	0	6	1	7.14
	344	188	133	23	57.86

British Lions's Record

Opposition	P	W	L	D	%
Australia	14	12	2	0	85.71
South Africa	40	14	20	6	42.50
New Zealand	32	5	24	3	20.31
	86	31	46	9	41.27

1957	**England**
1958	**England**
1959	**France**
1960	**England** / **France**
1961	**France**
1962	**France**
1963	**England**
1964	**Scotland** / **Wales**
1965	**Wales**
1966	**Wales**
1967	**France**
1968	**France**
1969	**Wales**
1970	**France** / **Wales**
1971	**Wales**
1972	**incomplete**
1973	**Quintuple tie**
1974	**Ireland**
1975	**Wales**
1976	**Wales**
1977	**France**
1978	**Wales**
1979	**Wales**
1980	**England**
1981	**France**
1982	**Ireland**
1983	**France** / **Ireland**

Wales have been champions most times, 21; England have won 18 times, Scotland 11, Ireland 9, and France 7.

CYRIL LOWE

CYRIL LOWE—
BOY'S OWN HERO

When Cyril Nelson Lowe died in February 1983, at the age of 91, one of the last links with the past, indeed the early days of rugby football, was severed. Lowe was remarkable in many ways, not the least being that his involvement in the game spanned 75 years: from the age of 16, when he abandoned Association Football to take up rugby at Dulwich College, in 1906, right through until he was honoured at the 100th University Match celebrations in 1981. It is astonishing to realise that when Lowe was born, the son of a clergyman, on 7 October 1891, the game too was in its infancy: a try was worth one point, the International Championship was only 8 years old, a British Isles team had just returned from a first ever tour of South Africa and Oxford and Cambridge were playing their warm-up matches for the 21st University Match.

If Lowe's chief claim to fame is that he is still England's leading try-scorer—he scored 18 in 25 consecutive appearances between 1913 and 1923, which is a record no one has even remotely challenged—the rest of his rugby career and life reads like a chapter from a Boy's Own Hero book. A natural, gifted athlete at school and at Cambridge, where he excelled not only in rugby, but cricket, boxing, athletics, swimming and tennis, he seemed to succeed in everything to which he applied himself. Incredibly, Lowe hardly possessed the physique for success at the top level of sport—he was barely 5ft 6in and at his heaviest he was a featherweight 9 stone, although for most of his early rugby career he was not much more than 8st 7lb.

When I visited him in his Surrey home in 1981 he disarmingly dismissed the idea that he was physically ill-equipped. 'It was true then, and I'm sure it's true now' he told me 'that if you set your mind to something, and you want to enjoy doing it, you can do anything.' Lowe added that rugby for him was everything, a way of life, and right from the first moment he took up the game until he retired he had worked to improve his skill and ability.

That Lowe was the sensation of his day is an understatement. At no matter what level he played he was a scoring machine. England enjoyed one of the greatest periods in history when he was on the right wing: only twice to Wales and once to South Africa did they lose, and they won four Grand Slams and four Championships in six seasons between 1913 and 1923. Until Wavell Wakefield

(Colorsport.)

beat the record, Lowe also was England's most capped player; only four players have scored more career points; no one scored more international tries in a season; only seven players scored more points in a season; and only six have made more consecutive appearances. Another measure of his contribution to England is that he helped them to their all-time record of 20 tries in a season, 1913–14.

Just what sort of fantastic additions Lowe would have made to the list of records but for the interruption of the First World War, can only be conjecture. For him, he thanked God for surviving it, while many of his contemporaries were wiped out, 14 of them with whom he had played in the last match before the outbreak, against Scotland at Inverleith where, incidentally, he scored a hat-trick of tries. The Great War, however, proved another challenge and as an officer in the Royal Flying Corps, his was another remarkable contribution. Although officially he was credited with shooting down nine enemy aeroplanes, he told me that the figure was nearer 30. 'In those days' he explained 'everyone was claiming a shoot-down, even infantrymen in the trenches, so many of mine could not be officially verified.' Regardless of the numbers, Captain Lowe, as he was, won the MC and DFC, and returned a hero.

When his playing days were over, Lowe became an England selector—'I wasn't very good at it, mind you'—but his love of flying became more important. Here again he broke new ground, being one of the proponents of the famous RAF aerobatic displays which led up to the creation of today's Red Arrows. One of his only regrets was that the bad weather prevented his appearing as guest-of-honour at the 100th Varsity Match in 1981. He was to have been introduced to Prince Andrew at Twickenham, 67 years after he had been similarly honoured by the Prince's great grandfather before the match with Ireland.

WHAT THE PAPERS SAID ....

'Lowe showed great pace and got through all the opposition'

The type of aircraft Lowe flew during aerobatic displays between the wars.

Among his many souvenirs, the programme for the 1913 University Match.

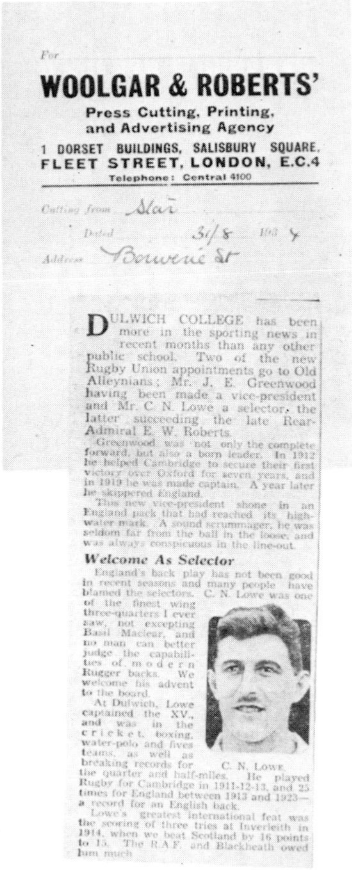

For

WOOLGAR & ROBERTS'
Press Cutting, Printing, and Advertising Agency
1 DORSET BUILDINGS, SALISBURY SQUARE, FLEET STREET, LONDON, E.C.4
Telephone: Central 4100

Cutting from Star
Dated 31/8 1934
Address Bouverie St

DULWICH COLLEGE has been more in the sporting news in recent months than any other public school. Two of the new Rugby Union appointments go to Old Alleynians; Mr. J. E. Greenwood having been made a vice-president and Mr. C. N. Lowe a selector, the latter succeeding the late Rear-Admiral E. W. Roberts.

Greenwood was not only the complete forward, but also a born leader. In 1912 he helped Cambridge to secure their first victory over Oxford for seven years, and in 1919 he was made captain. A year later he skippered England.

This new vice-president shone in an England pack that had reached its high-water mark. A sound scrummager, he was seldom far from the ball in the loose, and was always conspicuous in the line-out.

Welcome As Selector

England's back play has not been good in recent seasons and many people have blamed the selectors. C. N. Lowe was one of the finest wing three-quarters I ever saw, not excepting Basil Maclear, and no man can better judge the capabilities of modern Rugger backs. We welcome his advent to the board.

C. N. LOWE

At Dulwich, Lowe captained the XV., and was in the cricket, boxing, water-polo and fives teams, as well as breaking records for the quarter and half-miles. He played Rugby for Cambridge in 1911-12-13, and 25 times for England between 1913 and 1923—a record for an English back.

Lowe's greatest international feat was the scoring of three tries at Inverleith in 1914, when we beat Scotland by 16 points to 15. The R.A.F. and Blackheath owed him much

(Dulwich College v Bedford School 1910, anon cutting)

'Lowe, after a fine dribble, picked up the ball and made a great run, ultimately scoring between the posts. It was a brilliant and well-deserved try' (Dulwich College v St Paul's 1910, anon cutting)

'C N Lowe, who has great speed and is clever at making openings' (Richmond Fettesian-Lorettonians, January 1911, *The Times*)

'The outstanding personality in all the Old Boys' attacking movements was C N Lowe ... he has pace that is effective; he has resource, and he is unselfish, and though he has not the physique to make him strong in defence he is nevertheless not lacking in pluck ... against Rosslyn Park he displayed great form for so young a player' (Rosslyn Park v Old Alleynians, 1911, *The Morning Post*)

Lowe's schoolboy associates at Dulwich. (Right.)

32

MR. LEAKE'S HOUSE.

Form.	HEAD OF THE HOUSE.
M. VI.	Bentley, G. W. H.
	HOUSE PREFECTS.
M. VI.	Goulder, A. D. G.
Army VI.	King, J. F.
Math. V.	Lowe, C. N.
Eng. VI.	Raikes, H. R.
Cl. U. V.	Shand, E. G.
Eng. V.	Baxter, E. E. i.
Army L. IV.	Baxter, G. D. ii
L. III. B.	Chai, H.
II. B.	Criswick, J.
Sc. R.	Dowling, G.
M. L. V.	Evans, W. E.
Eng. R.	Eyre, G. L.
A. R.	Harman, L.
L. III. B.	Hovil, F. A.
L. III. B.	Howard, H. R.
Sc. V.	Marlowe, J. M.
Eng. V.	Mayne, W. E.
Eng. L. IV.	Odell, R. F.
M. U. V.	Peet, F. W.
Eng. U. IV.	Pharazyn, W. N.
Eng. R.	Roberts, J. S. i.
L. III. B.	Roberts, F. E. ii.
M. U. V.	Spinney, R. E.
II. B.	Springfield, R. W.
L. III. B.	†Townessend, C. J. D.
Army L. IV.	Volkers, F. C. S.
L. III. B.	Waite, E. B.

Lowe earned his nickname of 'Kid' whilst at Dulwich College, because of his small stature. Diminutive or not, Kid Lowe tried his hand at almost every sport in the school's curriculum.

1911 The Oval: Young Amateurs 117 and 335 (C N Lowe 37) Young Players of Surrey 222 and 145-4

1911 Dulwich: Dulwich College Sports—100 yards C N Lowe, 1st, 11 secs. 120 yards hurdles: C N Lowe, 1st, 19.45 secs. 440 yards C N Lowe 1st, 53.5 secs. 880 yards C N Lowe, 1st, 2 mins 6.5 secs (College record)

'Lowe quite confirmed his school and other form. Small, but strong, he was quick in all he did, breaking through cleverly and timing his passes well' (Cambridge University Freshmen's Trial, November 1911, anon cutting)

'The outstanding player—quite in a class by himself—was C N Lowe (Dulwich & Pembroke). Here is a natural player, and knows the game' (Cambridge University Freshmen's Trial, November 1911, *Daily Express*)

'There was at least one truly fine footballer ... he was C N Lowe, the Old Alleynian ... we may be certain that he is one of our coming young men ... he carries himself like a good and accomplished footballer' (Surrey Trial, 1911, anon cutting)

'The sight of Birkett opposite Lowe at Cambridge on Saturday, reminded me of W G batting to the bowling of W G

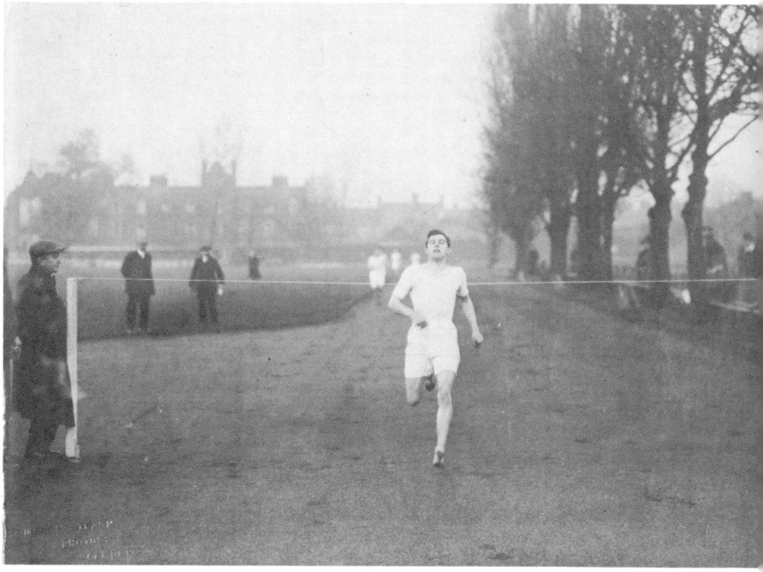

Lowe winning the Freshman's half mile in his first year at Cambridge. (Right.)

A rare event . . . Lowe being tackled.

Quaife. I am sure that Birkett could have given Lowe what in our childish days we used to call a "piggy-back", and have run in from halfway. But for all his smallness and lightness Lowe was never out of the picture. David and the Giant is a very old story, and most of us know who won. Birkett was well stopped by Lowe on one occasion when he had just begun to move, and I believe the little 'un has the pluck to have a genuine go at him even in full stride' (Cambridge match November 1911, *The Sportsman*)

'Lowe, the little Dulwich Freshman, overshadowed them all. Even admitting that the defence was weak, he gave a brilliant display ... he feigned passing and doubled back in an extraordinary manner, and repeatedly shook himself free from a couple of opponents, and then beat several more for pace. He scored five tries himself, and played a prominent part in obtaining most of the others' (Cambridge University v Liverpool, November 1911, *The Morning Post*)

A master of the dropped goal—Lowe shows how during his University days.

Although most of these pictures were 'posed' they were intended to highlight individual skills.

A. W. SYMINGTON
(Clare).

J. G. WILL
(Downing).

H W. THOMAS
(King's).

C. McG. URE
(Pembroke).

C. THORNE
(Clare).

A. H. WILSON
(Pembroke).

J. E. GREENWOOD
(King's)

A. E. KITCHING
(*Captain*) (Jesus).

W. C. NEILD
(Clare).

C. N. LOWE
(Pembroke).

B. R. LEWIS (*Hon. Secretary*)
(Trinity Hall).

B. S. CUMBERLEGE
(Emmanuel).

P. C. B. BLAIR
(King's).

T. G. FOWLER
(Caius).

L. L. PIENAAR
(King's).

'One of the "Admirable Crichtons" of sport is young CN Lowe, whose greatest claim to fame at present is the fact that he obtained his Rugby "blue" as a threequarter for Cambridge. He is only a freshman, and is certain to make his mark in several other forms of sport before he leaves the University. Lowe is short, but finely built and as hard as nails, as is proved by the fact that he can stand all the knocking about that comes so frequently to a centre threequarter. At Dulwich Lowe was a phenomenon. He was a first-class cricketer —both as a batsman and a bowler—and as an athlete he carried everything before him. He has already given a taste of his quality at Cambridge as a runner. Another of his accomplishments is boxing, at which he represented his school in the public schools championships at Aldershot. Though he did not actually win, he proved that if he devoted his attention seriously to the gloves he would be as good with them as he is in nearly every other sport' (Anon cutting, December 1911)

'There were some pretty touches by Lowe' (Oxford v Cambridge 1911, *The Times*)

'... their wings, Will and Lowe, were usually starved ... rarely did they come into effective action' (Oxford v Cambridge 1912, *The Morning Post*)

The 1911 Cambridge side which lost to Oxford at Queen's club.

'I may say that the South Africans hold a very high opinion of Lowe's abilities' (Cambridge University v South Africa 1912, *The Sporting Life*)

'Lowe was in the position of a man who had to make his own chances and we did not see the best of him ... he did this though: he showed that for such a little, light man he is a

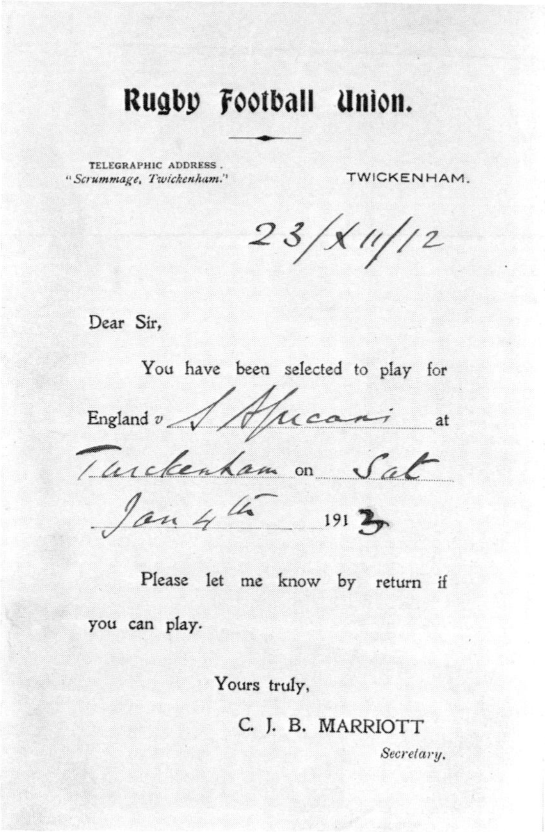

Rugby Football Union.

TELEGRAPHIC ADDRESS.
"*Scrummage, Twickenham.*"

TWICKENHAM.

23/XII/12

Dear Sir,

You have been selected to play for England v S Africans at Twickenham on Sat Jan 4th 1913.

Please let me know by return if you can play.

Yours truly,

C. J. B. MARRIOTT
Secretary.

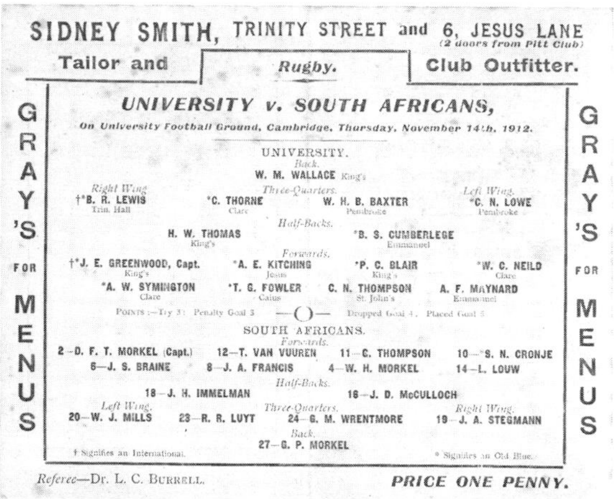

SIDNEY SMITH, TRINITY STREET and 6, JESUS LANE
(2 doors from Pitt Club)
Tailor and *Rugby.* Club Outfitter.

GRAY'S FOR MENUS

UNIVERSITY v. SOUTH AFRICANS,
On University Football Ground, Cambridge, Thursday, November 14th, 1912.

UNIVERSITY.

Back.
W. M. WALLACE King's

Right Wing / *Three-Quarters.* / *Left Wing.*
†*B. R. LEWIS Trin. Hall — *C. THORNE Clare — W. H. B. BAXTER Pembroke — *C. N. LOWE Pembroke

Half-Backs.
H. W. THOMAS King's — *B. S. CUMBERLEGE Emmanuel

Forwards.
†*J. E. GREENWOOD, Capt. King's — *A. E. KITCHING Jesus — *P. C. BLAIR King's — *W. C. NEILD Clare
*A. W. SYMINGTON Clare — *T. G. FOWLER Caius — C. N. THOMPSON St. John's — A. F. MAYNARD Emmanuel

POINTS:—Try 3: Penalty Goal 3 —()— Dropped Goal 4. Placed Goal 5

SOUTH AFRICANS.

Forwards.
2—D. F. T. MORKEL (Capt.) — 12—T. VAN VUUREN — 11—C. THOMPSON — 10—*S. N. CRONJE
6—J. S. BRAINE — 8—J. A. FRANCIS — 4—W. H. MORKEL — 14—L. LOUW

Half-Backs.
18—J. H. IMMELMAN — 16—J. D. McCULLOCH

Left Wing. / *Three-Quarters.* / *Right Wing.*
20—W. J. MILLS — 23—R. R. LUYT — 24—G. M. WRENTMORE — 19—J. A. STEGMANN

Back.
27—G. P. MORKEL

† Signifies an International. * Signifies an Old Blue.

Referee—Dr. L. C. BURRELL. ***PRICE ONE PENNY.***

GRAY'S FOR MENUS

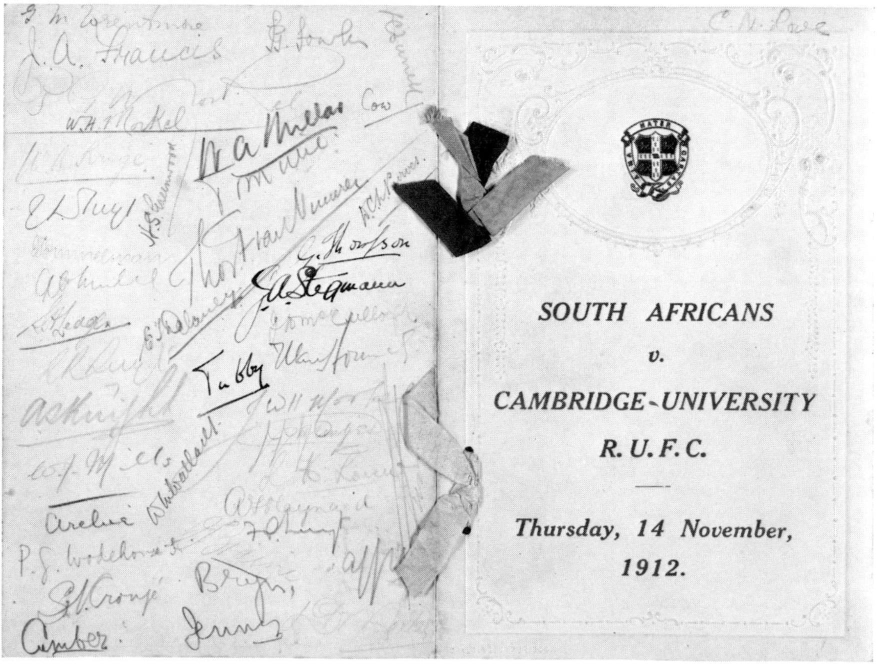

Mementoes of Lowe's first tas of overseas oppositi

remarkably fine tackler' (England v South Africa 1913, *The Morning Post*)

'Steinthal was also smitten with the "holding-on" fever, and in this way Lowe did not get a pass throughout the match. This is his third international, and he has yet to receive a pass. The fact did not depress him. For he was the best of the English line, and mastered Failliot, a man four stone heavier than he and a foot taller, from start to finish. Though he did not actually score, Lowe's clever play led up to the second and sixth tries, and it is abundantly clear that he has come to stay' (England v France, 1913, by E H D Sewell)

'Lowe has been condemned to an inglorious isolation ... he only had the ball given to him once by his new centre, and then it was forward. Now, there must be a reason for this state of things . . .' (England v Ireland, 1913, by 'Astral')

London Opinion, 22 February 1913

RUGBY INTERNATIONAL.

C. N. Lowe Among England's Representatives.

Boston gains a reflected credit from the inclusion in England's Rugby football team that met the South Africans and is to meet Wales on Saturday of Mr. C. N. Lowe, whose portrait we here reproduce. Mr. Lowe's grandfather was Lecturer at the Parish Church for about 30 years, and his father was born at Boston, educated at Boston Grammar School, and married a Boston lady—Miss Ridlington, a sister of the wine and spirit merchant. Mr. Lowe's grandmother lives in Spilsby-road, Boston.

C. N. LOWE.

Referring to Mr. C. N. Lowe's performance against the South Africans, and his selection to play against Wales, Mr. T. A. Beare, the great authority on Rugby football, writes:—"I am glad Lowe is chosen again. I said I thought him too small and light to oppose the big South Africans; and I still think so. His pluck and pace are beyond question; but I would have preferred to see that 'good big 'un' who is always better than the 'good little 'un' playing opposite McHardy. Still, Lowe played very well indeed. If he was once beaten by McHardy, he had an ample revenge, for he in turn slipped by the big Springbok and made a daring single-handed raid on the South African line. McHardy had the foot of him when it came to a race for the ball after Lowe's punt up the field, but the little man was on him like a flash, and prevented his kicking or running. Lowe justified his place in the team, and is well worthy of being played against Wales."

Lowe was featured in many newspaper and magazine articles, occasionally for no other reason than reflected glory (as left).

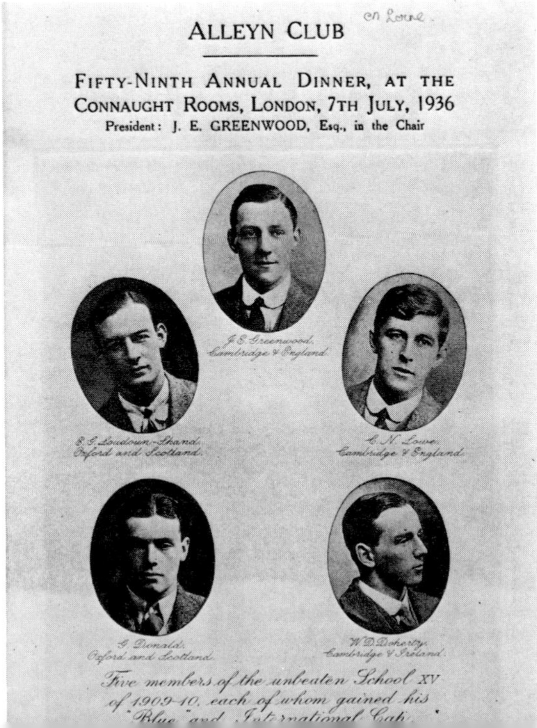
ALLEYN CLUB
FIFTY-NINTH ANNUAL DINNER, AT THE CONNAUGHT ROOMS, LONDON, 7TH JULY, 1936
President: J. E. GREENWOOD, Esq., in the Chair
J. E. Greenwood, Cambridge & England.
E. G. Loudoun-Shand, Oxford and Scotland.
C. N. Lowe, Cambridge & England.
G. Donald, Oxford and Scotland.
W. D. Doherty, Cambridge & Ireland.
Five members of the unbeaten School XV of 1909-10, each of whom gained his "Blue" and International Cap.

In many of his early matches Lowe was often starved of possession. He rarely received a pass. P G Wodehouse was among many to comment on this travesty, and the following poem summarised what many of Lowe's fans thought and felt at the time.

THE GREAT DAY

('Lowe has yet to receive a pass in international football')—(The Press passim).

I can recollect it clearly,
Every detail pretty nearly,
Though it happened many,
many years ago.
Yes, my children, I, your
grand-dad
A reserved seat in the stand
had
On the afternoon when
someone passed to Lowe.

There he stood, poor little
chappie,
Looking lonely and unhappy,
While the other players
frolicked with the ball.
For he knew he could not
mingle
In the fun with Coates and
Dingle;
He could simply go on
tackling—that was all.
I had stopped to light my briar,
For the wind was getting
higher,
When a thousand voices
screamed a startled 'Oh!'
I looked up. A try or
something?
Then sat gaping like a dumb
thing.
My children, somebody had
passed to Lowe!

I remember how he trembled
(For to him the thing resembled
A miracle), then gave a little
cry;

And spectators who were near
him
Were too overcome to cheer
him;
There were sympathetic
tears in every eye.

His astonishment was utter.
He was heard to gulp, and
mutter,
'What on earth has happened
now, I'd like to know?'
And incredulous reporters
Shouted out to the
three-quarters:
'Do we dream? Or did you
really pass to Lowe?'

There was sweat upon his
forehead
And his stare was simply
horrid:
He stood and goggled feebly
at the ball.
It was plain he suffered badly,
For the crowd, now cheering
madly,
Saw him shudder, start to
run, then limply fall.

Then a doctor*, who was
handy,
Fanned his face and gave him
brandy;
And at last, though his
recovery was slow,
He regained his health and
reason
By the middle of next season;
But the shock came very near
to killing Lowe.

P G WODEHOUSE

* Non-panel

'Lowe once more demonstrated what a truly marvellous little player he is, and his second try was one of the greatest things he has ever done' (Cambridge University v Newport, November 24 1913, *The Times*)

C N Lowe, the International, by scoring nineteen tries this term for Cambridge, holds the record for the number of tries scored by a 'Varsity player previous to the 'Varsity match. (Anon cutting 1913)

'C N Lowe is indisputably one of the greatest right-wing three-quarters Rugby has yet produced. No player of such distinction has been seen in the Cambridge team since the days of Kenneth G Macleod, the famous Scottish international . . . when going at top speed, he can swerve, too, in the most bewildering manner, and time after time he has eluded three or four opponents without one of them being able to put a hand on him. Moreover his defence is very sound. Though very small, he is as hard as nails, and no game is too robust or strenuous for this wiry and sturdy little player' (*Pall Mall Gazette* 1913)

'It was at once clear to me that Lowe possesses two qualities

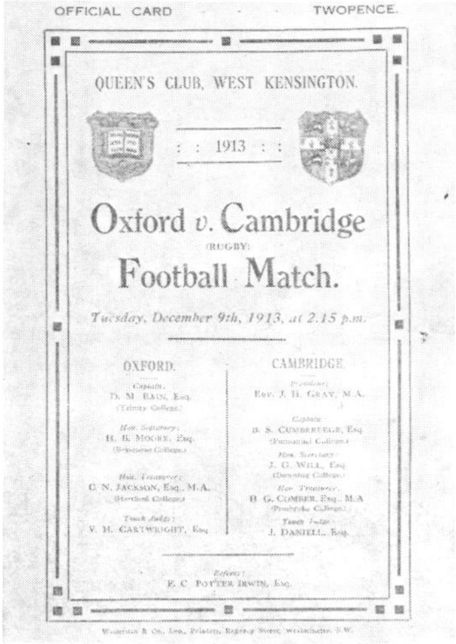
OFFICIAL CARD — TWOPENCE.

QUEEN'S CLUB, WEST KENSINGTON.

1913

Oxford *v.* Cambridge

(RUGBY)

Football Match.

Tuesday, December 9th, 1913, at 2.15 p.m.

OXFORD.	CAMBRIDGE.
Captain: D. M. BAIN, Esq. (Trinity College)	*President:* Rev. J. H. GRAY, M.A.
Hon. Secretary: H. B. MOORE, Esq. ([illegible] College)	*Captain:* B. S. CUMBERLEGE, Esq. (Emmanuel College)
Hon. Treasurer: C. N. JACKSON, Esq., M.A. (Hertford College)	*Hon. Secretary:* J. G. WILL, Esq. (Downing College)
Touch Judge: V. H. CARTWRIGHT, Esq.	*Hon. Treasurer:* H. G. COMBER, Esq., M.A. (Pembroke College)
	Touch Judge: J. DANIELL, Esq.

Referee: E. C. POTTER IRWIN, Esq.

[illegible] & Co., Ltd., Printers, Regency Street, Westminster, S.W.

The University Match programme of 9 December 1913.

The academic side of Lowe's life at Cambridge—his contemporaries at Pembroke College.

that are inseparable from really great, as apart from merely good, three-quarters. These are hands and pace—not merely the pace of a 100 yards racer, but the pace that is governed by a seemingly born knowledge of football. He has almost perfect fielding hands and in this I rank him second only to Knott, whose hands are the best ... in first-class football. As to field kicking, he can punt from all positions (mainly right-footed, it is true) and drop-kick well. Add to the virtues I have attempted to narrate an absolute fearlessness of any opponent, whatever his size (as Birkett and Stegmann will corroborate), and a very wiry and sound physique, in spite of his lack of inches ... we have the greatest wing player since Teddy Morgan, with whom Lowe shares the title of being the finest exponent of the game for his size ever seen. Lowe is certainly the greatest for his size that England has owned' (By E H D Sewell, 1913)

Lowe was a natural subject for the cartoonists of his day with rugby action photography in its infancy, the cartoons often were the only way matches could be illustrated.

'Lowe's try was the best thing of the match. His wonderful pace and swerve enabled him to beat both the opposing wing three-quarter, Crole, and the back, Reid. Later on he dropped a goal. He is, without much doubt, the finest wing three-quarter in the kingdom' (Oxford v Cambridge, *The Bystander*, 17 December 1913)

'... there was the marvellous play of Lowe, who was well looked after by his friends, and was therefore responsible for four tries, as well as a brilliant dropped goal' (England Trial, 1914, *The Morning Post*)

'Lowe was at his best, obtaining three tries' (France v England, 1914, *The Times*)

'There has been a great number of air fights during the past week of perfect flying weather, and astounding tourneys have taken place in the wide arena of the sky, only known to us earth-tethered folk by a glimpse now and then of squadrons mingled far up like a swarm of midges, and the high tattoo of machine-gun fire in the clouds, and afterwards by the sight of a German machine lying wrecked in some field behind our lines ...' (Front Line report from Philip Gibbs, *Daily Telegraph* correspondent, France, May 25 1919)

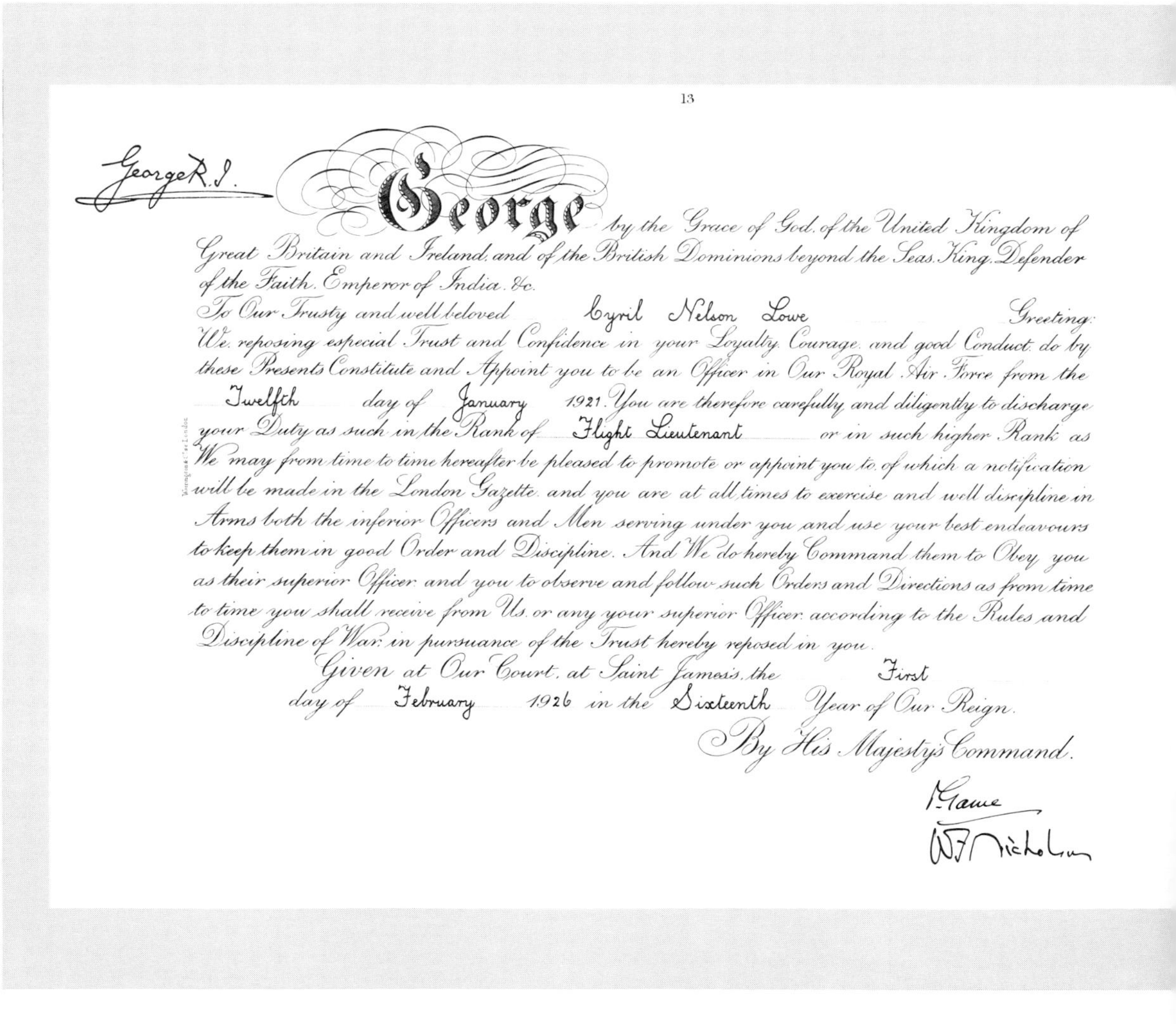

13

George R.I.

George by the Grace of God, of the United Kingdom of Great Britain and Ireland, and of the British Dominions beyond the Seas King, Defender of the Faith, Emperor of India &c.

To Our Trusty and well beloved Cyril Nelson Lowe Greeting:

We, reposing especial Trust and Confidence in your Loyalty, Courage, and good Conduct, do by these Presents Constitute and Appoint you to be an Officer in Our Royal Air Force from the Twelfth day of January 1921. You are therefore carefully and diligently to discharge your Duty as such in the Rank of Flight Lieutenant or in such higher Rank as We may from time to time hereafter be pleased to promote or appoint you to, of which a notification will be made in the London Gazette, and you are at all times to exercise and well discipline in Arms both the inferior Officers and Men serving under you and use your best endeavours to keep them in good Order and Discipline. And We do hereby Command them to Obey you as their superior Officer, and you to observe and follow such Orders and Directions as from time to time you shall receive from Us, or any your superior Officer, according to the Rules and Discipline of War, in pursuance of the Trust hereby reposed in you.

Given at Our Court, at Saint James's, the First day of February 1926 in the Sixteenth Year of Our Reign.

By His Majesty's Command.

[illegible]

[illegible]

Cyril Lowe, hero of the Royal Flying Corps, was commissioned in the newly formed Royal Air Force on 12 January 1921. Three days later he scored a try in England's 18–3 win over Wales at Twickenham.

How Capt. C N Lowe, MC, RAF, the English international and Cambridge Rugby footballer, won the Distinguished Flying Cross is described in a supplement to the *London Gazette* as follows:

'This officer has destroyed five enemy machines and driven down two others out of control. On one occasion he attacked two enemy triplanes, although at the time only one of his guns was serviceable; he shot down one of the machines in flames. On another occasion, while leading a formation of eight scouts, he engaged a hostile formation of 26 machines. Having shot down a Fokker biplane, he went to the assistance of one of our scouts, and drove the enemy machine down to 500 feet; at this low altitude half of a blade of his propeller was shot off by fire from the ground'

... the list of the casualties published on Saturday bore the intelligence that the old Cantab had been wounded. The nature of his injuries, sustained presumably in some aerial action, have not been indicated, but it is to be hoped that the spry, little threequarter back ... will soon be alright.

Lt. W. D. Doherty. Lt. T. Whittington. Major Lapham. Sec. Lt. E. C. O'Brien. Sec. Lt. A. Jacobson. Sec. Lt. L. H. Fetherstonhaugh. Sec Lt. F. W. J. White. Sec Lt. A. L. Wilson.
Major Millman. Capt. the Earl of Carrick. Lt. E. G. S. Stevens. Capt. C. L. Prior (Adjutant). Col. A. J. Erskine (Col. Commanding Depôt). Capt. S. W. Dixon. Lt. & Qtmr. T. W. Morris. Lt. W. W. Briggs. Sec. Lt. W. M. O. Kelly.
Sec. Lt. C. N. Lowe. Sec. Lt. A. A. Morphy. Sec. Lt. A. R. Whittington.

THE FIRST RESERVE HORSE TRANSPORT.

A GROUP of officers of the First Reserve Horse Transport, taken at their depôt, Deptford. They are responsible for the continuous supply of horses and vehicles for the use of our soldiers at the Front—a task of great magnitude. The group is also interesting on account of its composition. Capt. the Earl of Carrick is holding an axe presented to him by the Colonel and officers of the depôt, to commemorate his good work in sawing off the tilts of wagons which would not go under an arch at Waterloo Station recently, when 550 vehicles, 1,300 horses, and 700 men left for France to equip the Indian contingent. This is the largest transport ever despatched at one time. Twenty-seven trains were needed, and were despatched within twelve hours. Lt. W. W. Briggs may perhaps be better recognised as an actor, his stage name being Warwick Wellington. His last stage appearance was at the Playhouse, when he appeared with Miss Marie Tempest in *The Wynmartens*. Sec. Lt. C. N. Lowe will be remembered as the brilliant young international Rugby player.

When Lowe volunteered for First World War duty he joined the RASC in 1914 (above), later transferring to the Royal Flying Corps 'because it might be more fun'.

'C N Lowe, in particular, distinguished himself by scoring six tries' (Blackheath v Rosslyn Park, September 1920, *Daily Telegraph*)

'Lowe did a wonderful amount of defensive work, sometimes on his own wing and sometimes on the other. He is not quite as fast as he was, but he is still the best wing in England' (Ireland v England, 1920, *The Times*)

'Lowe was as resourceful as ever. There is brains at the back of everything he does, and his fifteenth consecutive appearance for England was a personal success. His dropped goal was as fine a one as you could wish to see. A grand little player is Lowe' (England v Ireland, 1921, *Daily Telegraph*)

'It was a case of Lowe, Lowe and again Lowe ... the speedy three-quarter had a real field day, scoring four tries, one of them a masterpiece of brilliant execution' (RAF v The Army, 1921, *The Times*)

VICTORIOUS IN AN ANGLO-IRISH STRUGGLE IN DUBLIN: THE ENGLISH RUGBY FOOT-BALL TEAM WHICH DEFEATED IRELAND.

Lowe (third left seated) in the England side . . .

. . . in action for Surrey . . .

'England owed a great deal to C N Lowe, who was the best man on the field' (England v France, 1922, *Daily Mail*)

'Harding was well looked after by Lowe, who made some beautiful tackles of the Welsh sprint champion before he could get into his stride. Otherwise, Lowe, in his 22nd consecutive appearance for England, had much the same experience as is so often his lot. He never had a chance in attack' (England v Wales, 1923, *Daily Telegraph*)

'The fact that C N Lowe, the famous English threequarter back, was making his first appearance for the West of Scotland in club football in Scotland was the means of attracting a large crowd to the West ground at Partick' (West of Scotland v Hillhead HSFP, 1925, anon report)

. . . England again, before their match against Scotland . . .

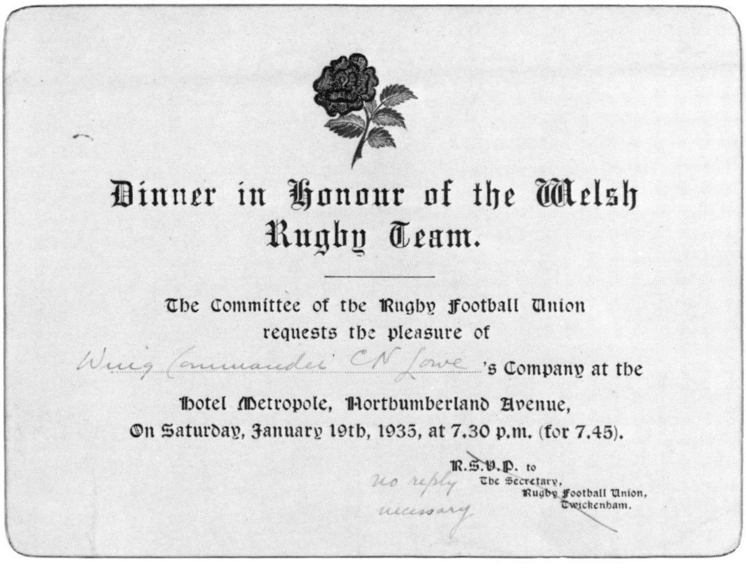

Dinner in Honour of the Welsh Rugby Team.

The Committee of the Rugby Football Union requests the pleasure of

Wing Commander C N Lowe's Company at the

Hotel Metropole, Northumberland Avenue,

On Saturday, January 19th, 1935, at 7.30 p.m. (for 7.45).

R.S.V.P. to The Secretary, Rugby Football Union, Twickenham.

no reply necessary

. . . and an invitation to dinner when Lowe had retired from international rugby.

The Sketch March 8, 1922

Captained by a 20-Cap Three-Quarter.

AS OUR ARTIST SEES THEM: SOME OF THE BLACKHEATH FIFTEEN.

Blackheath, which claims to be the oldest Rugger Club in existence, has just elected Mr. C. N. Lowe, the famous International three-quarter, captain for the remainder of the season. It is worthy of note that the new Blackheath skipper has just made his twentieth consecutive appearance for England, and with one more "cap" will equal the numerical record of Mr. J. G. G. Birkett.

Lowe was one of many international rugby players who occasionally was induced to reflect on his playing career in Newspapers . . . the RFU frowned upon the practice, allowing it provided no payment accrued.

THE WOES OF A WING THREE-QUARTER.

"If I Had My Time Over Again . . . . " ∴ All the Kicks and None of the Glory ∴ Oh! for the Happy Life of a Forward!

By C. N. LOWE

(who played wing-threequarter in 25 successive matches for England.)

THIS is the first of a series of articles written specially for "The Evening News" by famous athletes.

In these articles the writers will discuss what parts they would play in their own sports if they had to live through their athletic careers again, and what reformations they would make in present-day sport.

PETER McWILLIAM will deal with Association football; GEORGE DUNCAN with Golf; Cricket will be treated by that great master, JACK HOBBS; MLLE. SUZANNE LENGLEN, the most magnetic Lawn Tennis figure who ever stepped on to a court, will deal with her own game; and Boxing will be in the hands of Great Britain's former heavy-weight champion, JOE BECKETT.

I SUPPOSE every Rugby player imagines he could fill some other position on the field better than the one he has adopted. I know many forwards who imagine they would make wonderful three-quarters, and many three-quarters and halves who fancy themselves as forwards, and I believe everyone thinks he can play full-back.

Perhaps it is natural therefore that, on looking back upon my career, I think that in many ways wing three-quarter is the most uninteresting position on the Rugby field. Given the physique, I

MR. C. N. LOWE.
By Tom Webster.

would rather have been a forward or a centre three-quarter.

I started Rugby as a half and then a centre three-quarter, and only in my second year at Cambridge did I play wing three-quarter. That was against the South Africans, and from that time onward, except when playing for the Old Alleynians or Royal Air Force, I have always played on the wing.

In pre-war days a wing three-quarter saw a lot more of the ball than he does nowadays, and one of the reasons was, I think, that teams played to their wings, relying on them to score tries and knowing that if the wings could not get through, then by intelligent backing up they would receive a reverse pass or a kick across.

One saw many excellent wings score lots of tries, notably John George Will, of Cambridge and Scotland.

Stalemate.

Another reason was, I think, that outsides set out with the intention of trying to score tries and in consequence [illegible] back for attack, [illegible] and nowadays this is even more pronounced—three-quarters began to line up so straight that if both sides tackled there was little chance of either side scoring except through a mistake of their opponents.

This is now carried to such an extreme that in the last two International matches at Twickenham we have had glaring examples of three-quarters standing offside while the ball is in the scrum.

In fact, we are coming to a state of stalemate, in which neither side is willing to take a chance.

Since the war, the idea of making openings seemed to obsess all stand-off halves and centre three-quarters, with the result that a wing three-quarter seldom gets the ball except when it is too late and therefore useless to him.

A good wing wants the ball early, with some room to move in. He does not want his openings made for him.

The Good Old Days.

Again, halves and centre three-quarters feel that they must draw their opposite number before passing, but in many cases, in doing this, either they run across or slow up, and in some cases do both, before passing, whereas if they had turned slightly away from the man to whom they are passing, and thus put the defence on the wrong foot, the object of drawing their man would be achieved, and the ball could still be passed in plenty of time to give the wing room in which to move.

To bear this out, I would point out that J. G. Will and myself scored a great number of tries for Cambridge, not because we had brilliant centres who made openings, but because we had orthodox centres who ran straight and did not stop before giving their passes.

From my earliest days in Rugby I set out to learn to tackle, and to tackle correctly; that is, by the legs. This was not achieved without considerable pain in my school days, but after I had learnt to "grasp my nettle firmly" the painful times were past.

As I said before, I consider that wing three-quarter is the most uninteresting place on the field. I feel this because, after the war, playing on the wing, I got very few passes. Consequently, I gradually began to absorb a policy wrong in any game, and became a defensive rather than an offensive player, so that I developed into a kind of deputy assistant full-back.

A Human D.O.R.A.

"To the English side," wrote a cartoonist when describing a match during this stage of my career, "Lowe was a human Defence of the Realm Act."

Exactly!

This must have been obvious to other people, for I can well remember one day a father (an ex-International) whose son was playing full-back for the first time in a first-class game, coming to me before the game and asking me to give his son a hand and help to see him through the game.

I confess I look back on the later games I played with little pleasure, because as time went on chances of scoring tries became rarer and rarer, quite apart from approaching senility.

I had to rely on my defence for my [illegible] a team, and so every game became for me a personal encounter between myself and my opposing wing three-quarter, and I felt that I was falling more and more from my idea of the functions of a wing three-quarter.

It may be that, following the course of nature, I tend to join the ranks of *laudatores temporis acti*, but I do feel that, unless there is a reversion to the principles of Rugby and more adherence to the spirit of the game, we have reached the peak of its popularity.

If I had my Rugger days over again I would like to be either a centre three-quarter or a forward. In those positions one is more in the game.

MONDAY'S NOTTINGHAM

RUGBY AROUND THE WORLD

ABU DHABI

Headquarters	c/o Les Byrne, PO Box 705, Abu Dhabi
Colours	Green, black and white hoops
Number of clubs	2
Number of players	100
Season	September–April
Temperatures	50°F (10°C) to 90°F (30°C)

1982 results

Bahrain	L	0–36	(A)			
Dhahran	L	0–14	(H)	L	3–8	(A)
Dubai	W	13–0	(H)	L	0–3	(A)
Kuwait	W	3–6	(H)	L	0–35	(A)
Muscat	L	10–28	(H)	L	0–10	(A)
Qatar	W	20–4	(H)	W	12–0	(A)

1983 result

Qatar L 4–8 (A)

Gulf League 1983
Semi-final: Abu Dhabi 3 Bahrain 9

ANDORRA

Foundation	1963
Headquarters	Edifico Automovil Club, 2° la, Andorra La Vella
Colours	Blue and red jerseys
Number of clubs	1
Number of players	50
Season	September–May
Temperatures	45°F (7°C) to 70°F (21°C)
Population	29 000

ARGENTINA

Foundation	1899
Headquarters	Union Argentina de Rugby, UAR Pacheco de Melo 2120, Buenos Aires
Main stadium	Ferrocarril Oeste Stadium, Buenos Aires (capacity 55 000)
Colours	Blue and white striped jerseys
Number of clubs	198
Number of players	21 000
Season	April–November
Temperatures	40°F (4°C) to 77°F (25°C)

First match
1873 at Buenos Aires Football Club

First club
1886 Buenos Aires Cricket and Rugby Club (then Buenos Aires Football Club)

The Argentine Pumas gave a good account of themselves when they entered the 1982 Hong Kong Sevens—losing only to the Barbarians (below) and to Australia, the eventual winners, in the quarter-finals. (Colorsport.)

Club champions

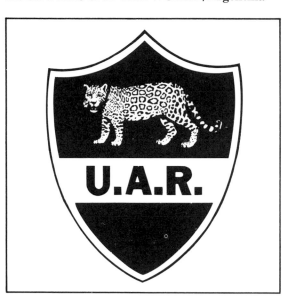

1899 Lomas
1900–04 Buenos Aires
1905–06 Rosario Athletic
1907 Belgrano
1908–09 Buenos Aires
1910 Belgrano
1911–12 Gymnasia y Escrima
1913 Lomas
1914 Belgrano
1915 Buenos Aires
1916 Not held
1917–18 Atletico San Isidro
1919 Not held
1920–30 Atletico San Isidro
1931 Universitario
1932 Gymnasia y Escrima
1933–34 Atletico San Isidro
1935 Rosario Athletic
1936–40 Not held
1941 San Isidro Club
1942 Universitario
1943 Atletico San Isidro

The Pumas saved their most impressive performance in the 1982 Hong Kong Sevens for their Group match against Sri Lanka (above), whom they beat 30–0, a win which earned them a quarter-final place. (Colorsport.)

1944–45 Universitario
1946 Pucara
1947 Universitario
1948 San Isidro Club
1949 Atletico San Isidro & Universitario
1950 Universitario & Pucara
1951–52 Universitario
1953 Obrias Sanitarias
1954–57 Atletico San Isidro
1958–59 Buenos Aires
1960 Not held
1961–62 Atletico San Isidro
1963 Belgrano
1964 Atletico San Isidro
1965 Not held
1966 Belgrano
1967 Atletico San Isidro & Belgrano
1968 Universitario & San Isidro
1969 Universitario
1970 San Isidro Club & Universitario
1971–73 San Isidro Club
1974–76 Atletico San Isidro
1977–80 San Isidro Club
1981–82 Atletico San Isidro

First championship
1899, won by Lomas AC

First official coach
Izak van Heerden 1964

First club tour
1963 Atletico San Isidro to British Isles

First incoming tour
1910 Rugby Football Union team

Most titles
30 Atletico San Isidro (including 2 shared)
12 Universitario (including 4 shared)
10 San Isidro Club (including 1 shared)
10 Buenos Aires
7 Belgrano (including 2 shared)
3 Rosario Athletic
3 Gymnasia y Esgrima
2 Pucara (including 1 shared)
2 Lomas
1 Obrias Sanitarias

1982 championship

	P	W	D	L	F	A	Pts
Atletico San Isidro	22	18	2	3	530	271	38
San Isidro Club	22	18	1	3	599	298	37
Banco Nacion	22	15	2	5	517	319	32
Hindu	22	15	1	6	386	297	31
Pueyrredon	22	13	1	8	392	303	27
Alumni	22	11	0	11	353	381	22
Universitario	22	9	1	12	343	308	19
Cardenal Newman	22	9	1	12	355	386	19
San Cirano	22	7	0	15	273	447	14
Pucara	22	6	1	15	262	388	13
Curupayti	22	3	2	17	272	583	8
Belgrano	22	2	0	20	199	500	4

NB Belgrano relegated to second division for first time since club became founder member of Argentine Rugby Union in 1899

Record points total
307 Hugo Porta (Banco Nacion) 1982

1982 Tour of France
W 38–15 French selection (Clermont-Ferrand)
L 15–25 French selection (Valence)
L 9–27 French Army (Aurillac)
W 22–8 French Barbarians (Dax)
L 12–25 France (Toulouse)
W 12–9 French selection (Angoulême)
L 6–13 France (Paris)

Tour summary: P 7 W 3 L 4 F 114 A 122

1982 Tour of Spain
W 28–19 Spain (Madeira)

Incoming tours

		P	W	D	L	F	A
1932	Junior Springboks	8	8	0	0	268	24
1949	France	9	9	0	0	154	18
1952	Ireland	8	5	2	1	96	43
1959	Junior Springboks	8	8	0	0	249	38
1966	South African Gazelles	12	12	0	0	497	53
1972	South African Gazelles	9	8	1	0	463	35
1979	Australia	7	6	0	1	180	83
1980	Fiji	7	4	0	3	243	158
1981	Canada	5	4	0	1	132	71
1981	England	7	6	1	0	193	100

Outgoing tours

		P	W	D	L	F	A
1965	South Africa/Rhodesia	16	11	1	4	305	183
1971	South Africa	8	4	1	3	84	66
1973	Ireland/Scotland	8	2	2	4	117	132
1975	France	7	3	0	4	95	125
1976	Wales/England	6	3	0	3	112	111
1978	UK, Ireland/Italy	9	5	1	3	157	133
1979	New Zealand	9	6	0	3	165	111
1982	France/Spain	8	4	0	4	142	141

International results

		W	D	L
Australia				
1979	Buenos Aires			12–17
	Buenos Aires	24–13		
Brazil				
1951	Buenos Aires	72–0		
1961	Montevideo	66–0		
1964	São Paulo	30–6		
1971	Montevideo	50–6		
1973	São Paulo	96–0		
1975	Asuncion	64–6		
1977	Tucuman	78–6		
1979	Santiago	109–3		
Canada				
1981	Buenos Aires	35–0		
Chile				
1951	Buenos Aires	13–3		
1958	Santiago	14–0		
1961	Montevideo	11–3		
1964	São Paulo	30–8		
1967	Buenos Aires	18–0		
1969	Santiago	54–0		
1971	Montevideo	20–3		
1973	São Paulo	60–3		
1975	Asuncion	45–3		
1977	Tucuman	25–10		
1979	Santiago	34–15		
1983	Buenos Aires	46–6		
England				
1978	Twickenham		13–13	
1981	Buenos Aires			6–12
	Buenos Aires		19–19	
Fiji				
1980	Buenos Aires	38–16		
	Buenos Aires	33–22		
France				
1949	Buenos Aires			3–12
	Buenos Aires			0–5
1954	Buenos Aires			8–22
	Buenos Aires			3–30
1960	Buenos Aires			6–29
	Buenos Aires			3–12
	Buenos Aires			3–37
1974	Buenos Aires			27–31
	Buenos Aires			15–20
1975	Paris			21–36
	Lyon			6–29
1977	Buenos Aires		18–18	
	Buenos Aires			3–26
1982	Toulouse			12–25
	Paris			6–13
Ireland				
1952	Buenos Aires			0–6
	Buenos Aires		3–3	
1969	Buenos Aires			3–6
	Buenos Aires			9–16
1970	Buenos Aires	6–3		
	Buenos Aires	8–3		
1976	Dublin			8–21
Italy				
1978	Rovigo			6–19
New Zealand				
1976	Buenos Aires			6–26
	Buenos Aires			9–21
1979	Wellington			6–15
	Dunedin			9–18
Paraguay				
1971	Montevideo	61–0		
1973	São Paulo	98–3		
1975	Asuncion	93–0		
1977	Tucuman	77–3		
1979	Vina del Mar	76–13		
1983	Buenos Aires	43–3		
Peru				
1958	Santiago	44–0		
Rhodesia				
1965	Salisbury			12–17
Romania				
1973	Buenos Aires	24–3		
	Buenos Aires	15–7		
Scotland				
1969	Buenos Aires	20–3		
	Buenos Aires			3–6
1973	Murrayfield			11–12
Spain				
1982	Madrid	28–19		
Uruguay				
1951	Buenos Aires	62–0		
1958	Vina del Mar	50–3		
1961	Montevideo	36–3		
1964	São Paulo	25–6		
1967	Buenos Aires	38–6		
1969	Santiago	41–6		
1971	Montevideo	55–6		
1973	São Paulo	55–0		
1975	Asuncion	30–15		
1977	Tucuman	70–0		
1979	Santiago	19–16		
1983	Buenos Aires	29–6		

Wales

1968	Buenos Aires		9–9	
	Buenos Aires	9–5		
1976	Cardiff			19–20

Other matches
1927 British Team (Buenos Aires) L 0–37, L 0–46, L 3–34, L 0–43
1978 Wales B (Llanelli) W 17–14

Junior internationals
Brazil 1972 W 144–0 1974 W 97–0 1978 W 84–0 1982 W 63–3. *Chile* 1972 W 35–0 1974 W 69–4 1976 W 68–9 1978 W 58–3 1982 W 41–6. *Paraguay* 1972 W 84–3 1974 W 82–0 1976 W 88–4 1978 W 118–0 1982 W 30–7. *Uruguay* 1972 W 16–9 1974 W 32–9 1976 W 41–15 1978 W 13–3 1982 W 31–6

AUSTRIA

Foundation 1978
Headquarters Celtic Vienna Rugby Club, c/o Wilhelm Zrisp, Business International, Prins Wilhelm Str. 4, 1040 Wien
Number of clubs 1 (Celtic Vienna)
Number of players 40
Season September–May
Temperatures 32°F (0°C) to 60°F (16°C)

Celtic Vienna, Austria's one club, usually rely on players from France, New Zealand, Scotland, South Africa, Wales and Zimbabwe but encouraged local players in 1982/83 by introducing a junior XV. Celtic Vienna usually play against international agency teams in Vienna and against sides from neighbouring west European countries.
In 1980 Celtic Vienna lost 6–7 to TV 1834 Pforzheim, the Federal Republic of Germany second division club.

THE BAHAMAS

Foundation 1962
Headquarters Freeport RFC, c/o PO Box 170, Freeport, Grand Bahama, Bahamas
Number of clubs 2
Number of players 100

BAHRAIN

Foundation 1972
Headquarters c/o Dave Maconachie, Box 5246, Gulf Air Commercial Division, Bahrain
Main stadium Sadr Road, Budaiya
Colours Green and white hoops
Number of clubs 1
Number of players 150
Season September–April
Temperatures 60°F (16°C) to 90°F (30°C)
Population 360 000

Bahrain, in the white shirts met Canada in the 1983 Hong Kong Sevens. (Colorsport.)

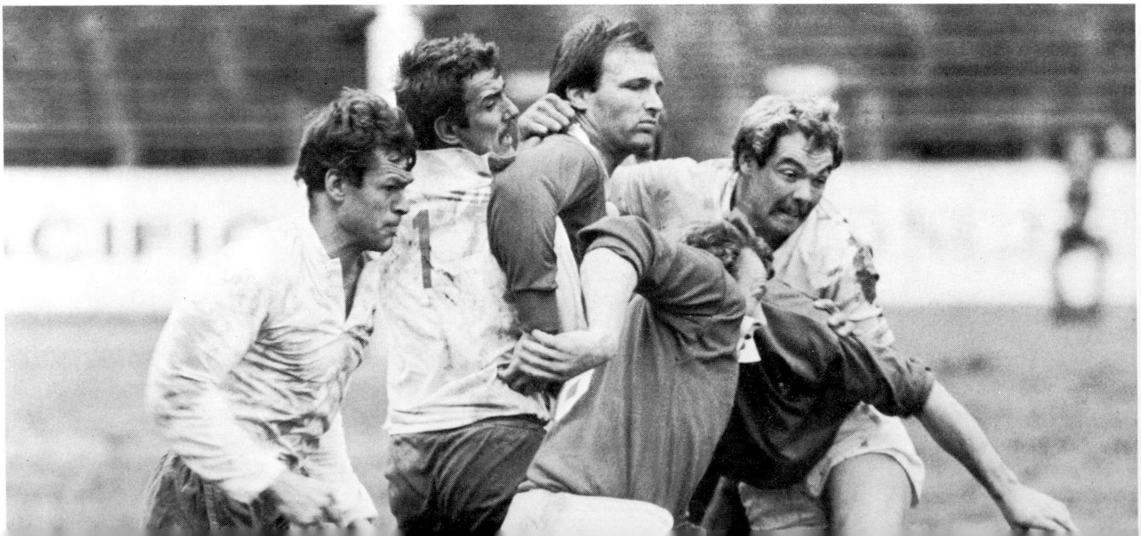

1982 results

Abu Dhabi	W 36–0	(H)		
Dhahran	W 10–3	(H)	L 3–4	(A)
Dubai	W 6–0	(H)	W 4–0	(A)
Kuwait	L 4–12	(H)	L 6–12	(A)
Muscat	W 19–3	(H)	W 17–10	(A)
Qatar	W 44–3	(H)	W 20–3	(A)

1983 results

Dhahran	W 14–12	(H)	W 22–4	(A)
Kuwait	L 3–15	(H)	L 7–10	(A)
Qatar	W 15–8	(A)	W 24–9	(H)

Gulf League 1983
Semi-final: Bahrain 9 Abu Dhabi 3
Final: Bahrain 9 Kuwait 7

Dubai Sevens
Bahrain won in 1975, 1976, 1977 and 1978

Hong Kong Sevens
1978 Bahrain won Plate competition

BARBADOS

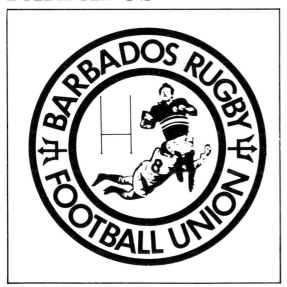

Foundation 1964
Headquarters Barbados Rugby Football Union, The Garrison, St Michael, PO Box 6W, Worthing, Barbados
Main stadium The Garrison, Savannah
Colours Gold and black hooped jerseys, black shorts and socks
Number of clubs 1
Number of players 50
Season June–November
Temperatures 75°F (24°C) to 85°F (29°C)
Population 254 000

First match
1933 Barbados 'Night Club' XV played Trinidad XV

First official match
1963 Barbados 0 HMS *Devonshire* 21

First club
Barbados RFC 1964

Best season
1965 Barbados played and won 19 matches

First tour
1965 to Trinidad and Tobago

First UK tour
1979 to England and Wales

Joined Rugby Football Union
1967

Schools Rugby
Introduced 1975 (established at four schools 1982)

Mini-rugby
Introduced 1975

International result

	W	D	L
Bermuda 1981 Trinidad			0–51

BELGIUM

Foundation 1931
Headquarters Federation Belge de Rugby, Anneke Wijmans, Bredabaan 702. 2170 Wuustwezel
Main stadium FBR Ground, Brussels
Capacity 7500

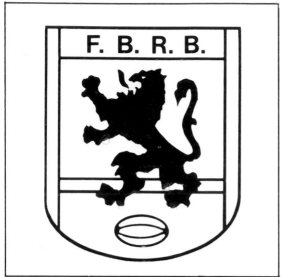

Colours Red, black, yellow hoops, black sleeves
Number of clubs 33
Number of players 1500
Season September–June
Temperatures 30°F (−1°C) to 65°F (18°C)
Population 9 837 413

Affiliation
FIRA 1934

First international
1930 Netherlands, The Hague

First FIRA competition
1979 III Division

Biggest win
52–8 Denmark, Brussels 1979

Biggest defeat
3–52 Fed. Rep. of Germany, Offenbach 1961

FIRA Division III results
1981/82 L 9–15 Sweden
W 9–0 Yugoslavia
W 10–6 Switzerland
W 16–12 Denmark
(Belgium runners-up to Sweden)

Outgoing tours
1973 Belgium to England
1974 Belgium to England

Incoming tour
1983 Sutton and Epsom Under 16s
W 17–3 Bodtsfort Cadets, W 25–0 Belgium

International results

	W	D	L
Czechoslovakia			
1967 Prague			6–46
1971 Ricany			12–25
1979 Prague			9–44
1982 Brussels			6–21
Denmark			
1973 Brussels	38–0		
1975 Copenhagen	10–6		
1979 Brussels	52–8		
1981 Dinant	34–9		
1982 Copenhagen	16–12		
Fed. Rep. of Germany			
1937 Dusseldorf			0–34
1952 Hanover			9–16
1956 Huy			0–16
1957 Cologne			3–33
1959 Luttich			6–8
1961 Offenbach			3–52
1962 Tirlemont			3–50
1964 Hurth			3–11
1971 Luttich			9–27
1972 Bonn			3–28
1973 Verviers			9–20
1974 Varel			3–24
1975 Hanover			3–43
Italy			
1937 Paris			0–45
1969 Brussels			0–30
Netherlands			
1930 The Hague	6–0		
1930 Brussels	11–0		
1932 Amsterdam		6–6	
1933 Wilrijch			5–14
1934 Utrecht			3–6
1935 Antwerp			6–8
1938 The Hague	28–8		
1939 Antwerp	23–6		
1945 Bussum			6–9
1946 Brussels	13–3		
1947 Brussels	9–6		
1947 Bussum	6–3		
1947 Bussum			3–5
1948 Leuven	9–0		
1948 Brussels		6–6	
1949 Amsterdam	6–3		
1949 Brussels	15–5		
1952 Brussels	9–0		
1956 Brussels			12–14
1965 Rijwijk			3–14
1968 Brussels			9–14
1969 Brussels	9–5		
1977 Hilversum			4–17
1978 Hilversum			3–10
1978 Hilversum			4–17
1982 Beek	13–9		
1982 Vise			10–19
Spain			
1954 Treviso			0–14

1958 Charleroi		5–11
1959 Brussels		14–17
1960 Madrid		0–21
1968 Brussels		0–14
1969 Madrid		3–41
1971 Brussels		0–44
Sweden		
1966 Brussels	24–3	
1971 Sollentu	7–3	
1973 Brussels	18–6	
1975 Vanersborg		0–3
1976 Brussels	14–3	
1981 Karlstad		9–15
Switzerland		
1974 Lausanne	18–10	
1975 Brussels	11–3	
1977 Lausanne	25–16	
1980 Brussels	7–0	
1982 Antwerp	10–6	
Tunisia		
1980 Tunis		7–11
1983 Brussels		12–13
Yugoslavia		
1972 Brussels	3–0	
1976 Brussels	8–6	
1978 Markarska	20–0	
1981 Liege	9–0	

FIRA Junior tournament
1982 (Geneva) Belgium 0 Ivory Coast 13

Colts Match
1982 Fed. Rep. Germany 18 Belgium 13 (Lüttich)

BERMUDA

Foundation	1964
Headquarters	Bermuda Rugby Football Union, P.O. Box 1909, Hamilton
Main stadium	National Sports Club, Devonshire (capacity 2000)
Colours	Blue jerseys, black shorts
Number of clubs	5
Number of players	420
Season	October–April
Temperatures	65°F (18°C) to 80°F (27°C)
Population	57 000

First matches
1854–9, Regimental XVs played

First club
Bermuda Athletic Association 1922

First competition
The Nicholl Shield 1924

Caribbean Tournament
Bermuda won 1977, 1979 and 1981

Easter Classic
1972 Bermuda 20 Irish 9. 1973 Bermuda 7 Irish 36. 1975 Bermuda 9 Irish 22. 1977 Bermuda 4 Irish 13. 1978 Bermuda 14 Irish 27. 1979 Bermuda 22 Irish 20. 1980 Bermuda 23 Irish 18. 1981 Bermuda 11 Irish 23. 1982 Bermuda 13 Irish 24. 1983 Bermuda 36 Irish 13

Nicholl Shield winners
1968 Police & Teachers. 1969 Teachers. 1970 Police & Teachers. 1971 Police. 1972 Police. 1973 Renegades. 1974 Bermuda Athletic Association. 1975 Renegades. 1976 Teachers. 1977 Police. 1978 Teachers. 1979 Police. 1980 Police. 1981 Police. 1982 Police. 1983 Police

Incoming tours

1980	Bermuda	0	Coventry 28
1982	Bermuda	21	Penguins 21
1983	Bermuda	12	Blackheath 9

Biggest international win
52–0 Guadeloupe 1979

Biggest international defeat
14–27 Trinidad & Tobago 1981

One of the highlights of the Bermuda season is the Easter Classic against an Invitation XV, comprised largely of Irish international players. In 1981 (above) John Moloney and Stuart McKinney link up in an Irish victory by 23–11.

International results

	W	D	L
Barbados			
1981 Trinidad	51–0		
Guadeloupe			
1977 Martinique	30–3		
1979 Guyana	52–0		
Guyana			
1979 Guyana	23–4		
1981 Trinidad	32–3		
Jamaica			
1975 Bermuda	16–10		
1976 Jamaica	14–3		
1977 Martinique	26–3		
Martinique			
1977 Martinique	7–3		
1979 Guyana		18–18	
1981 Trinidad	45–16		
Trinidad & Tobago			
1979 Guyana	42–8		
1981 Trinidad			14–27

BOTSWANA

Foundation	....
Number of clubs	2
Number of players	100
Season	May–October
Temperatures	55°F (13°C) to 85°F (29°C)
Population	726 000

BRAZIL

Foundation	1972
Headquarters	Associação Brasileira de Rugby, Rua Prof. Vahia de Abreu 189, 04549 São Paulo, S.P.
Main stadium	None
Colours	Yellow and green stripes
Number of clubs	22 (including universities and schools: 44 teams)
Number of players	1200 (1982)
Season	April to November
Temperatures	53°F (12°C) to 95°F (35°C)
Population	120 000 000

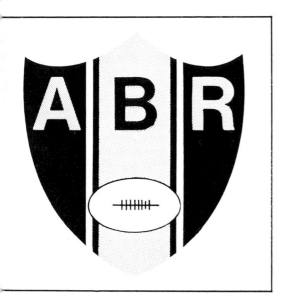

First match
1895

First inter-state match
1926 Rio de Janeiro v São Paulo (Niterói)

First university match
1966 Escola de Engenharia da Universidade Mackenzie v Faculdade de Medicina da Universidade de São Paulo (São Paulo)

First rugby school
1971 Colégio São Bento (São Paulo)

New Rugby Union formed
20 December 1972—Associacao Brasileira de Rugby, replaced União de Rugby do Brasil, founded 1963

Oldest club
São Paulo Athletic Club 1888

Number of referees
35

Number of coaches
4 (B class)

Biggest international victory
22–3 Paraguay 1973

Biggest international defeat
3–109 Argentina 1979

Beilby Alston Cup (Inter-State)
São Paulo won 23, Rio de Janeiro 16

University match results
Escola de Engenharia da Universidade Mackenzie won 4, Faculdade de Medicina da Universidade de São Paulo 13

Most capped players
13 Waldo Hoffmann (Fac. de Medicina da Universidade de São Paulo) 12 Alberto Moraes Barros Neto (São Paulo Athletic Club) 12 Paule Henry Bishop (São Paulo) 12 Robert Sydney Smith (São Paulo Athletic Club)

Brothers capped
D J, L K and J L V Bush (1964), A R and M H Truscott (1964), W E and J S Bennett (1971, 1973, 1975, 1977), R C and P H Bishop (1975, 1977), J L and J R Hughes (1961, 1964)

Double international
Brian Keen (4 caps for England 1968) won 4 caps for Brazil in 1971

Brazilian Championship winners
First Division: 1964 São Paulo Athletic Club. 1965 São Paulo Athletic Club. 1966 São Paulo Athletic Club. 1967 São Paulo Athletic Club. 1968 São Paulo Athletic Club. 1969 São Paulo Athletic Club. 1970 São Paulo Barbarians RFC. 1971 São Paulo Barbarians RFC. 1972 Fed. Universitária Paulista de Esportes. 1973 Fac. de Medicina da Universidade de São Paulo. 1974 São Paulo Athletic Club and Pasteur RC (shared). 1975 São Paulo Athletic Club. 1976 São Paulo Athletic Club and Niterói RFC (shared). 1977 São Paulo Athletic Club. 1978 São Paulo Athletic Club. 1979 Niterói RFC. 1980 Alphaville Tennis Club. 1981 Fac. de Medicina da Universidade de São Paulo. 1982 Alphaville Tennis Club

National Sevens winners
1966 São Paulo Athletic Club. 1967 São Paulo Athletic Club. 1968 Not held. 1969 São Paulo Athletic Club. 1970 São Paulo Athletic Club. 1971 São Paulo Barbarians RFC. 1972 Fac. de Medicina da Universidade de São Paulo and

Niteroi, 31 August 1936. The touring British team (above) before their match with a Brazilian Select XV (below). The team (from left to right) was: J A Waters (Selkirk, Scotland), W H Weston (Northampton, England), R W Shaw (Glasgow HSFP, Scotland), P Cooke (Richmond, England), Prince A Obolensky (Oxford University, England), R E Prescott (Harlequins, England), J S Moll (Lloyds Bank), J G A'Bear (Gloucester), R G S Hobbs (Richmond, England), E J Unwin (Rosslyn Park, England), J A Tallent (Blackheath, England), H J M Uren (Waterloo), W E Pratten (Blackheath, England), Brig. Glyn Hughes (Barbarians, referee). Middle row: C E Beamish (RAF, Ireland), P E Dunkley (Harlequins, England), T B Knowles (Birkenhead Park, England), B C Gadney (Leicester, England), F D Prentice (manager), P C Hordern (Gloucester, England), C V Boyle (Dublin University, Ireland). Front row: G E Hancock (Birkenhead Park, England), W O Chadwick (Cambridge University), J A Brett (Oxford University). One absentee from the photograph was Fred Hoskisson, president of Old Merchant Taylors in their centenary 1982.
The Brazilian team was (left to right): R Holland, H Tiplady, G A Turnbull, G Baker, J B N Wilson, A B P Smither, I J Swanson, J A Anderson. Seated: R G Tate, N Abdalla, R G Betts, A V Mackay, F E Trilsbach, M V Tilley, A Mitchell (touch-judge). Front: D Anderson.

Escola de Engenharia da Universidade Mackenzie (shared). 1973 Fac. de Medicina da Universidade de São Paulo. 1974 Fac. de Medicina da Universidade de São Paulo. 1975 São Paulo Athletic Club. 1976 Not held. 1977 São Paulo Barbarians RFC. 1978 São Paulo Barbarians RFC. 1979 Alphaville Tennis Club. 1980 Pasteur RC. 1981 Alphaville Tennis Club. 1982 Alphaville Tennis Club

International results

	W	D	L
Argentina			
1951 Buenos Aires			0–72
1961 Montevideo			0–66
1964 São Paulo			6–30
1971 Montevideo			6–50
1973 São Paulo			0–96
1975 Asuncion			6–64
1977 Tucuman			6–78
1979 Santiago			3–109
Chile			
1951 Buenos Aires			0–68
1961 Montevideo			5–34
1964 São Paulo		16–16	
1971 Montevideo			3–45
1973 São Paulo			3–22
1975 Asuncion			10–31
1977 Tucuman			27–33
1979 Vina del Mar			6–53
1981 Montevideo			3–33
Paraguay			
1971 Montevideo	12–6		
1973 São Paulo	22–3		
1975 Asuncion	19–6		
1977 Tucuman			13–25
1979 Santiago	16–6		
1981 Montevideo			3–35
Uruguay			
1951 Buenos Aires			10–17
1961 Montevideo			8–11
1964 São Paulo	15–8		
1971 Montevideo			11–37
1973 São Paulo			6–16
1975 Asuncion			7–38
1977 Tucuman			15–47
1979 Santiago			0–48
1981 Montevideo			0–77

Other matches

1965 Brazil 5 Oxford-Cambridge 49 (São Paulo). 1971 Brazil 8 Oxford-Cambridge 53 (São Paulo). 1962 Brazil 13 Uruguay 5 (São

The South African team which played a Rio de Janeiro XV at Niteroi during their tour of 1932. The team included two players who went on to become full Springboks—G D'Alton and J T Apsey, both of Western Province.

Paulo). 1970 Brazil 12 Paraguay 3 (Asuncion). 1974 Brazil 7 France 99 (São Paulo). 1981 Brazil 13 Chile 9 (São Paulo).

Junior internationals
Argentina 1972 L 0–144 1974 L 0–97 1978 L 0–84 1982 L 6–63. *Chile* 1972 L 0–54 1974 L 10–35 1978 L 7–27 1980 L 0–25 1982 L 4–56. *Paraguay* 1972 L 6–12 1974 W 17–7 1978 L 9–13 1980 L 3–34 1982 L 9–36. *Uruguay* 1972 L 9–36 1974 L 6–39 1978 L 3–58 1980 L 0–32 1982 L 4–21

BRITISH VIRGIN ISLANDS

Headquarters	British Virgin Islands RFC, Road Town, Tortola
Number of clubs	1
Number of players	30
Season	September–April
Temperatures	70°F (21°C) to 75°F (24°C)
Population	12 000

BRUNEI

Foundation	1975
Headquarters	c/o RBMR, CMM, BFPO 605
Main stadium	Panaga RFC Ground
Number of clubs	8
Number of players	500
Season	February–June
Temperatures	74°F (23°C) to 87°F (31°C)
Population	201 260

First match
1950

Most points in a season
72 Rick Preston (Panaga), 1978–9

Most tries in a season
14 David Dachtler (Panaga), 1975–6

Biggest club score
1978–9 Kukris 64, Royal Brunei Police 16

Most points in a match
32 (3T, 7C, 2P) Cliff Berry (Kukris 56, RBMR 0), 1978–9

Biggest representative match score
West of State 60 East of State 0, 1976–7

1978 Tour
New Zealand Armed Forces P 4 W 4 F 144 A 3

Brunei battle it out with Hong Kong in the Hong Kong Sevens in March 1983. Hong Kong won 26–0. (Colorsport.)

BULGARIA

Foundation	1967
Headquarters	c/o Conseil Central de L'Union Bulgare de Culture Physique etc des Sports, Boulevard Tolbukhine 18, Sofia
Colours	Red and white jerseys
Number of clubs	12
Number of players	900
Season	September–December and March–June
Temperatures	32°F (0°C) to 70°F (21°C)
Population	8 814 000

Affiliation
FIRA 1967

International results

	W	D	L
Czechoslovakia			
1973 Prague			0–45
1975 Kostinbrod			0–40
1976 Budejovice			6–28
German Dem. Rep.			
1963 Birlad			3–9
1974 Varna	12–0		
1976 Potsdam			0–6
1977 Nessebar	10–0		
1978 Varna	18–8		
1978 Varna	8–0		
1979 Magdeburg			7–8
1979 Berlin	13–4		
1979 Burgas	15–4		
1980 Rathenow			3–8
1980 Brandenburg			7–10
1981 Constinbrod	7–0		
1981 Sofia	16–0		
1982 Leipzig			3–6
1982 Sofia	16–3		
Italy			
1969 Sofia			0–17
Soviet Union			
1976 Burgas			13–27
Yugoslavia			
1968 Zagora	29–6		
1969 Pancevo			6–22

Under 19 Tournament
1982 (Prague) Romania 47 Bulgaria 0, Soviet Union 42 Bulgaria 0, Czechoslovakia 24 Bulgaria 0, German Dem. Rep. 4 Bulgaria 0.

CAMEROON

Number of clubs	2
Number of players	100
Season	April–November
Temperatures	75°F (24°C) to 90°F (32°C)
Population	7 914 000

CANADA

Foundation	1929, re-formed 1965
Headquarters	333 River Road, Ottawa, Ontario, K1L 8B9
Colours	Red jerseys with white maple leaf vests
Number of clubs	192 (110 in 1972, 154 in 1975)
Number of players	9800 (5200 in 1972, 6300 in 1975)

During England's tour of Canada and USA in 1982 Steve Smith gave his fellow tourists a laugh when he turned out for a training session with a few items borrowed from some gridiron friends. (Colorsport.)

Season May–October (September–May, British Columbia)
Temperatures 30°F (−1°C) to 63°F (17°C)
Population 23 499 000

First match
1865 in Montreal

Oldest club
Montreal FC 1868

Number of referees
240

Longest playing career
26 years D L 'Buzz' Moore (Vancouver Meralomas) 1938–64

Oldest player
Campbell Forbes (Victoria Ebb Tide), aged 69 in 1979

Longest unbeaten sequence
59 matches The Kats September 1960 to October 1963

Most points in an international
9 Barrie Burnham v Fiji 1970

Most capped players
19 Ro Hindson (British Columbia)
18 Spence McTavish (British Columbia)
15 Mike Luke (Newfoundland)

Interprovincial championship
1958 British Columbia 18 Eastern Canada 9 (Toronto). 1959 British Columbia 24 Eastern Canada 3 (Vancouver). 1960–65 not played. 1966 British Columbia 51 Ontario 3 (Vancouver). 1967 British Columbia 27 Quebec 6 (Montreal). 1968 British Columbia 13 Quebec 3 (Vancouver). 1969 British Columbia 21 Quebec 9 (Toronto). 1970 British Columbia 26 Ontario 6 (Vancouver). 1971 Ontario 27 British Columbia 17 (Toronto). 1972 Ontario 7 Alberta 3 (Victoria). 1973 Ontario 17 Alberta 7 (Ottawa). 1974 British Columbia 49 Nuffield 3 (Vancouver). 1975 British Columbia 43 Ontario 6 (Halifax). 1976 British Columbia 35 Ontario 6 (Victoria). 1977 British Columbia 7 Ontario 3 (Toronto). 1978 British Columbia 41 Quebec 3 (Calgary). 1979 British Columbia 36 Ontario 7 (Ottawa). 1980 British Columbia 48 Ontario 7 (Burnaby). 1981 British Columbia 9 Ontario 3 (Ottawa). 1982 Ontario 21 British Columbia 9 (Edmonton).

England toured Canada and the USA in 1982, when the highlights were matches against the Pacific Coast Grizzlies (top), against the Cougars (above) and a rousing international against Canada at Barnaby (facing page). (Colorsport.)

Rounsfell Cup
1983 Mevalomas 17 James Bay AA 16

Miller Cup
1983 Mevalomas 28 Kats 21

Hong Kong Sevens
1983 L 0–14 Scottish Border Club, L 0–16 Western Samoa, W 28–0 Papua New Guinea, W 26–0 Sri Lanka, W 14–4 Bahrain, W 14–8 Hong Kong. Plate final: L 6–30 South Korea

Incoming tours 1983
Middlesex: D 9–9 Vancouver, L 10–16 British Columbia.
Selkirk: W 14–3 Bolmy Beach, W 33–0 Toronto Branch Union, W 35–9 Mid Ontario Branch, W 19–12 Ontario.
West of Scotland: W 13–9 Toronto Saracens, W 21–9 Toronto XV, W 13–6 Ontario, W 11–0 Ottawa Beavers Bytown Blues.
Gosforth: W 17–3 Toronto Barbarians XV, W 12–0 Niagara Branch Union, W 20–6 Bytown Blues, W 30–16 E. Ontario Branch, L 12–14 Ontario.

Outgoing tours 1982
British Columbia to USA L 6–26 Pacific Coast Grizzlies, W 15–3 Northern California, W 13–0 Southern California

Edmonton Tigers to GB, Ireland
W 16–4 Bancroft, W 29–12 Machen, W 21–15 Llanelli Wanderers, W 29–7 Dolphin XV, L 9–11 Old Wesley XV, L 6–22 London Welsh XV

International results

	W	D	L
British Isles			
1966 Toronto			8–19
England			
1967 Vancouver			0–29
1977 Ottawa			13–26
1982 Burnaby			6–43
England U23			
1977 Toronto			9–29
Fiji			
1970 Burnaby			17–35
France			
1978 Calgary			9–24
1979 Paris			15–34
Italy			
1983 Vancouver	19–13		
1983 Toronto			9–37
Japan			
1932 Osaka			8–9
1932 Tokyo			5–38
1982 Osaka			18–24
1982 Tokyo			6–16
New Zealand			
1980 Burnaby			10–43
Tonga			
1974 Vancouver			14–40
USA			
1977 Burnaby	17–6		

Incoming tours

	P	W	D	L	F	A
1905 New Zealand	2*	2	0	0	108	12
1913 New Zealand	3	3	0	0	102	0
1925 New Zealand	2	2	0	0	117	4
1930 Japan	7	6	1	0	134	61
1936 New Zealand	2	2	0	0	59	3
1948 Australia	3	3	0	0	104	17
1954 New Zealand	3	3	C	0	118	17
1957 Barbarians	6	6	0	0	227	23
1958 Australia	3	2	0	1	56	31
1959 British Isles	2	2	0	0	86	17
1963 Japan	5	4	0	1	84	60
1964 New Zealand	2	2	0	0	45	6
1964 Scotland	5	5	0	0	172	16
1964 Fiji	2	2	0	0	36	8
1966 British Isles	2	1	0	1	22	16
1967 Australia	2	2	0	0	35	17
1967 England	5	5	0	0	164	9
1967 New Zealand	2	2	0	0	76	6
1970 Fiji	1	1	0	0	35	17
1972 New Zealand	1	1	0	0	31	3
1973 Wales	5	5	0	0	288	41
1974 Tonga	2	2	0	0	59	30
1976 Japan	5	1	0	4	80	153
1976 Barbarians	6	6	0	0	346	26
1977 England U23	6	6	0	0	147	63
1978 France	2	2	0	0	41	19
1980 New Zealand	1	1	0	0	43	10
1980 Wales 'B'	3	3	0	0	82	18
1982 England	2	2	0	0	95	9

*matches played in USA

Outgoing tours

	P	W	D	L	F	A
1902 British Isles	23	8	2	13	114	243
1932 Japan	7	5	0	2	150	82
1962 British Isles	16	1	1	14	89	289
1971 Wales	5	2	0	3	66	141
1979 Britain/France	6	3	1	2	68	75
1981 Argentina	5	4	0	1	71	132
1982 Japan	6	4	0	2	145	67

1978 Baltimore			7–12
1979 Toronto	19–12		
1980 Saranac Lake	16–0		
1981 Calgary	6–3		
1982 Albany		3–3	
Wales U23			
1962 Cardiff			0–8
Wales XV			
1971 Cardiff			10–56
1973 Toronto			20–58
Wales B			
1980 Burnaby			7–24

Other matches

1962 D 3–3 Barbarians (Gosforth)
1976 L 4–29 Barbarians
1979 W 14–4 France B (Lille)

CAYMAN ISLANDS

Foundation 1972
Headquarters Cayman RFC, c/o Allan Gee, PO Box 1519, Grand Cayman
Main stadium Cayman RFC Ground
Colours Green jerseys, white collars
Number of clubs 3
Number of players 60
Season September–April
Temperatures 60°F (16°C) to 80°F (27°C)
Population 20 000

Joined Rugby Football Union
1971

Outgoing tours
1978 to England
1982 Bahamas
1983 Australia, New Zealand

Trophy wins
Mayfair Cup (v Jamaica)
Cafenol Shield (Jamaican League Trophy)

CHILE

Foundation 1948
Headquarters Federacion de Rugby de Chile, Santa Beatriz 191, Provindecia, Santiago
Number of clubs 25
Number of players 2500
Season April–November
Temperatures 45°F (7°C) to 65°F (18°C)
Population 10 857 128

International results

	W	D	L
Argentina			
1951 Buenos Aires			3–13
1958 Santiago			0–14
1961 Montevideo			3–11
1964 São Paulo			8–30

1967 Buenos Aires			0–18
1969 Santiago			0–54
1971 Montevideo			3–20
1973 São Paulo			3–60
1975 Asuncion			3–45
1977 Tucuman			10–25
1979 Santiago			15–34
1983 Buenos Aires			6–46
Brazil			
1951 Buenos Aires	68–0		
1961 Montevideo	34–3		
1964 São Paulo		16–16	
1971 Montevideo	45–3		
1973 São Paulo	22–3		
1975 Asuncion	31–10		
1977 Tucuman	33–27		
1979 Vina del Mar	53–6		
1981 Montevideo	33–3		
1981 São Paulo			9–13
France			
1960 Santiago			6–55
Paraguay			
1971 Montevideo	40–0		
1973 São Paulo	27–3		
1975 Asuncion	44–3		
1977 Tucuman	22–3		
1979 Santiago	27–13		
1981 Montevideo	33–3		
1983 Buenos Aires	24–12		
Peru			
1958 Vina del Mar	31–3		
Uruguay			
1951 Buenos Aires			3–8
1958 Santiago	34–9		
1961 Montevideo	28–5		
1964 São Paulo			8–15
1967 Buenos Aires	16–11		
1969 Santiago	13–6		
1971 Montevideo	11–6		
1973 São Paulo			10–13
1975 Asuncion	15–7		
1977 Tucuman			18–21
1979 Santiago		9–9	
1981 Montevideo			3–33
1983 Buenos Aires			3–25

Junior internationals

Brazil 1972 W 54–0 1974 W 35–10 1978 W 27–7 1980 W 25–0 1982 W 56–4. *Argentina* 1972 L 0–35 1974 L 4–69 1976 L 9–68 1978 L 3–58 1982 L 6–41. *Paraguay* 1972 W 36–7 1974 W 44–6 1976 W 44–7 1978 W 35–3 1980 W 13–6 1982 L 14–19. *Uruguay* 1972 W 12–10 1974 L 10–20 1976 L 3–23 1978 L 9–17 1980 L 3–10 1982 L 12–27

COOK ISLANDS

Number of clubs 3
Number of players 200
International results
1981 Cook Islands 15 Italy 6 (Rarotonga)
1982 French Polynesia 28 Cook Islands 14; Cook Islands 42 French Polynesia 24

CYPRUS

Headquarters	Dhekelia Lions RFC (founded 1961)
Number of clubs	2 (including RAF Cyprus)
Number of players	60

CZECHOSLOVAKIA

Foundation	1926
Headquarters	Československá Sekce Rugby, Praha 1, NA Poříči 12
Main stadium	Prague Stadium
Colours	Red, blue and white jerseys, white shorts
Number of clubs	20
Number of players	2000
Season	September – December and April–June
Temperatures	34°F (1°C) to 60°F (16°C)
Population	15 178 000

First official match
1926 Brno v Prague

Oldest clubs
SK Moravská Slavia Brno, AFK Žižka Brno, Slavia Bratislava, 1926

Referees
95

Coaches
110

Tour matches
1982 (Tunisia): Tunisian XV 4 TJ Praga 23, Tunisia 22 TJ Praga 32

National Cup winners
1977 Sokol Vyškov 1978 TJ Praga 1979 TJ Praga 1980 Tatra Smíchov 1981 Tatra Smíchov 1982 TJ Praga

Club championship
1948 TJ Praga 1949 ATK 1950 Sokol Brno 1951–4 ATK 1955 TJ Praga 1956–8 Slávie Praha 1959–60 TJ Praga 1961 Slávie Praha 1962–3 TJ Praga 1964 Slávie Praha 1965 Zbrojovka Brno 1966 TJ Praga 1967–8 Sparta Praga 1969 Slávie Praha 1970 ATK 1971 Slávie Praha 1972 TJ Praga 1973 Sparta Praha 1974–80 TJ Vyškov 1981 Vyskov 1982 TJ Praga 1983 TJ Praga

Biggest international win
54–0 German Dem. Rep. 1976

Biggest international defeat
3–68 France 1972

Longest international career
1946–65 A. Barchánek (Slávie Praha)

International results

	W	D	L
Belgium			
1967 Prague	46–6		
1971 Ricany	25–12		
1979 Prague	44–9		
1982 Brussels	21–6		
Bulgaria			
1973 Prague	45–0		
1975 Kostinbrod	40–0		
1976 Budejovice	28–6		
Denmark			
1971 Gothenburg	29–3		
Fed. Rep. Germany			
1931 Leipzig			0–38
1934 Prague			9–19
1957 Brunn	9–3		
1958 Hanover	11–0		
1963 Prague			3–6
1965 Odenwald			6–25
1967 Prague	9–6		
1969 Hamburg	18–11		
1972 Ostrava	47–3		
1974 Hanover		6–6	
1976 Ricany	22–6		
1979 Brno	27–6		
France			
1957 Toulouse			3–28
1957 Liberec			3–30
1957 Moscow			19–38
1966 Prague			12–36
1968 Prague			6–19
1969 Besançon			14–34
1970 Prague			6–53
1972 Colmar			3–68
1974 Bourg-en-Bresse			3–28
1977 Hagondange			0–63

TJ Praga, the Czechoslovakian club champions, during their tour of Tunisia in October 1982. (Eduard Krutzner.)

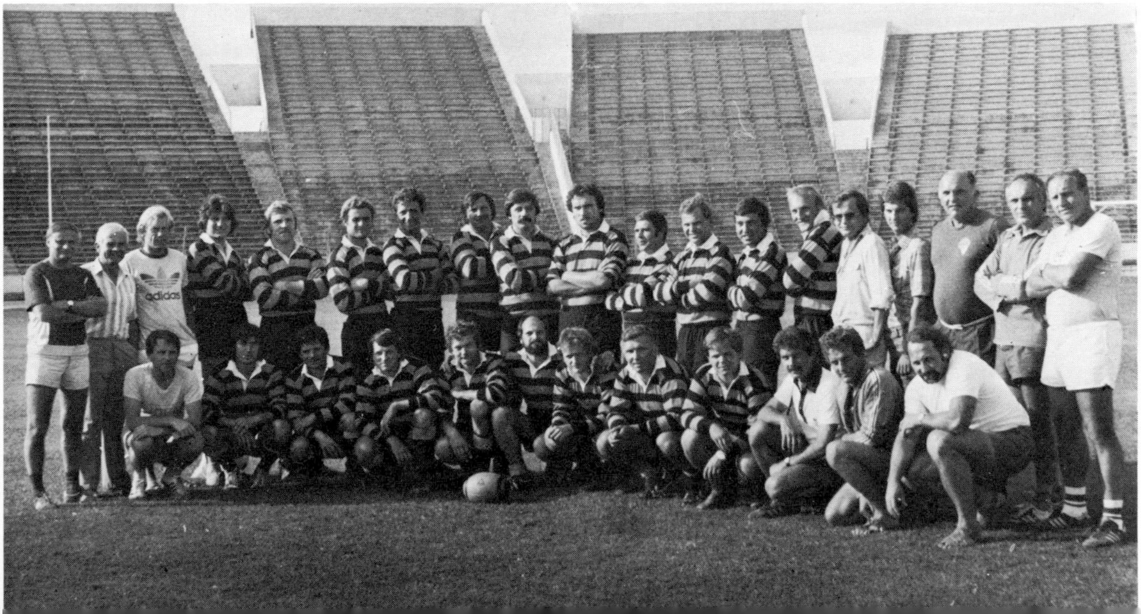

German Dem. Rep.			
1954 Gottwaldov	26–6		
1954 Kuadno	44–11		
1959 Bucharest	22–0		
1959 Berlin		0–0	
1959 Weibenfels		3–3	
1960 Zwickau	9–0		
1961 Prague	16–10		
1962 Plock	8–6		
1964 Ostritz			3–11
1971 Prague	8–0		
1972 Hennigsdorf			11–13
1973 Sumperk	44–6		
1974 Varna	56–4		
1974 Potsdam	16–9		
1976 Prague	54–0		
1978 Varna	17–3		
Italy			
1933 Milan			3–7
1933 Prague			3–12
1948 Parma			0–17
1949 Prague			6–14
1955 Rome			6–17
1956 Prague			9–19
1965 Prague			5–14
1965 St Dona			0–3
1965 Livorno			0–11
1970 Prague			3–11
1973 Rovigo		3–3	
1975 Reggio			9–49
1977 Prague			4–10
Morocco			
1967 Casablanca	6–0		
1972 Millau			3–21
Netherlands			
1946 Bussum	14–8		
1966 Prague	16–5		
1977 Hilversum	9–7		
Poland			
1959 Bucharest			6–9
1960 Gera	6–5		
1961 Brno	9–3		
1962 Pruzskow	17–0		
1963 Hunedvara		0–0	
1969 Havirov	25–8		
1972 Warsaw			9–23
1973 Prague	16–6		
1974 Varna			15–22
1975 Leningrad			6–27
1976 Warsaw	16–15		
1976 Lvov			3–16
1977 Tbilisi	21–4		
1978 Warsaw			3–14
1978 Kharkov	10–9		
Romania			
1927 Presburg			6–26
1949 Prague			5–20
1955 Brno			0–3
1957 Moscow			11–12
1959 Bucharest			0–11
1960 Glaucau			3–13
1961 Prague			12–19
1962 Piotrokow/ Tribunalski			6–11
1963 Bucharest			3–23
1963 Deva			0–3
1964 Bauzen			3–14
1966 Prague		9–9	
1968 Bucharest			3–17
1968 Ricany			9–18
1969 Bucharest			6–42
1972 Vyskov			3–22
1974 Varna			15–18
1974 Sumperk			6–16
1976 —			10–29
1978 Bucharest			6–60
1978 Kharkov			0–28
Soviet Union			
1974 Moscow			4–18
1975 Leningrad			6–27
1976 Lvov	12–7		
1976 Ricany	9–6		
1976 Lvov			6–15
1977 Tblisi			12–39
1978 Kharkov			4–18
Spain			
1967 Madrid	9–8		
1971 Madrid	12–6		
1975 Prague			7–13
1978 Barcelona			13–20
Sweden			
1965 Prague	42–0		
1967 Uppsala	27–3		
1971 Gothenburg		9–9	
1977 Gothenburg	50–12		
Switzerland			
1975 Lausanne	23–6		
1983 Nafels	14–9		
Tunisia			
1983 Prague	14–7		
Yugoslavia			
1968 Split	12–10		
1970 Havirov	19–3		
1970 Zagreb	9–0		
1973 Prague	32–3		
1975 Gottwaldov	28–3		
1982 Prague	17–9		

Under 19 Tournament

1982 (Prague): Romania 47 Bulgaria 0, Czechoslovakia 9 German Dem. Rep. 4, Soviet Union 42 Bulgaria 0, Romania 30 Czechoslovakia 4, Czechoslovakia 24 Bulgaria 0, Soviet Union 22 German Dem. Rep. 3, German Dem. Rep. 4 Bulgaria 0, Romania 18 Soviet Union 16, Romania 54 German Dem. Rep. 0, Soviet Union 11 Czechoslovakia 6. Summary: Romania 1, Soviet Union 2, Czechoslovakia 3, German Dem. Rep 4, Bulgaria 5

DENMARK

Foundation 1950

Headquarters Dansk Rugby Union, Idraettens hus, Brøndby Stadion 20, 2600 Glostrup

Main stadium	Brøndby Stadium, Copenhagen (capacity 5000)
Colours	Red jerseys, white shorts
Number of clubs	19
Number of players	1814
Season	April–June and September–November
Temperatures	32°F (0°C) to 60°F (16°C)
Population	5 111 000

Oldest club
Rugbyklubben Speed, 31 March 1950

Principal clubs
IHF-Aarhus, If. Comet, CSR/Nanok, RK Speed, Odense RC, PTI Exiles, Farum RK, Frederiksberg RK, Lindo RSC, RK Lynet, Holluf Pile, Brøndby RK, Tonder RK, Gladsaxe RK, Holstebro RK, Hamlet RK, Köbenhaun Old Boys Rugby Football Club

Cup finals
1973 Odense 7 Speed 46 1974 Comet 12 Speed 6 1975 Comet 28 CSR 3 1976 Comet 4 Exiles 20 1977 Comet 9 Exiles 27 1978 Comet 6 Exiles 0 1979 Lynet 6 Exiles 15 1980 Exiles 11 Lynet 3 1981 Exiles 30 Speed 15 1982 Lynet 18 CSR 0

International results

	W	D	L
Belgium			
1973 Brussels			0–38
1975 Copenhagen			6–10
1979 Brussels			8–52
1981 Dinant			9–34
1982 Copenhagen			12–16
Czechoslovakia			
1971 Gothenburg			3–29
German Dem. Rep.			
1964 Malmö			0–21
1972 Rostock			12–20
Netherlands			
1971 Gothenburg			3–24
1973 Hilversum			0–62
1978 Hilversum			9–52
1979 Copenhagen			3–12
1983 Hilversum			3–25
Norway			
1979 Copenhagen	30–12		
1980 Oslo			3–41
Poland			
1964 Malmö			6–25
Portugal			
1981 Copenhagen			16–45
Sweden			
1949 Stockholm			0–6
1950 Copenhagen			0–14
1951 Stockholm			3–30
1953 Gothenburg			6–16
1954 Copenhagen			6–9
1958 Norkopping		5–5	
1959 Copenhagen			6–8
1960 Stockholm			3–11
1961 Odense		12–12	
1962 Malmö			8–9
1963 Copenhagen	6–0		
1964 Malmö			3–14
1965 Aalborg			3–6
1966 Gothenburg			0–18
1967 Copenhagen			6–9
1968 Helsinborg			0–11
1969 Copenhagen		9–9	
1970 Vanersborg			0–8
1971 Koge			5–18
1971 Gothenburg			3–11
1972 Vasteras			12–26
1973 Aarhus	12–7		
1974 Enkoping			0–24
1975 Copenhagen			9–20
1976 Karlstad			9–36
1977 Odense			3–26
1978 Malmö			3–40
1980 Aarhus			4–20
1981 Copenhagen			6–35
1982 Lund			0–25
Switzerland			
1981 Lausanne	20–16		
1981 Lausanne			21–34
Tunisia			
1980 Copenhagen			13–19
Yugoslavia			
1982 Zenica			4–46

DHAHRAN

Foundation 1980
Headquarters c/o Dhahran Rugby Union Football Club, Box 1129, Aranco, Dhahran, Saudi Arabia
Colours Red jerseys, white shorts
Number of clubs 2
Number of players 100
Season September–April
Temperatures 50°F (10°C) to 90°F (30°C)

1982 results

Abu Dhabi	W	8–3	(H)	W	14–0	(A)
Bahrain	W	4–3	(H)	L	3–10	(A)
Dubai	W	21–0	(H)	L	0–12	(A)
Kuwait	L	0–3	(H)	L	8–24	(A)
Muscat	W	12–10	(H)	L	3–10	(A)
Qatar	W	20–7	(H)	W	14–6	(A)

1983 results

Bahrain	L	4–22	(H)	L	12–14	(A)
Qatar	L	6–12	(A)	W	17–3	(H)

DUBAI

Foundation 1969
Headquarters Dubai Exiles RFC, c/o The Secretary, PO Box 4987, Dubai, U.A.E.
Main stadium Country Club Ground, Quarry/Dwir Road, Dubai
Colours White with black hoop
Number of clubs 1 (2 teams)
Number of players 50
Season September–April
Temperatures 50°F (10°C) to 90°F (30°C)

1982 results

Abu Dhabi	W	3–0	(H)	L	0–13	(A)
Bahrain	L	0–4	(H)	L	0–6	(A)
Dhahran	W	12–0	(H)	L	0–21	(A)
Kuwait	L	6–10	(H)			
Muscat	L	9–25	(H)	L	8–9	(A)
Qatar	W	44–3	(H)	W	4–3	(A)

1983 results

Qatar	L	6–15	(A)

Outgoing tour
1982 Manila

Incoming tour
1982 Egypt

ECUADOR

Headquarters Quito RFC
Number of clubs 1
Number of players 30
Season April–November
Temperatures 50°F (10°C) to 75°F (24°C)
Population 7 814 000

EGYPT

Foundation 1980
Headquarters Cairo Rugby c/o PO Box 2034, International Telephone & Telegraph Corporation (ITT), 1 Sharia Bustan, Cairo, Egypt
Main stadium Ma'adi Club, Ma'adi, Cairo
Colours Red, white & black hoops
Number of clubs 1
Number of players 25
Season September–April
Temperatures 50°F (10°C) to 100°F (38°C)
Population 46 000 000

First club
Cairo RFC, 1980

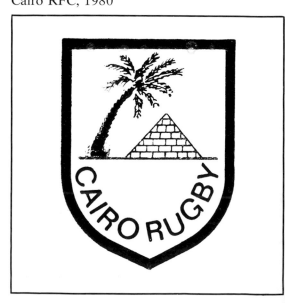

Outgoing tours
1980 Cyprus, Dubai
1981 Dubai, USA, Cyprus
1982 Sharjah, Bahrain, Dubai
1983 Sharjah, Jordan

Incoming tours
1981 Gulf, Lebanon, Bahrain
1982 Cyprus, Sharjah, Dhahran
1983 Kuwait, Muscat, Paris, Jordan, Cyprus

Dubai sevens
1980 Plate finalists
1981 Final: Cairo 12 Muscat 16

Sharjah tournament
1981 Won Plate competition
1982 Final: Cairo 3 Dubai 0

DHL Middle East tournament
1982 (Bahrain) Final: Cairo 0 Abu Dhabi 3

FEDERAL REPUBLIC OF GERMANY

Foundation	1900
Headquarters	Deutscher Rugby Verband, Bundesleistungszentrum Nord, Ferdinand Wilhelm Fricke Weg 2A, 3000 Hanover 1
Main stadium	Maifield, Berlin
Colours	White jerseys
Number of clubs	67
Number of players	3581
Season	September–June
Temperatures	32°F (0°C) to 60°F (16°C)
Population	61 332 000

Oldest club
Heidelberger Ruderklub, 1872

Player of the year poll 1981
1 Horst Kemmling (TSV Victoria) 2 Manfred Wundram (1897 Linden) 3 Hans-Joachim Schmitt (TSV Handschuhsheim) 4 Peter Mehl (RC Rottweil) 5 Dexter Landell (Germania List) 6 Jurgen Merz (RG Heidelberg) 7 Roger Sloane (Germania List) 8 Martin Haas (Frankfurt 1880) 9 Werner Morgenroth (1878 Hanover) 10 Claus Himmer (1878 Hanover)

League championship finals
1980 Rudergesellschaft Heidelberg 16 FV 1897 Linden Hanover 10
1981 SC Germania-List (Hanover) 28 Heidelberger Ruderklub 19
1982 DSV 1878 Hanover 15 Rudergesellschaft Heidelberg 6

National cup finals
1980 Rudergesellschaft Heidelberg 3 SC Germania List (Hanover) 7
1981 DSV 1878 Hanover 28 Deutscher RC Hanover 12
1982 TSV Victoria Hanover 9 Rudergesellschaft Heidelberg 3

Universities championship 1982
1 Berlin Combined Colleges, 2 Tübingen University, 3 Bonn University

Most capped player
36 Robert Twele (DSV Hanover)

Incoming tours
1981 Queen's College Cambridge
W 19–11 Baden-Württemberg District
W 30–10 Rudergesellschaft Heidelberg
1981 Finchley
W 19–12 Berlin Combined Clubs
Finchley II L 0–96 Berlin and L 0–92 Berlin Sports Verein 1892
1981 Other matches: TSV Pforzheim 20 Norkopping (Sweden) 10—TSV Handschuhsheim Heidelberg 30 RC Marciac (France) 22—Baden-Württemberg XV 44 Wellington XV (New Zealand) 15—SV Ricklingen 1908 Hannover 10 Fiji Military XV 80

Outgoing tours
1981 Berlin Sports Verein 92
W 30–27 Fittja RC Stockholm
L 0–12 City of Stockholm

1981 RC Rottweil
L 15–26 TJ Prague
L 37–40 RC Colmar (France)

1981 Other matches: Lok Olomouc (Czechoslovakia) 33 TV 1834 Pforzheim 16—APSAP (Paris) 0 ASV Köln 8

Rugby action in the Federal Republic of Germany . . . the FRG Colts (above) line-up against Scotland Colts in Berlin in 1982, Berlin RC in their match against a USA Forces XV (above right) for the Simper Cup in Berlin in 1982, and (right) Hanover 1878 play Berlin RC in 1982. (Deutsher Rugby Verband.)

1983 To Wales: South Wales Police 37 Federal Republic of Germany 16, Maesteg 21 Federal Republic of Germany 4

Olympic Games
1900 Frankfurt 17 France 27 (Paris)

First overseas club match
Frankfurt 1880 v Blackheath, 14 April 1890

Centenary
SC 1880 Frankfurt celebrated centenary in 1980

International results

	W	D	L
Belgium			
1937 Dusseldorf	34–0		
1952 Hanover	16–9		
1956 Huy	16–0		
1957 Cologne	33–3		
1959 Luttich	8–6		
1961 Offenbach	52–3		
1962 Tirlemont	50–3		
1964 Hurth	11–3		
1971 Luttich	27–9		
1972 Bonn	28–3		
1973 Verviers	20–9		
1974 Varel	24–3		
1975 Hanover	43–3		
Czechoslovakia			
1931 Leipzig	38–0		
1934 Prague	19–9		
1957 Brunn			3–9
1958 Hanover			0–11
1963 Prague	6–3		
1965 Odenwald	25–6		
1967 Prague			6–9
1969 Hamburg			11–18
1972 Ostrava			3–47
1974 Hanover		6–6	
1976 Ricany			6–22
1979 Hanover			6–27
France			
1927 Paris			5–30
1927 Frankfurt	17–16		
1928 Hanover			3–14
1929 Paris			0–24
1930 Berlin			0–31
1931 Paris			0–34
1932 Frankfurt			4–20
1933 Paris			17–38
1934 Hanover			9–13
1935 Paris			3–18
1936 Berlin			14–19
1936 Hanover			3–6
1937 Paris			6–27
1938 Frankfurt	3–0		
1938 Bucharest			5–8
1954 Grenoble			3–25
1954 Parma			3–28
1955 Hanover			0–16
1956 Toulon			6–32
1957 Berlin			3–11
1958 Nantes		6–6	
1959 Hanover			0–27
1960 Clermont-Ferrand			6–14
1961 Heidelberg			9–27
1962 Dijon			11–53
1963 Frankfurt			9–16
1964 Vichy			3–34
1965 Hanover			3–8
1966 Chalon-sur-Saone			6–8
1967 Hamburg			0–22
1968 Lons–Le Saunier			8–26
1969 Cologne			6–20
1969 Le Creusot			6–33
1970 Heidelberg			3–18
1972 Besancon			9–35
1972 Hanover			0–11
1973 Le Creusot			0–31
1975 Heidelberg			12–24
1977 Auxerre			3–50
1982 Heidelberg			15–53
1983 Bourg-en-Bresse			0–84
Italy			
1936 Berlin	19–8		
1937 Milan	6–3		
1937 Paris			7–9
1938 Stuttgart	10–0		
1939 Milan	12–3		
1940 Stuttgart			0–4
1952 Padua			6–14
1953 Hanover			3–21
1955 Milan			8–24
1956 Heidelberg			3–12
1957 Milan			0–8
1960 Hanover			5–11
1961 Piacenza			0–19
1962 Berlin			11–13
1964 Bologna			3–17
1966 Berlin		3–3	
1968 Venice			14–22
1974 Milan			10–16
1981 Rovigo			0–23
1982 Hanover			3–23
Morocco			
1975 Heidelberg	19–11		
1976 Casablanca			3–30
1979 Hanover			6–13
1980 Casablanca			6–22
Netherlands			
1933 Dusseldorf	23–0		
1934 Maastricht	21–0		
1935 Cologne	11–5		
1936 Hilversum	28–16		
1937 Hilversum	23–6		
1958 Eindhoven	24–0		
1959 Heidelberg	39–0		
1960 Breukelen	42–6		
1961 Hurth	14–6		
1962 The Hague	37–6		
1963 Russelsheim			12–13
1964 The Hague	18–5		
1965 Berlin	48–8		
1966 The Hague	12–0		
1967 Hanover	6–0		
1968 The Hague	11–0		
1969 Offenbach	14–13		
1970 The Hague	29–3		

1971	Bonn	14–9		
1972	Apeldoorn	17–13		
1974	Wageningen			21–32
1976	Hilversum		13–13	
1976	Hanover		13–13	
1977	Hilversum			9–10
1980	Hilversum			10–16
1981	Hanover	13–10		
Poland				
1958	Krakow	11–3		
1959	Braunschweig			8–9
1960	Rzeszow	8–3		
1961	Hanover	11–3		
1975	Warsaw			6–29
Portugal				
1974	Hanover	20–10		
Romania				
1936	Hamburg	37–9		
1937	Paris	30–0		
1938	Bucharest	8–3		
1958	Brussels			0–9
1964	Bucharest			3–19
1965	Hanover			8–9
1967	Bucharest			5–27
1969	Hanover			3–6
1972	Bucharest	11–10		
1973	Heidelberg			9–33
1982	Bucharest			18–60
1983	Heidelberg			12–26
Soviet Union				
1977	Hanover			16–22
1978	Kharkov			9–64
1981	Hanover	10–7		
1982	Moscow			9–31
Spain				
1929	Barcelona	24–15		
1930	Dresden	5–0		
1952	Madrid	17–6		
1954	Frankfurt		6–6	
1957	Barcelona	16–3		
1959	Heidelberg	19–14		
1960	Barcelona			3–9
1962	Hanover	14–6		
1979	Heidelberg			0–13
Sweden				
1977	Stockholm	32–9		
1977	Berlin			11–16
1979	Stockholm	10–4		
Switzerland				
1978	Geneva	18–0		
Tunisia				
1981	Heidelberg	30–9		
Yugoslavia				
1974	Markarska	20–8		
1980	Hanover		6–6	
1980	Kardeljevo	16–0		

Representative matches

1980 Federal Republic of Germany 13 BAOR 16—Federal Republic of Germany 15 RAF Germany 26

1981 Federal Republic of Germany 8 BAOR 13

1982 Federal Republic of Germany 11 BAOR 3—Federal Republic of Germany 10 RAF Germany 23

Colts matches

1980 Federal Republic of Germany 12 Netherlands 12—Federal Republic of Germany 28 Belgium 4

1982 Federal Republic of Germany 15 Scotland 12 (Berlin)—Federal Republic of Germany 16 Spain 10 (Geneva)—Federal Republic of Germany 10 Italy 48 (Geneva)—Federal Republic of Germany 0 Morocco 29 (Geneva)—Federal Republic of Germany 18 Belgium 13 (Lüttich)

1983 Federal Republic of Germany 29 Netherlands 3 (Heidelberg)

Under 23s

1980 Federal Republic of Germany 25 Belgium 3

Berlin Tournament 1983

GB and USA Services 22 Berlin XV 19, Racing Club of France 56 Colmar 7, Racing Club of France 68 Berlin XV 16, GB and USA Services 11 Colmar 33

FIJI

Foundation	1913
Headquarters	FRU Offices, PO Box 1234, Suva
Main stadium	Fiji National Stadium, (Fiji Sports Council) (capacity 30 000)
Colours	White jerseys, blue shorts
Number of clubs	600
Number of players	11 000
Season	April–October
Temperatures	70°F (21°C) to 75°F (24°C)
Population	650 000

First match

1884

First clubs

Civil Service, Fiji Constabulary 1904

F.R.U.

First overseas match
1924 v Western Samoa, Apia

Number of sub-unions
54

First major incoming tour
Maoris 1938

First major outgoing tour
New Zealand 1939 (Fiji won 8, drew 1 of 9 matches)

Record win on major tour
Western Provinces (Argentina) 0 Fiji 84

Recent major tours

		P	W	D	L	F	A
1964	Wales	5	2	1	2	90	80
1970	Britain	14	6	1	7	168	163
1974	New Zealand	13	8	0	5	252	188
1976	Australia	13	5	0	8	250	201
1980	New Zealand	12	4	0	8	164	271
1980	Argentina	7	4	0	3	245	158
1982	Scotland/England	10	0	0	10	126	327

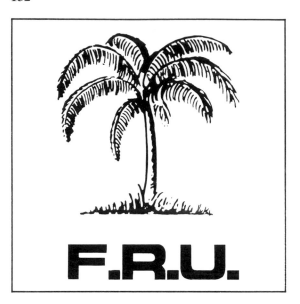

Fiji's pre-match 'war dance' before playing England at Twickenham 1982. (Geo. Herringshaw.)

Stuart Barnes races through to score a try for the South and South West against Fiji at Redruth in 1982. (Colorsport.)

Hong Kong Sevens

1983 W 16–0 Tonga, W 32–4 Thailand, W 40–0 Brunei, W 42–0 Hong Kong, W 20–0 Japan, W 14–8 Scottish Border Club. *Final*: L 4–14 Australia

International results

	W	D	L
Argentina			
1980 Buenos Aires			22–34
1980 Buenos Aires			16–38
Australia			
1952 Sydney			9–15
1952 Sydney	17–15		
1954 Brisbane			19–22
1954 Sydney	18–16		
1961 Brisbane			6–24
1961 Sydney			14–20
1961 Melbourne		3–3	
1976 Sydney			6–22
1976 Brisbane			9–21
1976 Sydney			15–27
1980 Suva			9–22
England			
1973 Suva			12–13
1979 Suva			7–19
1982 Twickenham			19–60
France			
1964 Paris			3–21
1979 Suva			4–13
Ireland			
1976 Suva			0–8
Italy			
1980 Suva	12–3		
Maoris			
1939 Hamilton	14–4		
New Zealand			
1968 Suva			6–33
1980 Suva			6–30
1980 Auckland			0–33
Scotland			
1982 Murrayfield			12–32
Wales			
1969 Suva			11–31

Other matches

	W	D	L
British Lions			
1977 Suva	25–21		
Barbarians			
1970 Gosforth	29–9		
England Under 23s			
1970 Twickenham			3–8
Wales Under 23s			
1964 Cardiff			22–28

Outgoing Tour 1982

Fiji to Scotland and England

L 12–47 Edinburgh
L 17–23 South of Scotland
L 19–29 Anglo Scots
L 12–32 Scotland XV
L 4–19 Northern Division
L 6–36 South & South-West
L 16–25 Midland Division
L 12–30 Cambridge University
L 9–26 English Students
L 19–60 England XV

Tour summary: P 10 W 0 L 10 F 126 A 327

Pacific Tournament 1983

Suva: W 13–8 Tonga, L 0–6 Western Samoa

FINLAND

At the time of publication no information was available, except that Finland lost 0–40 to Switzerland in Helsinki in 1982. There are two clubs and 65 players in Helsinki.

FRENCH POLYNESIA (Tahiti and Taravao)

Foundation ....Affiliated to French RU
Headquarters BP 983, Papeete, Tahiti
Main stadium Papeete (capacity 10 000)
Colours Red and black jerseys
Number of clubs 11
Number of players 600
Season April–October
Temperatures 60°F (16°C) to 85°F (29°C)
Population 137 382

International result
1979 French Polynesia 12 France 92 (Papeete)

GERMAN DEMOCRATIC REPUBLIC

Deutscher Rugby-Sportverband

Foundation 1948
Headquarters 1500 Potsdam, Kunersdorferstr. 8
Colours Blue jerseys with white sleeves
Number of clubs 21
Number of players 1200
Season September–December and March–July
Temperatures 32°F (0°C) to 60°F (16°C)
Population 16 757 857

First match
1948 in Hennigsdorf

Affiliation
FIRA 1956

World Youth Games
German Democratic Republic won in 1951 (Berlin)

GDR Club league
BSG Stahl Hennigsdorf 19 wins

GDR Cup
BSG Stahl Hennigsdorf 6 wins

Most capped player
Gerhard Schubert 40 appearances

International results

	W	D	L
Bulgaria			
1963 Birlad	9–3		
1974 Varna			0–12
1976 Potsdam	6–0		
1977 Nessebar			0–10
1978 Varna			8–18
1978 Varna			0–8
1979 Magdeburg	8–7		
1979 Berlin			4–13
1979 Burgas			4–15
1980 Rathenow	8–3		
1980 Brandenburg	10–7		
1981 Constinbrod			0–7
1981 Sofia			6–16
1982 Leipzig	6–3		
1982 Sofia			3–16
Czechoslovakia			
1954 Gottwaldov			6–26
1954 Klatno	11–44		
1959 Bucharest			0–22
1959 Berlin		0–0	
1959 Weissenfels		3–3	
1960 Zwickau			0–9
1961 Prague			10–16
1962 Plock			6–8
1964 Ostritz	11–3		
1971 Prague			0–8
1972 Hennigsdorf	13–11		
1973 Sumperk			6–44
1974 Varna			4–56
1974 Potsdam			6–16
1976 Prague			0–54
1978 Varna			3–17
Denmark			
1964 Malmö	21–0		
1972 Rostock	20–12		
Netherlands			
1958 Ostend	32–8		
1979 Copenhagen			3–12
Poland			
1958 Lodz			8–9
1959 Bucharest		3–3	
1959 Frankfurt/Oder	14–8		
1960 Plauen			0–3
1961 Brno	3–0		
1962 Cheakowice			0–11
1963 Pitesti	11–6		
1964 Malmö			3–22
1967 Polawi			0–3
1971 Grimma			9–23
1973 Radzibor			3–21
1973 Dresden			0–16
1974 Grojez			3–50

1975 Berlin			6–27
1975 Pilar			0–73
1979 Burgas			12–30
1981 Sofia			3–21
1982 Sofia			3–42
Romania			
1951 Bucharest			26–64
1952 Berlin			12–46
1952 Hennigsdorf			3–36
1958 Brandenburg		5–5	
1959 Bucharest			6–21
1959 Bucharest			6–38
1960 Pirna			0–5
1961 Brno			0–34
1961 Bucharest			0–27
1962 Siedlce			5–25
1962 Bucharest			6–53
1963 Birlad			0–15
1964 Gorlitz			6–28
1974 Varna			0–49
1979 Potsdam	8–7		
1979 Burgas			0–60
1980 Bucharest			10–46
1981 Sofia			0–70
1982 Sofia			0–56
Soviet Union			
1977 Nessebar			3–46
Sweden			
1964 Malmö	28–0		
1965 Zehdenick	18–5		
1973 Berlin	22–12		
Yugoslavia			
1977 Nessebar			11–15

Under 19 Tournament

1982 (Prague) Czechoslovakia 9 German Democratic Republic 4, Soviet Union 22 German Democratic Republic 3, German Democratic Republic 4 Bulgaria 0, Romania 54 German Democratic Republic 0

GHANA

Number of clubs 3
Number of players 200

GUADELOUPE

Number of clubs 1
Number of players 50
Season October–April
Temperatures 65°F (18°C) to 80°F (27°C)

International results

	W	D	L
Bermuda			
1977 Martinique			3–30
1979 Guyana			0–50

GUYANA

Number of clubs 1
Number of players 50
Season October–April
Temperatures 60°F (18°C) to 80°F (27°C)

First Inter-island tournament
1926 Trinidad played Guyana

International results

	W	D	L
Bermuda			
1979 Guyana			4–23
1981 Trinidad			3–32

GIBRALTAR

Foundation 1971
Headquarters c/o Cmdr J E Highton, HMS *Rooke*, BFPO 163
Number of clubs 5
Number of players 150
Season September–May
Temperatures 50°F (10°C) to 75°F (24°C)
Population 29 278

HAWAII

Foundation 1966
Headquarters Hawaii Harlequin RFC, PO Box 4533, Honolulu, Hawaii 96813
Main stadium Kapioloni Park
Colours Red and yellow
Number of clubs 9
Number of players 450
Season Throughout year
Temperatures 75°F (24°C) to 80°F (27°C)
Population 769 913

First match
1930

First club
Hawaii Harlequin RFC, 1964

League Division A teams
Barbarians, Harlequins, Diamond Head, Laie,

University of Hawaii, Hawaii Loa College, Brigham Young University Hawaii

League Division B teams
Barbarians, Harlequins, Diamond Head, Elemakule, Maui, Brigham Young University Hawaii, Tanoa, Seagulls, Freeway, Low Riders

Pan Am tournament
1979 Tokanui of New Zealand
1981 Semi-finals Kolofo'ou of Tonga 13 Hawaii Harlequins 6—NSW Combined Colleges 13, Viala (Western Samoa) 11. Final: Kolofo'ou 19 NSW Combined Colleges 10. Old Boys winner: Bald Eagles (USA)

Hawaii club champions
1980 Laie 1981 Laie 1982 Barbarians 1983 B.Y.U. 10 Harlequins 6 (A.E.T.)

Outgoing tour 1983
Hawaii Harlequins to New Zealand, Australia L 6–20 Invitation XV (Auckland), W 6–0 Ngatapa RFC (Gisborne), W 20–4 Manly (Manly) W 17–9 Campbelltown Harlequins (Sydney)

HONG KONG

Foundation 1952
Headquarters PO Box 1088, Hong Kong

Number of clubs 8
Number of players 350
Season September–April
Temperatures 50°F (10°C) to 80°F (26°C)
Population 5 287 000

Clubs
8 Hong Kong FC, Royal Hong Kong Police, Kowloon RFC, Valley RFC, Tigers RFC, Flying Kukris RFC, British Forces, Stanley Fort RFC

International Board countries

	W	D	L
England			
1971 Hong Kong			0–26
France			
1978 Hong Kong			6–26
Scotland			
1977 Hong Kong			6–42
Wales			
1975 Hong Kong			3–57

Incoming Tours
1958 New Zealand Under 23s
1980 New Zealand Universities
1982 Hong Kong 0 English Students 40

HUNGARY

Headquarters c/o National Office of Physical Recreation, Orszagos Testenevelesi es Sportivatal, Nemzetkosi Oszataly, Budapest V, Hungary H-1442
Number of clubs 1
Number of players 20
Season September–March
Population 10 699 000

INDIA

Foundation ....Rugby Federation of India 1980
Headquarters Rugby Federation of India, 5A/75 WEA Sat Nagar, Karol Bagh, New Delhi

Main stadium	Calcutta Cricket and Football Club
Number of clubs	150
Number of players	7000
Season	October–June
Temperatures	60°F (16°C) to 85°F (29°C)
Population	638 388 000

All India Tournament winners
1924 Calcutta FC (Bombay). 1925 1st Bn The Welch Regiment (Calcutta). 1926 Calcutta FC (Madras). 1927 2nd Bn South Lancashires (Bombay). 1928 Prince of Wales Volunteers (Calcutta). 1929 Bombay Gymkhana Club (Madras). 1930 Ceylon Gymkhana Club (Bombay). 1931 Bombay Gymkhana Club (Calcutta). 1932 2nd Bn The Welch Regiment (Madras). 1933 Ceylon (Bombay). 1934 2nd Bn The Welch Regiment (Calcutta). 1935 Calcutta FC (Madras). 1936 Ceylon (Bombay). 1937 Calcutta FC & 2nd Bn Duke of Wellington's Regiment shared (Calcutta). 1938 Ceylon (Madras). 1939–45 No tournament. 1946 RAF Mauripur, Karachi (Bombay). 1947 Calcutta FC (Calcutta). 1948 Calcutta FC (Madras). 1949 Ceylon (Colombo). 1950 Ceylon (Calcutta). 1951 Ceylon (Madras). 1952 Singapore Civilians (Colombo). 1953 Calcutta FC & Ceylon shared (Calcutta). 1954 Calcutta FC (Madras). 1955 Bombay Gymkhana (Colombo). 1956 Calcutta FC (Calcutta). 1957 South India (Madras). 1958 Ceylon (Colombo). 1959 Calcutta FC (Calcutta). 1960 Calcutta FC (Madras). 1961 Ceylon (Colombo). 1962 Ceylon (Calcutta). 1963 Ceylon (Madras). 1964 Ceylon & Ceylon Combined Services shared (Colombo). 1965 No tournament. 1966 Ceylon (Calcutta). 1967 Ceylon (Bombay). 1968 Ceylon (Colombo). 1969 Ceylon (Calcutta). 1970 Calcutta FC (Calcutta). 1971 Bombay Gymkhana (Bombay). 1972 Armenians (Calcutta). 1973 Ceylon R & FC (Bombay). 1974 Bombay Gymkhana and La Martiniere Old Boys shared (Calcutta). 1975 Armenians (Bombay). 1976 Wilson Gymkhana (Calcutta). 1977 Bombay Gymkhana (Bombay). 1978 Bombay Gymkhana (Calcutta). 1979 Bombay Gymkhana (Bombay)

All India Sevens winners
1956 South India. 1957 Bengal Tigers. 1958 South India. 1959 Ceylon. 1960 Ceylon. 1961 South India. 1962 South India. 1963 Karachi. 1964 Bengal Tigers. 1965 No competition. 1966 Ceylon Combined Services. 1967 Calcutta C & FC. 1968 Colombo H & FC. 1969 Ceylon. 1970 No competition. 1971 Armenians. 1972 Ceylon Combined Services. 1973 Sri Lanka Police. 1974 Armenians. 1975 La Martiniere Old Boys. 1976 Calcutta C & FC. 1977 La Martiniere Old Boys. 1978 Calcutta Police

Calcutta Cup Tournament
1978 La Martiniere Old Boys

INDONESIA

Foundation	1971
Headquarters	Indonesian Rugby Union, PO Box 311, Ciputat, Jakarta
Number of clubs	5
Number of players	100
Season	April–September
Temperatures	40°F (4°C) to 75°F (24°C)
Population	150 000 000

Hong Kong Sevens results
1976 L 3–34 Cantabrians, L 4–16 Thailand, L 0–14 Sri Lanka
1977 L 0–20 Australia, W 22–4 Sri Lanka, W 16–4 Singapore, W 12–3 Thailand, L 4–20 Tonga (Plate final)
1978 W 14–6 Hawaii, L 4–14 Malaysia, L 0–36 New Zealand

1979 W 22–26 Japan, L 0–22 Western Samoa, L 10–12 Hawaii, W 20–4 Brunei, L 9–24 Papua New Guinea
1980 L 0–28 Fiji, L 0–7 Korea, L 10–22 Papua New Guinea, L 10–12 Singapore
1983 L 0–44 Australia, L 0–30 Japan, L 4–28 Malaysia, D 10–10 Solomon Islands

Incoming tours 1981–2
ISCI 10 OMT 17—ISCI President's XV 4 OMT 17—ISCI 12 Australian Navy XV 15—ISCI 3 Hong Kong 12—ISCI President's XV 0 Hong Kong 17

Outgoing tour 1982
Singapore CC 7 ISCI 7

IRAN

Foundation 1950
Number of clubs 1
Number of players 30

Club
Tehran RFC 1975

First tour
1975 Dubai (reached quarter-finals of Dubai Sevens)

First sevens tournament
1976 (Tehran)

NB Since the 1978 Revolution, most rugby activity has been limited to occasional matches. In 1982 efforts were being made to revive interest in the clubs in Anwaz, Bandabash and Tehran.

IRAQ

Foundation 1920

As far as is known, no rugby is now played in Iraq. In 1926 most of the rugby activity was centred on British service units: Cyril Lowe, England's leading try scorer, served as a squadron leader with the RAF in Iraq at the time and is believed to have played in several services matches.

ISRAEL

Foundation	1971
Headquarters	Israel Rugby Football Union, Box 6062, Tel Aviv
Main stadiums	Kibbutz Yizreel, Kibbutz Hadgen
Colours	Light blue jerseys
Number of clubs	14
Number of players	500
Season	September–May
Temperatures	50°F (10°C) to 75°F (24°C)
Population	3 709 000

Affiliations
Rugby Football Union and FIRA

First outgoing tour
1981 France and Switzerland (D 9–9)

Other tours
1981 Israeli youth to South Africa

Incoming tours
1975 Northern Transvaal
W 78–8 Israel
1977 University of Cape Town
W 78–6 Combined Kibbutzim
W 74–3 Tel Aviv University
W 88–0 Combined Universities
W 90–0 Israel
1978 University of Pretoria
W 80–10 Tel Aviv Inv. XV
1979 British Forces Cyprus
L 9–24 Israel
1980 New South Wales Maccabi
W 16–0 Combined Universities
W 15–0 Jerusalem XV
W 38–3 Northern Israel
W 12–3 Combined Kibbutzim
L 3–6 Israel

1981 British Forces Cyprus
L 15–19 Israel
1981 Hebraica Youth (Argentina)

First representative match
1952 Israeli Army XV v South African Settlers XV

Most points in a season
299 Tel Aviv University, 1978–9

Biggest win
106–0 Haogen/Nir Eliyahu v Arad, 1982

Most points by one player
19 Mervyn Woolf, Jerusalem University v Kiryat Shmone, 1978

National League champions
1971 Hebrew University. 1972 Kibbutz Yizreel. 1975 Tel Aviv University. 1976 Holon/Na'an. 1977 Haogen/Nir Eliyahu. 1978 Tel Aviv University. 1979 Hebrew University. 1980 Haogen/Nir Eliyahu. 1981 Kibbutz Yizreel. 1982 Kibbutz Yizreel. 1983 Kibbutz Yizreel

National Sevens winners
1975 Holon/Na'an. 1976 Haogen/Nir Eliyahu. 1977 Haogen/Nir Eliyahu. 1978 Haogen/Nir Eliyahu. 1979 Haogen/Nir Eliyahu. 1980 Haogen/Nir Eliyahu. 1981 Kibbutz Yizreel. 1982 Kibbutz Yizreel. 1983 Kibbutz Yizreel

Youth League
1982 Raanana. 1983 Kibbutz Yizreel

Youth Sevens
1983 Raanana

ITALY

Foundation	1928
Headquarters	Viale Tiziano 70, 00100 Roma
Main stadium	FIR Stadium, Rome (capacity 27 000)
Colours	Blue jerseys
Number of clubs	265
Number of players	15 200
Season	September–June

C. O. N. I.

Temperatures	32°F (0°C) to 75°F (24°C)
Population	56 799 000

Italian League winners
1929 Ambrosiana Milano. 1930 Amatori Milano. 1931 Amatori Milano. 1932 Amatori Milano. 1933 Amatori Milano. 1934 Amatori Milano. 1935 Roma. 1936 Amatori Milano. 1937 Roma. 1938 Amatori Milano. 1939 Amatori Milano. 1940 Amatori Milano. 1941 Amatori Milano. 1942 Amatori Milano. 1943 Amatori Milano. 1944–5 not played. 1946 Amatori Milano. 1947 Ginnastic Turin. 1948 Roma. 1949 Roma. 1950 Parma. 1951 Rovigo. 1952 Rovigo. 1953 Rovigo. 1954 Rovigo. 1955 Parma. 1956 Treviso Faema. 1957 Parma. 1958 Fiamme Oro PD. 1959 Fiamme Oro PD. 1960 Fiamme Oro PD. 1961 Fiamme Oro PD. 1962 Rovigo. 1963 Rovigo. 1964 Rovigo. 1965 Partenope Naples. 1966 Partenope Naples. 1967 L'Aquila. 1968 Fiamme Oro PD. 1969 L'Aquila. 1970 Petrarca Padua. 1971 Petrarca Padua. 1972 Petrarca Padua. 1973 Petrarca Padua. 1974 Petrarca Padua. 1975 Brescia La Concordia. 1976 Sanson Rovigo. 1977 Petrarca. 1978 Treviso Metalcrom. 1979 Rovigo Sanson. 1980 Petrarca Padua

League record score
249 points, Robin Williams (Brescia), 1978–9

Biggest winning margin
45–0 v Belgium, 1937

Biggest losing margin
0–69 v Romania, 1977

Highest away score
30–0 v Belgium, 1969

Most individual tries in a match
4 Renzo Cova v Belgium, 1937
Roberto Mariani v Poland, 1977

Most team tries in a match
10 v Belgium, 1937

Most individual points in a match
21 (6 C, 3 PG) Carlo Ponzi v Czechoslovakia, 1975

Most caps
32 Marco Bollesan (1963–75)

Highest international score
49–9 v Czechoslovakia, 1975

Rovigo Sevens 1983
Aberavon 36 Moseley 12

Outgoing tour
1980 New Zealand P 5 W 2 D 0 L 3
F 65 A 94

Incoming tours
1982 England Under 23s
W 15–0 Italian Under 23s (Treviso)
W 21–10 Italy B (Mantua)
L 7–12 Italy (Padua)

International results

	W	D	L
Argentina			
1978 Rovigo	19–6		
Australia			
1973 Aquila			21–59
1976 Milan			15–16
Belgium			
1937 Paris	45–0		
1969 Brussels	30–0		
Bulgaria			
1969 Sofia	17–0		
Czechoslovakia			
1933 Milan	7–3		
1933 Prague	12–3		
1948 Parma	17–0		
1949 Prague	14–6		
1955 Rome	17–6		
1956 Prague	19–9		
1965 Prague	11–0		
1965 St Dona	14–5		
1965 Livorno	3–0		
1970 Prague	11–3		
1973 Rovigo		3–3	
1975 Reggio	49–9		
1977 Prague	10–4		
Fiji			
1980 Suva			3–12
France			
1935 Rome			6–44
1937 Paris			5–43
1948 Rovigo			6–39
1949 Marsiglia			0–27
1952 Milan			8–17
1953 Lyon			8–22
1954 Rome			12–39
1955 Grenoble			10–24
1955 Barcelona			8–16
1956 Padua			3–16
1957 Agen			6–38
1958 Naples			3–11
1959 Nantes			0–22
1960 Treviso			0–26
1961 Chambery			0–17
1962 Breschia			3–6
1963 Grenoble			12–14
1964 Parma			3–12
1965 Pau			0–21
1966 Naples			0–21
1967 Toulon			13–60
1969 Catania			8–22
1971 Nice			13–37
1975 Rome			9–16
1976 Milan			11–23
1977 Grenoble			3–10
1978 Aquila			9–31
1979 Padua			9–15
1981 Rovigo			9–17
1982 Carcassonne			19–25
1983 Rovigo		6–6	
Fed. Rep. Germany			
1936 Berlin			9–18
1937 Milan			3–6
1937 Paris	9–7		
1938 Stuttgart			0–10
1939 Milan			3–12
1940 Stuttgart	4–0		
1952 Padua	14–6		
1953 Hanover	21–3		
1955 Milan	24–8		
1956 Heidelberg	12–3		
1957 Milan	8–0		
1960 Hanover	11–5		
1961 Piacenza	19–0		
1962 Berlin	13–11		
1964 Bologna	17–3		
1966 Berlin		3–3	
1968 Venice	22–14		
1974 Milan	16–10		
1981 —	23–0		
Japan			
1976 Padua	25–3		

	W	D	L
Madagascar			
1970 Tananarive	17–9		
1970 Tananarive	9–6		
Morocco			
1971 Naples			6–8
1977 Casablanca			9–10
1980 —	34–6		
1983 Casablanca	13–6		
Netherlands			
1975 Apeldoorn	24–0		
1981 Hilversum	9–0		
New Zealand			
1976 Padua			9–17
1979 Rovigo			12–18
Poland			
1975 Treviso	28–13		
1977 Catania	29–3		
1977 Warsaw			6–12
1979 Aquila	18–3		
1979 Warsaw	13–3		
Portugal			
1967 Genoa	6–3		
1968 Lisbon	17–3		
1972 Padua		0–0	
1972 Lisbon	15–7		
1973 Coimbra			6–9
1974 Lisbon	11–3		
Romania			
1934 Milan	7–0		
1936 Berlin	8–7		
1937 Bucharest		0–0	
1939 Rome	3–0		
1940 Bucharest			0–3
1942 Milan	22–3		
1953 Bucharest	16–14		
1958 Catania	6–3		
1962 Bucharest			6–14
1966 Aquila	3–0		
1967 Bucharest			3–24
1970 Rovigo			3–14
1971 Bucharest			6–32
1975 Bucharest		3–3	
1976 Parma	13–12		
1977 Bucharest			0–69
1977 Reggio		10–10	
1979 Bucharest			0–44
1980 Aquila	24–17		
1981 Brailia			9–35
1982 Rovigo			15–21
1983 Buzau			6–13
Soviet Union			
1978 Rome			9–11
1979 Moscow			0–9
1980 —			3–4
1981 Moscow		12–12	
Spain			
1929 Barna			0–9
1930 Milan	3–0		
1951 Rome	12–0		
1952 Barna	6–0		
1954 Naples	16–6		
1955 Barna	8–0		
1969 Aquila	12–5		
1972 Madrid			0–10
1972 Ivrea		6–6	
1975 Madrid	19–3		
1975 Madrid	19–6		
1976 Rome	17–4		
1977 Madrid			3–10
1978 Treviso	35–3		
1979 Split	16–9		
1980 Madrid	18–13		
Yugoslavia			
1968 Dona di Piave	22–3		
1972 Aosta	13–12		
1973 Zagreb	25–7		
Zimbabwe			
1973 Salisbury			4–42

Other match
1982 Italy 12 England Under 23s 7

IVORY COAST

Foundation 1960
Headquarters Federation Ivoirienne de Rugby, BP 2357, Abidjan 01, Ivory Coast
Colours White jerseys
Number of clubs 11
Number of players 800
Season October–May
Temperatures 58°F (15°C) to 70°F (21°C)
Population 7 500 000

International results

	W	D	L
Tunisia			
1976 Tunis	22–6		
Senegal			
1977 Dakar	15–9		
1983 Abidjan	25–0		

Outgoing tours
1975 (W 4 L 2 v French clubs)
1979 (W 6 L 0 v French clubs)

Incoming tours
1974, 1982 (W 2 L 6 v French clubs)

FIRA Junior tournaments
1980 (Tunis) Ivory Coast 16 Yugoslavia 11, Ivory Coast 3 Tunisia A 11, Ivory Coast 14 Tunisia B 0
1982 (Geneva) Ivory Coast 20 Switzerland 4, Ivory Coast 13 Belgium 0, Ivory Coast 21 Sweden 6

Other matches
1982 Ville Franche 8 Ivory Coast 29, Stade Toulousain 10 Ivory Coast 22

JAMAICA

Foundation	1959
Headquarters	Jamaica Rugby Union, 15 Caledonia Avenue, Kingston 5
Main stadium	Caymanas Field, Kingston
Number of clubs	8
Number of players	200
Season	October–April
Temperatures	60°F (16°C) to 75°F (24°C)
Population	2 084 000

Affiliation
Caribbean RFU 1973

First match
1959

Incoming tour 1983
Jamaica RFU Chairman's XV 4 Worcester Polytechnic Inst. (Mass., USA) 26 (Kingston). *Women's 7-a-side match*: Worcester Polytechnic Inst. 24 Jamaica Amazons 0 (Kingston)

International results

	W	D	L
Bermuda			
1975 Barbados			10–16
1976 —			3–14
1977 Martinique			3–26

JAPAN

Foundation	1926
Headquarters	c/o Shiggy Konno, Shanshin Enterprises, Ichibancho Central Building, 22–1 Ichibancho, Chiyoda-Ku Tokyo 102
Main stadium	National Stadium, Tokyo (capacity 60 000)
Colours	Red and white hoops
Number of clubs	3000
Number of players	180 000
Season	September–June
Temperatures	45°F (7°C) to 65°F (18°C)
Population	114 898 000

Number of clubs
3000 (including schools)

Number of players
180 000 (note: in 1971 there were 764 clubs and 60 000 players)

Oldest club
Keio University, 1899

First University match
1923 Keio v Washeda

Asian Championships
1982 *Final*: South Korea 12 Japan 9 (Singapore)

Hong Kong Sevens
1983 L 0–42 Australia, W 30–0 Indonesia, W 28–0 Malaysia, W 40–0 Solomon Islands, L 0–20 Fiji

Major tours

	P	W	D	L	F	A
1973 Britain and France	11	2	0	9	149	286
1974 New Zealand	11	5	1	5	292	344
1975 Australia	9	4	0	5	185	341
1976 Britain	8	3	0	5	160	291
1976 Italy	2	0	0	2	33	56
1980 France	4	0	0	4	37	163

International results

	W	D	L
Australia			
1975 Sydney			7–37
1975 Brisbane			25–50
England			
1971 Osaka			19–27
1971 Tokyo			3–6
1979 Osaka			19–21
1979 Tokyo			18–38
France			
1973 Bordeaux			18–30
1978 Tokyo			16–55
1980 Paris			3–23
Holland			
1980 Hilversum			3–15

Hong Kong			
1979 Hong Kong			17–21
1982 Singapore	29–0		
Italy			
1976 Padua			3–25
Scotland			
1976 Murrayfield			9–34
1977 Tokyo			9–74
South Korea			
1978 Kuala Lumpur	16–4		
1980 Taiwan	21–12		
1982 Singapore			9–12
Sri Lanka			
1978 Kuala Lumpur	34–8		
1980 Taiwan	108–0		
Taiwan			
1982 Singapore	31–6		
Thailand			
1978 Kuala Lumpur	47–18		
1982 Singapore	43–6		
Wales			
1973 Cardiff			14–62
1975 Osaka			12–56
1975 Tokyo			6–82

Asian Championships
1982 final: Japan 9 South Korea 12 (Singapore)

Incoming tours
1958 New Zealand Under 23s
1980 New Zealand Universities
1982 English Students

Results
Kyushu Provinces 0 English Students 71, Kansai Provinces 14 English Students 51, All Japan 0 English Students 43, New Zealand Universities 9 English Students 19, Japan B 0 English Students 99, Tour summary: P 5 W 5 F 283 A 23

Fiji hack through against Japan in the 1983 Hong Kong Sevens. (Colorsport.)

KENYA

Foundation	1921
Headquarters	Kenya Rugby Football Union, PO Box 48322, Nairobi
Main stadium	East Africa RFU Ground, Ngong Road (capacity 6500)
Colours	Royal blue jerseys, lion badge
Number of clubs	11
Number of players	600
Season	March–August
Temperatures	55°F (13°C) to 85°F (29°C)
Population	15 427 000

Japan play France at Bordeaux 27 October 1973. (Colorsport.)

Administrative history
Kenya RFU (1921) took over administration of Rugby Football Union of East Africa (1953) in 1980

First match
1909 Officials v Settlers, Mombasa

Outgoing tours
1954 Copperbelt
1962 Copperbelt
1966 England
1972 Ireland
1975 Zambia
1977 Zambia
1979 Zambia
1982 Zambia, Zimbabwe

Incoming tours
1929 South African Universities
1935 Stellenbosch University
1949 Cape Town University
1957 Oxford and Cambridge Universities
1958 Barbarians
1963 Oxford and Cambridge Universities
1972 Rosslyn Park, Richmond
1973 Wasps
1976 Zambia

Enterprise Cup winners 1980–2
Nondescripts 15 Eldoret 6, Impala 6 Nakuru 5, Kampala 3 Harlequins 3

East Africa's international results

	W	D	L
British Isles			
1955 Nairobi			8–39
1962 Nairobi			0–50
South Africa			
1961 Nairobi			0–39
Wales			
1964 Nairobi			8–26
Zambia			
1975 Lusaka			15–18
1979 Lyansta	21–13		

Kenya's results

	W	D	L
Tanzania			
1955	11–3		
Uganda			
1958 Kampala	21–11		
Zambia			
1980 Nairobi	23–10		
Zimbabwe			
1981 Nairobi			24–34
1982 Salisbury			12–15

KOREA

Number of clubs 25
Number of players 1500
Season April–September
Temperatures 40°F (4°C) to 70°F (21°C)

Asian Championships
1978 Korea 40 Singapore 3—Korea 7 Hong Kong 0—Korea 62 Malaysia 0. Final: Japan 16 Korea 4
1980 Final: Japan 21 Korea 12
1982 W 12–0 Sri Lanka, W 40–12 Malaysia, W 12–0 Singapore. Final: W 12–9 Japan

Hong Kong Sevens
1983 L 0–18 New Zealand, W 16–6 American Eagles, L 4–10 Bahrain, W 24–3 Singapore, W 4–0 Papua New Guinea, W 36–0 Solomon Islands. Plate final: W 30–6 Canada

Mud goes flying in the 1983 Hong Kong Sevens Plate final in which Korea beat Canada 30-6. (Colorsport.)

KUWAIT

Headquarters	c/o Jim Hughes, PO Box 70, SAFAT, Kuwait
Colours	Black and amber hoops
Number of clubs	1
Number of players	60
Season	September–April
Temperatures	50°F (10°C) to 90°F (30°C)

1982 results

Abu Dhabi	W 35–0 (H)	L 3–6 (A)
Bahrain	W 12–6 (H)	W 12–4 (A)
Dhahran	W 24–8 (H)	W 3–0 (A)
Dubai	W 10–6 (A)	
Muscat	W 14–3 (H)	W 25–6 (A)

1983 results

Bahrain	W 10–7 (H)	W 15–3 (A)

Gulf League 1983
Final: Bahrain 9 Kuwait 7

LAOS

No information is available on rugby in Laos, except that they entered a side in the 1974 Asian championships in Colombo, Sri Lanka.

LA RÉUNION

Headquarters	Caserne Beaulieu, rue Montfleury, Saint-Benoit
Number of clubs	12
Number of players	420
Season	April–October
Temperatures	50°F (10°C) to 75°F (24°C)
Population	496 000

LEBANON

Number of clubs	1
Number of players	60
Population	2 126 325

Outgoing tour
1981 to Egypt

LIBERIA

Headquarters	Liberia Rugby Football Union, PO Box 360, Monrovia
Number of clubs	3
Number of players	100
Population	1 684 000

LUXEMBOURG

Foundation	1973
Headquarters	Rugby Club Luxembourg, Boite Postale: 1162 Luxembourg
Main stadium	Terrain de Sports, Cessange
Colours	White jerseys, blue shorts, red socks
Number of clubs	2
Number of players	50
Season	September–May
Temperatures	32°F (0°C) to 65°F (18°C)
Population	360 200

First match
1973

Affiliations
French Rugby Federation 1973, FIRA 1975

First competitive rugby
1973 Alsace-Lorraine Regional Championships

International results

	W	D	L
Switzerland			
1977 Luxembourg			4–7
1980 Berne			7–10

MADAGASCAR

Headquarters Federation Malgache de Rugby, Stade Antanimena, Tananarive
Colours Red, white and green jerseys
Number of clubs 54
Number of players 2720
Season February–August
Temperatures 60°F (16°C) to 90°F (32°C)
Population 8 290 000

First match
1950, played Mauritius

Affiliation
FIRA, 1976

International results

	W	D	L
Italy			
1970 Tananarive			9–17
1970 Tananarive			6–9

MALAWI

Foundation 1922
Headquarters Rugby Football Union of Malawi, PO Box 5542, Limbe, Malawi
Main stadium Blantyre Sports Club
Colours Black jerseys with gold hoop
Number of clubs 3
Number of players 100
Season January–April
Population 5 571 567

First match
1908

First representative match
1930 Nyasaland v Rhodesia

Outgoing tours
1980 Zambia
L 16–18 Mufulira
W 32–6 Ndola
W 15–6 Roan Antelope
1980 Zimbabwe
L 12–42 Mashonaland
L 12–16 Rhobank Select
1982 Zimbabwe
L 12–14 Marandellas
W 13–9 Manicaland

Club tour
1982 Blantyre to Mauritius

Grenager Trophy
1947 Cholo/Mlanje. 1950 Blantyre/Limbe. 1951–53 Limbe. 1954 Cholo. 1955–57 Limbe. 1958 Blantyre. 1959 Limbe. 1962 Limbe. 1965 Limbe. 1966–67 Lilongwe. 1968 Limbe. 1969–71 Blantyre. 1972 Limbe. 1973–79 Blantyre. 1980–81 Limbe. 1982 Blantyre

Leslie Sevens
1948 Blantyre. 1949 Limbe. 1950 Blantyre. 1951–57 Limbe. 1958 Blantyre. 1959 Limbe. 1960 Blantyre. 1961 Limbe. 1962 Blantyre. 1963–65 Limbe. 1968 Thyolo. 1969–78 Blantyre. 1979 Lilongwe. 1980–82 Blantyre

Milward Trophy
1953–56 Southern Province. 1958 Lilongwe. 1962 Blantyre. 1963 Lilongwe. 1965 Limbe. 1968–69 Thyolo. 1970 Limbe. 1972–74 South. 1975 North. 1976 Limbe. 1977–78 Blantyre. 1979 Limbe. 1980 Lilongwe. 1981–82 Blantyre

Knock-out Cup
1958 Eagles. 1959 Limbe. 1962 Limbe. 1965 Limbe. 1969 Zomba. 1970 Limbe. 1971 Blantyre. 1972–73 Limbe. 1974–78 Blantyre. 1979 Lilongwe. 1980 Limbe. 1981 Lilongwe. 1982 Lilongwe

Limbe Festival
1962 Blantyre. 1963 Limbe. 1964 Zomba. 1965–66 Lilongwe. 1967 Limbe. 1968–69 Thyolo. 1970 Limbe. 1971–73 Blantyre. 1974 Limbe. 1975 Lilongwe. 1976–77 Blantyre.

1978 Thyolo. 1979 Limbe. 1980 Lilongwe. 1981 Limbe. 1982 Limbe

Easter Festival
1981 Malawi 'B'. 1982 Malawi

MALAYSIA

Headquarters	Kesatuan Ragbi Malaysia, PO Box 393, Kuala Lumpur 01–02
Number of clubs	10
Number of players	300
Population	12 600 000

First match
1892

First competition
1922 HMS *Malaya* Cup

Hong Kong Sevens
1983 L 0–38 Australia, L 0–28 Japan, W 28–4 Indonesia, L 4–20 Solomon Islands, L 4–24 Hong Kong

International results

	W	D	L
Singapore			
1982 Singapore	15–6		
South Korea			
1982 Singapore			12–40
Sri Lanka			
1982 Singapore	23–12		
Hong Kong			
1982 Singapore			4–10

MALTA

The 36-year history of rugby in Malta came to a formal end on 11 January 1982 when the island's one club, Overseas, was disbanded. Overseas' demise was because there were insufficient Maltese to take over from a dwindling number of Britons in both playing and administrative capacities.

MARTINIQUE

Number of clubs	10
Number of players	310
Season	July–December
Temperatures	60°F (16°C) to 85°F (29°C)

Affiliation
FIRA, 1976

International results

	W	D	L
Bermuda			
1977 Martinique		18–18	
1981 Trinidad			16–45

MAURITIUS

Foundation	1976
Headquarters	Mauritius Rugby Football Union, c/o PO Box 209, Port Louis
Main stadium	Mauritius Football and Hockey Club
Number of clubs	3
Number of players	100
Season	March–August
Temperatures	65°F (18°C) to 80°F (27°C)
Population	908 819

Clubs
3 (Mauritius Football and Hockey Club Stags, Dodo Club, Police Club)

League Cup winners
1971 Dodo. 1972 Dodo. 1973 Stags. 1974 Stags. 1975 Stags. 1976 Dodo. 1977 Dodo. 1978 Stags

France Vallet Knock-out trophy
1972 HMS *Mauritius*. 1973 HMS *Mauritius*. 1974 HMS *Mauritius*. 1975 Stags. 1976 Dodo. 1977 Stags. 1978 Dodo

Challenge Shield
1976 Dodo. 1977 Dodo. 1978 Dodo

Mee Goupille Sevens trophy
1973 Dodo. 1975 Stags A. 1976 Dodo A. 1977 Juniors A. 1978 Dodo A

Representative matches against La Réunion
1966 W 21–0 (Mauritius), W 16–3 (Réunion). 1967 no records. 1968 W 20–16 (Mauritius). 1969 L 6–11 (Réunion), W 29–11 (Réunion), W 21–6 (Mauritius). 1970 lost. 1971 lost. 1972 won. 1973 W 19–4 (Mauritius). 1974 L 0–40 (Réunion). 1975 L 13–14 (Mauritius). 1976 L 6–11 (Réunion). 1977 L 6–9 (Réunion). 1978 no match

Biggest win
Mauritius 80, Air France 0, 1978

Biggest defeat
Mauritius 0, Racing Club of France 80, 1972

Oldest current player
Edouard Nairac, 47

International result
1953 Tananarive, Madagascar L 3–80 France

MEXICO

Foundation 1972
Headquarters Union Mexicana de Rugby AC, Apartado Postal 5–835, Mexico 5, D.F.
Colours Green jerseys, white shorts
Number of clubs 13
Number of players 280
Season September–March
Temperatures 60°F (16°C) to 90°F (32°C)
Population 66 943 976

First match
1925

First clubs
1935 Reforma, RFC France, Wachachara

Affiliation
FIRA, 1975

Senior champions
1979–80 Instituto Anglo Mexicano

Junior champions
1978–9 Liceo Franco Mexicano

Biggest score known
British Army Belize 0, Mexico Select XV 92 (Mexico City, 25 November 1978)

Under 19 tour
1979 USA P 4 W 2 L 2

MOROCCO

Foundation 1956
Headquarters Federation Royale Marocaine de Rugby, Maison de Sport, Parc de la Ligue Arabe, Casablanca
Colours Red and green jerseys
Number of clubs 17
Number of players 1300
Season October–May
Temperatures 55°F (13°C) to 80°F (27°C)
Population 18 245 000

Affiliation FIRA, 1956

Incoming tour
1958 Oxford and Cambridge

International results

	W	D	L
Czechoslovakia			
1967 Casablanca			0–6
1972 Millau	21–3		
Fed. Rep. Germany			
1975 Heidelberg			11–19
1976 Casablanca	30–3		
1979 Hanover	13–6		
1980 Casablanca	22–6		
France			
1972 Casablanca			3–72
1973 Marmande			6–73
1974 La Rochelle			3–54
1977 Casablanca			0–69
1980 Casablanca			4–33
1983 Casablanca			9–16
Italy			
1979 Split			6–15
1980 —			6–34
1983 Casablanca			3–13
Netherlands			
1970 Casablanca	23–8		
1975 Hilversum			7–26
1979 Hilversum	21–17		
1981 Casablanca			6–10
1981 Hilversum	10–3		
Poland			
1980 Warsaw			13–28
1981 Casablanca	6–3		
Portugal			
1968 Lisbon		6–6	
1969 Casablanca	15–6		
1970 Barreiro	9–8		
1982 Casablanca	26–7		
Romania			
1980 Bucharest			11–41
1983 Casablanca			3–28
Soviet Union			
1980 Casablanca			3–11
Spain			
1931 Rabat			6–14
1932 Madrid			8–14
1932 Rabat			0–14
1967 Madrid	3–0		
1968 Casablanca			5–6
1969 Madrid	18–0		
1970 Casablanca			8–11
1973 Casablanca	20–9		
1974 Madrid	22–0		
1977 Madrid	21–3		
1979 Split	16–4		
1982 —	Forfeit		
Switzerland			
1979 Casablanca	43–0		
Tunisia			
1981 Tunis			10–13
1982 Casablanca	6–4		
Yugoslavia			
1979 Split	22–7		
1981 Split	13–0		

Junior international
1973 Morocco 3 France 58

MUSCAT

Foundation	1971
Headquarters	c/o Chris Morton, Naval HG, PO Box 6804, Muscat, Sultanate of Oman
Main stadium	Wattayeh, Muscat
Colours	Red, green and white hoops
Number of clubs	1 (2 teams)
Number of players	40
Season	September–April
Temperatures	75°F (24°C) to 110°F (43°C)
Population	1 500 000

1982 results

Abu Dhabi	W 10–0	(H)	W 28–10	(A)
Bahrain	L 10–17	(H)	L 3–19	(A)
Dhahran	W 10–3	(H)	L 10–12	(A)
Dubai	W 9–8	(H)	L 3–14	(A)
Qatar	W 23–12	(H)	L 3–7	(A)

1983 result
Qatar L 8–24 (H)

Dubai Sevens
Muscat winners in 1978, 1980, 1981

Muscat Sevens
Muscat winners in 1979, 1980, 1981, 1982

Gulf League
Muscat champions in 1980

Outgoing tours
Singapore, Kenya, Hong Kong, Thailand, Egypt

NETHERLANDS

Foundation	1932
Headquarters	Nederlandse Rugby Bond, Schaepmanlaan 5, 1272 GJ Huizen—NH

NEDERLANDSE RUGBY BOND
50 JAAR 1932 1982

Main stadium	Gemeentelijk Sportpark, Hilversum (capacity 23 000)
Colours	Orange jerseys
Number of clubs	95
Number of players	6500
Season	September–May
Temperatures	35°F (2°C) to 54°F (25°C)
Population	14 000 000

First match
1879, in Amsterdam

Growth of clubs
1969—16, 1975—60, 1977—64, 1978—76, 1981—93, 1982—95

Van Swol Trophy
1975 Noord-Oost, 1976 West. 1977 Midden. 1978 South. 1979 West. 1980 Midden. 1981 Noord-West. Nat. Students

Oldest club
DSRC (Delft Students), formed 24 September 1918

Biggest club
HRC (The Hague RFC), 1932

Referees
33 full-time, 47 part-time

Coaches
120

Longest international career
John van Altena (RC Hilversum), flanker, 106 caps over 14 seasons

National cup winners
1929 Groningen University. 1938 Delft University. 1939 Delft University. 1968 HRC. 1969 AAC (Amsterdam). 1971 HRC. 1972 HRC. 1973 HRC. 1974 RCH (Hilversum). 1975 RCH. 1976 RCH. 1977 AAC. 1977 HRC. 1979 cancelled because of bad weather. 1980 HRC. 1981 DIOK. 1982 RCH. 1983 RCH

National sevens winners
1971 HRC, 1972 AAC, 1973 AAC, 1977 AAC, 1978 LSRG, 1979 AAC, 1980 DSR-C, 1981 NFC, 1982 Castricum. 1983 NFC

Amsterdam sevens winners
1972 Walsall, 1973 Walsall, 1974 The Voyagers (London Welsh), 1975 The Voyagers, 1976 Edinburgh Wanderers, 1977 The Voyagers, 1978 The Musketeers, 1979 The Musketeers, 1980 The Musketeers, 1981 Steepholm, 1982 Steepholm, 1983 Kemp and Horley

Preston Grasshoppens Schools Festival
1983 Plate winners: Netherlands Youth

Biggest international win
62–0 Denmark, 1973

Biggest international defeat
6–73 France B, 1976

International results

	W	D	L
Belgium			
1930 The Hague			0–6
1930 Brussels			0–11
1932 Amsterdam		6–6	
1933 Wilrijch	14–5		
1934 Utrecht	6–3		
1935 Antwerp	8–6		
1938 The Hague			8–28
1939 Antwerp			6–23
1945 Bussum	9–6		
1946 Brussels			3–13
1947 Brussels			6–9
1947 Bussum			3–6
1947 Bussum	5–3		
1948 Leuven			0–9
1948 Brussels		6–6	
1949 Amsterdam			3–6
1949 Brussels			5–15
1952 Brussels			0–9
1956 Brussels	14–12		
1965 Rijswijk	14–3		
1968 Brussels	14–9		
1969 Brussels			5–9
1977 Hilversum	17–4		
1978 Hilversum	10–3		
1978 Hilversum	17–4		
1982 Beek			9–13
1982 Visé	19–10		

Czechoslovakia			
1946 Bussum			8–14
1966 Prague			5–16
1977 Hilversum			7–9
Denmark			
1971 Gothenburg	24–3		
1973 Hilversum	62–0		
1978 Hilversum	52–9		
1983 Hilversum	25–3		
Fed. Rep. Germany			
1932 Eindhoven	24–11		
1933 Dusseldorf			0–23
1934 Maastricht			0–21
1935 Cologne			5–11
1936 Hilversum			16–28
1937 Hilversum			6–23
1958 Eindhoven			0–24
1959 Heidelberg			0–39
1960 Breukelen			6–42
1961 Murth			6–14
1962 The Hague			6–37
1962 The Hague	18–5		
1963 Russelsheim	13–12		
1964 The Hague			5–18
1965 Berlin			3–48
1966 The Hague			0–12
1967 Hanover			0–6
1968 Hilversum			0–12
1968 The Hague			0–8
1969 Offenbach			13–14
1970 The Hague			3–29
1971 Bonn			9–14
1972 Apeldoorn			13–17
1974 Wageningen	32–21		
1976 Hilversum		13–13	
1977 Hilversum	10–9		
1980 Hilversum	16–10		
1981 Hanover			10–13
France			
1975 Hilversum			18–26
1976 Lille			6–71
Italy			
1975 Apeldoorn			0–24
1981 Hilversum			0–9
Japan			
1980 Hilversum	15–13		
Morocco			
1970 Casablanca			8–23
1975 Hilversum	26–7		
1979 Hilversum			17–21
1981 Casablanca	10–6		
1981 Hilversum			3–10
Poland			
1968 Hilversum			8–16
1973 Hilversum			3–24
1979 Hilversum		6–6	
1981 Hilversum			9–19
1982 Warsaw	13–6		
Portugal			
1970 Hilversum		9–9	
1982 Hilversum			12–16
1983 Hilversum			6–13
Romania			
1937 Paris			3–42
1938 Alkmaar		3–3	
1976 Hilversum			3–27

Scotland			
1975 Hilversum			3–29
1978 Hilversum			0–19
Spain			
1967 Amsterdam			5–14
1975 Uden		4–4	
1977 Hilversum			0–28
1980 Barcelona			3–24
1982 Barcelona			12–25
1983 Hilversum			3–32
Sweden			
1966 Hilversum	23–5		
1968 Helsinborg	35–3		
1971 Gothenburg			0–6
1973 Amsterdam	21–0		
1976 Hilversum	34–3		
1978 Hilversum	4–0		
1982 Malmö	16–7		
Tunisia			
1979 Hilversum	12–0		
1981 Hilversum	21–9		
1982 Tunis	15–6		
Yugoslavia			
1972 The Hague	9–3		
1978 Split	30–11		
1979 Ljubljana			6–10
1981 Hilversum	17–0		

Other matches

1978 Netherlands 3, England Under 23s 24 (Hilversum)
1981 England Under 23s 51, Netherlands 3 (Leicester)
1982 Women's match: Netherlands 0, France 4 (Utrecht)

NEW CALEDONIA

Foundation	(Affiliated to French RU)
Headquarters	c/o M. Donneau Marcel, BP 1190, Nouméa
Main stadium	Stade Noméen
Colours	Blue and white jerseys
Number of clubs	9
Number of players	500
Season	April–November
Temperatures	50°F (10°C) to 80°F (27°C)
Population	135 500

South Pacific Games

1979 New Caledonia 17 Papua New Guinea 8—New Caledonia 3 Tonga 58 (Suva, Fiji)

NIGERIA

Number of clubs 6
Number of players 400
Season April–November
Temperatures 80°F (27°C) to 90°F (32°C)

First match
1950

First major incoming tour
1981 London Welsh

International results

	W	D	L
Denmark			
1979 Copenhagen			12–30
1980 Oslo	41–3		
Sweden			
1980 Vänersborg			0–20

NORWAY

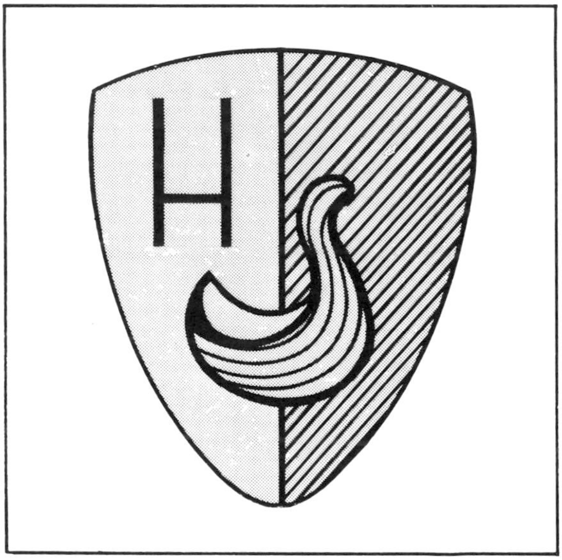

Headquarters ....Norwegian Rugby Union, PO Box 1943 Vika, Oslo 3
Main stadium Oslo RFC
Colours Navy: light blue hoops
Number of clubs 2
Number of players 100
Season May–September/October
Temperatures 30°F (−1°C) to 73°F (23°C)
Population 4 059 000

First club
Oslo RFC 1964

Affiliations
Nordic Rugby Union, FIRA

PAPUA NEW GUINEA

Headquarters Papua New Guinea RFU, PO Box 704, Port Moresby
Number of clubs 5
Number of players 200

International results
1970 New Caledonia 17 Papua New Guinea 8 (South Pacific Games, Suva, Fiji)

Hong Kong Sevens
1983 L 0–28 Scottish Border Club, L 0–28 Canada, L 4–24 Western Samoa, W 8–4 Sri Lanka, L 0–4 South Korea

PARAGUAY

Foundation 1968
Headquarters Union de Rugby de Paraguay, Palma 670, Asuncion

Main stadium	Asuncion RFC
Number of clubs	8
Number of players	380
Season	March–October
Temperatures	35°F (2°C) to 58°F (14°C)
Population	2 880 000

Oldest club
Asuncion, 1968

International results

	W	D	L
Argentina			
1971 Montevideo			0–61
1973 São Paulo			3–98
1975 Asuncion			0–93
1977 Tucuman			3–77
1979 Vina del Mar			13–76
1983 Buenos Aires			3–43
Brazil			
1970 Asuncion			3–12
1971 Montevideo			6–12
1973 São Paulo			3–22
1975 Asuncion			6–19
1977 Tucuman	25–13		
1979 Santiago			6–16
1981 Montevideo	35–3		
Chile			
1971 Montevideo			0–40
1973 São Paulo			3–27
1975 Asuncion			3–44
1977 Tucuman			3–22
1979 Santiago			13–27
1981 Montevideo			3–33
1983 Buenos Aires			12–24
South Africa			
1980 Asuncion			6–84
Uruguay			
1971 Montevideo			3–56
1973 São Paulo			9–31
1975 Asuncion			18–38
1977 Tucuman			7–16
1979 Santiago			9–53
1981 Montevideo			14–54
1983 Buenos Aires			12–20

Junior internationals
Brazil 1972 W 12–6 1974 L 7–17 1978 W 13–9 1980 W 34–3 1982 W 36–9 *Chile* 1972 L 7–36 1974 L 6–44 1976 L 7–44 1978 L 3–35 1980 L 6–13 1982 W 19–14 *Argentina* 1972 L 3–84 1974 L 0–82 1976 L 4–88 1978 L 0–118 1982 L 7–30 *Uruguay* 1972 L 0–58 1974 L 18–70 1976 L 12–17 1978 L 24–66 1980 W 13–7 1982 L 7–9

PERU

Headquarters	Lima Bullfrogs RFC, Lima
Number of clubs	1
Number of players	40
Season	April–November
Temperatures	50°F (10°C) to 75°F (24°C)
Population	16 819 000

Oldest club
Lima Bullfrogs, 1977

International results

	W	D	L
Argentina			
1958 Santiago			0–44
Chile			
1958 Vina del Mar			3–31
Uruguay			
1958 Santiago			6–10

THE PHILIPPINES

Foundation	1975
Headquarters	c/o Ben Bennett, Clark Air Base 'Outlaw' RFC, Angeles City, Philippines
Number of clubs	1
Number of players	30

POLAND

Foundation	1956
Headquarters	Polski Zwiazek Rugby, 03–727 Warszawa Stadion X-lecia
Main stadium	Polski Zwiazek Rugby, Warsaw
Colours	White and red jerseys
Number of clubs	17
Number of players	1820
Season	September–December and March–June
Temperatures	28°F (−2°C) to 58°F (14°C)
Population	35 048 000

Affiliation
FIRA 1957

Most capped player
51 J Olejnieczaic

Club championship
1980 AZS Warsaw. Division II RFC Lech Poznon

International results

	W	D	L
Czechoslovakia			
1959 Bucharest	9–6		
1960 Bera			5–6
1961 Brno			3–9
1962 Pruzskow			0–17
1963 Hunedoara		0–0	
1969 Havirov			8–25
1972 Warsaw	23–9		
1973 Prague			6–16
1974 Varna	22–15		
1975 Leningrad	27–6		
1976 Warsaw			15–16
1976 Lvov	16–3		
1977 Tblisi			4–21
1978 Warsaw	14–3		
1978 Kharkov			9–10
Denmark			
1964 Malmö	25–6		
Fed. Rep. Germany			
1958 Kracow			3–11
1959 Braunschweig	9–8		
1960 Rzeszow			3–8
1961 Hanover			3–11
1975 Warsaw	29–6		
France			
1969 Warsaw			0–67
1977 Warsaw			9–26
1977 Albi			24–35
1977 Czestochova			9–26
1980 Lodz			0–42
1981 —			6–49
German Dem. Rep.			
1958 Lodz	9–8		
1959 Bucharest		3–3	
1959 Frankfurt/Oder			8–14
1960 Plauen	3–0		
1961 Brno			0–3
1962 Cheakowice	11–0		
1963 Pitesti			6–11
1964 Malmö	22–3		
1967 Polawi	3–0		
1971 Grimma	23–9		
1973 Radzibor	21–3		
1973 Dresden	16–0		
1974 Grojez	50–3		
1975 Berlin	27–6		
1975 Pilar	73–0		
1979 Burgas	30–12		
1981 Sofia	21–3		
1982 Sofia	42–3		
Italy			
1975 Treviso			13–28
1977 Catania			3–29
1977 Warsaw	12–6		
1979 L'Aquila			3–18
1980 Lodz			3–13
1981 —			12–37
1983 —			6–13
Morocco			
1980 Warsaw	28–13		
1981 —			3–6
Netherlands			
1968 Hilversum	16–8		
1973 Hilversum	24–3		
1979 Hilversum		6–6	
1981 Hilversum	19–9		
1982 Warsaw			6–13
Portugal			
1982 Warsaw	38–13		
Romania			
1977 Bucharest			21–38
1978 Warsaw			9–30
1979 Bucharest			15–48
1980 Sochaczew			0–33
Soviet Union			
1975 Leningrad	21–15		
1976 Lvov			16–22
1977 Tblisi			3–37
1978 Kharkov			13–28
1979 Moscow			7–19
1980 Moscow			10–54
1981 —			3–7
Spain			
1970 Poznan			6–8
1972 Madrid			0–3
1974 Poznan			0–4
1976 Bialystok	17–14		
1977 Madrid			3–11
1978 Warsaw			22–28
1978 Barcelona	16–4		
1980 Madrid	25–20		
1982 Lublin	32–6		
1983 Valencia	16–7		
Sweden			
1964 Malmö	12–0		
1965 Gdansk	35–0		
1966 Eskiltuna		12–12	
1968 Warsaw	38–3		
1982 Poznan	54–6		
Tunisia			
1982 Tunis	16–3		
Yugoslavia			
1970 SM. Palanka			9–12
1970 Sisak			15–19

PORTUGAL

Foundation 1957

Headquarters Federacao Portuguesa de Rugby, Rue Sociedade Farmaceutica 56–2^{e} — 1199 Lisboa Codex, Portugal

Main stadium Estadio Universitario Lisbon (capacity 10 000)
Colours Red jerseys, white shorts
Number of clubs 38
Number of players 6350
Season August–June
Temperatures 45°F (7°C) to 85°F (29°C)
Population 9 798 000

First match
1907

Referees
35, two of them international

Coaches
30

Principal rugby centres
Coimbra, Lisbon, Setubal, Elvas (the game is played periodically in Oporto and the Algarve)

Portuguese League
1979 Academica. Second division: Agronomia

Portuguese cup
1979 Academica

Oldest club
Sport Lisboa e Benfica, 1922

First club
Casa Pia de Lisboa, 1919

Biggest international win
39–0 v Switzerland 1980

Biggest international defeat
14–56 v France, Lisbon 1967

Representative match
Portugal 13, Middlesex Clubs 28, Lisbon 1980

International results

	W	D	L
Belgium			
1966 Brussels		3–3	
1968 Lisbon	8–6		
1980 —	15–7		
Denmark			
1980 —	45–16		
Fed. Rep. Germany			
1974 Hanover			10–20
France			
1967 Lisbon			14–56
Italy			
1967 Genoa			3–6
1968 Lisbon			3–17
1972 Padua		0–0	
1972 Lisbon			7–15
1973 Coimbra	9–6		
1974 Lisbon			3–11
Morocco			
1968 Lisbon		6–6	
1969 Casablanca			6–15
1970 Barreiro			8–9
1982 Lisbon			7–26
Netherlands			
1970 Hilversum		9–9	
1982 Hilversum	16–12		
1983 Hilversum	13–6		
Poland			
1973 Warsaw			13–35
1973 Coimbra	13–3		
1982 Warsaw			13–38
Romania			
1967 Lisbon			6–46
Spain			
1935 Lisbon			5–6
1936 Madrid			9–16
1954 Madrid			0–23
1965 Lisbon			9–12
1966 Madrid	9–3		
1967 Lisbon			5–9
1968 Madrid			5–14
1969 Barreiro			11–15
1970 Madrid			0–17
1982 Lisbon			13–32
1983 Madrid			4–25
Switzerland			
1973 Neuchatel	23–4		
1979 Lisbon	31–0		
1981 Lisbon	39–0		

Sweden			
1970 Hilversum		9–9	
1981 Trelleborg	15–10		
Tunisia			
1982 Lisbon	25–16		

QATAR

Foundation	1974
Headquarters	Qatar Rugby Union, PO Box 8453, Doha-Qatar
Main stadium	Salwa Road
Colours	Maroon and white hoops
Number of clubs	1
Number of players	65
Season	September–April
Temperatures	50°F (10°C) to 90°F (32°C)
Population	250 000

1982 results

Abu Dhabi	L 0–12 (H)	L 4–20 (A)	
Bahrain	L 3–20 (H)	L 3–44 (A)	
Dhahran	L 6–14 (H)	L 7–20 (A)	
Dubai	L 3–4 (H)	L 3–44 (A)	
Muscat	W 7–3 (H)	L 12–23 (A)	

1983 results

Abu Dhabi	W 8–4 (H)	
Bahrain	L 8–15 (H)	L 9–24 (A)
Dhahran	W 12–6 (H)	L 3–17 (A)
Dubai	W 15–6 (H)	
Muscat	W 24–8 (A)	
Al Khobar	W 20–3 (H)	

Other match
W 30–3 HMS *Ambuscade*

ROMANIA

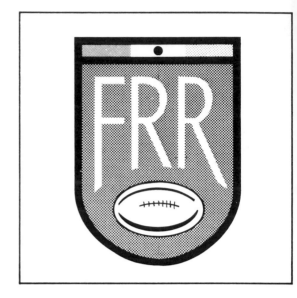

Foundation	1914
Headquarters	Str Vasile Conta 16 Bucharest
Main stadium	Giulesti Stadium, Bucharest (capacity 17 000)
Colours	Yellow jerseys
Number of clubs	197
Number of players	13 400
Season	September–November and April–June
Temperatures	30°F (−1°C) to 65°F (18°C)
Population	21 855 000

Growth of clubs and players

Year	*Clubs*	*Players*
1913	3	100
1924	14	270
1936	50	1000
1944	62	1200
1950	76	1550
1960	108	3600
1965	165	7500
1980	197	13 400

Oldest club
Tennis Club Roman Bucharest, 1913

Biggest club
Grivitza Rosie Bucharest (1933), 600 players

Number of rugby playing schools
50

Referees	**Coaches**
192	314

Most capped player
Constantin Dinu, Grivitza Rosie (67 appearances 1970–82)

Longest international career
Georghi Pircalabescu (Grivitza Rosie) 1940–60 (15)

First major overseas tour
1955 to UK

Biggest crowd
95 000, Romania 15 France 18 (23 August Stadium, Bucharest, 19 May 1957)

Club champions
1914 Tennis Club Roman Bucharest. 1915 Tennis Club Roman Bucharest. 1916 Tennis Club Roman Bucharest. 1919 Stadiul Roman Bucharest. 1920 Educatia Fizica Bucharest. 1921 Tennis Club Roman Bucharest. 1922 Tennis Club Roman Bucharest. 1923 Tennis Club Roman Bucharest. 1924 Stadiul Roman Bucharest. 1925 Sportul Studentesc Bucharest. 1926 Stadiul Roman Bucharest. 1927 Tennis Club Roman Bucharest. 1928 Stadiul Roman Bucharest. 1929 Sportul Studentesc Bucharest. 1930 Stadiul Roman Bucharest. 1931 Stadiul Roman Bucharest. 1932 Sportul Studentesc Bucharest. 1933 PTT Bucharest. 1934 PTT Bucharest. 1935 Sportul Studentesc Bucharest. 1936 Sportul Studentesc Bucharest. 1938 Tennis Club Roman Bucharest. 1939 Sportul Studentesc Bucharest. 1940 Tennis Club Roman Bucharest. 1941 Viforul Dacia Bucharest. 1942 Tennis Club Roman Bucharest. 1943 Viforul Dacia Bucharest. 1944 Viforul Dacia Bucharest. 1945 Viforul Dacia Bucharest. 1946 Sportul Studentesc Bucharest. 1947 Stadiul Roman Bucharest. 1948 CFR Bucharest. 1949 CCA Bucharest. 1950 CFR Bucharest. 1951 Dinamo Bucharest. 1952 Dinamo Bucharest. 1953 CCA Bucharest. 1954 CCA Bucharest. 1955 Locomotiva Grivitza Rosie. 1956 Dinamo Bucharest. 1957 Locomotiva Grivitza Rosie. 1958 CFR Grivitza Rosie Bucharest. 1959 CFR Grivitza Rosie Bucharest. 1960 CFR Grivitza Rosie Bucharest. 1961 Steaua Bucharest. 1962 Grivitza Rosie Bucharest. 1963 Steaua Bucharest. 1964 Steaua Bucharest. 1965 Dinamo Bucharest. 1966 Grivitza Rosie Bucharest. 1967 Grivitza Rosie Bucharest. 1968/69 Dinamo Bucharest. 1970 Grivitza Rosie Bucharest. 1971 Steaua Bucharest. 1972 Universitea Timisoara. 1973 Steaua Bucharest. 1974 Steaua Bucharest. 1975 Farul Constanta. 1976 Farul Constanta. 1977 Steaua Bucharest. 1978 Farul Constanta. 1979 Steaua Bucharest. 1980 Steaua Bucharest. 1981 Steaua Bucharest. 1982 Dinamo Bucharest. 1983 Steaua.

First provincial club champions
Universitea Timisoara 1972

Biggest international win
100–0 v Bulgaria, Burgas 1976

Biggest international defeat
3–59 v France, Paris 1924

Incoming tour 1982
Middlesex County Clubs, L 6–7
Constructilor Constanta, W 9–6
Constanta XV, D 9–9 Regional XV

Outgoing tours

1982 to Zimbabwe
L 27–33 Mashonoland
W 25–23 Zimbabwe
W 61–6 Matabeleland
W 44–6 Midland
W 25–24 Zimbabwe
W 37–9 Invitation XV

Tour summary: P 6 W 5 L 1 F 219 A 101

1980 to UK
W 32–9 Munster
L 10–24 Leinster
W 15–13 Ulster
W 28–9 Connacht
D 13–13 Ireland XV
W 39–7 Leicester

Tour summary: P 6 W 4 D 1 L 1 F 137 A 75

International results

	W	D	L
Argentina			
1973 Buenos Aires			9–15
1973 Buenos Aires			3–24
Belgium			
1957 Brussels	35–5		
Bulgaria			
1963 Birlad	70–3		
1963 Giurgiu	29–11		
1968 Stara Zagora	25–3		
1976 Burgas	100–0		
Czechoslovakia			
1927 Presburg	26–6		
1949 Prague	20–5		
1955 Brno	3–0		
1957 Moscow	12–11		
1959 Bucharest	11–0		
1960 Glaucau	13–3		

1961 Prague	19–12		
1962 Piotrkow Tribunalski	11–6		
1962 Bucharest	40–0		
1963 Bucharest	23–3		
1963 Deva	3–0		
1964 Bauzen	14–3		
1966 Prague		9–9	
1968 Bucharest	17–3		
1968 Ricany	18–9		
1969 Bucharest	42–6		
1972 Vyskov	22–3		
1974 Varna	18–15		
1974 Svmperk	16–6		
1976 —	29–10		
1978 Bucharest	60–6		
1978 Kharkov	28–0		
Fed. Rep. Germany			
1936 Hamburg			9–37
1937 Paris			3–30
1938 Bucharest			5–8
1958 Brussels	9–0		
1964 Bucharest	19–3		
1965 Hanover	9–8		
1967 Bucharest	27–5		
1969 Hanover	6–3		
1972 Bucharest			10–11
1973 Heidelberg	33–9		
1982 Bucharest	60–18		
1983 Heidelberg	26–12		
France			
1919 Paris			5–48
1924 Paris			3–59
1936 Berlin			5–26
1937 Paris			11–27
1938 Bucharest			8–11
1957 Bucharest			15–18
1957 Bordeaux			0–39
1960 Bucharest	11–5		
1961 Bayonne		5–5	
1962 Bucharest	3–0		
1963 Toulouse		6–6	
1964 Bucharest			6–9
1965 Lyon			3–8
1966 Bucharest			3–9
1967 Nantes			3–11
1968 Bucharest	15–14		
1969 Tarbres			9–14
1970 Bucharest			3–14
1971 Béziers			12–31
1972 Constanta			6–15
1973 Valencia			6–7
1974 Bucharest	15–10		

RUGBY ACTION IN ROMANIA

Every picture tells a story . . . rugby has become a major sport in Romania and the quality of their pitches and spectator facilities is borne out in these pictures of the Romania v France international played in Bucharest on 31 October 1982. Romania have been in the process of re-building the side which won the 1981 European Championship and this victory over France, by 13–9, suggests the new side is going to be a major force during the coming seasons. The referee for the match was Alan Hosie, of Scotland, which is another indication that the Romanians are eager to develop their game at all levels.

Pictures supplied by Federaţia Română de Rugbi

1975 Bordeaux			12–36
1976 Bucharest	15–12		
1977 Clermont-Ferrand			6–9
1978 Bucharest			6–9
1979 Montauban			12–30
1980 Bucharest	15–0		
1981 Narbonne			9–17
1982 Bucharest	13–9		
German Dem. Rep.			
1951 Bucharest	64–26		
1952 Berlin	46–12		
1952 Hennigsdorf	36–3		
1958 Brandenberg		5–5	
1959 Bucharest	21–6		
1959 Bucharest	38–6		
1960 Pirna	5–0		
1961 Brno	34–0		
1961 Bucharest	27–0		
1962 Siedlce	25–5		
1962 Bucharest	53–6		
1963 Birlad	15–0		
1964 Gorlitz	28–6		
1974 Varna	49–0		
1979 Potsdam			7–8
1979 Burgas	60–0		
1980 Bucharest	46–10		
1981 Sofia	70–0		
1982 Sofia	56–0		
Ireland			
1980 Dublin		13–13	
Italy			
1934 Milan			0–7
1936 Berlin			7–8
1937 Bucharest		0–0	
1939 Rome			0–3
1940 Bucharest	3–0		
1942 Milan			3–22
1953 Bucharest			14–16
1958 Catania			3–6
1962 Bucharest	14–6		
1966 Aquila			0–3
1967 Bucharest	24–3		
1970 Rovigo	14–3		
1971 Bucharest	32–6		
1975 Bucharest		3–3	
1976 Parma			12–13
1977 Bucharest	69–0		
1977 Reggio Calabria		10–10	
1979 Bucharest	44–0		
1980 Aquila			17–24
1981 Brailia	35–9		
1982 Rovigo			15–21
1983 Buzau	13–6		
Morocco			
1971 Casablanca	25–0		
1972 Bucharest	58–6		
1973 Bucharest	69–9		
1974 Casablanca	22–9		
1980 Constanta	41–11		
1983 Casablanca	28–3		
Netherlands			
1937 Paris	42–3		
1938 Alkmaar		3–3	
1976 Hilversum	27–3		
New Zealand			
1981 Bucharest			6–14
Poland			
1959 Bucharest	43–3		
1960 Altenburg	6–0		
1960 Cojow	25–0		
1960 Zelonia Gora	15–0		
1961 Bratislava	24–6		
1961 Galati Romana	8–0		
1961 Bucharest	28–3		
1962 Zyrardow	26–6		
1962 Bucharest	22–0		
1963 Deva	9–0		
1967 Gdansk	28–3		
1968 Bucharest	15–3		
1971 Bucharest	16–3		
1974 Bucharest	20–6		
1975 Burgas	58–6		
1975 Nowy-Dwor	38–8		
1977 Bucharest	38–21		
1978 Warsaw	39–9		
1979 Bucharest	49–15		
1980 Sochaczew	33–0		
Portugal			
1967 Lisbon	46–6		
Scotland			
1981 Murrayfield			6–12
Soviet Union			
1974 Varna	26–6		
1976 Burgas	14–3		
1979 Kharkov	15–9		
1980 Bucharest	23–6		
1981 Bucharest	18–10		
1982 Bucharest	18–3		
Spain			
1959 Liège	14–12		
1973 Constanta	16–3		
1974 Timisoara	20–9		
1975 Madrid	16–12		
1976 Bucharest	16–7		
1977 Barcelona	22–11		
1978 Bucharest	76–3		
1979 Madrid	22–6		
1981 Barcelona	56–6		
USA			
1920 Antwerp			0–21
1924 Paris			0–37
Wales			
1978 Cardiff			12–13
Yugoslavia			
1968 Stara Zagora	11–3		
1979 Split	32–6		

SABAH

Foundation 1966

Headquarters Sabah Rugby Union, PO Box 1242, Kota Kinabalu, Sabah

Number of clubs 8

Number of players	300
Season	September–March
Temperatures	74°F (23°C) to 80°F (27°C)
Population	1 550 000

Affiliations
Malaysian RFU, 1972

First competition
Campbell Sevens 1953

First outgoing tour
1970 Sabah Police

State championship
1979 Semi-finals: Kota Kinabalu 25 Police 3, Armed Forces 0 Tawau 24. Final: Kota Kinabalu 7 Tawau 9

Borneo Cup
1982 Final: Sabah 9 Brunei 27 (Kota Kinabalu)

SARAWAK

Number of clubs	10
Number of players	250
Season	September–March
Temperatures	74°F (23°C) to 80°F (27°C)

Borneo Cup
1979 Sarawak beat Brunei

SHARJAH

Foundation	1976
Headquarters	c/o Clive Buckley, National Bank of Sharjah, PO Box 4, Sharjah
Main stadium	Sharjah Wanderers Sports Club
Colours	Red and black hoops
Number of clubs	1
Number of players	30
Season	September–April
Temperatures	50°F (10°C) to 90°F (30°C)
Population	800 000

ST LUCIA

Headquarters	St Lucia RFC
Number of clubs	1
Number of players	30

SENEGAL

Foundation	Affiliated to French RU
Headquarters	Hotel Croix du Sud, Dakar
Colours	Yellow and green jerseys
Number of clubs	7
Number of players	210
Season	October–June
Temperatures	60°F (16°C) to 85°F (29°C)
Affiliation	FIRA

Senegal also has 2 junior clubs and 5 school sides.

International results

	W	D	L
Ivory Coast			
1977 Dakar			9–15
1983 Abidjan			0–25

SEYCHELLES

Headquarters	Seychelles RFC, Victoria
Number of clubs	2
Number of players	60
Season	March–October
Temperatures	60°F (16°C) to 80°F (27°C)
Population	61 898

First match
1940

First outgoing tour
1972 Kenya

SINGAPORE

Headquarters	Singapore Rugby Union, c/o Seek Khoon Hiong, Singapore Cricket Club, Esplanade, Singapore 6
Number of clubs	18

Singapore in action against Bahrain in the Hong Kong Sevens, 1983. (Colorsport.)

Number of players	750
Population	2 334 400

First match
1902

First competition
HMS *Malaya* Cup 1922

Hong Kong Sevens
L 0–48 New Zealand, L 3–24 South Korea, L 0–42 American Eagles, L 0–18 Bahrain

Representative matches

	W	D	L
England			
1971 Singapore			9–39
1978 Kuala Lumpur	16–15		
Malaysia			
1982 Singapore			6–15
New Zealand Universities			
1980 Singapore			6–27
South Korea			
1982 Singapore			0–12
Sri Lanka			
1982 Singapore	9–8		

SOLOMON ISLANDS

Number of clubs	10
Number of players	300
Season	May–November
Temperatures	65°F (18°C) to 85°F (29°C)
Population	215 000

South Pacific Games
1969 L 13–113 Fiji
1979 W 35–5 French Polynesia, W 35–3 Tahiti, L 3–92 Tonga

Hong Kong Sevens
1983 L 0–40 Japan, L 0–26 Australia, D 10–10 Indonesia, W 20–4 Malaysia, W 14–0 Thailand, L 0–36 South Korea

SOVIET UNION

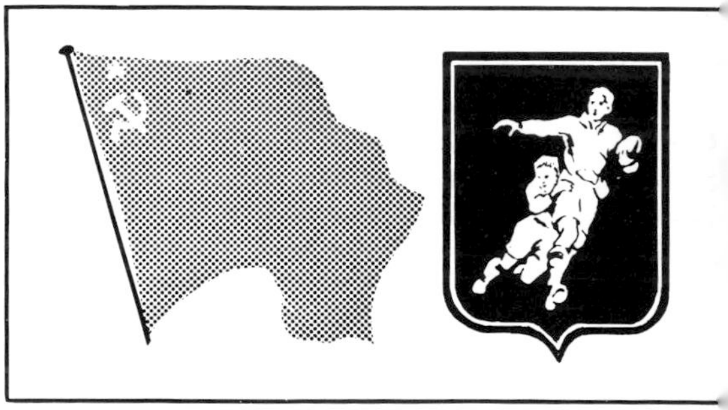

Foundation	1966
Headquarters	4 bid Skatortni, Moscow 69
Main stadium	National Stadium, Moscow (capacity 30 000)
Colours	Red jerseys, white shorts
Number of clubs	222
Number of players	45 000
Season	September–November and April–June
Temperatures	25°F (−4°C) to 65°F (18°C)
Population	262 442 000

Oldest club
VVA, formed 1939. Foundation of other leading clubs—Dynamo Kiev (1946), Fili Moscow (1945), Lokomotive Tblisi (1948), Slava Moscow (1948), Lokomotive Moscow (1947), Elva Tblisi (1950), Poly Krasnoyarsk (1951)

League champions—Division I
1969 VVA. 1970 Fili Moscow. 1971 VVA. 1972 Fili Moscow. 1973 Fili Moscow. 1974 Fili Moscow. 1975 Fili Moscow. 1976 VVA. 1977 VVA. 1978 Aviator Kiev

Biggest victory
Slava Moscow 93 University Moscow 0, 1977

First British club to play in Soviet Union
Llanelli, 1957

Soviet Cup
1978 Lokomotive Tblisi 30 Slava Moscow 3

Most capped players
B Schapavalov (VVA), 32 caps. A Cheverev (Aviator Kiev), 27

Biggest international win
72–0 v Sweden, 1976

Biggest international defeat
7–29 v France, 1978

Outgoing tour 1983
Slava Moscow to Zimbabwe W16–15 Mashonaland (Harare) W 16–12 Matabeleland (Bulawayo) L 9–42 Zimbabwe (Bulawayo) W 33–16 Midlands (Redcliff) L 9–21 Zimbabwe (Harare)

World's most northerly international venue
Leningrad

International results

	W	D	L
Bulgaria			
1976 Burgas	27–13		
Czechoslovakia			
1974 Moscow	18–4		
1975 Leningrad	28–0		
1975 Leningrad	27–6		
1976 Lvov			7–12
1976 Lvov	15–6		
1976 Ricany			6–9
1977 Tblisi	39–12		
1978 Kharkov	18–4		
Fed. Rep. Germany			
1977 Hanover	22–16		
1978 Kharkov	64–9		
1981 Hanover			7–10
France			
1978 Toulouse			7–29
1980 Moscow			7–18
1981 —			10–23
1982 Moscow		10–10	
1982 Merigna	12–6		
German Dem. Rep.			
1977 Nessebar	46–3		
Italy			
1979 Rome	11–9		
1980 Moscow	9–0		
1980 —	4–3		
1981 Moscow		12–12	
Morocco			
1980 Moscow	11–3		
Poland			
1975 Leningrad			15–21
1976 Lvov	22–16		
1977 Tblisi	37–3		
1978 Kharkov	28–13		
1979 Moscow	19–7		
1980 Moscow	54–10		
1981 —	7–3		
Romania			
1974 Varna			6–26
1976 Burgas			3–14
1978 Kharkov			4–16
1979 Bucharest			9–15
1980 Bucharest			6–23
1981 —			10–18
1982 Bucharest			3–18
Spain			
1979 Madrid	15–9		
1981 Kiev	40–7		
Sweden			
1976 Tblisi	72–0		
1977 Vanersborg	38–6		
Yugoslavia			
1978 Sarajevo	18–3		
1978 Travnic	16–6		

Under 19 tournament
1982 (Prague) Soviet Union 42 Bulgaria 0, Soviet Union 22 German Dem. Rep. 3, Romania 18 Soviet Union 16, Soviet Union 11 Czechoslovakia 6

SPAIN

Foundation	1923
Headquarters	FER, Ferraz 16, Madrid 8
Main stadium	Madrid
Colours	Red and blue jerseys
Number of clubs	174
Number of players	11 160
Season	September–May
Temperatures	45°F (7°C) to 70°F (21°C)
Population	36 780 000

Oldest club
Club de Natacion Barcelona, 1922

Number of referees
128

Spanish League champions
1953 CF Barcelona. 1954 CF Barcelona. 1970 Atletico de San Sebastian. 1971 Canoe Natacion Club. 1972 Canoe Natacion Club. 1973 Canoe Natacion Club. 1974 CD Arquitectura de Madrid. 1975 CD Arquitectura de Madrid. 1976 CM Cisneros. 1977 CD Arquitectura de Madrid. 1978 Atletico de San Sebastian. 1979 North Atletico San Sebastian. 1980 CAU Madrid. 1981 CD Arquitectura. 1982 CD Arquitectura. 1983 Valencia RC. (*Group Centro*: CAU Madrid. *Group Levante*: FC Barcelona. *Group Nor-Oeste*: CDU Valladolid. *Group Norte*: Hernani RC)

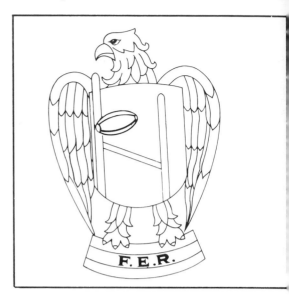

National Cup finals
1941 SEU Madrid 14, RCD Espanol Barcelona 10. **1942** CF Barcelona 17, SEU de Madrid 8. **1943** UD Samboyana 16, Tabernes de Valldigna 0. **1944** CF Barcelona 9, SEU de Madrid 0. **1945** CF Barcelona 3, SEU de Madrid 0. **1946** CF Barcelona 23, SEU de Madrid 13. **1947** SEU de Madrid 6, CF Barcelona 3. **1948** UD Samboyana 13, SEU de Leon 9. **1949** Atletico Madrid CF 8, UD Samboyana 3. **1950** CF Barcelona beat Atletico Madrid CF (score not known). **1951** CF Barcelona 14, SEU de Madrid 0. **1952** CF Barcelona 10, Atletico Madrid CF 3. **1953** CF Barcelona 6, Atletico de Madrid 3. **1954** SEU de Madrid 16, CN Barcelona 3. **1955** CF Barcelona beat Atletico de Madrid CF (score not known). **1956** CF Barcelona 6, UD Samboyana 3. **1957** CN Barcelona 8, CF Barcelona 0. **1958** UD Samboyana 11, CF Barcelona 9. **1959** UD Samboyana 20, Picadero Juventud 14. **1960** UD Samboyana 8, CN Barcelona 3. **1961** UD Samboyana 3, CN Barcelona 0. **1962** UD Samboyana 6, C. Aitor de Madrid 3. **1963** CN Barcelona 3, UD Samboyana 0. **1964** Canoe Natacion 3, UD Samboyana 0. **1965** CF Barcelona 3, C. Universitario Barcelona 0. **1966** Canoe Natacion 12, C. Universitario Barcelona 0. **1967** CM Cisneros 14, UD Samboyana 3. **1968** A. San Sebastian 8, CF Barcelona 6. **1969** CM Cisneros 11, CF Barcelona 8. **1970** Canoe Natacion 17, A. San Sebastian 13. **1971** Canoe Natacion 6, El Salvador Valladolid 3. **1972** A. San Sebastian 31, C Natacion Barcelona 10. **1973** A San Sebastian 21, CD Arquitectura 13. **1974** Canoe Natacion 13, CA San Sebastian 9. **1975** A San Sebastian 14, C Universitario Valladolid 0. **1976** CD Arquitectura 24, CA Uros Madrid 12. **1977** CAU Madrid 26, CM Cisneros 6. **1978** CAU Madrid 22, CD Arquitectura 9. **1979** Cisneros Madrid 26, Valencia RC 14. **1980** CD Arquitectura 19, CAU Madrid 0. **1981** CD Arquitectura 25, Canoe NC 7. **1982** RC Cisneros 7, CD Arquitectura 6. **1983** RC Cisneros

FER Cup
1983 CD Arquitectura

Incoming tours
1982 Maoris
W 62–13 Spain B (Barcelona)
W 66–3 Spain (Madrid)

1982 Argentina
W 28–19 Spain (Madrid)

1983 Wales
W 24–3 Basque XV (Guernica)
W 32–6 Spain Under 23s (Gijon)
W 71–0 Valencia Select XV
W 83–3 Castille–Leon XV (Valladolid)
W 65–16 Spain (Madeira)

Outgoing tour
1983 Spain to England

International results

	W	D	L
Argentina			
1982 Madrid			19–28
Belgium			
1954 Treviso	14–0		
1958 Charleroi	11–5		
1959 Brussels	17–14		
1960 Madrid	21–0		
1968 Brussels	14–0		
1969 Madrid	41–3		
1971 Brussels	44–0		
Czechoslovakia			
1967 Madrid			8–9
1971 Madrid			6–12
1975 Prague	13–7		
1978 Barcelona	20–13		
Fed. Rep. Germany			
1929 Barreiro			15–24
1930 Dresden			0–5
1952 Madrid			6–17
1954 Frankfurt		6–6	
1957 Barna			3–16
1959 Heidelberg			14–19
1960 Barna	9–3		
1962 Hanover			6–14
1973 Bucharest	11–9		
1979 Heidelberg	13–0		
France			
1927 Madrid			6–66
1928 Bordeaux			6–53
1954 Barna			26–45
1955 Limoges			6–50
1965 Barna			3–45
1967 Valencia			3–42
1970 Madrid			6–58
1973 Barna			23–30
1974 Madrid			7–15
1975 Mauleon			3–46
1976 Madrid			0–36
1977 Hendaye			21–28
1978 Madrid			3–20
1979 Oloron			0–92
1981 Barcelona			19–40
Italy			
1929 Barna	9–0		
1930 Milan			0–3
1951 Rome			0–12
1952 Barna			0–6
1954 Naples			6–16
1956 Barna			0–8
1969 Aquila			5–12
1972 Madrid	10–0		
1972 Ivrea		6–6	
1975 Madrid			3–19
1975 Madrid			6–19
1976 Rome			4–17
1977 Madrid	10–3		
1978 Treviso			3–35
1979 Split			9–16
1980 Madrid			13–18
Morocco			
1931 Rabat			6–14
1932 Madrid			8–14
1932 Rabat			0–14
1967 Madrid	3–0		
1968 Casablanca			5–6
1969 Madrid	18–0		
1970 Casablanca			8–11
1973 Casablanca	20–9		
1974 Madrid	22–0		
1977 Madrid	21–3		
1979 Split			4–16
1982 forfeit			
Netherlands			
1967 Amsterdam	14–5		
1975 Uden		4–4	
1977 Hilversum	28–0		
1980 Barcelona	24–3		
1982 Barcelona	25–12		
1983 Hilversum	32–3		
Poland			
1970 Poznan	8–6		
1972 Madrid	3–0		
1974 Poznan	4–0		
1976 Bialystok			14–17
1977 Madrid	11–3		
1978 Warsaw	28–22		
1978 Barcelona			4–16
1980 Madrid			20–25
1982 Lublin			6–32
1983 Valencia			7–16
Portugal			
1935 Lisbon	6–5		
1936 Madrid	16–9		
1954 Madrid	23–0		
1965 Lisbon	12–9		
1966 Madrid			3–9
1967 Lisbon	9–5		
1968 Madrid	14–5		
1969 Barreiro	15–11		
1970 Madrid	17–0		
1982 Lisbon	32–13		
1983 Madrid	25–4		
Romania			
1958 Liège			12–14
1971 Madrid			3–20
1972 Constanza			13–16
1974 Timisoara			9–20
1975 Madrid			12–16
1976 Bucharest			7–16
1977 Barcelona			11–22
1978 Bucharest			3–76
1979 Madrid			6–22
1981 Barcelona			6–56
Soviet Union			
1979 Moscow			9–15
1981 Kiev			7–40
Sweden			
1980 Uppsala	39–27		
Tunisia			
1979 Split	62–0		
1981 Madrid	7–3		
1982 Burgos	15–3		
Yugoslavia			
1969 Madrid	14–3		
1971 Madrid	26–4		

	W	D	L
1972 Split	21–7		
1979 Madrid	25–3		

Other match

1982 Maoris 66 Spain 3 (Madrid)

SRI LANKA

Foundation 1878
Headquarters Sri Lanka RFU, c/o Sqn. Ldr. E Y Buell, 28 Longden Place, Colombo 7
Main stadium Colombo
Number of clubs 15
Number of players 300
Population 13 971 000

British Lions' tour

1950 Sri Lanka 6 British Lions 44, Colombo

Results against International Board countries

	W	D	L
British Lions			
1950 Colombo			6–44
England			
1971 Colombo			11–40
1971 Colombo			6–34
Japan			
1978 Kuala Lumpur			8–34
1980 Taiwan			0–108
Thailand			
1978 Kuala Lumpur			10–19

Sri Lanka going for the tackle in their 1983 Hong Kong Sevens match against Papua New Guinea. (Colorsport.)

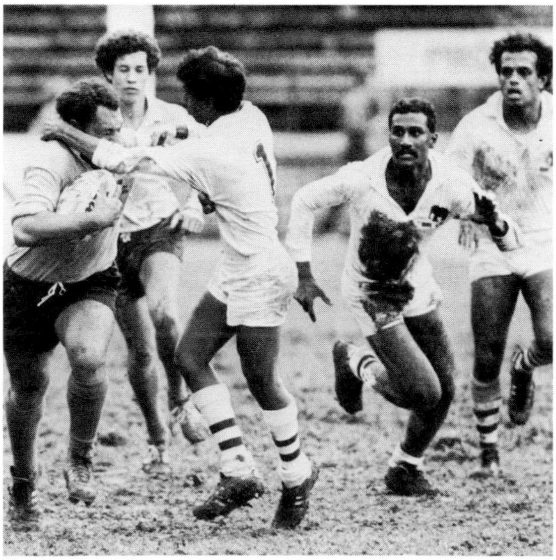

International results

	W	D	L
Malaysia			
1982 Singapore			12–23
Singapore			
1982 Singapore			8–9
South Korea			
1982 Singapore			0–12

Hong Kong Sevens

1983 L 0–16 Scottish Border Club, L 0–26 Canada, L 0–28 Western Samoa, L 4–8 Papua New Guinea

SWAZILAND

Number of clubs 2
Number of players 100
Season April–October
Temperatures 55°F (13°C) to 70°F (21°C)
Population 507 000

SWEDEN

Foundation 1931
Headquarters Svenska Rugbyförbundet, Idrottens Hus, 123 87 Farsta
Main stadium Stockholm
Colours Yellow jerseys
Number of clubs 56
Number of players 2480
Season August–November and March–July
Temperatures 32°F (0°C) to 60°F (16°C)
Population 8 285 000

First match

1931 Stockholm

First club

IK Balder 1933

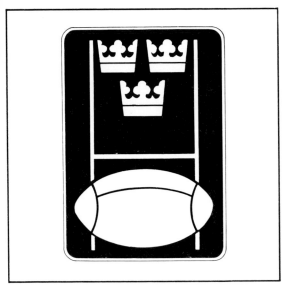

Oldest club
Älvsjö AIK 1946

Affiliation
FIRA, founder members 1934

League champions
1943–44 Göta. 1945 Stockholms RK. 1946 RK Pantern. 1947–48 IK Göta. 1949 Västerås RK. 1950–51 IK Göta. 1952–56 Älvsjö AIK. 1957–58 IF Attila. 1959 Malmö RC. 1960 Ingen Mästere. 1961 IF Attila. 1962–65 Malmö RC. 1966 Exiles RFC. 1967 Malmö RC. 1968 IF Attila. 1969–70 Uppsala RFC. 1971 IFK Vänersborg. 1972 Exiles RFC. 1973–76 Enköpings RK. 1977 Uppsala RFC. 1978–82 Enköpings RK

Junior champions
1947 Tranebergspojkarna. 1948–49 IK Skuru. 1950 Älvsjö AIK. 1951 IF Attila. 1952–54 Uppehåll. 1955 RK Vikingarna. 1956 Farsta IF. 1957–60 Älvsjö AIK. 1961–70 Uppehåll. 1971 IFK Vänersborg. 1972–73 Malmö RC. 1974 Enköpings RK. 1975–80 Malmö RC. 1981 IFK Vänersborg. 1982 Malmö RC

Swedish Cup
1971–72 Exiles RFC. 1973–74 Enköpings RK. 1975 Exiles RFC. 1976 Enköpings RK. 1977 Uppsala RFC. 1978–82 Enköpings RK

Number of referees 60

Biggest international win
40–3 v Denmark, 1978

Biggest international defeat
0–72 v Soviet Union, 1976

Most tries in internationals
6 Torbjorn Johansson (Enköping), Christer Lindahl (Malmö)

Longest playing international
Nils Rolf (Attila), 1958–73

Leading scorer in internationals
Kjell Olsson (Attila), 80 points

Most capped player
Jörgen Pettersson (Vasteras) 36 caps

Outgoing tour
1981 Gothenburg to Barbados

Incoming tour
1981 Rugby School

International results

	W	D	L
Belgium			
1966 Brussels			3–24
1971 Sollentuna			3–7
1973 Brussels			6–18
1975 Vänersborg	3–0		
1976 Brussels			3–14
1978 Brussels			6–12
1980 Enköping			0–7
1981 Karlstad	15–9		
Czechoslovakia			
1965 Prague			0–42
1967 Uppsala			3–27
1971 Gothenburg		9–9	
1977 Gothenburg			12–50
Denmark			
1949 Stockholm	6–0		
1950 Copenhagen	14–0		
1951 Stockholm	30–3		
1953 Gothenburg	16–6		
1954 Copenhagen	9–6		
1958 Norrkoping		5–5	
1959 Copenhagen	8–6		
1960 Stockholm	11–3		
1961 Odense		12–12	
1962 Malmö	9–8		
1963 Copenhagen			0–6
1964 Malmö	14–3		
1965 Aarhus	6–3		
1966 Gothenburg	18–0		
1967 Copenhagen	9–6		
1968 Helsinborg	11–0		
1969 Copenhagen		9–9	

1970 Vänersborg	8–0		
1971 Gothenburg	11–3		
1971 Koge	18–5		
1972 Vasteras	26–12		
1973 Aarhus			7–12
1974 Enköping	24–0		
1975 Copenhagen	20–9		
1976 Karlstad	36–9		
1977 Odense	26–3		
1978 Malmö	40–3		
1980 Aarhus	20–4		
1981 Copenhagen	35–6		
1982 Lund	25–0		
Fed. Rep. Germany			
1977 Berlin	16–11		
1977 Sollentuna			9–32
1979 Sollentuna			4–10
German Dem. Rep.			
1964 Malmö			0–28
1965 Zehdenick			5–18
1973 Berlin			12–22
Netherlands			
1966 Hilversum			5–23
1968 Helsingborg			3–35
1971 Gothenburg	6–0		
1973 Amsterdam			0–21
1976 Hilversum			3–34
1978 Hilversum			0–4
1979 Hilversum			0–12
1982 Malmö			7–16
Norway			
1980 Vänersborg	20–0		
Poland			
1964 Malmö			0–12
1965 Gdansk			0–32
1966 Eskilstuna	12–12		
1968 Warsaw			3–38
1982 Poznan			6–54
Portugal			
1970 Hilversum		9–9	
1981 Trelleborg			10–15
Soviet Union			
1976 Tblisi			0–72
1977 Vänersborg			6–38
Spain			
1980 Uppsala			27–39
Switzerland			
1980 Yverdon	7–4		
1982 Enköping	10–3		
1982 Enköping	6–4		
Yugoslavia			
1978 Enköping			3–7
1980 Split			4–14
1982 Ljubljana	17–9		

FIRA Junior tournament

1982 (Geneva) Sweden 6 Ivory Coast 21

SWITZERLAND

Foundation	1971
Headquarters	Fédération Suisse de Rugby, Case Postale 325, 1001 Lausanne
Main stadium	Stade Municipal de Vidy/Lausanne (capacity 10 000)
Colours	Red jerseys, white shorts
Number of clubs	20
Number of players	800
Season	September – December and March–June
Temperatures	32°F (0°C) to 60°F (16°C)
Population	6 298 000

Oldest active player

Antoine Cazorla (CERN-Meyrin), aged 51

Most capped player

Daniel Henry (Neuchâtel Sports), 14 caps

Longest international career

Gerard Nicod (Albaladéjo Lausanne) 1972–80

First overseas tour

1979 L 0–43 v Morocco, L 0–31 v Portugal

Other tours

1982 L 4–6 v Sweden, W 40–0 v Finland

Oldest clubs
CERN-Meyrin 1967, Neuchâtel-Sports 1968, Albaladéjo, Stade Lausanne, International Genève, RC Zurich 1969

Highest club scores
82–0 Bern v Riviera, 100–0 CERN v Monthey, 108–3 Stade Lausanne v Albaladéjo Lausanne (1st Div. match, 1983)

National Cup winners
1971 RC Genève. 1972 RC Genève. 1973 RC CERN-Meyrin. 1974 RC CERN-Meyrin. 1975 International RC Genève. 1976 International RC Genève. 1977 RC CERN-Meyrin. 1978 International RC Genève. 1979 RC Hermance. 1980 RC Hermance. 1981 Stade Lausanne. 1982 Stade Lausanne

National championship
1971 Stade Lausanne. 1972 RC Genève. 1973 RC Nyon and RC IOS. 1974 RC CERN-Meyrin. 1975 Stade Lausanne. 1976 Stade Lausanne. 1977 RC CERN-Meyrin. 1978 RC CERN-Meyrin. 1979 RC CERN-Meyrin. 1980 RC CERN-Meyrin. 1981 Stade Lausanne. 1982 CERN-Meyrin

League Champions
Stade Lausanne

Cup Winners
RC Hermance beat Stade Lausanne 16–10

Monthey tournament
1972 RC Genève. 1973 RC Monthey. 1974 RC IOS. 1975 RC IOS. 1976 RC Stade Lausanne. 1977 RC International. 1978 RC International. 1979 RC Saint-Florent (France). 1980 RC Saint-Florent (France). 1981 Balma Toulouse. 1982 LOU Lyon. 1983 Thonon (France)

Max Bangerter Sevens (Neuchâtel)
1975 US Douanes (Paris). 1976 Lyon Olympique Universitaire. 1977 Neuchâtel-Sports. 1978 Lyon Olympique Universitaire. 1979 SOC Chambéry. 1980 Heidelberg Magicians. 1981 Heidelberg Magicians. 1982 Haguenau. 1983 Heidelberg Magicians

International results

	W	D	L
Belgium			
1974 Lausanne			10–18
1975 Brussels			3–11
1977 Lausanne			16–25
1980 Brussels			0–7
1982 Antwerp			6–10
1983 Geneva			9–23
Czechoslovakia			
1975 Lausanne			6–23
1983 Nafels			9–14
Denmark			
1980 Geneva			16–20
1981 Lausanne	34–21		
Fed. Rep. Germany			
1978 Geneva			0–18
Finland			
1982 Helsinki	40–0		
Israel			
1981 Geneva		9–9	
Luxembourg			
1977 Luxembourg	7–4		
1980 Berne	10–7		
Morocco			
1979 Casablanca			0–43
Portugal			
1973 Neuchâtel			4–23
1979 Lisbon			0–31
1981 Lisbon			0–39
Sweden			
1980 Yverdon			4–7
1982 Enköping			3–10
1982 Enköping			4–6
Tunisia			
1982 Tunis			0–3
Yugoslavia			
1975 Geneva	12–3		
1976 Split			4–31
1976 Lausanne			6–18
1981 Lausanne			0–10
1982 Split			19–36

FIRA Junior tournament
1982 (Geneva) Switzerland 4 Ivory Coast 20

TAIWAN

Headquarters	Republic of China RFU, 10 Pa-Te Road, Sec. 10, Taipei, Taiwan
Number of clubs	10
Number of players	300

Hosted 1980 Asian championships

International results

	W	D	L
Hong Kong			
1982 Singapore			3–21
Japan			
1982 Singapore			6–31
Thailand			
1982 Singapore	20–0		

TANZANIA

Foundation ....1953 (ceased in 1959)
Headquarters Dar-es-Salaam Gymkhana RFC
Main stadium Dar-es-Salaam Gymkhana RFC
Number of clubs 1
Number of players 30
Season April–August
Temperatures 55°F (13°C) to 75°F (24°C)
Population 16 553 000

According to the Rugby Football Union of East Africa, there was little or no rugby played in Tanzania in 1981–3

THAILAND

Foundation 1937
Headquarters Royal Bangkok Sports Club
Main stadium National Stadium, Bangkok (capacity 10 000)
Number of clubs 40
Number of players 1400
Season July–December
Temperatures 40°F (4°C) to 65°F (18°C)
Population 45 500 000

First overseas tour
To England, 1950

Royal Trophy
The Vajiralongkorn Cup, donated by the King of Thailand in 1954

First inter-port match
Penang Sports Club v Royal Bangkok Sports Club, 1920

British Council Cup
Instituted 1938

Other tournaments
University Shield, Inter-Scholastic Shield, General Praphas Charusathira's Cup, Inter-Scholastic Knock-out Competition Shield

Hong Kong Sevens
1983 L 4–32 Fiji, L 6–20 Tonga, W 10–0 Brunei, L 4–20 Hong Kong, L 0–14 Solomon Islands

International results

	W	D	L
Hong Kong			
1982 Singapore			6–39
Japan			
1970 Tokyo			12–44
1978 Kuala Lumpur			18–47
1982 Singapore			6–43
Scotland			
1977 Bangkok			6–82
Singapore			
1978 Kuala Lumpur			15–16
Taiwan			
1982 Singapore			0–20

TONGA

Foundation 1923
Headquarters PO Box 369, Nuku' Alofa

Main stadium	Teufaiva Park (capacity 18 000)
Colours	Scarlet jerseys
Number of clubs	80
Number of players	3000
Season	April–September
Temperatures	60°F (16°C) to 80°F (27°C)
Population	160 000

Oldest clubs
Kolofo'ou and Kolomotu'a 1939

Largest scores
St John Under-20s 120 v Wairarapa (New Zealand) Under-20s, March 1979; Nukunuku scored 112 v Talafo'ou, in May 1979 (in this match, Matini Tu'iono, 21, a wing, scored 6 tries and kicked 16 conversions, which gave him a world record of 56 points)

Biggest international win
92–3 v Solomon Islands, 1979

Biggest defeat
4–46 England Under-23s, 1974

Longest career
15 seasons Uaisele Latukefu 1957–73

Other results
1974 beat Australian Capital City 21–9
East Wales 18–13
lost Wales XV 7–26

Major tours

	P	W	D	L	F	A
1973 Australia	10	4	0	6	125	158
1974 British Isles	10	1	0	9	95	237
1975 New Zealand	12	8	0	4	268	231

Pan Am tournament
Hawaii, 1981, won by Kolofo'ou

District Championship
1980 A—Town. B—Town
1981 A—Country. B—Country
1983 A—Country. B—Town. C—Town

Sub-district
1981 A—Vahe Kolomotu'a. B—Ha'apai
1983 A—Vahe Kolomotu'a

Club champions

	Grade	*Trophy*	*Winners*
1977	Senior A	Shield	Hihifo and Kolomotu (tie)
		Cup	Kolomotu'a
	Senior B	Shield	Hua' Atolitoli
		Cup	Kauvai
	Reserve	Shield	Kolofo'ou
1978	Senior A	Shield	Hihifo
	A I	Cup	Hihifo
	A II	Cup	Ha' Ateiho
	Senior B	Shield	Tahimate
	B I	Cup	Tahimate
	B II	Cup	Ha' Asini
	Reserve	Shield	Tavatu'utolu
	Reserve I	Cup	Liahona
	Reserve II	Cup	Nukunuku and Kauvai (tie)

	Grade	*Trophy*	*Winners*
	Sevens	Shield	Lapaha
1979	Senior A	Shield	Hihifo and Kolomotu'a (tie)
	B	Shield	Nukunuku
	Reserve I	Shield	Tavatu'utolu
	Reserve II	Shield	Fatai/Lakepa
	Colts		Vahekolo
1980	Senior A	Shield	Polisi
	B I	Shield	Tahimate and Ma' Ufanga (tie)
	B II	Shield	Tavatu'utolu
	Reserve I	Shield	Ma' Ufanga and Houmakelikao (tie)
	Reserve II	Shield	Sopu'o Taufa'ahau
1981	Senior A		Hihifo
	Senior B I		Ha'asini and Hihifo
	Senior B II		THS Old Boys
	Reserve I		Kolovai
	Reserve II		Kotongo and Houma 'Utulau
1982	Senior A		Tavatu'utolu
	Senior A II		Tavatu'utolu and Kolomotu'a
	Senior B I		Kolovai
	Senior B II		Hihifo
	Reserve I		Sopu 'o Taufa'ahau
	Reserve II		Puke
1983	Senior A I		Hihifo
	Senior A II		Hihifo
	Senior B I		Polisi
	Senior B II		Haveluloto
	Senior C I		Tahimate
	Senior C II		Tavatu'utolu

Hong Kong Sevens
1983 L 0–16 Fiji, W 20–6 Thailand, W 20–0 Brunei, W 10–8 Hong Kong, L 6–12 Australia

International results

	W	D	L
Australia			
1973 Sydney			12–30
1973 Brisbane	16–11		
England			
1979 Nuku' Alofa			17–37

Fiji			
1924 Nuku' Alofa			3–14
1924 Nuku' Alofa	9–6		
1924 Nuku' Alofa		0–0	
1926 Suva			3–10
1926 Suva	13–8		
1926 Suva	6–3		
1928 Nuku' Alofa	9–6		
1928 Nuku' Alofa			5–9
1928 Nuku' Alofa	11–8		
1932 Suva			0–11
1932 Suva			5–24
1932 Suva			0–30
1934 Nuku' Alofa			6–16
1934 Nuku' Alofa	6–5		
1934 Nuku' Alofa			8–30
1947 Suva			3–25
1947 Suva			9–19
1958 Nuku' Alofa			14–17
1958 Nuku' Alofa	16–11		
1958 Nuku' Alofa			10–11
1959 Suva	14–11		
1963 Suva			5–8
1963 Suva			9–25
1967 Nuku' Alofa			6–18
1967 Nuku' Alofa		6–6	
1967 Nuku' Alofa			6–9
1968 Suva	8–6		
1968 Lautoka			10–12
1968 Suva			6–11
1972 Nuku' Alofa			6–12
1972 Nuku' Alofa			8–15
1972 Nuku' Alofa			6–16
1977 Suva			9–13
1977 Lautoka			7–33
1977 Suva			9–43
1979 Suva	6–3		
1981 Nuku' Alofa	10–4		
1981 Nuku' Alofa			8–10
1981 Nuku' Alofa			8–18
1982 Nuku' Alofa			4–37
1983 Suva			8–13

New Caledonia			
1979 Suva (S. Pacific Games)	58–3		
New Zealand			
1960 Nuku' Alofa	27–16		
Maoris			
1969 New Zealand	26–19		
1969 New Zealand	19–6		
1973 Nuku' Alofa	11–3		
1975 New Zealand			16–23
1975 New Zealand			7–37
1979 Nuku' Alofa			9–26
Scotland			
1974 Murrayfield			8–44
Solomon Islands			
1979 Suva (S. Pacific Games)	92–3		
Tahiti			
1979 Suva (S. Pacific Games)	74–0		
Western Samoa			
1956 Nuku' Alofa	24–8		
1957 Apia	26–9		
1957 Apia	24–7		
1957 Apia		9–9	
1963 Suva (S. Pacific Games)	12–8		
1972 Apia	26–18		
1972 Apia	16–14		
1975 Apia	15–10		
1975 Apia			9–14
1978 Nuku' Alofa	18–9		
1979 Suva (S. Pacific Games)	18–10		
1980 Apia	15–12		
1982 Nuku' Alofa			7–13
1983 Suva	15–6		

TRINIDAD AND TOBAGO

Headquarters	c/o Chief State Solicitor, 7 St Vincent Street, Port of Spain
Main stadium	Carib RFC, Port of Spain (capacity 2000)
Colours	Red jerseys, white shorts
Number of clubs	10
Number of players	350
Season	July–December
Temperatures	60°F (16°C) to 85°F (29°C)
Population	1 133 000

First match
1927

Oldest club
Carib, 1926

Affiliation
Caribbean RFU 1973

International results

	W	D	L
Bermuda			
1979 Guyana			8–42
1981 Trinidad	27–14		

TUNISIA

Headquarters	22 rue Gamei, Abdenasser, Tunis
Main stadium	Cité Bourguiba, Tunis
Colours	Red and white jerseys
Number of clubs	30
Number of players	4000
Season	September–May
Temperatures	50°F (10°C) to 70°F (21°C)
Population	6 080 000

Cup finals
1978 OB 16 CSS 10. 1979 L'Asmt 13 OB 9. 1980 CSMI 23 OB 0. 1981 CA 12 ASS 6. 1982 CSL. 1983 EST 16 SN 10

League winners
1978 CSL. 1979 O Béja 10. 1980 CSMI. 1981 OB. 1982 CA. 1983 CA

International results

	W	D	L
Belgium			
1978 Brussels			8–26
1980 Tunis	11–7		
1983 Brussels	13–12		
Czechoslovakia			
1983 Prague			7–14
Denmark			
1980 Copenhagen	19–13		
Fed. Rep. Germany			
1981 Heidelberg			9–30
France			
1979 Split			3–104
Ivory Coast			
1976 Tunis			6–22
Morocco			
1981 Tunis	13–10		
1982 Casablanca			4–6
Netherlands			
1981 Hilversum			9–21
1982 Tunis			6–15
Poland			
1982 Tunis			3–16
Portugal			
1982 Lisbon			16–25
Spain			
1979 Split			0–62
1982 Madrid			3–7
1982 Burgos			3–15
Switzerland			
1982 Tunis	3–0		
Yugoslavia			
1979 Split			0–23
1982 Split			0–4
1983 Tunis	41–6		

Junior internationals
1980 (Tunis) Tunisia B 3 Yugoslavia 15, Tunisia A 19 Yugoslavia 3, Tunisia A 11 Ivory Coast 3, Tunisia B 0 Ivory Coast 14
1983 (Casablanca) Tunisia 16 Spain 16, Tunisia 3 Italy 32, Tunisia 14 Morocco 28

UGANDA

Foundation	1955
Headquarters	c/o Kenyan RU
Main stadium	Kampala RFC (capacity 8000)
Colours	Black, crested crane badge
Number of clubs	1
Number of players	30
Season	April–September
Temperatures	55°F (13°C) to 70°F (21°C)
Population	12 780 000

Kampala RFC are still in existence, but according to the Rugby Football Union of East Africa no rugby was played in Uganda 1981–3

URUGUAY

Foundation	1951
Headquarters	Union de Rugby del Uruguay, Yaguaron 1093, Montevideo

Uruguay National Team May 1981. Taken during South American Championship played in Montevideo. (Union de Rugby del Uruguay.)

Main stadium	None
Colours	Sky blue jerseys
Number of clubs	14
Number of players	1300
Season	April–November
Temperatures	55°F (13°C) to 68°F (20°C)
Population	2 900 000

First match
1880

First club
Montevideo Cricket Club, 1929

Club champions
1951 Montevideo Cricket Club. 1952 Old Boys/Carrasco Polo Club. 1953 Montevideo Cricket Club. 1954 Trouville. 1955 Colonia Rowing. 1956 Old Boys, Trouville/Montevideo Cricket Club. 1957 Old Boys. 1958 Colonia Rowing/Trouville. 1959 Old Boys. 1960 Los Cuervos. 1961 Carrasco Polo Club. 1962 Old Boys. 1963 Old Boys. 1964 Old Boys. 1965 Old Boys. 1966 Carrasco Polo Club. 1967 Old Boys. 1968 Old Christians/Old Boys. 1969 Old Boys. 1970 Old Christians. 1971 La Cachila. 1972 La Cachila. 1973 La Cachila/Old Christians. 1974 La Cachila. 1975 La Cachila/Old Boys. 1976 Old Christians. 1977 Old Christians. 1978 Old Christians. 1979 Old Christians. 1980 Old Christians. 1981 Carrasco Polo Club. 1982 La Cachila 0 MVCC 26—Old Boys 42 Circulo Tennis 0—Los Cuervos 3 Old Christians 22—Old Christians 31 La Cachila 0—Old Boys 17 MVCC 13—Los Cuervos 0 Carrasco Polo 12—La Cachila 3 Los Cuervos 17—MVCC 15 Old Christians 15—Circulo Tennis 10 Carrasço Polo 44—Los Cuervos 7 Old Boys 9—Carrasco Polo 37 MVCC 6—La Cachila 9 Circulo Tennis 3—MVCC 18 Los Cuervos 16—Carrasco Polo 13 Old Boys 12—Circulo Tennis 14 Old Christians 45—Carrasco Polo 28 La Cachila 0—Old Boys 6 Old Christians 22—Circulo Tennis 3 Los Cuervos 32—Old Boys 17 La Cachila 16—MVCC 33 Circulo Tennis 7—Old Christians 6 Carrasco Polo 6—Old Christians 14 Los Cuervos 9—MVCC 36 La Cachila 3—Circulo Tennis 16 Old Boys 54—Carrasco Polo 25 Los Cuervos 7—La Cachila 3 Old

Christians 20—MVCC 4 Old Boys 11—Carrasco Polo 24 Circulo Tennis 9—Los Cuervos 10 La Cachila 7—Old Christians 40 MVCC 0—MVCC 3 Carrasco Polo 21—Circulo Tennis 12 La Cachila 21—Old Boys 21 Los Cuervos 6—Old Christians 38 Circulo Tennis 4—Old Boys 3 Carrasco Polo 20—Los Cuervos 19 MVCC 28—Old Christians 36 Old Boys 6—La Cachila 0 Carrasco Polo 28—Los Cuervos 32 Circulo Tennis 4—MVCC W.O. Circulo Tennis—Carrasco Polo 6 Old Christians 10—La Cachila 4 Old Boys 24. *Final Positions:* 1 Old Christians 2 Carrasco Polo 3 Old Boys 4 MVCC 5 Los Cuervos 6 La Cachila 7 Circulo Tennis

Biggest international win
77–0 Brazil, Montevideo 1981

Biggest international defeat
0–70 Argentina, Tucuman 1977

Incoming tours
1975 The Oribis (South Africa) 1976 New Zealand 1980 South Africa 1981 South Africa Country Team 1982 Northern Transvaal

Outgoing tours
1980 Old Boys to South Africa. 1981 Los Cuervos to South Africa. 1982 Carrasco Polo Club to South Africa. 1982 Old Christians to South Africa (Results: L 18–20 Paratus—W 35–6 Durban Collegians—W 34–3 Durban Technical College—W 33–13 East London XV—L 3–13 Patensie—W 19–0 Hamilton—D 14–14 Christian Brothers College—W 21–18 Libertas)

International results

	W	D	L
Argentina			
1951 Buenos Aires			0–62
1958 Vina del Mar			3–50
1961 Montevideo			3–36
1964 São Paulo			6–25
1967 Buenos Aires			6–38
1969 Santiago			6–41
1971 Montevideo			6–55
1973 São Paulo			0–55
1975 Asuncion			15–30
1977 Tucuman			0–70
1979 Santiago			16–19
1983 Buenos Aires			6–29
Brazil			
1951 Buenos Aires	17–10		
1961 Montevideo	11–8		
1964 São Paulo			8–15
1971 Montevideo	37–11		
1973 São Paulo	16–6		
1975 Asuncion	38–7		
1977 Tucuman	47–15		
1979 Santiago	48–0		
1981 Montevideo	77–0		
Chile			
1951 Buenos Aires	8–3		
1958 Santiago			9–34
1961 Montevideo			5–28
1964 São Paulo	15–8		
1967 Buenos Aires			11–16
1969 Santiago			6–13
1971 Montevideo			6–11
1973 São Paulo	13–10		
1975 Asuncion			7–15
1977 Tucuman	21–18		
1979 Santiago		9–9	
1981 Montevideo	33–3		
1983 Buenos Aires	25–3		
Paraguay			
1971 Montevideo	56–3		
1973 São Paulo	31–9		
1975 Asuncion	38–18		
1977 Tucuman	16–7		
1979 Santiago	53–9		
1981 Montevideo	54–14		
1983 Buenos Aires	20–12		
Peru			
1958 Santiago	10–6		

Junior internationals
Brazil 1972 W 36–9 1974 W 39–6 1978 W 58–3 1980 W 32–0 1982 W 21–4. *Chile* 1972 L 10–12 1974 W 20–10 1976 W 23–3 1978 W 17–9 1980 W 10–3 1982 W 27–12. *Argentina* 1972 L 9–16 1974 L 9–32 1976 L 15–41 1978 L 3–13 1982 L 6–31. *Paraguay* 1972 W 58–0 1974 W 70–18 1976 W 17–12 1978 W 66–24 1980 L 7–13 1982 W 9–7

UNITED STATES OF AMERICA

Foundation	1975
Headquarters	United States of America Rugby Football Union, 525 Mason Avenue, St Louis, MO 63119
Main stadium	Various venues
Colours	Red, white and blue jerseys
Number of clubs	1000
Number of players	65 000
Season	September–May
Temperatures	32°F (0°C) to 75°F (24°C)

Population 218 502 000

First match
1840

Affiliation
Rugby Football Union

National Club champions
1979–82 Old Blues (Berkeley) 1983 Old Blues 23 Dallas Harlequins 0

Territorial winners
1977 Pacific Coast 1978 Pacific Coast, Midwest & Eastern 1979–82 Pacific Coast

University champions
1980–82 University of California 1983 University of California 13 US Air Force Academy 3

Olympic Games
USA won title in 1920 (Antwerp) and 1924 (Paris)

National coaches
1974–77 Dennis Storer, 1978–82 Ray Cornhill, 1983+ Ron Mays (Old Blues, California)

National club championships
1982 Denver Barbarians 35 Norfolk 24—Old Blues 20 Chicago Lions 15. *Final:* Old Blues 36 Denver 7. *3rd place:* Norfolk 20 Chicago Lions 16

National University championship
1982 Life College 34 New Mexico State 11—California 19 Michigan 8. *Final:* California 16 Life College 14. *3rd place:* Michigan 26 New Mexico State 3 (**NB** Michigan disqualified for playing an ineligible player)

Inter-territorial tournament 1977–82

	W	D	L
Pacific	16	1	1
Midwest	10	0	8
East	8	1	9
West	1	0	17

Oldest player
Skip Niebauer, 37, USA captain 1982

Most capped player
7 John Fowler (Santa Monica) 1979–82, Steve Gray (Los Angeles) 1979–82

Incoming tours

		P	W	D	L	F	A
1905	New Zealand	*2	2	0	0	108	12
1913	New Zealand	13	13	0	0	508	6
1954	New Zealand	2	2	0	0	34	6
1971	Australia	1	1	0	0	22	3
1972	New Zealand	1	1	0	0	41	9
1980	New Zealand	1	1	0	0	53	6
1980	Wales	2	2	0	0	52	18
1981	South Africa	3	3	0	0	125	19
1982	England	6	6	0	0	127	19

* Both matches against British Columbia, at Berkeley and San Francisco

Hong Kong Sevens
1983 American Eagles 0 New Zealand 26, South Korea 16 American Eagles 6, American Eagles 12 Bahrain 10, American Eagles 42 Singapore 0, American Eagles 0 Scottish Border Club 12

Other tours
1982 Pacific Coast Grizzlies 26 British Columbia 6 (Sacramento), Northern California 3 British Columbia 15, Southern California 0 British Columbia 13, California XV 15 Manawatu (New Zealand) 14

Outgoing tours

		P	W	D	L	F	A
1924	England	3	1	0	2	—	—
1977	England	6	2	0	4	75	124

USA Cougars
1978 South Africa/Zimbabwe P 7 W 1 L 6

Les Cusworth, the England fly-half comes under pressure in the match against USA at Hartford in 1982. (Colorsport.)

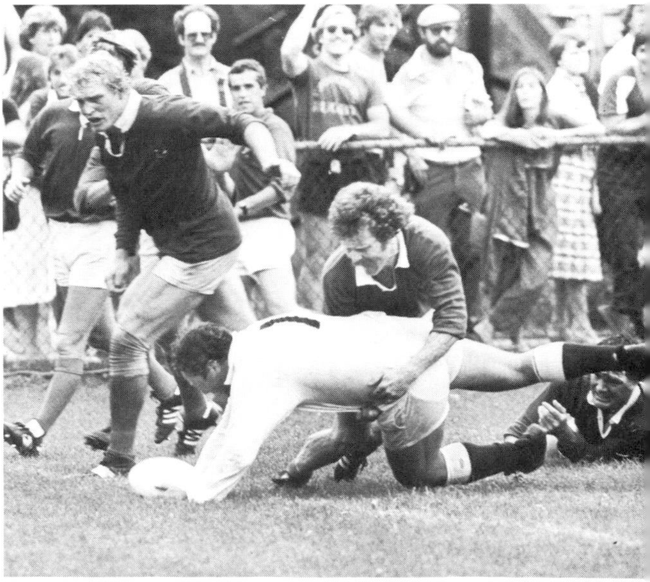

Left: Trampled underfoot! An incident during the South African tour in 1980 when Chicago Lions met Western Province. (All Sport.) Above: Paul Rendell dives in to score a try in England's 59–0 victory over USA at Hartford in 1982. (Colorsport.)

International results

	W	D	L
Australia			
1912 Berkeley			8–12
1971 New York			3–22
1976 Anaheim			12–24
1983 Sydney			3–49
Canada			
1977 Vancouver			6–17
1978 Baltimore	12–7		
1979 Toronto			12–19
1980 Saranac Lake			0–16
1981 Calgary			3–6
1982 Albany		6–6	
1983 Vancouver			9–15
England			
1977 Twickenham			11–37
1982 Hartford			0–59
France			
1920 Antwerp	8–0		
1924 Paris	17–3		
1976 Chicago			14–33
New Zealand			
1913 San Francisco			6–51
1980 San Diego			6–53
Romania			
1920 Antwerp	21–0		
1924 Paris	37–0		
Wales			
1980 Long Beach			18–24

Other matches
1910 USA 8 New Zealand Maoris 0 (San Francisco)
1978 USA Cougars 15 Zimbabwe 32 (Salisbury)

National women's champions
1979 Florida State University. 1980 Florida State University. 1981 Belmont Shore (California). 1982 Beantown (Boston)

US VIRGIN ISLANDS

Headquarters US Virgin Islands RFC
Number of clubs 1
Number of players 30

VENEZUELA

Foundation 1973
Number of clubs 9
Number of players 400

WALLIS AND FUTUNA

Number of clubs 1
Number of players 30
Season April–November
Temperatures 50°F (10°C) to 80°F (27°C)
Population 9000

Affiliation
French Federation

South Pacific Games
1969 Wallis and Futuna 8 Fiji 84 (Port Moresby)

WESTERN SAMOA

Foundation 1927
Headquarters Apia
Number of clubs 10
Number of players 350
Population 154 000

Affiliation
New Zealand RFU 1927

Mark Ella gets the ball away in Australia's 16–0 win over Western Samoa in the 1983 Hong Kong Sevens. (Colorsport.)

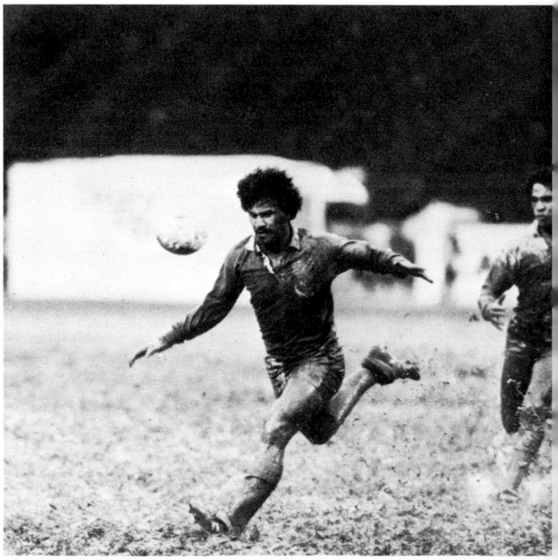

First match
1924 v Fiji (Apia)

Representative match
1979 New Zealand Maoris 26 Western Samoa 3

Hong Kong Sevens
1979 Final: Australia 39 Western Samoa 3
1983 L 4–8 Scottish Border Club, W 16–0 Canada, W 24–4 Papua New Guinea, W 28–0 Sri Lanka, L 0–16 Australia

YUGOSLAVIA

Foundation	1954
Headquarters	Ragbi Savez Jugoslavije, 58 000 Split, Kruzićeva 1
Colours	Blue jerseys, white shorts
Number of clubs	23
Number of players	2700
Season	March–June & September–December
Temperatures	37°F (3°C) to 65°F (18°C)
Population	22 418 000

First club
Partizan Belgrade 1953

Affiliation
FIRA 1964

First club championship
1957

Club champions
1957 Jedinstvo Pančevo. 1958 Mladost Zagreb. 1959 Partizan Beograd. 1960 Partizan Beograd. 1961 Partizan Beograd. 1962–7 Nada Split. 1968 Dinamo Pančevo. 1969 Dinamo Pančevo. 1970–3 Nada Split. 1974 Dinamo Pančevo. 1975–8 Zagreb. 1979 Dinamo Pančevo. 1980 Zagreb. 1981 Zagreb. 1982 Celik Zenica.

National Cup winners
1958 Jedinstvo Pančevo. 1959 Mladost Zagreb. 1960 Partizan Beograd. 1961 Mladost Zagreb. 1962 Mladost Zagreb. 1963— 1964 Nada Split. 1965 Brodarac Beograd. 1966— 1967 Mladost Zagreb. 1968–70 Nada Split. 1971 Brodarac Beograd. 1972 Nada Split. 1973 Dinamo Pančevo. 1974 Zagreb. 1975 Dinamo Pančevo. 1976 Nada Split. 1977 Dinamo Pančevo. 1978 Nada Split. 1979 Dinamo Pančevo. 1980 Zagreb. 1981 Zagreb. 1982 Nada Split

Number of referees
30

Number of coaches
39

Biggest recorded score
134–3 Zagreb v Student 15 April 1978

First international
Yugoslavia v Romania, Stara Zagora 1968

Most capped players
42 Dragan Kesić (Dinamo) 41 Branko Radić (NADA) 39 Nikola Stančević (Dinamo)

Longest international career
1968–81 Dragan Kesić (Dinamo)

International results

	W	D	L
Belgium			
1972 Brussels			0–3
1976 Brussels			6–8
1978 Markarska			0–20
1981 Liége			0–9
1983 Ljubljana	23–3		
Bulgaria			
1968 Zagora			6–29
1969 Pančevo	22–6		
Czechoslovakia			
1968 Split			10–12
1970 Havirov			3–19
1970 Zagreb			0–9
1973 Prague			3–32
1975 Gottwaldov			3–28
1982 Prague			9–17
Denmark			
1982 Zenica	46–4		

Fed. Rep. Germany			
1974 Markarska			8–20
1980 Hanover		6–6	
1980 Kardeljevo			0–16
France			
1979 Split			6–86
Italy			
1968 S. Donadi Piave			3–22
1972 Aosta			12–13
1973 Zagreb			7–25
Morocco			
1979 Split			7–22
1981 Split			0–13
Netherlands			
1972 The Hague			3–9
1978 Split			11–30
1979 Ljubljana	10–6		
1981 Hilversum			0–17
Poland			
1970 Sm. Palanka	12–9		
1970 Sisak	19–15		
Portugal			
1973 Markarska		3–3	
Romania			
1968 Zagora			3–11
1979 Split			6–32
Soviet Union			
1978 Sarajevo			3–18
1978 Travnik			6–16
Spain			
1969 Madrid			3–14
1971 Madrid			4–26
1972 Split			7–21
1979 Madrid			3–25
Sweden			
1978 Enköping	7–3		
1980 Split	14–4		
1982 Ljubljana			9–17
Switzerland			
1975 Geneva			3–12
1976 Split	31–4		
1976 Lausanne	18–6		
1981 Lausanne	10–0		
1982 Split	36–19		
Tunisia			
1979 Split	23–0		
1982 Split	4–0		
1983 Split			6–41

ZAMBIA

Foundation ....1900 (circa)
Headquarters PO Box 20917, Kitwe
Main stadium Lusaka
Colours Green jerseys
Number of clubs 13
Number of players 300
Season April–October
Temperatures 55°F (13°C) to 70°F (21°C)
Population 5 472 000

First match
1900

International results
1979 Zambia 13 Kenya 21
1981 Zambia 4 Zimbabwe 54

ZIMBABWE

Foundation ....1980 (formerly Rhodesian RFU founded 1895)
Headquarters Zimbabwe Rugby Union, PO Box 1129, Harare
Main stadium National Stadium Harare (capacity 20 000)
Colours White jerseys with olive green hoops
Number of clubs 30
Number of players 1000
Season April–October
Temperatures 50°F (10°C) to 70°F (21°C)
Population 6 934 000

Inter-provincial championship
1982 Matabeleland 38 Midlands 12, Mashonaland 26 Country Districts 6. *Final*: Mashonaland 18 Matabeleland 3

Russell Cup final
1982 Mashonaland 31 Matabeleland 3

Globe and Phoenix Shield
1982 Harare Sports Club 15 Zisco 6

Inter-Cities League
1982 *Winners*: Harare Sports Club

Catsicas Cup
1982 Matabeleland 10 Mashonaland 9

Mashonaland Leagues 1982
1st: OG I. 2nd: Marandellas I. 3rd (A): Beatrice. 3rd (B): Zimbank II

Matabeleland/Midlands Leagues 1982
1st: Old Miltonians II. 2nd: Zisco II

English Schools Tour 1982
W 47–6 Matabeleland, W 38–18 Midlands, W 25–9 Mashonaland, W 38–18 Mashonaland B, W 62–6 Country Districts, W 17–14 Zimbabwe, W 21–16 Zimbabwe Under 19s

Outgoing Schools Tour 1981/82
Prince Edward's School to UK W 40–12 Douai, W 24–10 Christ College Brecon, W 31–3 King's College Taunton

Most appearances
92 Iain Buchanan

Most internationals
9 Des van Jaarsveldt

Most points in career
437 Ian Robertson

Most points in a season
205 Frank Inocco, 1980

Most points in a match
30 Ian Robertson v South Western Districts, Bulawayo, 1974

Most tries in season
12 Norman Mellett, 1980

Most career tries
34 Ray Mordt

Biggest victory
58–0 v Mombasa Coastal XV, Mombasa, 1981

Biggest defeat
3–57 v Griqualand West, Kimberley, 1968

Most points conceded
67 (13–67) v Northern Transvaal, Pretoria, 1976

Incoming tours 1982
Romania
L 27–33 Mashonaland
W 61–6 Matabeleland
W 25–23 Zimbabwe
W 44–6 Midland
W 25–24 Zimbabwe
W 37–9 Invitation XV

Tour summary: P 6 W 5 L 1 F 219 A 101

Kenya
L 18–40 Matabeleland
W 35–16 Midlands
L 12–15 Zimbabwe

Tour summary: P 3 W 1 L 2 F 65 A 71

Other tours 1982
Swansea
W 26–19 Matabeleland
W 28–6 Zimbabwe
W 23–22 Mashonaland
L 30–31 Zimbabwe

Leicester
L 23–28 Mashonaland
W 25–12 Matabeleland
W 22–18 Zimbabwe
W 46–0 Midlands
D 15–15 Zimbabwe

1983
Bristol
W 52–0 Matabeleland
W 16–12 Zimbabwe
W 19–12 Mashonaland
L 20–31 Zimbabwe

International results

	P	W	D	L	F	A
Argentina	1	1	0	0	17	12
Australia	8	0	1	7	66	162
British Isles	9	0	0	9	83	265
France	3	0	0	3	24	89
Ireland	1	0	0	1	0	24
Italy	1	1	0	0	42	4
Kenya	2	2	0	0	49	36
New Zealand	6	1	1	4	58	124
Romania	2	0	0	2	47	50
USA	1	1	0	0	32	15

THE GULF RUGBY FOOTBALL UNION

The first organised rugby club in the Arabian Gulf was Kuwait, who have now been playing the game since 1947 and number amongst their patrons, Lord Wakefield of Kendal and Sir Philip Southwell. Over the past 20 years, the game has spread through the region with clubs starting up in Bahrain, Dubai, Muscat, Abu Dhabi, Sharjah, Doha, Dhahran, Jeddah, Riyadh, Al Khobar and Al Ain. Fixtures between these clubs were initially few and far between, mainly because of the distances involved (Kuwait to Muscat for example is 750 miles, *1207km*) and the associated cost of making such a journey by scheduled international carriers.

However, the increasing expatriate population and the consequential demand for outside fixtures aided and abetted by sympathetic employers and sponsors soon promoted a regular exchange of fixtures between clubs over an ever-widening area. The staging of the Gulf's first tournament, the Dubai Exiles Seven-a-side Tournament, in 1969 produced an ideal forum for clubs to get together on an annual basis, exchange contact addresses and organise fixtures. The tournament now attracts some 40 teams representing all the clubs and nations of the Gulf, plus an occasional guest entry such as the RAF teams from Cyprus, Cairo RFC and in 1979, the Benson and Hedges Golden 7 with such household rugby names as Peter Dixon, Clive Rees, Roger Shackleton and Roger Uttley.

The Gulf Rugby Football Union was formed in 1978 and accepted as a member of the RFU the same year. The Gulf RFU co-ordinates the game throughout the Gulf and now has a membership of 13 clubs: Dubai, Cairo, Kuwait, Al Ain, Muscat, Doha, Bahrain, Sharjah, Dhahran, Al Khobar, Abu Dhabi, Ras al Khaimah and Jebel Ali; with three more clubs, Jeddah, Riyadh and Jordan soon expected to join.

The Union organises a Merit Table Championship each season based on a home and away fixture list. The 1982 winners were Kuwait with Bahrain runners-up. There are also two XV-a-side knock-out tournaments each year, in Bahrain and Sharjah and two seven-a-side tournaments in Dubai and Muscat. The 1982 winners of these tournaments were Bahrain, Cairo, Muscat and Muscat respectively.

The winners of the Dubai Seven-a-side Tournament have, for the past 4 years represented Gulf Rugby at the Hong Kong Sevens. This honour has fallen to Bahrain, Dubai and Muscat (twice). Although often outlcassed by the major international sides, these Gulf sides have always given a good account of themselves on and off the field—Bahrain even won the Plate Competition in 1978, and the Gulf representative side has now become a firm favourite with the Hong Kong crowd.

All teams in the GRFU have made a point of honouring that most traditional expression of the game—the seasonal tour. Bahrain have visited the UK (the Bournemouth Festival), East Africa and the Far East. Dubai, the Gulf's most seasoned travellers, have toured Sri Lanka, Singapore, Cyprus, Bangkok, Hong Kong and, this year Manila (what a tour schedule) where they met up with Dhahran. The UAE teams, Dubai, Abu Dhabi, Sharjah and Al Ain have also formed their own touring side—the Emirates Barbarians—whose exploits in Ireland must now be part of Dublin folklore.

The Gulf's chief ambition is to send a representative touring party to play in the UK and it is hoped to achieve this by the end of the 1983–4 season. Incoming tourists are also most welcome in the Gulf.

WORLDWIDE CHAMPIONSHIPS

FIRA Championship

1965–66 France 1967–68 France 1968–69 Romania 1969–70 France 1970–71 France 1971–72 France 1972–73 France.

Group A

1973–74 France 1974–75 Romania 1975–76 France 1976–77 Romania 1977–78 France 1978–79 France 1979–80 France 1980–81 Romania

Group B
1973–74 Italy 1974–75 Poland 1975–76 Morocco 1976–77 Czechoslovakia 1977–78 Soviet Union 1978–79 Morocco 1979–80 Spain 1980–81 Fed. Rep. Germany

Group C
1976–77 Belgium 1979–80 Tunisia 1980–81 Portugal

1981–82 Championships
Group A
1 France 2 Italy 3 Romania 4 Fed. Rep. Germany 5 Soviet Union
Soviet Union 12 Italy 12 (Moscow), Fed. Rep. Germany 10 Soviet Union 7 (Hanover), France 17 Romania 9 (Narbonne), Italy 23 Fed. Rep. Germany 0 (Rovigo), France 25 Italy 19 (Carcassone), Fed. Rep. Germany 15 France 53 (Heidelberg), Romania 60 Fed. Rep. Germany 18 (Bucharest), Italy 21 Romania 15 (Rovigo), Romania 18 Soviet Union 3 (Bucharest), Soviet Union 10 France 10 (Moscow)

Group B
1 Morocco 2 Poland 3 Spain 4 Portugal 5 Netherlands 6 Tunisia
Netherlands 9 Poland 19 (Hilversum), Morocco 6 Poland 3 (Casablanca), Tunisia 3 Poland 16 (Tunis), Netherlands 3 Morocco 10 (Hilversum), Tunisia 6 Netherlands 15 (Tunis), Morocco 13 Tunisia 32 (Casablanca), Portugal 13 Spain 32 (Lisbon), Spain forfeited v Morocco, Spain 25 Netherlands 12 (Barcelona), Portugal 7 Morocco 26 (Lisbon), Portugal 25 Tunisia 16 (Lisbon), Netherlands 12 Portugal 16 (Hilversum), Poland 38 Portugal 13 (Warsaw), Spain 7 Tunisia 3 (Madrid), Poland 32 Spain 6 (Warsaw)

Group C
1 Sweden 2 Belgium 3 Yugoslavia 4 Switzerland 5 Denmark
Switzerland 34 Denmark 21 (Lausanne), Sweden 15 Belgium 9 (Karlstad), Denmark 6 Sweden 35 (Copenhagen), Belgium 9 Yugoslavia 0 (Liége), Switzerland 0 Yugoslavia 10 (Lausanne), Belgium 10 Switzerland 6 (Antwerp), Denmark 12 Belgium 16 (Copenhagen), Yugoslavia 46 Denmark 4 (Zenica), Yugoslavia 9 Sweden 17 (Ljubljana), Sweden 10 Switzerland 3 (Enköping)

1982–83 Results
Group A
France 6 Soviet Union 12 (Mérignac), Romania 13 France 9 (Bucharest), Morocco 3 Italy 13 (Casablanca), Soviet Union 31 Fed. Rep. Germany 9 (Moscow), Fed. Rep. Germany 3 Italy 23 (Hanover), Italy 6 France 6 (Rovigo), France 84 Fed. Rep. Germany 0 (Bourg-En-Bresse), Morocco 3 Romania 28 (Casablanca), Fed. Rep. Germany 12 Romania 26 (Heidelberg), Romania 13 Italy 6 (Buzau), Morocco 9 France 16 (Casablanca), Italy 12 Soviet Union 10, Romania 15 Soviet Union 10, Morocco 16 Fed. Rep. Germany 13

Group B
Poland 54 Sweden 6 (Poznan), Sweden 7 Netherlands 16 (Malmö), Poland 6 Netherlands 13 (Warsaw), Netherlands 6 Portugal 13 (Hilversum), Spain 25 Portugal 4 (Madrid), Netherlands 3 Spain 32 (Hilversum), Sweden 3 Spain 19 (Malmö), Spain 7 Poland 16 (Valencia), Poland 6 Portugal 4, Portugal 17 Sweden 9

Group C
Tunisia 3 Czechoslovakia 0 (Tunis), Belgium 12 Tunisia 13 (Brussels), Belgium 6 Czechoslovakia 21 (Brussels), Yugoslavia 21 Belgium 6, Tunisia 3 Switzerland 0, Tunisia 41 Yugoslavia 6, Czechoslovakia 17 Yugoslavia 6, Czechoslovakia 14 Switzerland 9

Caribbean Tournament

1966 *Champions:* Guyana. *Runners-up* (in order of merit): Barbados, Trinidad & Tobago, Jamaica. **1967**: Trinidad & Tobago. *Runners-up:* Barbados, Guyana, Jamaica. **1969**: Jamaica. *Runners-up:* Barbados, Trinidad & Tobago, Guyana. **1971**: Guyana. *Runners-up:* Trinidad & Tobago, The Bahamas, Jamaica, Barbados. **1973**: Trinidad & Tobago. *Runners-up:* Barbados, Guyana, Martinique, The Bahamas. **1975**: Jamaica. *Runners-up:* Barbados, The Bahamas, Guyana, Martinique, Trinidad & Tobago. **1977**: Bermuda. *Runners-up:* Martinique, Trinidad & Tobago, Guyana, Barbados. **1979**: Bermuda. *Runners-up:* Trinidad & Tobago, Martinique, Guyana, Guadeloupe. **1981**: Bermuda. *Runners-up:* Trinidad & Tobago, Guyana, Martinique, Barbados

South American Championships

1951 (unofficial) Buenos Aires: Chile 68 Brazil 0—Argentina 62 Uruguay 0—Argentina 72 Brazil 0—Uruguay 8 Chile 3—Uruguay 17 Brazil 10—Argentina 13 Chile 3

1958 Chile: Argentina 44 Peru 0 (Santiago)—Chile 34 Uruguay 9 (Santiago)—Argentina 50 Uruguay 3 (Vina del Mar)—Chile 31 Peru 3 (Vina del Mar)— Uruguay 10 Peru 6 (Santiago)—Argentina 14 Chile 0 (Santiago)

1961 Montevideo: Argentina 11 Chile 3—Uruguay 11 Brazil 8—Argentina 66 Brazil 0—Chile 28 Uruguay 5—Chile 34 Brazil 5—Argentina 36 Uruguay 3

1964 São Paulo: Argentina 25 Uruguay 6—Brazil 16 Chile 16—Uruguay 15 Chile 8—Argentina 30 Brazil 6—Brazil 15 Uruguay 8—Argentina 30 Chile 8

1967 Buenos Aires: Chile 16 Uruguay 11—Argentina 38 Uruguay 6—Argentina 18 Chile 0

1969 Santiago: Argentina 41 Uruguay 6—Chile 13 Uruguay 6—Argentina 54 Chile 0

1971 Montevideo: Uruguay 56 Paraguay 3—Brazil 12 Paraguay 6—Argentina 20 Chile 3—Argentina 50 Brazil 6—Chile 11 Uruguay 6—Chile 40 Paraguay 0—Uruguay 37 Brazil 11—Chile 45 Brazil 3—Argentina 61 Paraguay 0—Argentina 55 Uruguay 6

1973 São Paulo: Brazil 22 Paraguay 3—Uruguay 13 Chile 10—Argentina 98 Paraguay 3—Argentina 55 Uruguay 0—Chile 22 Brazil 3—Chile 27 Paraguay 3—Uruguay 16 Brazil 6—Uruguay 31 Paraguay 9—Argentina 96 Brazil 0—Argentina 60 Chile 3

1975 Asuncion: Chile 31 Brazil 10—Argentina 30 Uruguay 15—Brazil 19 Paraguay 6—Uruguay 38 Brazil 7—Chile 44 Paraguay 3—Chile 16 Uruguay 7—Argentina 93 Paraguay 0—Argentina 64 Brazil 6—Uruguay 38 Paraguay 18—Argentina 45 Chile 3

1977 Tucuman: Chile 22 Paraguay 3—Uruguay 16 Paraguay 7—Argentina 78 Brazil 6—Paraguay 25 Brazil 13—Uruguay 21 Chile 18—Argentina 70 Uruguay 0—Chile 33 Brazil 27—Argentina 77 Paraguay 3—Uruguay 47 Brazil 15—Argentina 25 Chile 10

1979 Chile: Argentina 19 Uruguay 16 (Santiago)—Chile 27 Paraguay 13 (Santiago)—Uruguay 48 Brazil 0 (Santiago)—Argentina 34 Chile 15 (Santiago)—Argentina 76 Paraguay 13 (Vina del Mar)—Chile 53 Brazil 6 (Vina del Mar)—Uruguay 53 Paraguay 9 (Santiago)—Argentina 109 Brazil 3 (Santiago)—Brazil 16 Paraguay 6 (Santiago)—Chile 9 Uruguay 9 (Santiago)

1981 Montevideo: Uruguay 54 Paraguay 14—Chile 33 Brazil 3—Chile 33 Paraguay 3—Uruguay 77 Brazil 0—Paraguay 35 Brazil 3—Uruguay 33 Chile 3

1983 Buenos Aires: Uruguay 20 Paraguay 12—Argentina 46 Chile 6—Uruguay 25 Chile 3—Argentina 43 Paraguay 3—Chile 24 Paraguay 12—Argentina 29 Uruguay 6

South American Junior Championships

1972 Buenos Aires: Argentina 1974 (various venues): Argentina 1976 Santiago: Argentina 1978 São Paulo: Argentina 1980 Asuncion: Paraguay 1982 Montevideo: Argentina

Hong Kong Sevens

1976 Cantabrians 24 Wallaroos 8. 1977 Fiji 28 New Zealand 18. 1978 Fiji 14 New Zealand 10. 1979 Australia 39 Western Samoa 3. 1980 Fiji. 1981 Barbarians. 1982 Australia

1983 results

Group A—Australia 42 Japan 0, Australia 44 Indonesia 0, Australia 38 Malaysia 0, Australia 26 Solomon Islands 0, Japan 30 Indonesia 0, Japan 28 Malaysia 0, Japan 40 Solomon Islands 0, Indonesia 4 Malaysia 28, Indonesia 10 Solomon Islands 10, Malaysia 4 Solomon Islands 20

Group B—Fiji 16 Tonga 0, Fiji 32 Thailand 4, Fiji 40 Brunei 0, Fiji 42 Hong Kong 0, Tonga 20 Thailand 6, Tonga 20 Brunei 0, Tonga 10 Hong Kong 8, Thailand 10 Brunei 0, Thailand 4 Hong Kong 20, Brunei 0 Hong Kong 26

Group C—New Zealand 18 South Korea 0, New Zealand 26 American Eagles 0, New Zealand 22 Bahrain 0, New Zealand 48 Singapore 0, South Korea 16 American Eagles 6, South Korea 4 Bahrain 10, South Korea 24 Singapore 3, American Eagles 42 Singapore 0, American Eagles 12 Bahrain 10, Bahrain 18 Singapore 0

Group D—Scottish Border Club 14 Canada 0, Scottish Border Club 8 Western Samoa 4, Scottish Border Club 28 Papua New Guinea 0, Scottish Border Club 16 Sri Lanka 0, Canada 0 Western Samoa 16, Canada 28 Papua New Guinea 0, Canada 26 Sri Lanka 0, Western Samoa 24 Papua New Guinea 4, Western Samoa 28 Sri Lanka 0, Papua New Guinea 8 Sri Lanka 4

Plate Quarter-finals: Solomon Islands 14 Thailand 0, South Korea 4 Papua New Guinea 0, Hong Kong 24 Malaysia 4, Canada 14 Bahrain 4
Semi-finals: South Korea 36 Solomon Islands 0, Hong Kong 8 Canada 14
Final: South Korea 30 Canada 6

Cup Quarter-finals: Australia 12 Tonga 6, Western Samoa 4 New Zealand 0, Fiji 20 Japan 0, Scottish Border Club 12 American Eagles 0
Semi-finals: Australia 16 Western Samoa 0, Fiji 14 Scottish Border Club 8
Final: Australia 14 Fiji 4

Pacific Tournament (Suva)

1983 Tonga 15 Western Samoa 6, Fiji 13 Tonga 8, Fiji 0 Western Samoa 6

Asian Championships

1972 (Hong Kong): Japan 16 Hong Kong 0
1974 (Sri Lanka): Japan 44 Sri Lanka 6
1978 (Kuala Lumpur): Japan 16 South Korea 4
1980 (Taiwan): Japan 21 South Korea 12

1982 results (Singapore)
Group A—Singapore 6 Malaysia 15, South Korea 12 Sri Lanka 0, Singapore 9 Sri Lanka 8, South Korea 40 Malaysia 12, Malaysia 23 Sri Lanka 12, South Korea 12 Singapore 0

Group B—Japan 29 Hong Kong 0, Taiwan 20 Thailand 0, Japan 31 Taiwan 6, Hong Kong 39 Thailand 6, Japan 43 Thailand 6, Hong Kong 21 Taiwan 3

3rd/4th place final: Hong Kong 10 Malaysia 4
Final: South Korea 12 Japan 9

DID YOU KNOW?

DID YOU KNOW?

Gibraltar Tag Rugby

The Gibraltar Rugby Union have solved the problem of having no grass pitches on the Rock by inventing what they believe is a unique game called 'Tag Rugby'. Instead of tackling, players must achieve a 'tag', which is a piece of rope 10 inches long tucked into the waistband with eight inches of rope exposed. The tackle is achieved when the tag is pulled from the attacker's waistband and 'tag' is shouted. If by the fourth tag the attacking team have failed to score, the defending side are given the put-in at a tight scrummage.

Bunny Abbott plays for and against All Blacks
The most notable occasion when a player appeared against his own country was when Nick (now Sir Nicholas) Shehadie played for the Barbarians against Australia on 22 February 1958 at Cardiff Arms Park. Lesser-known 'duplicity' was that of Bunny Abbott, the Taranaki wing-threequarter, who having played against British Columbia in the penultimate match of New Zealand's 1905–6 tour of British Isles/France/USA played—and scored a try—for the Canadians when they found themselves short because of injury for the second, and the All Blacks' final tour match, at Berkeley, California, on 13 February 1906. Abbott, whose one international game for the All Blacks was against France on the same tour, appeared against New Zealand once again, in 1907, for Wellington Province at Wellington, a preparation match for New Zealand's tour of Australia.

Another New Zealander, Ian Clarke, 'did a Shehadie' when he played for the Barbarians against the All Blacks at Cardiff on 15 February 1964. Clarke also scored the Barbarians' only points, a dropped goal. Incredulity in the crowd preceded the score for Clarke, a prop-forward, had set himself up for the score by calling for a fair mark from a drop-out by his brother Don. The crowd's scoffing was unwarranted. Ian was an accomplished kicker and drop-goaler, having practised often with his younger brother, who was one of the finest goal-kickers of all time.

All Blacks wear white
The New Zealanders became known as the All Blacks on the 1905 tour of the British Isles/France/USA but on two notable occasions switched from conventional black and wore white jerseys: in the 1930 Test series against the British Isles, whose colours were then dark blue, and at Auckland on 14 June 1975, against Scotland, who also wore dark blue.

Morgenroth's example
One of the outstanding players for the past two seasons in the Bundesliga, the first division of the Federal Republic of Germany, has been Werner Morgenroth who plays for 1878 Hannover. Morgenroth was 40 when he was voted a creditable ninth in the ballot for German player of 1981. Morgenroth . . . 'still a shining example to all his colleagues for his fitness and enthusiasm' . . . now looks forward to playing a 20th season in 1983–4.

Obolensky scores 17 tries

The greatest number of tries scored in a representative match was 17 by Prince Alexander Obolensky, playing for the touring British team against a Brazilian XV at Niteroi on 31 August 1936. The British team, which also included B C Gadney, Charles Beamish and Robin Prescott, won 82–0 in a match postponed for two days because of the late arrival of the touring team's ship from Argentina. The match was originally to have been played at Santos and the switch of venue meant that the Brazilian XV was severely weakened by the enforced absence of players from São Paulo.

São Paulo players were also absent on another notable occasion. In 1932 a combined São Paulo and Rio XV were to have played the touring South Africans but 'owing to the Revolution São Paulo could not provide any assistance.' Rio thus provided all the players and were duly beaten 73–0.

First rugby match at Wembley

The first time the Rugby League Cup final was staged at Wembley was in 1929, but the first time a rugby union match was played there was four years earlier when the Army and the RAF drew 6–6 in the Inter-Services Tournament, watched by a crowd of 5000. The experiment was not without criticism. One newspaper wrote: 'Wembley Stadium is a magnificent conception of its kind, and its enclosed playing field with running players upon it a very fine sight, but to those who like to follow the points of a game it is rather unsatisfactory . . . the decisions of the referee were even more obscure than usual . . . one can imagine an uninstructed crowd expressing themselves very strongly on the matter.'

Curious scoring

The curiosity of the South American Championships staged in Montevideo, Uruguay, in 1981 was the scoring involving Chile. They beat Brazil and Paraguay and lost to Uruguay, the result of each match being 33–3. The loss to Uruguay cost Chile the chance of winning the Championship for a first time.

Blackheath forced to stop playing on Blackheath

In their early days Blackheath used to play on Blackheath and it was their match against Richmond on 20 January 1877 which was the cause of the club leaving the heath for a private ground: 'The spectators assembled in such numbers and were so unseemly in their behaviour that the game was brought to a premature conclusion . . . the crowds were a great nuisance for they invariably declined to keep in touch . . . a half-back did see his opportunity and dive in the thick of the shouting throng so soon as the ball was in his hands . . . no woodcock flushed in cover is more wary to keep a tree between itself and the gun than was the said half-back to dodge among the flying spectators in such a way as to have one or more of them between himself and his tacklers.'

Fastest try by replacement

The fastest try by a replacement in first-class rugby was that by David Evans, who came on as a flank-forward and scored within 30 seconds, for Llanelli against Ebbw Vale at Stradey Park on 11 December 1982.

Youngest international player

Daniel Brendan Carroll (born 17 February 1892) who was 16 years 149 days when he played for Australia against Great Britain in the 1908 Olympic Games final in London, qualifies as the youngest player to play in international rugby. A popular but spurious argument against Carroll's feat is that the Olympic final was not a 'full' international. Yet international it was and fully representative, too, for Australia's opponents, although in effect the Cornwall XV, were officially nominated as Britain's representatives, in precisely the same way as are British Lions teams when playing international matches.

The youngest player to play in an 'official' international was Ninian Jamieson Finlay (1858–1936) who was 17 years 36 days when he played for Scotland against England in 1875. Charles Reid (1864–1909) was also 17 years and 36 days when he played for Scotland against Ireland in 1881, but Finlay was reckoned to be a day younger because he had four leap years in his lifetime up to playing for Scotland, while Reid had five. Carroll had another interesting claim to fame. He played against France in the 1920 Olympic final—for the United States.

Most wasted effort

The most wasted effort by any player was that of Brunei player Dick Dover. Playing for Kukris against Panaga, Dover, completely disorientated by the wheeling of a scrum, broke with the ball and ran 75 yards to 'score' a try near his own posts.

One of the most unusual sendings-off also occurred in Brunei: Hugh Chalmers, a spectator at a match between Royal Brunei Yacht Club and Panaga in 1976, was ordered out of the ground by the referee T Peregrine, who threatened to abandon the match unless Chalmers obeyed. Chalmers' offence was the shouting of insults from the touchline at the referee.

Wales play at Birkenhead

The only occasion when Wales played a 'home' match outside the Principality was in 1887 at Birkenhead against Ireland. The Irish, acutely short of funds, suggested Birkenhead because of its proximity to the Dublin–Liverpool ferry arrival point.

Ranfurly Shield design error

When the Ranfurly Shield, New Zealand's most coveted trophy, was made and delivered to the New Zealand RFU in 1902 as a presentation trophy from the Earl of Ranfurly, the Governor of New Zealand, it was discovered that the embossed centrepiece depicted an association football match. The design was altered before its inaugural award to Auckland, who were unbeaten that season.

Cove-Smith's distinction

Although best remembered as captain of the British Isles team which had the worst record of any tourists to South Africa, winning only 9 of 21 matches in 1924, Dr Ronald Cove-Smith has one of the most distinguished international careers in the history of the game. The Cambridge University and Old Merchant Taylors' lock-forward played 29 times for England and was on a losing side only five times. In that period, 1921–9, England won four Grand Slams and Cove-Smith, who occasionally played at prop-forward, had the distinction of playing six times against Wales and being on the winning side each time, a record which no other player has achieved.

Odd abandonment
One of the oddest abandonments of a match was that between Barbados and Trinidad Northern, played in a thunderstorm in 1970. At half-time a Trinidadian player leaned against a Land Rover, which was parked on the touchline in its capacity as a temporary bar, only to be thrown violently to the ground because the vehicle had attracted static electricity. Some of the unfortunate player's colleagues were convinced he was suffering an epileptic fit but when moments later a bolt of lightning struck the ground a few feet from a pregnant bystander, the referee's wife, further play was considered unwise.

Best captain
Arguably the finest achievement in captaincy was that of Wilson Whineray. In 30 internationals as captain of New Zealand the Auckland prop-forward was on the losing side only five times. In all Whineray captained New Zealand in 68 out of the 77 matches he played between 1957–65.

Tom Kiernan of Ireland captained his country and the British Lions on 28 occasions.

Herbert Hayton Castens
Herbert Hayton Castens, the Western Province front row forward, who won rugby blues for Oxford against Cambridge in 1886–7, not only became South Africa's first rugby captain (he led against the British Isles in the first Test in Port Elizabeth in 1891) but he became South Africa's first captain at cricket on a tour overseas (to England in 1894).

Most ties
In what is believed to be the biggest tie presentation in the history of sport, the Argentine Rugby Union awarded Puma ties to over 300 past players at a special ceremony in Buenos Aires in 1982. The recipients included the six surviving players from the 1927 Argentine team which played against the British Isles tourists in Buenos Aires. Argentina have been awarding ties, rather than caps, for internationals since 1977.

Internationals at Leicester
England played four internationals at Leicester, against Ireland in 1902, 1906 and 1923 and against Wales in 1904. In the 1923 match England won 23–5, which at the time was a record total by England against Ireland, and has been bettered only three times since—36–14 in Dublin in 1938, 26–21 at Twickenham in 1974 and 24–9 at Twickenham in 1980.

Baron de Coubertin
Baron Pierre de Coubertin, who founded the modern Olympic movement, was also a referee of note. The Baron refereed France's first international, against New Zealand, at Parc des Princes on 1 January 1906, and France's first club championship final, between Stade Français and Racing Club, at Bois de Boulogne in 1892.

England nearly wear maroon
England ordered a set of maroon jerseys in anticipation of having to avoid a colour clash with Fiji at Twickenham on 16 October 1982. Both sides normally wear white, but England's first ever colour change never happened because Fiji agreed to play in striped jerseys.

Unique club tournament
One of the features of the USA rugby scene is the Weekend Club Tournament. Approximately 100 of these are played nationwide within a year and the theme is a knock-out competition of abbreviated matches involving as few as eight sides or as many as 64 at one location.

International Gala
Underlining the cosmopolitan nature of modern-day rugby, Gala, the Scottish club, met clubs from five different countries in successive matches: Santa Monica (USA), Gosforth (England), Jedforest (Scotland), Ebbw Vale (Wales) and Benetton Treviso (Italy).

Dropped goals
Naas Botha, of South Africa, holds the record for most dropped goals, 11, in internationals but his fellow-countryman, Gerry Brand, holds the record for the longest drop-goal in international rugby: a 90 yarder against England at Twickenham in 1932. Bob Hiller's two dropped goals against Ireland at Twickenham in 1970 were towering 45-yarders, but the most dropped goals in an international are 3, a feat achieved by Pierre Albaladejo (France v Ireland, Paris, 1960), Phil Hawthorne (Australia v England, Twickenham, 1967), Hugo Porta (Argentina v Australia, Buenos Aires, 1979) and Botha (South Africa v South America, Durban, 1980 and South Africa v Ireland, Durban, 1981).

Original tour fund-raising
The Poneke Club from Wellington in New Zealand, devised a highly original way of raising funds to finance their tour of the British Isles in October/November 1982. Using the services and skills of their members and players they planned, designed and built a house and when it was sold the resultant profit was allocated to the tour fund.

And the ref was a woman!
Women's Rugby has arrived in the Caribbean. Not only did a women's side from the Worcester Polytechnic Institute in Massachusetts play and beat the Jamaican Amazons 24–0 at sevens in March 1983 in Kingston, Jamaica, but a female referee, Barbara Apelian-Beall, from Worcester, officiated at the men's tour match in which Worcester Polytechnic beat the Jamaica RFU Chairman's XV 26–4 at Caymanas Field. Barbara Apelian-Beall, a member of the New England RFU Referees Society, is believed to have been the first female referee of any match in the Caribbean.

Schweppes Welsh Cup final at Cardiff, 30 April 1983 . . . Huw Davies (left), the Swansea scrum-half, dive-passes from a scrummage. A critical phase of the game was the line-out (below), which Pontypool dominated, due as much to their jumpers as to the accuracy of their thrower-in, Steve Jones (No. 2), one of Wales's most underrated hookers. (Colorsport.)

The splendour of the National Stadium at Cardiff is vividly portrayed in this panoramic shot of the 1983 Schweppes Welsh Cup Final. Arthur Emyr, the Swansea left wing (No. 11), is squeezed for room by the attentions of the Pontypool forwards, Martin Jones (left) and Mike Crowley, and clearly will need the support of his scrum-half, Huw Davies, and Richard Moriarty (right). (Colorsport.)

Daily Telegraph
GAS
National & Provincial
insurance
ICI

A heavy downpour and a greasy pitch made life difficult for the competitors in the 1983 Hong Kong Sevens. Adaptability, however, is second nature to sevens players and this popular cosmopolitan tournament went ahead like clockwork, with lesser known sides deriving just as much fun and enjoyment from the proceedings as did the eventual winners, Australia.

HONG KONG SEVENS

Possession, the art of obtaining it, support play and finishing power are illustrated in this pot-pourri of the action from the 1983 Hong Kong Sevens.

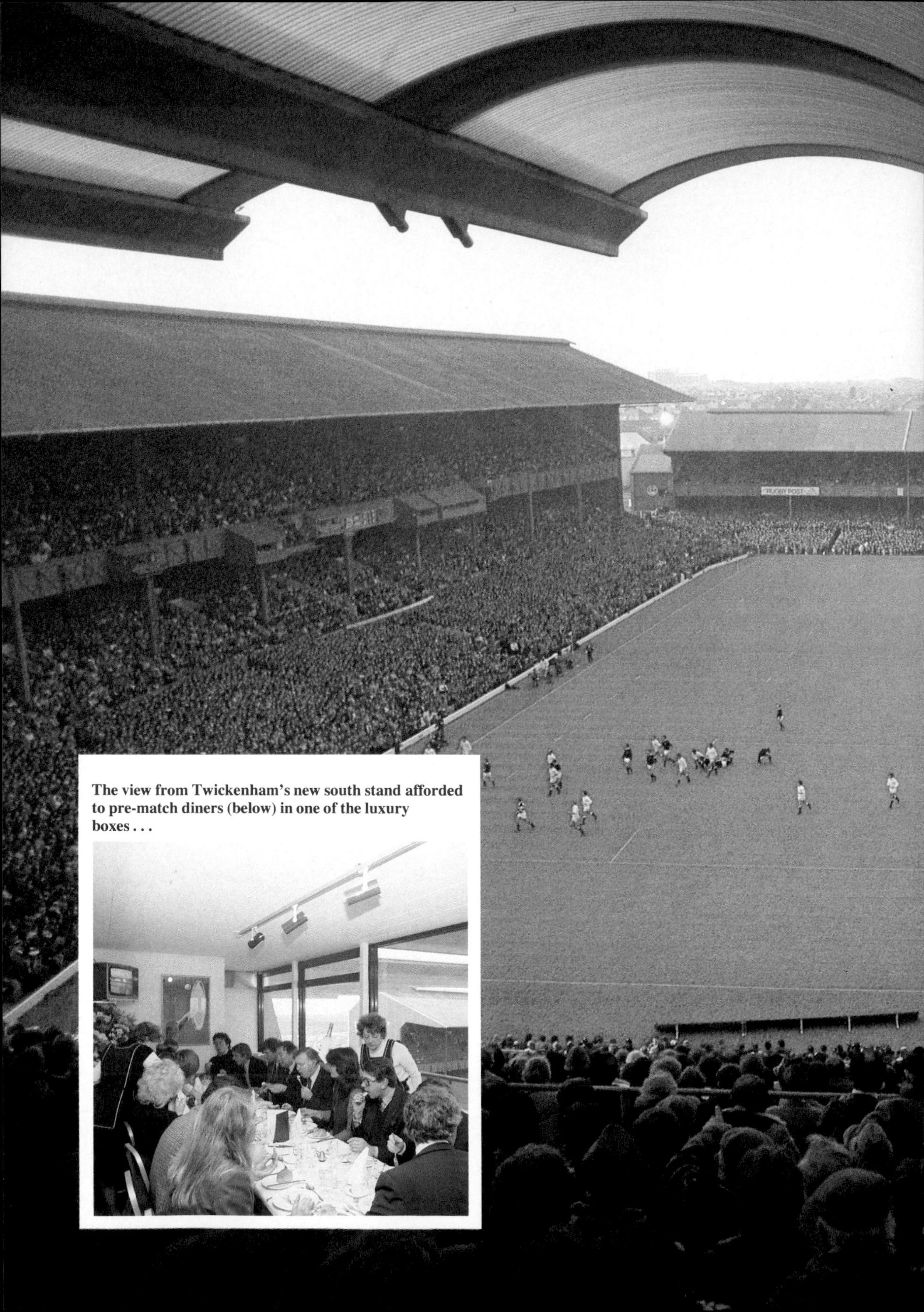

The view from Twickenham's new south stand afforded to pre-match diners (below) in one of the luxury boxes . . .

. . . a rare, possibly unique, colour photograph of the Calcutta Cup, the prize in all England v Scotland matches. (Colorsport.)

If it took an uncommonly long time for those who design or commission postage stamps to recognise that rugby football was a subject worthy of depiction, they have more than made up for it since the first rugby stamp was issued in March 1944. Produced by Romania to commemorate the 30th anniversary of their Rugby Federation, this first rugby stamp was the trail-blazer for 28 other stamps produced since in all parts of the world, apart from many other first day covers.

It might seem curious that Britain, the birthplace of postage stamps and rugby football, should have taken over 100 years to produce a rugby stamp, that of 1971 celebrating the centenary of the Rugby Football Union. Even odder, at first sight, was Monaco's issue of 1973, celebrating the 150th anniversary of William Webb Ellis's much-heralded exploit of 'originating the distinctive feature of the Rugby game'. Why should Monaco, hardly a rugby outpost, issue a rugby stamp? And why depict the legendary Webb Ellis? The answer seems to be that Webb Ellis spent the last few months of his life near Monaco and is buried in nearby Menton.

The reasons for rugby stamps issue are multifarious. Czechoslovakia marked 35 years of its federation in 1961; South Africa 75 years of its Board with two stamps in 1964; New Zealand likewise celebrated 75 years with two stamps in 1967; the Diamond Jubilee of the Fiji RFU produced three stamps in 1973; the Irish RFU centenary merited two issues in 1974; and the Welsh Rugby Union's centenary in 1980 was marked with one stamp.

Generally the design of rugby stamps has tended toward the obvious: a line-out, a player running or a match scene. There have been noteworthy exceptions. The 1971 RFU issue was based on W B Wollen's 1870 painting of a match between Cambridge University and (it is believed) Newport, which hangs in Twickenham. The Irish stamp had to be exceptional: it is the only one which portrays identifiable players—Colin Grimshaw, Donal Canniffe and Barrie McGann in action during the Combined Universities v Rest of Ireland at Lansdowne Road in December 1973.

A bare-footed player gets pride of place on the Solomons Islands issue of 1969 while the 1973 Singapore stamp shows players outside the City Hall.

Not all stamps actually commemorate rugby. Rugby posts are clearly depicted on Samoa's 1962 independence issue; posts and a ball are on a 1981 stamp from Equatorial Guinea for the 75th anniversary of FC Barcelona (Spanish rugby's first league champions as well as a renowned football club); and there was a sketch of a rugby stamp in the souvenir sheet from Stampex, Britain's national stamp exhibition, in 1982. (Colorsport.)

When Dusty Hare (above) is not adding to his world record number of points for Leicester, England or the British Lions, he has to turn his attentions to the matter of earning a living as a farmer. In contrast, the Muscat team (below) pose for a team photograph on the occasion of the high point in their country's short rugby history—entry to the 1982 Hong Kong Sevens. Muscat were beaten by the Barbarians, the Pumas, Western Samoa and Hong Kong—but for them participating was more important than winning. (Colorsport.)

Mike Rafter, the Bristol captain, acknowledges the appreciation of the Twickenham crowd after Bristol had beaten Leicester in a thrilling John Player Cup final on 30 April 1983. It was Bristol's first success in the competition, although they had reached the 1973 final when they were beaten 27–15 by Coventry. It was Leicester's fifth appearance in the final since 1978. (Colorsport.)

Right, Leicester are comprehensively the winners of this line-out in the John Player Cup final at Twickenham, but in the end Bristol engineered enough possession from all points to win 28–22.

Right, a shot taken at Loftus/Versfeld, Pretoria, when the American Club, the Chicago Lions, toured South Africa in 1980 (All Sport.)

The Irish players join with the Lansdowne Road crowd in acknowledging Ollie Campbell's first try for his country, scored against England on 19 March 1983. Roger Gould (right), who established an Australian record for the most points in internationals on tour when he scored 35 in the three-match series against New Zealand in 1982. Gould also became the first Australian full-back to score two tries in an international, against Scotland on 10 July 1982. (Colorsport.)

Ollie Campbell, the Irish fly-half (above left), who scored 52 points in Ireland's four Championship matches in 1983, a best-ever total by an Irish player. (Colorsport). Action (above and left) from the Queensland v Australian Barbarians match at Ballymore on 2 October 1982. The injury to Barbarians flanker, Gary Pearce, looks far worse than it was and he carried on playing. Two of the stars of the Queensland side were Paul McLean (left), holder of the Australian test record of 21 points, and Chris Roche (with ball). (Colorsport.)

Mobil
Clover
SUZUKI

Hugo Porta (above), who scored 307 points in the 1982 season for his club, Banco Nacion, a record for an Argentine player. Princess Anne (below) performs the official opening ceremony of the new stand at Murrayfield on 26 March 1983 when Scotland played the Barbarians to mark the occasion. (Colorsport.)

No, not Brand's Hatch or Silverstone (left). A section of the crowd at Durban watching the British Isles beating the South African Barbarians 25–14 on 2 July 1980. (All Sport.)

Entente cordiale, as
expressed by Englan
supporter Eddie Ba
and a French fan, a
Twickenham before
England v France
Championship mat
15 January 1983.
(Colorsport.)

Welsh referee Ken
Parfitt looks slightly
perplexed as Tohi L
(13) and Qele Ratu
the mud) slip and sl
during the Tonga v
Australia match at
1983 Hong Kong Se
(Colorsport.)

WORLD RECORDS

Gwyn Evans, of Wales, who equalled the record of most penalty goals in an international when he kicked six against France at Cardiff in 1982. (Colorsport.)

Highest score
55 South Africa 55–6 v France 1907 (unofficial international)
49 Wales 49–14 v France 1910

Biggest winning margin
44 South Africa 44–0 v Scotland 1951

Highest score by touring team
117 New Zealand 117–6 v South Australia 1974

Most points by touring team
976 New Zealand to British Isles, France, Canada 1905–6

Most tries on overseas tour
215 New Zealand to British Isles, France 1905–6 (33 matches)

Most tries in an international
11 Wales 47–5 v France 1909

Most tries by a touring team
22 New Zealand v Northern New South Wales 1962

Unbeaten teams on tour
New Zealand to British Isles 1924–5 played 32, won 32
British Isles to South Africa 1974 played 22 won 21, drawn 1
British Isles to South Africa 1891 played 19, won 19

Most points in international series
97 New Zealand v Australia 1972

Most tries in international series
16 South Africa v British Isles 1955 (4 matches)
16 New Zealand v Australia 1972 (3 matches)

International championship—most points

102 Wales 1976

Most tries
21 Wales 1910

INDIVIDUAL

Most capped player
Mike Gibson (Ireland) 81 (12 for British Isles)

Most consecutive international appearances
53 Willie John McBride (Ireland), Gareth Edwards (Wales)

Most points in internationals
301 Andy Irvine (Scotland & British Isles)

The five drop goals of David Shiel of Scotland is a record in first-class rugby. (Scottish & Universal Newspapers.)

Most points in an international
26 Allan Hewson (New Zealand v Australia 1982)

Most tries in internationals
24 Ian Smith (Scotland) 1924–33 (32 appearances)

Most tries in an international
5 D Lambert (England v France 1907)

Most penalty goals in international
7 Hugo Porta (Argentina) v France 1974
6 Don Clarke (New Zealand v British Isles 1959), Gerald Bosch (South Africa v France 1975), Gwyn Evans (Wales v France 1982), Ollie Campbell (Ireland v Scotland 1982)

Most tries by a prop in internationals
8 Robert Paparemborde (France 1975–83)

Most career tries
365 Alan Morley (Bristol) 1969–83

Most career points
4754 Dusty Hare (Leicester) 1970–83

Most times a replacement in internationals
3 Bob Hesford (England): 1981 v Scotland, 1982 v France, 1983 v France

Most drop goals in first-class rugby
5 David Shiel (Melrose v Langholm, 11 September 1982)

Most points on tour
230 Billy Wallace (New Zealand) in British Isles/France 1905–6

Most tries on tour
44 Jimmy Hunter (New Zealand) in British Isles/France 1905–6

Most points in tour match
41 Joe Karam (New Zealand v South Australia 1974)

Most tries in tour match
8 Rod Heeps (New Zealand v Northern New South Wales 1962)

Fastest 100 points on tour
6 matches Naas Botha (South Africa) in New Zealand 1981

Fastest 100 points in internationals
11 internationals Naas Botha (South Africa 1980–1)

Most international dropped goals
11 Naas Botha (South Africa) 15 internationals

Most capped prop forward
53 Graham Price (Wales 41, British Isles 12)

Youngest international player
Daniel Brendan Carroll (Australia) 16 years 149 days (Australia v Great Britain, Olympic Games Final, London, 1908)
Ninian Jamieson Finlay (Scotland) 17 years 36 days (Scotland v England, Raeburn Place, 8 March 1875)

Oldest international player
Ned Hughes (New Zealand) 40 years 123 days (New Zealand v South Africa 27 August 1921)

Longest international career
17 seasons G M Cooke (Australia) 1932–48 (13 internationals)

OTHER INTERNATIONAL RECORDS

Highest scores in internationals

49 Wales v France (49–14) *1910 Swansea*
44 South Africa v Scotland (44–0) *1951 Murrayfield*
41 England v France (41–13) *1907 Richmond*
40 New Zealand v Scotland (40–15) *1981 Auckland*
37 France v England (37–12) *1972 Paris*
35 Scotland v Wales (35–10) *1924 Inverleith*
33 Australia v Scotland (33–9) *1982 Sydney*
26 Ireland v Scotland (26–8) *1953 Murrayfield*
26 Ireland v England (26–21) *1974 Twickenham*

Other major international scores

113–13 Fiji v New Caledonia
113–3 Fiji v Solomon Islands
(both in Pacific Games, Port Moresby, 1969)

Biggest points margin

44 South Africa v Scotland (44–0) *1951 Murrayfield*
42 Wales v France (47–5) *1909 Paris*
37 England v France (37–0) *1911 Twickenham*
35 New Zealand v Australia (38–3) *1972 Auckland*
28 Scotland v France (31–3) *1912 Inverleith*
28 France v Australia (34–6) *1976 Paris*
24 Ireland v France (24–0) *1913 Cork*
24 Australia v Scotland (33–9) *1982 Sydney*

Most points conceded

49 France v Wales (14–49) *1910 Swansea*
44 Scotland v South Africa (0–44) *1951 Murrayfield*
38 Australia v New Zealand (13–38) *1936 Dunedin*
38 Australia v New Zealand (3–38) *1972 Auckland*
38 Ireland v South Africa (0–38) *1912 Dublin*
37 England v France (12–37) *1972 Paris*
35 Wales v Scotland (10–35) *1924 Inverleith*
30 New Zealand v Australia (16–30) *1978 Auckland*
28 South Africa v British Lions (9–28) *1974 Pretoria*

Biggest points margin defeat

44 Scotland v South Africa (0–44) *1951 Murrayfield*
42 France v Wales (5–47) *1909 Paris*
38 Ireland v South Africa (0–38) *1912 Dublin*
35 Australia v New Zealand (3–38) *1972 Auckland*
25 England v Wales (0–25) *1905 Cardiff*
England v France (12–37) *1972 Paris*
25 Wales v England (0–25) *1896 Blackheath*
Wales v Scotland (10–35) *1924 Inverleith*
19 South Africa v British Lions (9–28) *1974 Pretoria*
17 New Zealand v South Africa (0–17) *1928 Durban*

Most points in international championship season

102 Wales 1975–6 (record of 21 tries in 1910)
82 England 1913–14 (20 tries)
82 France 1975–6 (13 tries)
77 Scotland 1924–5 (17 tries)
71 Ireland 1982–3

Leading points scorers for each country in internationals

275 Andy Irvine (1973–83) Scotland
207 Don Clarke (1956–64) New Zealand
192 Ollie Campbell (1979–83) Ireland
166 Phil Bennett (1969–78) Wales
164 Dusty Hare (1974–83) England
163 Paul McLean (1974–82) Australia
139 Jean-Pierre Romeu (1973–7) France
130 Piet Visagie (1967–71) South Africa

Most tries in internationals for each country

23 Ian Smith (1924–33) Scotland
20 Gerald Davies (1966–78) Wales
Gareth Edwards (1967–78) Wales
19 Stewart Wilson (1977–83) New Zealand
18 Cyril Lowe (1913–23) England
14 Christian Darrouy (1957–68) France
12 Gerrie Germishuys (1974–81) South Africa

11 Alan Duggan (1964–72) Ireland
7 Colin Windon (1946–52) Australia

Most capped players

69 Mike Gibson (1964–79) Ireland
55 Colin Meads (1957–71) New Zealand
J P R Williams (1969–81) Wales
51 Andy Irvine (1972–82) Scotland
Jim Renwick (1972–83) Scotland
Benoit Dauga (1964–72) France
Roland Bertranne (1971–81) France
43 Tony Neary (1971–80) England
39 Peter Johnson (1959–71) Australia
Greg Davis (1963–72) Australia
38 Frik du Preez (1960–71) South Africa
Jan Ellis (1965–76) South Africa

Most points in total international career

301 Andy Irvine, Scotland, British Lions (60 internationals)
210 Phil Bennett, Wales, British Lions (37 internationals)
207 Don Clarke, New Zealand (31 internationals)
193 Tom Kiernan, Ireland, British Lions (59 internationals)

Most points in a series

97 New Zealand v Australia 1972 (29–6, 30–17, 38–3)

Most tries in a series

16 South Africa v British Lions 1955 (4 Tests)
New Zealand v Australia 1972 (3 Tests)

Most points scored in an international

30 Colin Mair Scotland v Japan, Tokyo 1977 (9 conversions, 4 penalties)
27 Guy Camberabero France v Italy, Toulon 1967
26 Allan Hewson New Zealand v Australia 1982
26 Phil Bennett Wales v Japan, Tokyo 1973
24 Fergie McCormick New Zealand v Wales, Second Test, Auckland 1969 (5 penalties, 3 conversions, 1 dropped goal)
Roger Blyth Wales v Overseas XV, Cardiff 1980 (3 tries, 3 conversions, 2 penalties)
23 Hugo Porta Argentina v France, Buenos Aires 1974 (7 penalties, 1 conversion)
22 D S Mare South Africa v France, Paris 1907 (8 conversions, 2 penalties)
Douglas Lambert England v France, Twickenham 1911 (5 conversions, 2 tries value 3 pts, 2 penalties)
Gerald Bosch South Africa v France, Second Test, Pretoria 1975 (6 penalties, 2 conversions)
21 Robbie Blair South Africa v World XV, Pretoria 1977 (5 penalties, 3 conversions)
Ollie Campbell Ireland v England, Dublin 1983 (1 try, 1 conversion, 5 penalties), Ireland v Scotland, Dublin 1982 (1 dropped goal, 6 penalties)
Paul McLean Australia v Scotland, Sydney 1983 (3 conversions, 5 penalties)

Most penalties in an international

7 Hugo Porta Argentina v France, Buenos Aires 1974
6 Don Clarke New Zealand v British Lions, Dunedin 1959
Gerald Bosch South Africa v France, Pretoria 1975
Hugo Porta Argentina v France, Buenos Aires 1975*
Jean Michel Aguirre France v Argentina, Buenos Aires 1975*
Gwyn Evans Wales v France, Cardiff 1982
Ollie Campbell Ireland v Scotland, Dublin 1982

(*In same match)

Most dropped goals in an international

3 Pierre Albaladejo France v Ireland, Paris 1960
Phil Hawthorne Australia v England, Twickenham 1967
Hugo Porta Argentina v Australia, Buenos Aires 1979
Naas Botha South Africa v Ireland, Durban 1981

Most international points in a series or season

52 Ollie Campbell Ireland v England, France, Scotland and Wales 1983

49 Guy Camberabero France v Ireland, England, Wales and Australia 1967
Bob Hiller England v Ireland, Scotland, Wales and Presidents XV 1971
43 Piet Visagie South Africa in four Tests v Australia 1969
39 Don Clarke New Zealand in four Tests v British Lions 1959

Biggest win by touring side

117–6 New Zealand v South Australia, Adelaide 1974
103–0 New Zealand v Northern NSW, Quirindi 1962

Most points by a touring team

976 New Zealand in British Isles, France and Canada 1905–6 (868 points in 33 matches in British Isles and France, also a record)

Most points in a tour match

41 Joe Karam New Zealand v South Australia, Adelaide 1974 (15 conversions, 1 penalty, 1 try)

Biggest club win

194–0 Comet 194 Lindo 0, Copenhagen 1973
160–6 Ammosal v Kimberley Defence, 1977 (29 tries)
164–0 Ponsonby II v De La Salle Gold, 1974 (28 tries)

Biggest Cup win

150–3 Old Askeans v Bredgar, Kent Cup 1977

Biggest points aggregate in an international

63 Wales 49 France 14, Swansea 1910
South Africa 38 France 25, Bloemfontein 1975

Record club representation on tour

12 players from Cambridge University in British team to South Africa in 1891

Longest international careers

17 seasons Graeme Cooke, Australia 1932–48
16 Tony O'Reilly, Ireland 1955–70
Mike Gibson, Ireland 1964–79
15 Haydn Tanner, Wales, 1935–49
Ned Hughes, New Zealand 1907–21
Colin Meads, New Zealand 1957–71
Tony Miller, Australia 1952–67

Top attendance for club match

48 000 Cardiff v Newport, Arms Park, 17 February 1951

Top attendance for non-test tour match

68 000 Northern Transvaal v British Lions, Loftus Versfeld, Pretoria, 21 June 1980

Points on tour (individual)

230 Billy Wallace New Zealand to Great Britain 1905–6
210 Don Clarke New Zealand to Australia and South Africa 1960
209 Gerry Brand South Africa to New Zealand 1937
188 Barry John British Lions to Australia and New Zealand 1971
163 Don Clarke New Zealand to Australia 1956–7
156 Andy Irvine British Lions to South Africa 1974
154 Paul McLean Australia to Great Britain 1975
145 Joe Karam New Zealand to Great Britain, France and North America 1972–3
136 Don Clarke New Zealand to Great Britain 1963–4
132 Laurie Mains New Zealand to South Africa 1976
Fergie McCormick New Zealand to South Africa 1970

Most international tries (individual)

5 Douglas Lambert England v France, Richmond 1907
4 Willie Llewellyn Wales v England, Swansea 1899
Duncan McGregor New Zealand v England, Crystal Palace 1905
A Hudson England v France, Paris 1906

4 Reggie Gibbs Wales v France, Cardiff 1908
W A Stewart Scotland v Ireland, Inverleith 1913
Ronnie Poulton-Palmer England v France, Paris 1914
Ian Smith Scotland v France, Inverleith 1925
Ian Smith Scotland v Wales, Swansea 1925
Maurice Richards Wales v England, Cardiff 1969
Greg Cornelsen Australia v New Zealand, Auckland 1978

NOTE: No Irish, French or South African player has reached the qualifying mark of 4 tries. G Lindsay (Scotland) scored 5 tries v Wales in 1887 and G Burton (England) scored 4 v Wales (1881) before modern scoring values were adopted.

Highest total points in a season

1454 Pontypridd RFC 1975–6

Allan Hewson, the Wellington full-back was one of the great successes against the 1983 British Isles tourists with his sound defence and immaculate touch-finding. Hewson also scored 46 points in the 4 Tests. (Peter Bush.)

JOHN BURGUM REFEREE FOR ALL SEASONS

JOHN BURGUM

When John Burgum, of the North Midlands Society, retired from refereeing in 1982, he had completed 29 years on the county panel and 36 years of service in all. No other referee has ever officiated for so long at that level and even now Burgum has not entirely divorced himself from the practice. He has become a touchjudge.

Which takes him back to where he started.

Many are the quirks of fate that drive sane men to become rugby referees but in Burgum's case it was a simple process.

'I was not big enough to play the game so I started running the line at school,' he says. 'From there it was a natural progression. I became secretary of the rugby club while I was at Exeter University and we had difficulty in finding referees. So I became one.'

Burgum joined the Devon Society in 1946, joined North Midlands on his return to Birmingham and went on to outlast all his colleagues. He became one of the best referees in the country and even now there are good judges who are astonished that he never got on to the international panel. Burgum was on the select list twice and was well fancied to make the top panel in the year when England, with a decision that might have demoralised scores of ambitious officials, decided to put only two men on the panel instead of three.

The word was put about that Burgum was too strict, too inflexible and he accepts this as the reason why he did not make it to the very top. He is philosophical. 'Like all selection policies, it is only a question of opinion. I had a style of refereeing and I stuck to it. I have no hard feelings. I would have liked to referee an international but it was not to be. I enjoyed my time. I always felt that you had to get a style of refereeing over. If you do that you get a reputation and the players respond accordingly. The trouble frequently starts when a referee compromises.'

Burgum's biggest game was the North Eastern Counties v Whineray's All Blacks. He has taken charge of an England trial and controlled 36 county games, including the Cornwall v Surrey semi-final that had to be replayed twice.

On the prevailing standards of refereeing he says: 'There have been problems in the last few years because of the flood of retirements of senior referees. They got old together and now there are a lot of young, inexperienced referees who are not as well known, who have not made their mark and are therefore not as well respected.' Of those who are left he singles out Roger Quittenton. 'He is head and shoulders above the rest,' he said.

TOURS, LIONS, BARBARIANS

INTERNATIONAL TOURS

Argentina to France, Spain

	P	W	D	L	F	A
1982	8	4	0	4	142	141

Argentina to New Zealand

	P	W	D	L	F	A
1979	9	6	0	3	165	111

Argentina to South Africa

	P	W	D	L	F	A
1965	16	11	1	4	183	62
1971	14	9	1	4	132	28

Australia to British Isles, France, Italy and USA

		P	W	D	L	F	A
1908–09	England/Wales	31	25	1	5	438	149
1927–28	British Isles	28	22	2	4	400	177
1927–28	France	3	2	0	1	32	30
1947–48	British Isles	30	25	0	5	429	197
1947–48	France	5	4	0	1	71	46
1957–58	British Isles	30	14	3	13	248	203
1957–58	France	4	2	0	2	37	41
1966–67	British Isles	30	15	2	13	303	280
1966–67	France	4	2	1	1	45	42
1968	Ireland/Scotland	5	2	0	3	38	40
1971	France	8	4	0	4	110	101
1973	England/Wales	8	2	1	5	85	131
1975–76	British Isles	25	18	1	6	472	337
1976	USA	1	1	0	0	24	12
1976	Italy	1	1	0	0	16	15
1976	France	9	3	0	6	98	148
1981–82	British Isles	23	16	1	6	431	219

Australia to Fiji

	P	W	D	L	F	A
1980	3	3	0	0	93	34

Australia to South Africa

	P	W	D	L	F	A
1933	23	12	1	10	299	195
1953	27	16	1	10	450	413
1961	6	3	1	2	90	80
1963	24	15	1	8	303	233
1969	26	15	0	11	465	353

England to Australia, Fiji and New Zealand

		P	W	D	L	F	A
1963	New Zealand	5	1	0	4	45	73
1963	Australia	1	0	0	1	9	18
1973	Fiji	1	1	0	0	13	12
1973	New Zealand	4	1	0	3	47	60
1975	Australia	8	4	0	4	217	110
1979	Fiji/Japan/Tonga	7	7	0	0	270	93

England to Argentina

	P	W	D	L	F	A
1981	7	6	1	0	193	100

NB England players were given caps for the two internationals against Argentina, the first non-International Board country to be so recognised.

England to South Africa

	P	W	D	L	F	A
1972	7	6	1	0	166	58

Fiji to Scotland/England

	P	W	D	L	F	A
1982	10	0	0	10	126	327

France to Australia and New Zealand

		P	W	D	L	F	A
1961	New Zealand	13	6	0	7	150	149
1961	Australia	2	2	0	0	30	20
1968	New Zealand	12	8	0	4	154	120
1968	Australia	2	1	0	1	41	22
1972	Australia	9	8	1	0	254	122
1979	New Zealand/Fiji	9	6	0	3	168	116
1981	Australia	9	6	0	3	189	112

France to South Africa

	P	W	D	L	F	A
1958	10	5	2	3	137	124
1964	6	5	0	1	117	55
1967	13	8	1	4	209	161
1971	9	7	1	1	228	92
1975	11	6	1	4	282	190
1980	4	3	0	1	90	95

Ireland to Australia

	P	W	D	L	F	A
1967	6	4	0	2	119	80
1979	8	7	0	1	184	75

Ireland to New Zealand and Fiji

		P	W	D	L	F	A
1976	New Zealand	7	4	0	3	88	68
1976	Fiji	1	1	0	0	8	0

Ireland to South Africa

	P	W	D	L	F	A
1961	4	3	0	1	59	36
1981	7	3	0	4	207	90

New Zealand to Australia/Fiji

	P	W	D	L	F	A
1980	16	12	1	3	507	126

New Zealand to British Isles and France

		P	W	D	L	F	A
1888–89	British Isles	74	49	5	20	394	188
1905–06	British Isles	32	31	0	1	830	39
1905–06	France	1	1	0	0	38	8
1924–25	British Isles	28	28	0	0	654	98
1924–25	France	2	2	0	0	67	14
1926–27	England/Wales	16	8	2	6	126	113
1926–27	France	15	14	0	1	333	81
1935–36	British Isles	28	24	1	3	431	180
1953–54	British Isles	29	25	2	2	438	115
1953–54	France	2	0	0	2	8	14
1963–64	British Isles	30	28	1	1	508	137
1963–64	France	4	4	0	0	60	16
1967	British Isles	11	10	1	0	207	78
1967	France	4	4	0	0	87	51
1972–73	British Isles	26	20	2	4	521	227
1972–73	France	4	3	0	1	47	27
1974	Ireland/UK	8	7	1	0	127	50
1977	France/Italy	9	8	0	1	216	86
1978	British Isles	18	17	0	1	364	147
1979	England/Scotland/ Italy	11	10	0	1	192	95
1981	France/Romania	10	8	1	1	170	108

New Zealand to South Africa

	P	W	D	L	F	A
1928	22	16	1	5	339	144
1949	24	14	3	7	230	146
1960	26	20	2	4	441	164
1970	24	21	0	3	687	228
1976	24	18	0	6	610	291

New Zealand to USA/Canada

	P	W	D	L	F	A
1980	2	2	0	0	96	16

New Zealand to Wales

	P	W	D	L	F	A
1980	5	5	0	0	101	25

Romania to Ireland

	P	W	D	L	F	A
1980	6	4	1	1	137	75

Romania to Scotland

	P	W	D	L	F	A
1981	3	2	0	1	42	35

Scotland to South Africa

	P	W	D	L	F	A
1960	3	2	0	1	61	45

Scotland to Australia

	P	W	D	L	F	A
1970	6	3	0	3	109	94
1982	9	6	0	3	220	113

Scotland to New Zealand

	P	W	D	L	F	A
1975	7	4	0	3	157	104
1981	8	5	0	3	189	125

South Africa to Australia and New Zealand

		P	W	D	L	F	A
1921	Australia	4	4	0	0	83	38
1921	New Zealand	19	15	2	2	244	81
1937	Australia	9	8	0	1	342	65
1937	New Zealand	17	16	0	1	411	104
1956	Australia	6	6	0	0	150	26
1956	New Zealand	23	16	1	6	370	177
1965	Australia	6	3	0	3	184	53
1965	New Zealand	24	19	0	5	485	232
1971	Australia	13	13	0	0	396	102
1981	New Zealand	14	11	1	2	410	171

South Africa to British Isles and France

		P	W	D	L	F	A
1906–07	British Isles	28	25	1	2	553	79
1912–13	British Isles	26	23	0	3	403	96
1912–13	France	1	1	0	0	38	5
1931–32	British Isles	26	23	2	1	407	124
1951–52	British Isles	27	26	0	1	499	143
1951–52	France	4	4	0	0	63	24
1960–61	British Isles	30	28	1	1	476	110
1960–61	France	4	3	1	0	91	22
1965	Ireland/Scotland	5	0	1	4	37	53
1968	France	6	5	0	1	84	43
1969–70	British Isles	24	15	4	5	323	157
1974	France	9	8	0	1	170	74

South Africa to South America

	P	W	D	L	F	A
1980	6	6	0	0	376	78

South Africa to USA

	P	W	D	L	F	A
1981	3	3	0	0	125	19

South America to South Africa

	P	W	D	L	F	A
1980	7	4	0	3	174	134
1982	7	6	0	1	218	109

Wales to South Africa

	P	W	D	L	F	A
1964	4	2	0	2	43	58

Wales to Australia, New Zealand and Fiji

		P	W	D	L	F	A
1969	New Zealand	5	2	1	2	62	76
1969	Australia	1	1	0	0	19	16
1969	Fiji	1	1	0	0	31	11
1978	Australia	9	5	0	4	227	106

British Lions on Tour

TO AUSTRALIA

	P	W	D	L	F	A
1888	16	14	2	0	210	65
1899	21	18	0	3	333	90
1904	14	14	0	0	265	51
1908	9	7	0	2	139	48
1930	7	5	0	2	204	113
1950	6	5	0	1	150	52
1959	6	5	0	1	174	70
1966	8	7	1	0	202	48
1971	2	1	0	1	25	27
	89	76	3	10	1702	564

Willie John McBride, manager of the 1983 British Isles tour of New Zealand, paid tribute to the quality of the All Blacks but during the tour complained of poor refereeing and dirty play by some New Zealand sides. (Colorsport.)

Test Matches in Australia

Matches played	14
Australia	2 wins
British Isles	12 wins
Australia	58 pts
British Isles	219 pts

Year	Results	Australia T	Australia C	Australia P	Australia D	British Isles T	British Isles C	British Isles P	British Isles D
1888	No Tests played								
1899	Australia: 13–3								
	British Isles: 11–0								
	British Isles: 11–10								
	British Isles: 13–0								
1904	British Isles: 17–0								
	British Isles: 17–3								
	British Isles: 16–0								
1908	No Tests played								
1930	Australia: 6–5	2				1	1		
1950	British Isles: 19–6			2		2	2	2	1
	British Isles: 24–3	1				5	3	1	
1959	British Isles: 17–6			2		2	1	2	1
	British Isles: 24–3			1		5	3	1	
1966	British Isles: 11–8	1	1	1		2	1	1	
	British Isles: 31–0					5	5	1	1
	TOTALS	4	1	6		22	16	8	3

Injuries forced New Zealand to employ a three-man scrum against the British Isles in the Fourth Test at Auckland on the 1977 tour. (Colorsport.)

TO NEW ZEALAND

	P	W	D	L	F	A
1888	19	13	4	2	82	33
1904	5	2	1	2	22	33
1908	17	9	1	7	184	153
1930	21	15		6	420	205
1950	23	17	1	5	420	162
1959	25	20		5	582	266
1966	25	15	2	8	300	281
1971	24	22	1	1	555	204
1977	25	20	1	4	586	295
1983	18	12	0	6	478	266
	202	145	11	46	3629	1898

Former prime minister Edward Heath (right) chats to members of the 1983 British Isles side at a pre-tour reception in London. The full Lions party (below) photographed before their departure for New Zealand. (Colorsport.)

Test Matches in New Zealand

		Year	Results	New Zealand				British Isles			
				T	C	P	D	T	C	P	D
Matches played	32	1888	No Tests played								
New Zealand	34 wins	1904	New Zealand: 9–3	2		1				1	
British Isles	5 wins	1908	New Zealand: 32–5	7	4	1		1	1		
Drawn	3		Drawn: 3–3			1		1			
New Zealand	470 pts		New Zealand: 29–0	9	1						
British Isles	254 pts	1930	British Isles: 6–3			1		2			
			New Zealand: 13–10	2	2		1*	2	2		
			New Zealand: 15–10	3	1		1	2	2		
			New Zealand: 22–8	6	2			1	1	1	
		1950	Drawn: 9–9	2		1		2		1	
			New Zealand: 8–0	2	1						
			New Zealand: 6–3	1		1				1	
			New Zealand: 11–8	2	1		1	1	1	1	
		1959	New Zealand: 18–17			6		4	1	1	
			New Zealand: 11–8	3	1			1	1	1	
			New Zealand: 22–8	4	2	1	1	1	1	1	
			British Isles: 9–6			2		3			
		1966	New Zealand: 20–3	3	1	2	1			1	
			New Zealand: 16–12	3	2	1				3	1
			New Zealand: 19–6	3	2	2		2			
			New Zealand: 24–11	4	3	1	1	2	1	1	
		1971	British Isles: 9–3			1		1		2	
			New Zealand: 22–12	5†	2	1		2		1	1
			British Isles: 13–3	1				2	2	1	
			Drawn: 14–14	2	1	2		1	1	2	1
		1977	New Zealand: 16–12	3	2					4	
			British Isles: 13–9			3		1		3	
			New Zealand: 19–7	2	1	2	1	1		1	
			New Zealand: 10–9	1		2		1	1	1	
		1983	New Zealand: 16–12	1		3	1			3	1
			New Zealand: 9–0	1	1	1					
			New Zealand: 15–8	1	1	3		2			
			New Zealand: 38–6	6	4	2			2		
			TOTALS	79	35	41	8	36	15	33	4

* Goal from a mark. † Including penalty try.

Jim Telfer, of Scotland, who coached the British Isles during their 1983 tour of New Zealand. (Colorsport.)

TEST RECORDS IN NEW ZEALAND

Most points
New Zealand 38 (1983 4th Test 38–6)
British Isles 17 (1959 1st Test 17–18)

Most points in a match
44 New Zealand 38 British Isles 6 (1983 4th Test)

Most points in a match lost
New Zealand 9 (1977 2nd Test 9–13)
British Isles 17 (1959 1st Test 17–18)

Most points scored in a series
New Zealand 79 (1966)
British Isles 48 (1971)

Least points scored in a series (4 Tests)

New Zealand	34 (1950)
British Isles	20 (1950)

Most tries in a series

New Zealand	16 (3 Tests 1908)
British Isles	9 (1959)

Least tries in a series

New Zealand	6 (1977)
British Isles	2 (3 Tests 1908)
	3 (4 Tests 1950, 1977)

Injuries hit the 1983 British Isles tour to New Zealand with the result that seven players were flown out as replacements: Steve

Bainbridge (top), Nick Jeavons, Nigel Melville, Donald Lenihan, Gerry McLoughlin, Steve Smith and Eddie Butler. (Colorsport.)

Most penalties in a series
New Zealand 9 (1959)
British Isles 9 (1977)

Most tries in a Test
New Zealand 9 (1908 1st Test)
British Isles 4 (1959 1st Test)

Biggest winning points margin
New Zealand 32 (1983 4th Test 38–6)
British Isles 10 (1971 3rd Test 13–3)

TOUR RECORDS

Most tries on a tour
In New Zealand: 17 J Bevan (1971), A J F O'Reilly (1959)
On Australasian tour: A J F O'Reilly 23 (1959)

Most points in a match
25 Andy Irvine v King Country-Wanganui (1977)
M C Thomas v Marlborough-Nelson-Golden Bay-Motueka (1959)

Biggest win
In New Zealand: 64–5 v Marlborough-Nelson-Golden Bay-Motueka (1959)
On Australasian tour: 70–6 v E Canada (1959)

Most tries in a match
In New Zealand and Australasian tour: 6 by David Duckham

Biggest loss
6–38 New Zealand (1983)

Most points on a tour
In New Zealand: 181 Barry John 1971
On Australasian tour: 188 Barry John 1971

TO SOUTH AFRICA

	P	W	D	L	F	A
1891	19	19	—	—	224	1
1896	21	19	1	1	310	45
1903	22	11	3	8	231	138
1910	24	13	3	8	290	236
1924	21	9	3	9	175	155
1938	23	17	—	6	407	272
1955	24	18	1	5	418	271
1962	24	15	4	5	351	208
1968	20	15	1	4	377	181
1974	22	21	1	0	729	207
1980	18	15	0	3	401	244
	238	172	17	49	3913	1958

TEST RECORDS IN SOUTH AFRICA

Most points
South Africa 34 (1962 4th Test 34–14)
British Isles 28 (1974 2nd Test 28–9)
(These are also the biggest winning points margins)

Most points in a match
48 South Africa 34 British Isles 14 (1962 4th Test)
South Africa 26 British Isles 22 (1980 1st Test)

Most points
South Africa 22 (1955 1st Test 22–23)
British Isles 22 (1980 1st Test 22–26)

Most points scored in a series
South Africa 77 (1980)
British Isles 79 (1974)

Least points scored in a series
South Africa 0 (1891)
British Isles 11 (1891)

Least points scored in a series (4 Tests)
South Africa 16 (1896)
British Isles 15 (1924)

Most tries in a series
South Africa 16 (1955)
British Isles 10 (1955, 1974)

Least tries in a series (4 Tests)
South Africa 1 (1974)
British Isles 1 (1968)

Most penalties in a series
South Africa 8 (1968, 1974)
British Isles 11 (1968)

Most tries in a Test
South Africa 7 (1955 2nd Test)
British Isles 5 (1955 1st Test; 1974 2nd Test)

INDIVIDUAL RECORDS

Most points in a Test match
South Africa K Oxlee 16 (1962 4th Test)
British Isles A Ward 18 (1980 1st Test)

Most points in a Test series
South Africa K Oxlee 27 (1962)
British Isles T Kiernan 35 (1968)

Test Matches in South Africa

Matches played	40
South Africa	20 wins
British Isles	14 wins
Drawn	6
South Africa	474 pts
British Isles	381 pts

			South Africa				British Isles			
Year	Venue	Results	T	C	P	D	T	C	P	D
1891	Port Elizabeth	British Isles: 4–0					2	1		
	Kimberley	British Isles: 3–0								1
	Newlands	British Isles: 4–0					2	1		
1896	Port Elizabeth	British Isles: 8–0					2	1		
	Johannesburg	British Isles: 17–8	2	1			3	2		1
	Kimberley	British Isles: 9–3	1				1	1		1
	Newlands	South Africa: 8–0	1	1						
1903	Johannesburg	Drawn: 10–10	2	2			2	2		
	Kimberley	Drawn: 0–0								
	Newlands	South Africa: 8–0	2	1						
1910	Johannesburg	South Africa: 14–10	4	1			2			1
	Port Elizabeth	British Isles: 8–3	1				2	1		
	Newlands	South Africa: 21–5	4	3	1		1	1		
1924	Durban	South Africa: 7–3	1			1	1			
	Johannesburg	South Africa: 17–0	4	1	1					
	Port Elizabeth	Drawn: 3–3	1				1			
	Newlands	South Africa: 16–9	4			1	2		1	
1938	Johannesburg	South Africa: 26–12	4	4	2				4	
	Port Elizabeth	South Africa: 19–3	3	2	2		1			
	Newlands	British Isles: 21–16	3	2	1		4	1	1	1
1955	Johannesburg	British Isles: 23–22	4	2	2		5	4		
	Newlands	South Africa: 25–9	7	2			2		1	
	Pretoria	British Isles: 9–6			2		1		1	1
	Port Elizabeth	South Africa: 22–8	5	2		1	2	1		
	Johannesburg	Drawn: 3–3	1				1			
	Durban	South Africa: 3–0			1					
	Newlands	South Africa: 8–3	1	1	1					1
	Bloemfontein	South Africa: 34–14	6	5	2		3	1	1	
1968	Pretoria	South Africa: 25–20	3	2	4		1	1	5	
	Port Elizabeth	Drawn: 6–6			2				2	
	Newlands	South Africa: 11–6	1	1	2				2	
	Johannesburg	South Africa: 19–6	4	2		1			2	
1974	Newlands	British Isles: 12–3				1			3	1
	Pretoria	British Isles: 28–9			2	1	5	1	1	1
	Port Elizabeth	British Isles: 26–9			3		3	1	2	2
	Johannesburg	Drawn: 13–13	1		3		2	1	1	
1980	Newlands	South Africa: 26–22	5	3			1		5	1
	Bloemfontein	South Africa: 26–19	4	2	2		2	1	3	
	Port Elizabeth	South Africa: 12–10	1	1	1	1	1		2	
	Pretoria	British Isles: 17–13	1		3		3	1	1	
		TOTALS	81	41	37	7	58	23	37	12

Most tries in a Test series
South Africa TPD Briers 5 (1955)
British Isles John J Williams 4 (1974)

TOUR RECORDS IN SOUTH AFRICA

Most tries on tour
30 RL Aston (1896)

Most points in a match
37 Alan Old v SW Districts (1974)

Biggest win
97–0 v SW Districts (1974)

Most tries in a match (individual)
6 John J Williams v SW Districts (1974)

Most tries in a match
16 v SW Districts (1974)

Biggest defeat
0–20 v Eastern Province (1955)
14–34 v South Africa (1962 4th Test)

Most points on tour
156 Andy Irvine (1974)

Best provincial records
1974 P 18 W 18, points 650–173

Most tries on tour
107 1974

Least number of tries on tour
45 1924 and 1980

ALL TOURS RECORDS

Highest score
31 Australia (31–0, 1966)

Highest score against
38 New Zealand (6–38, 1983)

Most points in a series
35 T Kiernan v South Africa (1968)
(in New Zealand 30 Barry John, 1971)

Most points in Internationals
44 Phil Bennett (1974–7)

Most points in an International
18 A Ward v South Africa (1980 1st Test)

Most tries in Internationals
6 Tony O'Reilly (1955–9)

Most tries in a series
4 John J Williams v South Africa (1974)

Most points on tour
842 Australia, New Zealand & Canada (33 matches, 1959)

TEST APPEARANCES

17 Willie John McBride (Ballymena, Ireland)
13 Dickie Jeeps (Northampton, England)
12 Mike Gibson (NIFC, Ireland)
Graham Price (Pontypool, Wales)
10 Gareth Edwards (Cardiff, Wales)
Tony O'Reilly (Old Belvedere, Ireland)
Rhys Williams (Llanelli, Wales)
9 Sid Millar (Ballymena, Ireland)
Andy R Irvine (Heriot's FP, Scotland)
8 Dewi Bebb (Swansea, Wales)
Phil Bennett (Llanelli, Wales)
Gordon Brown (West of Scotland, Scotland)
Mike Campbell-Lamerton (Halifax, The Army, Scotland)
Mervyn Davies (London Welsh, Swansea, Wales)
Ian McGeechan (Headingley, Scotland)
Ian McLauchlan (Jordanhill, Scotland)
Bryn Meredith (Newport, Wales)
Noel Murphy (Cork Constitution, Ireland)
Alun Pask (Abertillery, Wales)
J P R Williams (London Welsh, Wales)

Graham Price (above), the Pontypool and Wales prop, became one of the British Lions elite when he played four times against the All Blacks in 1983, bringing his total Lions appearances to 12. Only Willie John McBride and Dickie Jeeps have played more times for the Lions. Ollie Campbell (below) totalled 124 points on the same tour. (Colorsport.)

Highest Scores on Tour

97	v SW Districts, South Africa	1974	(97–0)
71	v Western Australia	1930	(71–3)
70	v Eastern Canada	1959	(70–6)
69	v Griqualand West	1974	(69–16)
64	v Marlborough–Nelson–Golden Bay–Motueka, New Zealand	1959	(64–5)
60	v Western Australia	1966	(60–3)
60	v King Country–Wanganui, New Zealand	1977	(60–9)
59	v Western Transvaal, South Africa	1974	(59–13)
58	v West Coast–Buller, New Zealand	1959	(58–3)
53	v Victoria, Australia	1959	(53–18)
52	v Hawkes Bay, New Zealand	1959	(52–12)
50	v Leopards, South Africa	1974	(50–10)
50	v East Africa	1962	(50–0)

100 Points on Tour

188	Barry John	1971
156	Andy Irvine	1974
127	J F Byrne	1896
125	Phil Bennett	1977
125	Ollie Campbell	1983
112	Dave Hewitt	1959
110	Bob Hiller	1971
104	Bob Hiller	1968
104	Terry Davies	1959
103	Phil Bennett	1974

Most Tours

5 Willie John McBride (Ireland)

Total number of tours

Tours	P	W	D	L	F	A
21	513	382	31	100	8808	4234

OTHER MATCHES

1950	Ceylon	44–6
1959	British Columbia	16–11
	Eastern Canada	70–6
1962	East Africa	50–0
1966	British Columbia	3–8
	Canada	19–8
1977	Fiji	21–25

Matches played	7
British Isles	5 wins
Others	2 wins
British Isles	223 pts
Others	64 pts

1983 Tour of New Zealand Results

W	47–15	Wanganui (Wanganui)
L	12–13	Auckland (Eden Park)
W	34–16	Bay of Plenty (Rotorua)
W	27–19	Wellington (Athletic Park)
W	25–18	Manawatu (Manawatu)
W	26–6	Mid-Canterbury (Ashburton)
L	12–16	New Zealand (Christchurch)
W	52–16	West Coast (Greymouth)
W	41–3	Southland (Invercargill)
W	57–10	Wairarapa–Bush (Masterton)
L	0–9	New Zealand (Wellington)
W	21–12	North Auckland (Whangarei)
L	20–22	Canterbury (Lancaster Park)
L	8–15	New Zealand (Canterbury)
W	25–19	Hawke's Bay (Napier)
W	25–16	Counties (Pukekohe)
W	40–3	Waikato (Hamilton)
L	6–38	New Zealand (Auckland)

Tour summary: P 18 W 12 D 0 L 6 F 478 A 266

The Barbarians

Results against touring sides

1948 Barbarians 9 (3T) Australia 6 (1P 1T) Cardiff
1952 Barbarians 3 (1T) South Africa 17 (1G 1T 3PG) Cardiff
1954 Barbarians 5 (1G) New Zealand 19 (2G 2T 1DG) Cardiff
1958 Barbarians 11 (1G 2T) Australia 6 (2T) Cardiff
1961 Barbarians 6 (2T) South Africa 0 Cardiff
1964 Barbarians 3 (1DG) New Zealand 36 (6G 2T) Cardiff
1967 Barbarians 11 (1PT 1T 1PG) Australia 17 (1G 4T) Cardiff
1967 Barbarians 6 (1T 1DG) New Zealand 11 (1G 1T 1DG) Twickenham
1970 Barbarians 12 (3T 1PG) South Africa 21 (3G 1PG 1DG) Twickenham
1973 Barbarians 23 (2G 2T 1PG) New Zealand 11 (2T 1PG) Cardiff
1974 Barbarians 13 (1T 3PG) New Zealand 13 (1G 1T 1PG) Twickenham
1976 Barbarians 19 (2G 1T 1PG) Australia 7 (1T 1PG) Cardiff
1978 Barbarians 16 (1G 1T 2PG) New Zealand 18 (3T 1PG 1DG) Cardiff

Errol Tobias, the coloured South African player who added flair to the Barbarian midfield play during their Easter tour of Wales in 1983. (Colorsport.)

Graham Mourie, who ended his international career by leading New Zealand to a 2–1 series win over Australia in October 1982, played his final representative match later that year when appearing for the Barbarians against Racing Club de Paris in Paris in a match to celebrate the French club's centenary. (Colorsport.)

Tony Bond in action for the Barbarians during their 52–25 victory over East Midlands at Northampton in March 1983.

Other match

1977 Barbarians 14 (1G 2T) British Lions 23 (1G 2T 3PG) Twickenham

Summary

	P	W	D	L	F	A
v Australia	4	3	0	1	50	36
v South Africa	3	1	0	2	21	38
v New Zealand	6	1	1	4	66	108
	13	5	1	7	137	182

1982 results

W 35–22 East Midlands
W 84–16 Penarth
L 31–36 Cardiff
W 25–22 Swansea
W 48–20 Newport
L 32–36 Leicester

1983 results

W 36–12 Penarth
D 32–32 Cardiff
L 6–58* Swansea

*Barbarians heaviest ever defeat.

Hong Kong Sevens

L 12–18 Scottish Borders (semi-final)

Centenary matches

L 14–24 Waterloo
L 17–22 Racing Club de Paris

A brilliant performance in the centre for the Barbarians against Cardiff in 1983 earned David Gerber rave notices in the British Press (Colorsport.)

1882 1982

RHYMNEY RFC

RHYMNEY RFC

Rhymney RFC in 1887–88, a team thought to be known as the 'Stars'. It is believed to be the first ever photograph of a Rhymney RFC side.

Rhymney, in common with many other clubs world-wide, celebrated their Centenary in 1982–3 and, although largely unheralded, this small Welsh club are in many ways typical of those who have reached this important milestone: their beginnings were humble and vaguely recorded, they suffered setbacks and threats to survival, but gradually they laid firm and lasting foundations which not only established their identity but instilled a purpose which will serve them well in the next 100 years.

Rhymney's *raison d'être* is simple: to provide facilities for players to play the game and to enjoy so doing. And like clubs with similar objectives, they cast no envious look to wealthier, bigger and more publicised clubs. Yet for all this 'contentedness' and acceptance of their role and status, Rhymney are far from dyed in the wool. Indeed they are an example to other minor clubs in that they organise and plan for the future, always looking to improve playing standards and fixtures.

More than 90 years on, the Rhymney side of 1980–81 pose with captain Alan Rodaway—the club's leading forward try scorer with 52.

The War Memorial Park, Rhymney

Grand Rugby Match

SLAVA-MOSCOW

versus

Rhymney

Wednesday, 10th November, 1976 K.O. 7 p.m.

Admission — 20p.

First ever visit of Russian Rugby Team to Britain

Ticket for first ever game of a Russian rugby side in Great Britain—Rhymney, November 1976. Won by Rhymney 10–8.

Where Rhymney have an edge over others is in touring, at least in the variety and quality of this phenomenon of the game during the last 10 years. Rhymney in fact have been 'at it' for 20 years, which is longer than most, and have undertaken ambitious trips to such intriguingly diverse places as South Africa, France, Germany, Czechoslovakia and the Soviet Union. At home, too, at The Park, their snug, well-appointed little ground, they have hosted Americans, Czechs, Russians, Frenchmen and Argentines—and they are justly proud that the home record against all overseas visitors is one hundred per cent.

Rhymney's J L Brown gets highest during 1982's 3–3 away draw with old French rivals L'isle Jourdain.

Rhymney line up before return game in Moscow July 1977. First ever British side to play Russians in Russia (Llanelli played non-Russians 1957) record Rhymney defeat 61–6!!

Ian Lewis sends Ken Barnes away during Slava Moscow/Rhymney game.

Rhymney claim that they are the only club to have toured both South Africa and the Soviet Union, though they hasten to explain that this was largely by accident rather than design. During their 1975 tour of Czechoslovakia, Rhymney were fog-bound at Prague Airport where they met a Soviet side en route for Moscow, and who were similarly grounded. Rugbymen, regardless of their persuasions, do not take long to strike up a common discussion and from this Prague parley emerged an arrangement for Slava Moscow to become the first Soviet Union side to tour Britain, in November 1976. A reciprocal visit was arranged for the 1977 close-season and so Rhymney became the first British side to play against Russians in the Soviet Union and, of course, the first British side to play against Russians in Great Britain (Note: an Irish side, St Mary's College, played in the Soviet Union the day before Rhymney, and when Llanelli toured in 1957 the west Wales side had Romanian opposition in Moscow). Rhymney, incidentally, won their home game against Slava Moscow 10–8, but went down 6–61 in the return—'hot, hard, out-of-season, big crowd, reffing eccentric, them super-fit and vengeful, our faces as red as their shirts' according to Philip Atkinson, researcher and writer of Rhymney's highly entertaining club history. Atkinson's

'Duw, it was hard'—Rhymney forwards (far left Dennis Humphreys, Colin Williams, Robert Wood and Phil Matthews wait for the next 'round' in the Slava encounter.

enthusiasm and painstaking research of Rhymney's early days is a feature of an outstanding contribution to the literature of the 100-year-old clubs. With one breath he claims Rhymney to be typical of 'your average valley club' but decidedly atypical in others.

The book traces the club's origins with a delicate balance of humour and cold hard fact.

Centenary Chairman David Lewis presents Bruzon, the Captain of French hosts Castelsarrasin, with the 'Farmer's Lilies' trophy. The cup recalls that won by the Lilies, a Rhymney side, 75 years ago and has been donated by Whitbread Wales for competition between Rhymney and their French rivals.

Centenary Spirit—players from 'the super Sixties' were amongst those who celebrated Rhymney's hundredth year in a splendid clubhouse reunion in 1982.

Captains from Rhymney's last four decades, including record scorer David Pulsford (far left, standing), are pictured here.

That a whole chapter is devoted to Rhymney's first home produced international, Bill Evans (two caps for Wales 1882–83), is hardly surprising but efforts to link Evans, who also played for Newport, with the first Rhymney sides were unavailing. At the time, Rhymney, once remote and rural, was invaded by 'traders, prospectors and work people . . . a hive of teeming industry; they came from all parts to make up a community varied in industry, religion, politics and culture'. The principal employer was the Rhymney Iron Company and with 'its furnaces, works, farms, brewery, coal pits, brickworks and Company shop' the population soared to 9000. It was against this backdrop of the industrial revolution that rugby took its first roots in Rhymney, and although Evans, the son of a clergyman and an Oxford graduate was an exception, the workforce of the original sides undoubtedly provided the nucleus of the first Rhymney sides.

Centenary Committee—some of the men who helped plan Rhymney's splendid Centenary Season 1982–83.

Twelve post-war Rhymney captains, including later Swansea coach Stan Addicot (seated extreme right) are amongst this clubhouse group.

The club was not formed when the Salmon Tin Dribblers and the Pig's Bladder Barbarians played as street sides but no doubt these wonderfully named outfits accentuated the need to establish a club that played rugby in the area. 'The Rhymney Stars' were proved to be founded in 1882 and were followed by 'The Farmer's Lilies' in 1887. The 'Lilies' were Rhymney RFC for the next 20 years, in which time they extended the fixture list to take on such opposition as Aberbargoed, Bedwas, Machen, Cwm, Maesycwmmer and Cyfarthfa. Rhymney entered the Monmouthshire League in 1910 when they were to 'survive rather than flourish', and often the club were hard pressed financially and to keep players often lured to better known, more established clubs in the area. In the Depression of the Twenties, too, the club hardly survived, with few games played until 1932. The Second World War left the club on its knees again, and although they lost their second most famous player, Bob Evans, to Newport, in 1945, enthusiasm was undimmed so that by 1956 the

Rhymney's record man, Sixties star and Welsh trialist David Pulsford (right) is congratulated by former Secretary John Meade. Pulsford scored over 2200 points including 200 plus tries (38 in one season) in some 350 games.

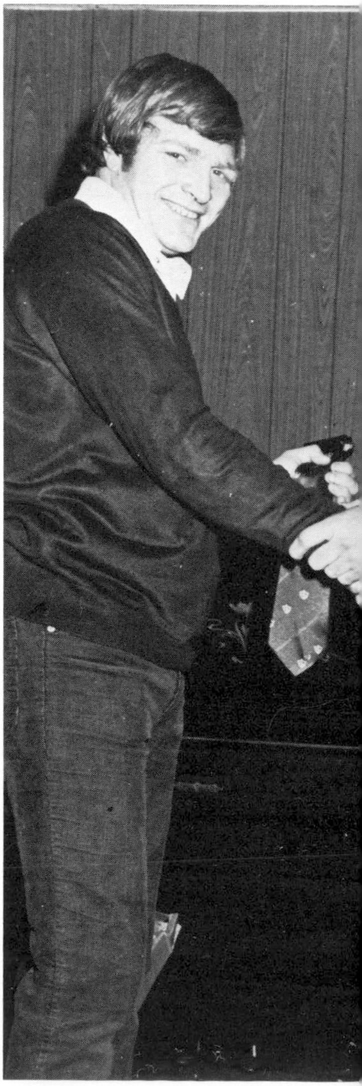

Rhymney's Captain, Alan Rodaway, exchanges souvenirs with Roberto Passaglia (right), Argentine International and skipper of La

club was set on a course of complete renovation: they aimed for a new ground, their own clubhouse, floodlights, tours and good fixtures. All this they achieved, and if most of the good things in Rhymney's life arrived in the later part of their first 100 years, they are stronger for it, and better prepared for the future.

Tablada (Cordoba) one of Rhymney's many overseas opponents. Rhymney with a 1002 record against foreign visitors, won 17–16 in 1980.

RHYMNEY'S RECORD AGAINST OVERSEAS OPPOSITION

At Home

1966 W 11–6 Oregon Universities (USA)
1975 W 22–13 Slavia Prague (Czechoslovakia)
1976 W 10–8 Slava Moscow (Soviet Union)
1977 W 20–3 Slavia Prague (Czechoslovakia)
1979 W 11–3 L'Isle Jourdain (France)
1979 W 16–9 Vyskov (Czechoslovakia)
1979 W 19–7 Michigan (USA)
1980 W 17–16 La Tablada (Argentina)
1982 W 18–9 L'Isle Jourdain (France)
Summary: P 9 W 9 L 0 F 144 A 74

Away

1964 South Africa L 16–27 Cape Town University, W 16–6 Wellington, L 9–41 Natal XV, W 19–11 Pretoria Harlequins, W 17–16 Johannesburg Wanderers
1966 France L 8–9 Gujan-La Teste, W 16–12 Mimizan
1967 France W 9–3 Bourg, L 0–16 Givors, W 14–11 Bourgoin
1972 France L 4–17 Castelsarassin
1975 Germany W 22–3 Hamburg Police
1975 Czechoslovakia W 24–10 Slavia Prague, W 18–8 Olomoue, W 16–7 Vyskov
1977 Soviet Union L 6–61 Slava Moscow, L 19–28 Kutaisi, L 3–15 Kutaisi
1978 France W 31–14 L'Isle Jourdain
1979 Czechoslovakia W 46–0 Slavia Prague, W 21–6 Zbrojovka Brno, W 25–10 Tatra Smichov
1982 France D 3–3 L'Isle Jourdain
Summary: P 23 W 14 D 1 L 8 F 362 A 334

CLUB RECORDS

Most wins in a season: 37 1963–4
Most points in a season: 836 1963–4
Highest score: 78 v Exmouth 1973
Longest winning sequence: 15 1973–4
Longest unbeaten sequence: 22 1963–4

Individual

Most points in career: 2200 D Pulsford 1953–70
Most points in a season: 360 D Pulsford 1964–5
Most points in a game: 31 D Pulsford 1964
Most tries in career: 200 D Pulsford 1953–70
Wales caps: W F Evans (1882–3), R T Evans* (1947–51), J Jeffery* (1967)

**capped after leaving club*

MILESTONES

A CHRONOLOGY OF WORLD RUGBY

Many and multi-various events shaped the world of rugby that we know today. The purpose of this Chronology is to provide a guide to the spread and development of the game to all corners of the globe. Events not catalogued in the Chronology are referred to elsewhere; any significant omissions are excused on the grounds of insufficient space.

Events Which Shaped The World of Rugby

1823 William Webb Ellis 'who with a fine disregard for the rules of football as played in his time first took the ball in his arms and ran with it' ... so states the plaque at Rugby School which more than any single historic fact gave rise to the most enduring legend in rugby football, that Ellis originated the distinctive feature of the game.

1827–40 Matches, of sorts, played in England, Wales, Scotland and Australia. Little documentary evidence has been obtained to verify the type of rugby played or the motivation for the early spread of the game. The chief source of what this embryonic game might have been like is contained in an admirably descriptive account of a game played at Rugby School in *Tom Brown's Schooldays*, by Thomas Hughes, written in 1835.

1839 There are claims that Arthur Pell, on leaving Rugby School and going up to Cambridge, introduced the game to the university. If that be so Pell, who later became an MP, would have been a far more significant figure in rugby's propagation than Webb Ellis. It was, after all, from the universities that the trickle of influence soon became a flood as graduates spread the game throughout Britain and the Empire.

1843 A club is formed at Guy's Hospital in London.

1845 Rugby's first set of rules was drawn up at Rugby School on 28 August. Although these rules were frequently amended, often for no obvious reason, they provided the framework from which the game has developed. Indeed today we still employ many of the terms used in that first set of rules—'fair catch', 'off side', 'knock on', 'try', 'punt', 'place kick' and 'touch'. (Bibliographic note: a well researched account of the development of the game at Rugby School is contained in *The World of Rugby*, by John Reason and Carwyn James, BBC.)

1848 Cambridge Rules drawn up (later they formed the basis for the rules of the Football Association).

1850 The Reverend Rowland Williams became Vice-Principal of St David's College Lampeter in west Wales in 1850 and introduced rugby there the same year. Williams had arrived in Lampeter from Cambridge, where he had been a student, a Fellow and a Tutor at King's College when Arthur Pell, an old Rugbeian, first brought the game to King's—and Cambridge—in 1839 (*qv*).

1854 Dublin University RFC founded, the game brought to Ireland by boys who had attended school at Rugby and Cheltenham. The first secretary of Trinity College (as Dublin University then was) was R H Scott, an old Rugbeian. What might have been the first newspaper publication of a rugby fixture concerned the club: 'Trinity College. The University Football Club. A match will be played today between the original and new members of the club at 2.0.' The newspaper was the *Dublin Daily Express* and the date was 1 December 1855 (source: *The Men In Green*, by Sean Diffley, Pelham Books).

1857 Clubs formed at Edinburgh Academicals and Liverpool.

1858 Lillywhite's *Football Annual* of 1868 (edited by C W Alcock) stated that the foundation of Blackheath Football Club was 1858, and described the club's colours as 'red and black jersey, ditto stockings'. Other sources gave 1860 (*qv*), and that the club, called the Old Blackheathean Football Club, changed its name in 1862 when it was found that the club could not be run without the aid of players who had not attended Blackheath Proprietary School. Blackheath's first captain was W Burnett, a New Zealander who became a prime motivator of the tour of the New Zealand Native Team to Great Britain in 1888–9. Blackheath, presumably because of Burnett's influence, staged the Native Team's match against England in 1889.
Sandy Thorburn in his *History of Scottish Rugby* (Johnston and Bacon) states that Merchiston played Edinburgh Academy on 11 December 1858 and this 'must surely be the oldest (fixture) in the history of the game'. In the same publication Thorburn traces the influence of English-educated Scots in introducing the game to Scotland.

1863 Blackheath published their club rules (*qv*).
South Africa's first recorded match, Civilians v Military, took place in August 1862, at Cape Town. One of the players was Adriaan Van der Byl, who was educated at Marlborough College in England and Merchiston in Scotland, where he was captain of the team which played Edinburgh High School on 13 February 1858 in the first inter-school game.

1864 The first code of rules was formulated in Canada at Trinity College Toronto and a rugby club was formed at Sydney University in Australia.

1867 Although some sources suggest an earlier date, the first of rugby's oldest club fixtures, Richmond v Blackheath, took place on 26 January 1867 on Richmond Green.

1870 Rugby introduced to New Zealand by Charles John Monro, who learned the game while a schoolboy at Christ's Hospital in England.
First New Zealand club match took place in Nelson on 14 May 1870 between Nelson FC and Nelson College.

1871 Neath, Wales's oldest club, founded.
Rugby football's first international was played at Raeburn Place, Edinburgh, on 27 March 1871, when Scotland beat England by a goal and a try against a try.
The Rugby Football Union was founded in London on 26 January 1871.

1872 France's first club was formed at Le Havre by British residents.
The first University Match took place at the Parks, Oxford, on 10 February 1872 when Oxford beat Cambridge by a goal and a try to nil.
William Webb Ellis died and was buried in Menton, France. Curiously also buried in Menton was Percy Carpmael, founder of the Barbarians in 1890 and who died, aged 73, on 27 December 1936.

1873 The Scottish Rugby Union founded on 3 March 1873 in Glasgow.
First game played in Argentina, Banks v City, in Buenos Aires.

1874 McGill University of Montreal played Harvard University in first game to be played in USA, at Cambridge, Massachusetts.

Irish Football Union and Southern Rugby Union in Australia founded.

1875 Teams are reduced from 20 to 15 players.
England played Ireland for first time, Kennington Oval, London, 19 February 1875.
First Hospitals' Cup tournament played.

1877 Calcutta Cup struck in Calcutta (it was formally accepted by the Rugby Football Union in 1878 and first played for in 1879).

1878 The South Wales Football Union superseded the South Wales FC.

1879 Canterbury became first New Zealand Union to be formed.

Hawick and Newport used floodlights for first time. Rugby introduced to the Netherlands.

The Irish Football Union (Dublin) and the Northern Football Union (Belfast) united to form the Irish Rugby Union in Cork, February 1879.

1880 Rugby Football Union agreed to pay expenses for first time for international matches.

Sides from Montevideo Cricket Club arranged a match, the first played in Uruguay, on 25 August 1880.

1881 England played Wales for first time, at Richardson's Field, Blackheath, 19 February 1881, the only time this ground used as venue for an international.

Neutral referees were appointed for international matches.

The Welsh Rugby Union founded on 12 March 1881 at the Castle Hotel, Neath.

1882 Blues were awarded for rugby at Oxford.

New South Wales played in New Zealand, the first visit by an overseas team.

USA adopted different rules, leading to creation of new sport: American Football.

1883 Scotland played Wales for first time at Raeburn Place, Edinburgh, on 8 January 1883 to start the official International Championship.

Seven-a-side rugby invented and played at Melrose, Roxburghshire.

1884 Cardiff played four threequarters, against Gloucester, on 23 February 1884.

First New Zealand team assembled and it toured New South Wales.

First rugby match played in Fiji, between Fijian soldiers and European soldiers, at Ba.

Points system is adopted: a try worth 1 point, a conversion 2, other goals 3.

1886 Wales played four threequarters for first time, against Scotland at Cardiff 9 January 1886.

Points Scoring Since 1886

Year	*Try*	*Conversion*	*Penalty Goal*	*Dropped Goal*	*Goal from Mark*
1890 ..	1	2	2	3	3
1892 ..	2	3	3	4	4
1894 ..	3	2	3	4	4
1905 ..	3	2	3	4	3
1948 ..	3	2	3	3	3
1971 ..	4	2	3	3	3

1887 First meeting of the International Board held in Manchester on 5 December.

1888 New Zealand Native Team toured British Isles. This was the biggest tour ever: they played 74 matches in 25 weeks and after games in Australia and New Zealand on their return the total rose to 107.

R L Seddon led side to Australia and New Zealand, Britain's first tourists.

1889 London Society of Referees formed. Provincial competition started in South Africa.

Rugby Football Union established a close season: 1 May–31 August.

South African Rugby Football Board founded.
The County Championship in England started.

1890 The Barbarian Football Club formed at 2 am in the morning of 9 April 1890 at the Alexandra Hotel, Bradford (*qv*).

1891 British team toured South Africa for first time: South Africa played her first international, against the tourists at Port Elizabeth on 30 July 1891.
Cyril Nelson Lowe, England's record try scorer, was born on 7 October 1891.
The Currie Cup inaugurated in South Africa.

1892 New Zealand Rugby Football Union founded.

The International Board revised score values (try 2 points, conversion 3, penalty 3, dropped goal 4), mauls-in-goal were abolished, and the Rugby Football Union decreed that all matches would be played 15-a-side.

1893 The Broken Time Dispute: clubs from Cheshire, Lancashire and Yorkshire withdrew from the Rugby Football Union and formed the Northern Union (later the Rugby League).

1894 Scoring values again revised: try 3 points, conversion 2, penalty 3, drop goal and goal from a mark 4.

1895 Rugby clubs formed in Geneva and Prague.

1896 J Hammond's British team toured South Africa.

1897 Rugby introduced to Japan.
Numbering of jerseys became common practice.

1899 British Isles toured Australia.
Argentina Rugby Union founded.

1900 Madras Gymkhana Challenge Cup inaugurated.
Federal Republic of Germany Rugby Union founded.

1901 Barbarians made four-match tour of Wales for first time.

1902 Ranfurly Shield inaugurated in New Zealand.
Canada toured British Isles.

1903 Mark Morrison's British Isles team toured South Africa.
New Zealand played first full international, against Australia, Sydney, 15 August 1903.

1904 British Isles toured Australia and New Zealand.

1905 New Zealand made first tour to British Isles.

1906 France played first international, against New Zealand, Parc des Princes, Paris, on 1 January 1906.
England played France for first time, Parc des Princes, Paris.

1908 Australia toured England and Wales for first time, their first fully representative tour.

Carcavelos played Lisbon Cricket Club in Lisbon in Portugal's first rugby match.

1909 The first match played at Twickenham was Harlequins v Richmond on 2 October 1909.
D G Herring became the first American to play in the University Match. Herring, from Princeton University, played for Oxford.
Officials played Settlers in Mombasa in the first recorded match in Kenya.

1910 England played Wales in the first international to be staged at Twickenham, 15 January 1910.
France played in Championship for first time.
Dr T Smyth's British Isles team toured South Africa.

1911 France gained first international victory, beating Scotland 16–15 at Colombes, Paris, on 2 January 1911.
The Hampshire Cup, Thailand's first trophy, is presented to the Royal Bangkok Sports Club.

1912 Blackheath celebrated Jubilee season.

South Africa toured British Isles and France.

1913 International Board reprimanded France over crowd indiscipline during match against Scotland at Parc des Princes, Paris, on 1 January 1913. The match should have been played at Colombes, which could not be used because of flooding. The referee, J Baxter, of England, had upset sections of the crowd by awarding frequent penalties against France. At the end the referee had to be escorted from the pitch by police and players. Scotland refused to play France in 1914 because of this match.
Fiji Rugby Union founded.

1914 Romania Rugby Federation founded.

1917 Royal Bangkok Sports Club formed a rugby section.

1918 DSRC (Delft Students) formed as Netherlands' first rugby club.

1920 The French Rugby Federation founded.
Sri Lanka (then Ceylon) played matches against Calcutta and Madras.

1921 The first University Match to be staged at Twickenham, Oxford beating Cambridge 11–5.

South Africa toured Australia and New Zealand for first time.

Kenya Rugby Football Union founded.

1922 Malawi Rugby Football Union founded.

1923 Cyril Lowe, England's record try scorer, played 25th successive and last international, against France, in Paris.

England beat Ireland 23–5 at Leicester, which at the time was a record total by England against Ireland.

Rugby Football Unions of Tonga and Spain founded.

RC Heidelberg of the Federal Republic of Germany became first side to tour Romania.

1924 USA won the Olympic title in Paris, the last time rugby was an Olympic sport. The Americans had made a three match tour of Britain as a 'warm up'.

Romania beat Poland 46–0 to gain first international victory.

Tonga played first international, against Fiji in Suva.

Bermuda Rugby Football Union and a Mauritius club founded.

First All India Tournament staged in Bombay.

1925 Cyril Brownlie, the Hawke's Bay back-row forward, became the first player to be sent off in an international, when he was dismissed by Albert Freethy, of Wales, in the England v New Zealand match at Twickenham, during the New Zealand tour of the British Isles and France.

First international played at Murrayfield, Scotland beat England 14–11 watched by a then record crowd of 70 000. Scotland, having also beaten France (in the last ever international at Inverleith, 24 January 1925), Wales and Ireland, won the Grand Slam for the first and only time.

First rugby union match played at Wembley, The Army and RAF drawing 6–6 in the Inter-Services Tournament.

International matches fixed at 40 minutes each way, with 5 minutes interval and referee sole judge of time.

Rugby introduced to Mexico.

1926 Australia, New Zealand and South Africa are given separate representation on the International Board.
Japanese Rugby Football Union, Caribbean Rugby Football Union

and Czechoslovakia Rugby Union founded.
First clubs formed in Czechoslovakia.
Middlesex Sevens staged for first time, at Twickenham.

1927 A Rugby Football Union team won all matches on a tour of Argentina.
Apia Rugby Union founded in Western Samoa.
Spain played first international, against France, in Madrid.
Federal Republic of Germany played first international, against France, in Paris.

1928 Italian Rugby Federation founded.

1929 Belgian Rugby Union, Canada Rugby Union and Montevideo RFC in Uruguay founded.
Italy played first international, against Spain, in Madrid.

1930 Japan toured Canada.

Netherlands played first international, against Belgium, The Hague.
International Board take over the framing of the Laws.

1931 Four Home Unions severed relationship with France.
Romania Rugby Federation, Belgian Federation and Swedish Rugby Board founded.

1932 South African Junior Springboks toured Argentina.
Netherlands Rugby Union founded.
Canada toured Japan.

1933 Australia toured South Africa for first time.
France, Italy and Federal Republic of Germany drew up principles for the formation of FIRA.
Barbarians refused permission to play in Italy because of the Italians' liaison with France.

1934 Moscow Dynamo won first Soviet Union club championship.
FIRA founded by France, Federal Republic of Germany, Portugal, Italy, Romania, Sweden, Czechoslovakia, Netherlands and Catalonia.

1935 Don Tarr, the Swansea hooker, broke his neck playing for Wales against New Zealand at Cardiff, 21 December 1935.
New Zealand Maoris toured Australia.
Cambridge University became first British team to tour USA.

1936 British team toured Argentina and Brazil.

1937 South Africa won series in New Zealand, the only time in the history of matches between the countries.

1938 First international to be televised, England v Scotland at Twickenham.
Thailand Rugby Football Union and Mexican clubs, Reforma, RFC France and Wachachara founded.
Maoris toured Fiji.

1939 Australia arrived in Britain for tour, but returned home without playing a match because of outbreak of war.
France re-admitted to Five Nations Championship.

1940 Prince Alexander Obolensky killed on 29 March 1940 in a flying training accident in Norfolk: first international to lose his life during war.
Romania beat Italy for first time, in Bucharest.
Spanish Cup competition inaugurated.
Seychelles RFC founded.

1941–5 War severely curtailed rugby activities: notable exceptions were Guy's Hospital Centenary matches at Honor Oak Park (1943), a services match between a Rugby League XV and a Rugby Union XV at Odsal Stadium (1943), the knighting of Wavell Wakefield (1944) and the Kiwis played Victory internationals against England, Wales, France and Scotland (1945).
Twickenham damaged by bomb blast (1944).

1946 France took part in Five Nations Championship for first time since 1931.
The war-time concession which allowed Rugby Union and Rugby League players to play together whilst in the services, was extended to peace-time.
Overseas RFC in Malta and Alvsjo Aik RFC in Sweden founded.

1947 Australia toured British Isles, and met Barbarians for first time.

1948 Cardiff supplied 10 players for Wales against Scotland at Cardiff to set a British record.
Value of dropped goal reduced from 4 to 3 points.
Australia, New Zealand and South Africa joined International Board.
Chilean Rugby Federation and German Democratic Republic Rugby Union founded.
Chile started a club championship.
Australian Rugby Union founded.

1949 Four Home Unions set up permanent Tours Committee.
East Africa fielded a full representative XV for first time against a touring side, Cape Town University, in Nairobi.
Sweden played first international, against Denmark in Stockholm.
France beat Argentina in Buenos Aires.
Romania played internationals against Czechoslovakia and the German Democratic Republic.

1950 A record crowd of 75 500 watched Wales beat England at Twickenham.
Danish Rugby Football Union founded.
Michel Pomathios, of Agen, became first Frenchman to play for Barbarians.

1951 France beat England, their first victory at Twickham.
Lansdowne Road became permanent headquarters of Irish Rugby Union.
Universities of Oxford and Cambridge toured South Africa and Kenya.
FIRA announced plans for a European Cup.
Uruguay Rugby Union founded.

1952 Ireland undertook first overseas tour, to Argentina.
Fiji toured Australia.
Thailand toured England.
Hong Kong Rugby Union founded.
First match played in Israel, between Army XV and South African settlers, at Sarafend.

1953 Lewis Jones turned professional, joined Rugby League for a then record signing fee of £6000.
Australia toured South Africa.

1954 Fiji toured Australia and New Zealand.
France beat New Zealand for first time, in Paris.
St Luke's College Exeter became first club to top 1000 points in a season, scoring 1082 from 42 matches.
Yugoslavia Rugby Union founded.
Llanelli and Swansea toured Romania.

1955 Romania toured England and Wales.
Ngong Road ground in Nairobi opened with match between British Lions and East Africa.
Fiji toured Western Samoa.
Uganda Rugby Union founded.

1956 Universities of Oxford and Cambridge toured Argentina.
Italy played at Twickenham for first time, losing to a London Counties XV.
Danie Craven became president of the South African Rugby Board.
Morocco Rugby Federation and Poland Rugby Union founded.

1957 Romania played France for first time, in Bucharest.
Swansea played three matches in Italy.
England won Grand Slam.
Portuguese Rugby Federation founded.

1958 France undertook first major tour, to South Africa.
Overseas countries vote on International Board increased to two each.
South American Championships staged for first time, in Chile.
Sweden joined FIRA.

1959 France won Five Nations Championship outright for first time.
Under-soil heating installed at Murrayfield.
Thailand staged first club tournament, in Bangkok.
Jamaica Rugby Union founded and Bermuda Rugby Union re-founded.

1960 Scotland toured for first time, to South Africa.
Tonga played Maoris for first time, in Nuku'Alofa.
Romania beat France for first time, in Bucharest.

1961 France toured Australia and New Zealand.
Australia toured South Africa.
FIRA inaugurated European Cup for clubs.

1962 Béziers of France beat Grivitza of Romania in final of first European Clubs Cup.
Tours undertaken: Canada to British Isles, New Zealand to Australia, British Isles to South Africa.
The Bahamas Rugby Union founded.

1963 England made first tour, to New Zealand and Australia.
Brazilian Rugby Union founded.
South Pacific Games staged for first time, in Suva.
Andorra's first club formed.

1964 Wales made first tour, to South Africa.
Fiji undertook first tour, to Wales, France and Canada.
Yugoslavia joined FIRA.
Barbados Rugby Union.

1965 Argentina toured South Africa.
Canadian Rugby Union re-formed.

1966 A coach, John Robins, accompanied a British Lions team for first time, to Australia and New Zealand.
Soviet Union Rugby Union and Hawaii Rugby Union founded.
First Caribbean Championships staged, in Barbados.
International Board decreed standardised numbering of players.

1967 Colin Meads sent off, playing for New Zealand against Scotland at Murrayfield, 2 December 1967.
Cardiff became first club side to tour South Africa.
Switzerland's first club founded—CERN-Meyrin RFC.
Bulgarian Rugby Union founded.

1968 Asian Rugby Union and Paraguayan Rugby Union founded.
Replacements permitted in international matches.
South Africa toured France.
Australia toured Ireland and Scotland.
Wales toured Argentina.
Japan undertook first major tour, to Australia and New Zealand.

1969 Anti-apartheid demonstrations disrupted South Africa tour of British Isles.
Wales toured Australia, New Zealand and Fiji.
First Asian Championships staged, in Tokyo.
Clubs in Moscow, Kiev and Tblisi formed Soviet Union League.
Dubai Rugby Union founded.

1970 Rugby Football Union stage World Convention to help celebrate their centenary.
Scotland toured Australia.
Ireland toured Argentina.

1971 The Rugby Football Union celebrated centenary.
England toured Japan and Far East.
Try revalued at 4 points.
Tonga toured British Isles.
Swiss Rugby Union, Gulf Rugby Union, Gibraltar Rugby Union,

Indonesian Rugby Union and Israeli Rugby Union founded.

1972 England toured South Africa.
Scotland formed leagues.
Wales and Scotland refused to play Ireland because of terrorist threats.
Brazilian Rugby Association, Bahrain RFC, Mexican Rugby Union and Cayman RFC founded.
France beat England in last international to be played at Colombes.

1973 Scotland celebrated centenary.
Argentina toured Europe for first time.
Tonga Rugby Union celebrated Jubilee.
Romania toured Argentina.
First Pan Pacific Tournament staged in Hawaii.
Ivory Coast Federation and Luxembourg RFC founded.
France beat Scotland in first international to be staged at the new Parc des Princes, Paris.

1974 British Lions enjoyed most successful tour ever, winning 21 and drawing one of 22 matches in South Africa.
Wales beat Scotland in 100th international to be staged in Cardiff.
Tunisia joined FIRA.

1975 Mike Burton became first England player to be sent off in an international, against Australia in Brisbane.
Norman Sanson, of Scotland, became first neutral referee to handle internationals, South Africa v France.
World record crowd of 104 000 watched Scotland beat Wales at Murrayfield, 1 March 1975.
Brunei Rugby Union and USA Rugby Union founded.
Club formed in The Philippines.

1976 Australia played USA for first time, in Anaheim.
Ireland toured New Zealand and Fiji.
New Zealand toured Uruguay and Argentina.
Mauritius Rugby Union founded.

1977 New Zealand toured France and Italy.
USA toured England.
France toured Argentina.
Thailand played Scotland for first time, in Bangkok.

1978 New Zealand beat four home countries for first time on tour of British Isles.
France undertook first tours of Japan and Canada.
France admitted as full member of the International Board.
Slava Moscow toured Wales.
Celtic Vienna, Austria's only club formed.

1979 Argentina toured New Zealand.
Wales won Triple Crown for a fourth time in succession, a record.
New Zealand and South Africa experimented with 'sin-bins' for players sent off.
England toured Japan, Fiji and Tonga.

1980 Wales celebrated centenary.
Chile toured Europe.
International Junior Tournament staged in Tunis.

1981 Demonstrations interrupted South Africa tour of New Zealand: in USA the one international played was staged at an unpublicised venue.
Australia toured British Isles.
Scotland toured New Zealand.
Ireland toured South Africa.
England undertook first tour of Argentina.
The 100th University Match took place at Twickenham on 8 December 1981, when Cambridge beat Oxford 9–6 to lead in the series for the first time, 44–43 with 13 draws (*qv*).

1982 Argentina toured France.
Fiji toured England and Scotland.
Maoris toured Wales and Spain.

1983 Centenary Tournament played at Melrose, birthplace of Sevens: French Barbarians won.

INDEX

This index is in six sections to facilitate easy reference—(1) People, (2) Countries, (3) Clubs, (4) Competitions, (5) Venues, and (6) General. Page numbers in bold type are the chief reference to the particular subject. Because of pressure on space, not every item is recorded in the Index. Cross-reference to the main Index subject will indicate where the omitted item will be.

PEOPLE

A

Aarvold, Carl 20, 22
Abbott, Bunny 187
Adair, A H B 22
Addicot, Stan 233
Aguirre, Jean-Michel 212
Albaladejo, Pierre 30, 192, 212
Alcock, C W 237
Anderson, E 22
Andrew, Prince 86
Anne, Princess 207
Apelian-Beall, Barbara 192
Arigho, Jack 36
Aston, R L 223
Atkinson, Philip 231, 232

B

Bailey, C B 22
Baily, Eddie 208
Bainbridge, Steve 221
Bancroft, Jack 56
Bannerman, J Mac D 73
Barchanek, A 123
Barker, Norman 24
Barnard, Ian 54
Barnes, Ken 231
Barnes, Stuart 133
Barros, Neto 113
Basquet, Guy 30
Baxter, J 240
Beamish, Charles 188
Beattie, J 22
Beaumont, Bill 15, 25, 62
Bebb, Dewi 224
Bennett, Ben 153
Bennett, J S 113
Bennett, Neil 25
Bennett, N O 22
Bennett, Phil 52, 54, 56, 211, 212, 224, 225
Bennett, W E 113
Bergiers, Roy 55
Berry, Cliff 116
Bertranne, Roland 30, 63, 212
Bevan, John 52, 222
Biggar, Mike 23
Birkett, J G G 88, 89, 97
Bishop, David 54
Bishop, Paule Henry 113
Bishop, R C 113
Black, B H 22
Blair, P C B 91
Blair, Robbie 212
Blakiston, A F 102
Blanco, Serge 30
Bollesan, Marco 140
Bond, Tony 226
Bosch, Gerald 48, 210, 212
Botha, Naas 48, 192, 210, 212
Boyce, Jim 9
Brand, Gerry 48, 192, 213
Bratherton, D G 22
Brook, P W P 22
Brown, Gordon 224
Brown, J L 230
Brown, Mark 55
Browne, W F 22
Brownlie, Cyril 240
Bruce, Doug 39
Bruel, Michel 30
Bruzon 232
Buchanan, A W B 22
Buchanan, Iain 181
Buckley, Clive 161
Burgum, John 215
Burnett, W 237
Burnham, Barrie 118
Burton, G 214
Burton, Mike 244
Bush, D J 113
Bush, J L V 113
Bush, L K 113
Butler, A G 22
Butler, Eddie 221
Butler, Peter 16
Butterfield, Jeff 25
Byrne, J F 225
Byrne, Sean 36

C

Camberabero, Guy 212, 213
Camilleri, Chris 55
Campbell, Ollie 34, 36, 37, 204, 205, 210, 211, 212, 224
Campbell-Lamerton, Mike 224
Carmichael, Sandy 45, 72
Carpmael, Percy 237
Carroll, Daniel Brendan 189, 210
Castens, H H 190
Cazorla, Antoine 168
Cester, Elie 30
Chick, J S 22
Chorlton, A B 22
Churchill, John 55
Claassen, J T 74
Clarke, Don 39, 40, 70, 187, 210, 211, 212, 213
Clarke, Ian 187
Coates, V H M 94
Cobner, Terry 52
Cockburn, H D 22
Cole, John 10
Cole, J R 22
Coles, W E 22
Connell, Gordon 44
Cooke, G M 210, 213
Cornelsen, Greg 9, 11, 214
Cornhill, Ray 176
Cotton, Fran 25, 63
Cova, Renzo 140
Cove-Smith, Ronald 189
Coverdale, H 102
Cowey, B T V 22
Cranfield, T 22
Crauste, Michel 30, 64
Craven, Danie 242
Crighton, R E 22
Crole, G B 98
Cumberlege, B S 91, 102
Cusworth, Les 177

D

Dachtler, David 116
Daniel, Henry 168
Darrouy, Christian 30, 211
Dauga, Benoit 212
Dauga, Bernard 64
Davey, E C 22
David, Tommy 52, 55
Davies, Gerald 56, 76, 211
Davies, Huw (England) 46
Davies, Huw (Swansea) 193, 194
Davies, L J 22
Davies, Mervyn 52, 56, 58, 76, 224
Davies, S 22
Davies, Terry 225
Davies, V G 22
Davies, W E N 22
Davies, W J A 25
Davies, W R 22
Davis, Greg 9, 10, 59, 212
Davis, Mike 26
Davy, Eddie O'D 36
Dawes, John 52
de Coubertin, Baron Pierre 191
De Villiers, Dawie 49
Dean, G J 22

Dehez, J L 30
Diffley, Sean 237
Dingle, A J 94
Dinu, Constantin 156
Doherty, W D 93
Donald, D G 93
Donneau, Marcel 151
Dospital, Pierre 29
Dover, Dick 189
Dryburgh, Roy 49
du Plessis, Morne 51
du Preez, Frik 48, 49, 73, 212
Duckham, David 62, 222
Dudley-Jones, Robert 55
Dufau, Gerard 30
Duggan, Alan 35, 36, 211
Duggan, Willie 36
Dunkley, P E 22
Dunn, R W 22
Dupuy, Jean 30

E

Edwards, Gareth 44, 52, 56, 75, 211, 224
Edwards, Ross 54
Ella, Mark 178
Elliott, W I D 45
Ellis, Jan 49, 74, 212
Emyr, Arthur 194
Enevoldson, Peter 20
Engelbrecht, Jannie 49, 74
Esteve, Patrick 30
Evans, Bill 233, 235
Evans, Bob 234, 235
Evans, David 188
Evans, Eric 63
Evans, Geoff 55
Evans, Gwyn 52, 209, 210, 212
Evans, M H 22

F

Fabre, Michel 29
Faithful, C K T 22
Fay, Garrick 10
Fenwick, Steve 54, 56, 57
Finlay, Ninian Jamieson 189, 210
Fitzgerald, Ciaran 34
Flannigan, Colin 44
Forbes, Campbell 118
Fowler, John 176
Fowler,T G 91
Francis, E L 22
Fraser, Bernie 39
Freethy, Albert 240
Fuller, Harry 20
Fyfe, K C 22

G

Gadney, B C 188
Gainsford, J L 49, 74
Gatherer, Don 26
Gerber, David 227
Germishuys, Gerrie 212
Gerrard, R A 22
Gibbs, J C 22
Gibbs, Reggie 56, 214
Gibbs, T W 22
Gibson, Mike 35, 36, 37, 65, 209, 212, 213, 224
Going, Sid 39, 40, 70
Gould, Roger 204
Grace, Tom 35
Grace, W G 88
Graham, J 22
Graham-Jones, J 22
Gray, Steve 176
Greenwood, J E 90, 93

H

Haas, Martin 127
Haden, Andy 70
Hale, G 22
Hamilton-Hill, R 22
Hamilton-Wickes, R H 22
Hammett, E D G 102
Hammond, J 239
Harding, W R 101
Hardy, J C 22
Hare, Dusty 18, 26, 200, 210, 211
Haslett, L W 102
Hawthorne, Phil 9, 10, 192, 212
Heath, Edward 219
Heatlie, Barrie 48
Heeps, Rod 41, 210
Herdman, Jeff 55
Herrero, Bernard 29
Herring, D G 239
Hesford, Bob 210
Hewitt, Dave 225
Hewson, Allan 40, 210, 212, 214
Hignell, Alistair 18, 20
Hill, Andy 53
Hiller, Bob 25, 192, 213, 225
Himmer, Claus 127
Hindmarsh, John 9
Hindson, Ro 118
Hipwell, John 9, 10, 60
Hodson, C J 22
Hoffmann, Waldo 113
Holmes, Terry 52
Hopkins, Ray 52
Hopwood, D 49
Horsburgh, G B 22
Hosen, Roger 26
Hosie, Alan 159
Hudson, A 213
Hudson, G E C 22
Hughes, J L 113
Hughes, J R 113
Hughes, Ned 210, 213
Hughes, Thomas (author) 236
Humphries, Denis 231
Hunter, Jimmy 41, 210

I

Inocco, Frank 181
Irvine, Andy 44, 45, 71, 209, 211, 212, 213, 222, 223, 224, 225

J

Jacklind, G S 22
James, Carwyn 236
Jarrett, Keith 56
Jeavons, Nick 221
Jeeps, Dickie 224
Jeffery, John 235
Jenkins, Viv 55
Johansson, Torbjorn 167
John, Barry 52, 55, 213, 222, 224, 225
Johnson, Peter 9, 10, 59, 212
Johnston, D J B 22
Jones, A H 22
Jones, Ken 56, 76
Jones, Lewis 242
Jones, Martin 194
Jones, Mike 55
Jones, R 22
Jones, Steve 193

K

Karam, Joe 41, 210, 213
Keane, Moss 38, 67
Keen, Brian 113
Kemmling, Horst 127
Kemp, T A 22
Kennedy, Ken 36, 68
Kesic, Dragan 179
Kiernan, Mike 36
Kiernan, Tom 34, 35, 36, 67, 190, 212, 224
Kirkpatrick, Ian 39, 69
Kitching, A E 90
Knapp, E R 22
Knight, Peter 25
Konno, Shiggy 142
Krutzner, Eduard 123
Kyle, Jackie 36, 68

L

Laidlaw, Frank 45
Laird, H C C 22
Lakin, Bob 54
Lambert, D 26, 210, 212, 213
Landell, Dexter 127
Lane, Stuart 55
Latukefu, Uaisele 171
Lauder, Wilson 55
Leha, Tohi 208
Lenihan, Donal 221
Lewis, B R 91
Lewis, David 232
Lewis, Ian 231
Lewis, W T 22
Lind, H 22
Lindsay, G 214
Llewellyn, Willie 56, 213
Lloyd, John 52
Loane, Mark 10
Lochore, Brian 39
Loudoun-Shand, E G 93
Lowe, Cyril 26, 84–103, 138, 211, 239, 240

Luke, Mike 118
Lux, J-P 65

M

McBride, Willie John 36, 37, 66, 209, 218, 224, 225
McCormick, Fergie 212, 213
McCrae, Ian 44
McCreight, C C 22
McGeechan, Ian 224
McGill, Arthur 10
McGregor, Duncan 40, 213
McHarg, Alistair 45, 72
McKinney, Stuart 112
McLaren, Bill 44
McLauchlan, Ian 72, 224
McLean, Paul 9, 10, 60, 205, 211, 212, 213
McLeod, Hugh 73
Macleod, K G 96
McLoughlin, Gerry 221
McLoughlin, Ray 36
McRae, F M 22
McTavish, Spence 118
Mains, Laurie 213
Mair, Colin 212
Malan, G F 49
Marais, J F K 49, 74
Mare, D S 212
Mariani, Roberto 140
Maritz, Piet 48
Marriott, C J B 92
Martin, Allan 56
Masters, R P 22
Matthews, Phil 231
Mays, Ron 176
Meade, John 234
Meads, Colin 39, 69, 212, 213, 243
Mehl, Peter 127
Mellett, Norman 181
Melville, Nigel 221
Meredith, Bryn 56, 224
Merz, Jurgen 127
Millar, Sid 224
Miller, Tony 59, 213
Moloney, John 112
Monro, Charles John 237
Moore, D L 118
Moraes, Alberto 113
Mordt, Ray 181
Morgan, B H 22
Morgan, Cliff 56
Morgan, E T 97
Morgan, Peter 55
Morgenroth, Werner 127, 187
Moriarty, Richard 53, 194
Morley, Alan 26, 210
Morris, Dai 56
Morrison, Mark 239
Morrison, R W 22
Mourie, Graham 40, 226
Murphy, Noel 224
Mycock, J 22

N

Nash, David 52
Neary, Tony 25, 61, 212
Neild, W C 90
Nelson, J B 45
Nicod, Gerard 168
Niebauer, Skip 176
Norden, G C 22
Norton, Tane 39

O

O'Reilly, Tony 213, 222, 224
Obolensky, Prince Alexander 188, 241
Old, Alan 223
Olejnieczaic, J 154
Olsson, Kjell 167
Owen, Dicky 77

P

Paco, Alain 30
Paparemborde, Robert 29, 30, 64, 210
Parfitt, Ken 208
Park, J 22
Parker, Dai 55
Pask, Alun 224
Passaghia, Roberto 234
Pattison, H C 22
Pearce, Gary 205
Pearn, Alan 18
Pell, Arthur 236
Peregrine, T 189
Perkins, John 53
Petterson, Jorgen 167
Pienaar, L L 91
Pircalabescu, Georghi 156
Pomathios, Michel 242
Ponzi, Carlo 140
Porta, Hugo 107, 192, 207, 210, 212
Porter, G L 22
Poulton-Palmer, Ronnie 214
Powell, Jackie 48
Powell, Wick 22
Prat, Jean 65
Preece, Peter 26
Prescott, Robin 188
Preston, Rick 116
Price, Graham 56, 57, 76, 210, 224
Price, H L 22
Pridmore, C A 22
Prosser, Bob 10
Pullin, John 18, 25, 61
Pulsford, D 232, 234, 235

Q

Quaife, W G 88
Quinn, Jerry 36
Quittenton, Roger 215

R

Radic, Branko 179
Rafter, Mike 202
Ranfurly, Earl of 189
Ratu, Qele 208
Reason, John 236
Reeves, J S R 22
Reid, Charles 189
Reid, N 98
Rendell, Paul 177
Renwick, Jim 45, 46, 71, 212
Reynolds, G J 22
Reynolds, R U 22
Richards, David 52, 54
Richards, Maurice 56, 214
Ripley, Andy 17, 25
Rives, Jean-Pierre 26, 29, 64
Robbie, John 20
Robertson, Bruce 39, 69
Robertson, Ian 181
Roche, Chris 205
Rodaway, Alan 229, 234
Rogers, Budge 62
Rolf, Nils 167
Rollo, David 73
Romeu, Jean-Pierre 30, 211
Rose, Alan 55
Roux, F du T 75
Rowlands, Clive 52
Russell, C J 9
Russell-Roberts, F D 22
Rutherford, John 45
Rylands, J E 22

S

Sanson, Norman 244
Schapavalov, B 163
Schmitt, Hans-Joachim 127
Schubert, Gerhard 134
Scott, John 26, 38
Scott, R H 236
Seddon, R L 238
Sewell, E H D 93, 97
Shaw, G D 22
Shaw, Geoff 10
Shaw, Tony 60
Shehadie, Nick 61, 187
Shiel, David 44, 210
Simpson, F W 22
Sinclair, R P 22
Slattery, Fergus 36, 37, 66
Slemen, Mike 25
Sloane, Roger 127
Smith, Arthur 45
Smith, Ian 44, 210, 211, 214
Smith, Robert Sidney 113
Smith, Steve 25, 117, 221
Smyth, Dr T 239
Spanghero, Walter 64
Spence, L 22
Squire, C M 22
Squires, Peter 25
Stancevic, Nikola 179
Stegmann, J A 97
Steinthal, F E 93
Stewart, W A 44, 214
Storer, Dennis 176

Style, H B 22
Sugden, Mark 36
Symington, A W 90

T
Tallent, J A 22
Tanner, Haydn 213
Tarr, Don 241
Telfer, Jim 45, 220
Thom, D A 22
Thomas, H W 90
Thomas, John 55
Thomas, Kevin 55
Thomas, Malcolm 222
Thomas, R 22
Thomas, W A V 22
Thompson, C 22
Thorburn, Sandy (historian) 237
Thorne, C 90
Thornett, John 9, 59
Titley, Mark 54
Tobias, Errol 225
Tremain, Kel 39, 69
Truscott, A R 113
Truscott, M H 113
Twele, Robert 127

U
Ure, C McG 90

V
Van Altena, John 150
Van der Byl, Adriaan 237
Van Heerden, Izak 107
Van Jaarsveldt, Des 181
Vannier, Michel 30
Visagie, Piet 48, 49, 211, 213

W
Wakefield, Wavell 22, 63, 85, 241
Wallace, Billy 40, 210, 213
Ward, Tony 36, 37, 224
Waters, J A 22
Watkins, David 55
Watson, R W 22
Webb Ellis, William 236, 237
Webber, H S 22
West, Peter 13
Westhuizen, Johnny van der 48
Wheeler, Peter 62
Whinerary, Wilson 39, 70, 190
Whineray, W J 215
Will, J G 90
Williams, Bryan 39, 69
Williams, Brynmor 55
Williams, Colin 231
Williams, Denzil 77
Williams, Gareth 54, 55
Williams, Gwynfor 55
Williams, J J 223, 224
Williams, John 55
Williams, J P R 52, 55, 56, 75, 212, 224
Williams, Rev Rowland 236
Williams, Rhys 224
Williams, Robin 139
Wilson, A H 90
Wilson, L G 49, 75
Wilson, Stewart 40, 70, 211
Windon, Colin 10, 212
Winterbottom, Peter 46
Wodehouse, P G 94–5
Wood, Robert 231
Woolf, Mervyn 139
Wooller, W 22
Worton, J R B 22
Wright, G T 22
Wundram, Manfred 127
Wynne, A M 22

Y
Young, A T 102
Young, A W 22
Young, C A 22

COUNTRIES

A
Abu Dhabi **104**, 109, 126, 127, 145, 149, 156, 182
Andorra **104**, 243
Argentina 12, 27, 31, 37, 38, 41, 42, 46, 57, 58, **104–8**, 115, 116, 120–2, 132, 133, 140, 153, 157, 164, 165, 175, 181, 183, 184, 191, 192, 210, 216, 235, 237, 239, 241–4
AUSTRALIA **9–12**, 24–6, 28, 30, 31, 36, 37, 40–5, 48–51, 56, 57, 59–62, 81–3, 107, 120, 121, 132, 133, 140, 142, 162, 171, 176, 178, 181, 187, 189, 192, 209–14, 216–18, 222, 224, 225, 227, 237–44
Austria **108**, 244

B
Bahamas, The **108**, 121, 183, 243
Bahrain 42, 104, **108**, 119, 126, 127, 144, 145, 149, 156, 162, 176, 182, 244
Barbados **109**, 112, 183, 190, 243
Belgium **109–11**, 123, 125, 130, 131, 139, 140, 141, 150, 155, 157, 165, 167, 169, 173, 179, 241
Bermuda 109, **111–12**, 135, 142, 147, 173, 183, 240, 242
Botswana **112**
Brazil 107, 108, **112–16**, 122, 153, 175, 183, 184, 188, 241, 243, 244
British Isles 9, 10, 12, 40–3, 47–51, 58, 85, 120, 133, 144, 166, 171, 181, **218–25**
British Virgin Islands **116**
Brunei **116**, 133, 138, 161, 170, 184, 189, 244
Bulgaria **116–17**, 123, 124, 134, 135, 140, 157, 163, 179, 243

C
Cameroon **117**
Canada 27, 31, 42, 46, 57, 58, 107, 108, **117–21**, 140, 144, 152, 166, 178, 179, 185, 217, 237, 239, 241, 243, 244
Cayman Islands **121**, 244
Chile 107, 108, 115, 116, **121–2**, 153, 175, 183, 184, 188, **242–4**
Cook Islands **122**
Cyprus **122**, 127
Czechoslovakia 31, 110, 117, **122–4**, 125, 130, 134, 135, 140, 149, 151, 154, 157, 163, 165, 167, 169, 173, 179, 183, 230, 231, 235, 241, 242

D
Denmark 110, **124–5**, 134, 150–2, 154, 155, 167, 169, 173, 179, 183, 242
Dhahran 104, 109, **126**, 127, 145, 149, 156, 182
Dubai 104, 109, **126**, 127, 138, 145, 149, 156, 182, 243

E
East Africa 57, 144, 242
Ecuador **126**
Egypt **126**, 145, 149
ENGLAND 10, 12, **13–27**, 28, 30, 34, 36, 38, 40, 42, 43, 45, 46, 49, 56, 59, 61–9, 81–3, 85, 86, 93, 100, 101–3, 107, 113, 117–21, 132, 133, 136, 141–4, 151, 164, 166, 171, 176–8, 189–92, 210–17, 224, 236–44.

F
Fiji 10, 12, 27, 32, 37, 41, 42, 46, 57, 107, 120, **131–3**, 138, 140, 142, 143, 162, 170–2, 178, 184, 185, 191, 216, 217, 238, 240–3
Finland **133**, 168, 169
FRANCE 3, 9, 12, 26, **28–32**, 36, 37, 40–5, 48–51, 56, 57, 59, 63–5, 69–73, 81–3, 93, 101, 106, 107, 120, 122, 123, 130, 133, 134, 140–2, 145, 149, 150, 154, 155, 157–9, 163, 165, 173, 178, 180–3, 191, 192, 209–14, 216, 217, 226, 230, 235, 237–44
French Polynesia **134**, 162

G
German Dem. Republic 117, 123, 124, **134–5**, 154, 160, 163, 168, 242
Germany, Fed. Republic of 32, 110, 111, 123, 127–31, 140, 149, 151, 154, 155, 158, 163, 165, 168, 169, 173, 180, 183, 187, 230, 235, 239–41
Ghana **135**
Gibraltar **135**, 243

Guadeloupe 111, 112, **135**, 183
Guyana 112, **135**, 183

H

Hawaii **135–6**, 137, 138, 184, 243, 244
Hong Kong 27, 42, 46, 58, 105, 116, 119, 133, **136**, 137, 143, 144, 147, 149, 152, 166, 170, 176, 178, 184, 185, 242
Hungary **136**

I

India **136–7**, 240
Indonesia **137–8**, 142, 147, 162, 184, 185, 243
Iran **138**
Iraq **138**
IRELAND 3, 10, 12, 26–30, **32–8**, 40–2, 45, 49–51, 56, 59, 64–70, 73–7, 81–3, 86, 93, 100, 107, 111, 112, 133, 157, 160, 181, 189, 191, 192, 209–14, 216, 217, 224, 236–44
Israel **138–9**, 169, 242, 243
Italy 12, 27, 32, 41, 42, 107, 110, 117, 123, 130, 131, 133, **139–41**, 142, 143, 146, 149, 151, 154, 155, 160, 163, 165, 180, 181, 183, 191, 212, 216, 241, 242, 244
Ivory Coast 111, **141–2**, 168, 173, 244

J

Jamaica 112, 121, **142**, 183, 192, 242
Japan 12, 27, 32, 46, 58, 120, 133, 138, 141, **142–3**, 144, 147, 151, 162, 166, 170, 184, 185, 212, 239–41, 243, 244

K

Kenya **143–4**, 149, 161, 180, 181, 239, 240
Korea 42, 119, 138, 142, 143, **144**, 147, 152, 162, 166, 176, 185
Kuwait 104, 109, 126, 127, **145**, 182

L

La Réunion **145**, 148
Laos **145**
Lebanon 127, **145**
Liberia **145**
Luxembourg **145–6**, 169, 244

M

Madagascar 141, **146**
Malawi **146–7**, 240
Malaysia 137, 138, 142, 144, **147**, 162, 166, 184, 185
Malta **147**, 242
Martinique 112, **147**
Mauritius 146, **147–8**, 240, 244
Mexico **148**, 240, 241, 244
Morocco 32, 124, 130, 131, 141, **148–9**, 151, 154, 155, 160, 163, 165, 168, 169, 173, 180, 183, 242
Muscat 104, 109, 126, 127, 145, **149**, 156, 182

N

Netherlands 32, 46, 110, 124, 125, 130, 131, 134, 140, 142, **149–51**, 154, 155, 160, 165, 168, 173, 180, 183, 240, 241
New Caledonia **151**, 152, 172
NEW ZEALAND 9–12, 25, 26, 28, 31, 36, 37, **39–43**, 45, 46, 48–51, 56, 57, 60, 61, 65, 69–71, 73, 78, 81–3, 107, 120, 121, 132, 133, 141, 143, 160, 171, 172, 176, 178, 179, 181, 187, 189–92, 209–22, 224, 225, 226, 237–44
Nigeria **152**
Norway 125, **152**, 168

P

Papua New Guinea 119, 138, 144, 151, 152, 166, 179, 184
Paraguay 107, 108, 115, 116, 122, **152–3**, 175, 185, 243
Peru 107, 122, **153**, 175
Philippines, The **153**, 244
Poland 32, 124, 125, 131, 134, 140, 141, 149, 151, **153–4**, 155, 160, 163, 165, 168, 173, 180, 183, 240, 242
Portugal 125, 131, 141, 149, 151, 155, **154–6**, 160, 165, 168, 169, 173, 180, 183, 239, 241, 242

Q

Qatar 104, 109, 126, 149, **156**, 182

R

Romania 32, 41, 58, 107, 117, 124, 131, 135, 140, 141, 149, 151, 154, 155, **156–60**, 163, 165, 178, 180–3, 217, 240–4

S

Sabah **160–1**
Sarawak **161**
SCOTLAND 9–13, 25, 26, 28, 36–8, 40–3, **44–6**, 48, 49, 56, 61, 66, 67, 71–5, 77, 78–83, 97, 101, 107, 120, 128, 132, 133, 136, 143, 151, 159, 160, 170, 172, 187, 189, 191, 209–14, 216, 217, 220, 224, 236–44
Senegal 141, **161**
Seychelles **161**, 241
Sharjah 127, **161**, 182
Singapore 27, 42, 137, 138, 144, 147, 149, **161–2**, 166, 170, 176, 185
Solomon Islands 138, 142, 144, 147, **162**, 170–2, 184
SOUTH AFRICA 10, 12, 24–6, 28, 30, 31, 36–8, 40–5, **47–51**, 56, 57, 61, 62, 67, 72–6, 78, 79, 81–3, 85, 92, 93, 107, 115, 144, 176, 181, 189, 190, 192, 209–14, 216, 217, 222–5, 227, 230, 235–44
South America 49
Soviet Union 32, 117, 124, 131, 135, 141, 149, 154, 160, **162–3**, 167, 168, 180, 183, 229, 230, 231, 235, 241, 243
Spain 32, 42, 58, 106, 107, 110, 111, 124, 131, 141, 149, 151, 154, 155, 160, **163–6**, 168, 173, 180, 183, 216, 240, 241
Sri Lanka 27, 119, 137, 143, 144, 147, 152, 162, **166**, 179, 185, 240
St Lucia **161**
Swaziland **166**
Sweden 110, 111, 124, 125, 131, 135, 151, 152, 154, 156, 163, 165, **166–8**, 169, 180, 183, 241–3
Switzerland 110, 111, 124, 125, 131, 141, 146, 149, 155, **168–9**, 173, 180, 183, 243

T

Taiwan 143, **169–70**
Tanzania 144, 170
Thailand 46, 133, 137, 143, 149, 162, 166, **170**, 171, 184, 185, 239, 242–4
Tonga 12, 27, 46, 58, 120, 133, 137, 151, 162, **170–2**, 185, 240, 242–4
Trinidad & Tobago 111, 112, **172–3**, 183
Tunisia 111, 123–5, 131, 141, 149, 151, 154, 156, 165, 169, **173**, 180, 183, 244

U

Uganda 144, **173**, 242
Uruguay 107, 108, 115, 116, 122, 153, **173–5**, 183, 184, 188, 238, 241, 242, 244
US Virgin Islands **178**
USA 12, 31, 32, 42, 49, 50, 57, 117–21, 127, 140, 144, 160, 162, **175–8**, 181, 185, 191, 216, 217, 235, 237, 238, 240, 244

V

Venezuela **178**

W

WALES 10, 12, 26, 28–31, 36, 40–5, 49, 51, **52–8**, 62, 68, 69, 72, 73, 75–83, 85, 101, 107, 109, 120, 121, 130, 132, 133, 136, 143, 144, 160, 176, 178, 189, 209–14, 216, 217, 224, 225, 227, 229–34, 236–44
Wallis & Futuna **178**
Western Samoa 42, 119, 132, 133, 138, 152, 166, 172, **178–9**, 185, 241, 242

Y
Yugoslavia 32, 110, 111, 117, 124, 125, 131, 135, 141, 149, 151, 154, 160, 163, 165, 168, 169, 173, **179–80**, 183, 242, 243

Z
Zambia 144, 146, **180**
Zimbabwe 107, 141, 144, 146, 157, 176, 178, **180–1**

CLUBS

This section includes county, representative and combined sides

A
A Bagnerais 28
A Bayonnais 28
A Beglais 28
Abbey 16
Aberaeron 55
Aberavon 42, 53, 55, 58
Aberbargoed 234
Abercynon 55
Aberdeen GSFP 44
Abertillery 53, 55
Abertillery & Ebbw Vale 57
Aberystwyth 55
Academy 35
Aire sur Adour 31
Alberton 48
Aldershot Services 16
All Japan 27
Alnwick 17
Alsager 16
Amman United 53
Ammosal 48
Ampleforth 24
Army, The 100
AS Montferrand 28, 29
Aspatria 16
Athlone 35
Auckland 39, 42, 50
Australian Capital Territory 10, 11, 30, 36
Avon & Somerset Police 17
Aylesbury 16
Ayr 44

B
Baglan 53
Ballina 35
Ballinsloe 35
Ballymena 34, 35
Bandon 34
Barbarians, The 22, 36, 50, **225–7**
Basque XV 58
Bath 13, 17
Bay of Plenty 39, 41, 42, 50
Bective Rangers 33, 35
Bedford 13, 17, 18
Bedford Athletic 16
Bedford School 87
Bedfordshire 16
Bedwas 234
Bedworth 17
Berkshire 16
Beziers 28, 29
Biarritz 01 28
Birkenhead Park 13, 16
Birmingham 13
Blackheath 13, 16, 22, 100, 102
Blackrock College 33–5
Boland 50
Border 47, 49, 50
Bournemouth 16, 18
Bradford 13
Brakpan 48
Bridgend 53–7
Bridgwater & Albion 17
Bristol 13, 17, 18
Bristol Polytechnic 21
Bristol University 21
British Colleges 21
British Police 21
Brixham 42
Bromsgrove 17
Brothers 9
Broughton 44
Broughton Park 13
Brownhill CC 55
Buckinghamshire 16
Builth Wells 54
Buller 41
Burry Port 55

C
CA Brive 28
Caerleon 53
Caius College, Cambridge 91
Caldicot 24
Caldy 16
Camberley 17
Camborne 13, 16
Cambridge University 13, 19, 20, 22, 24, 27, 85, 87, 89, 91, 92, 96, 98
Cambridgeshire 16
Cambuslang 44
Camp Hill 17
Canterbury 9, 39, 42, 50
Canterbury-South Canterbury 42
Cape Colony 50
Cape Town University 235
Carcassonne 28
Cardiff 22, 42, 53–6, 58
Cardiff College 21, 53
Cardigan 55
Carmaux 28
Carnarvon 48
Carnegie College 21
Castille-Leon XV 58
Cheshire 14–16
Chesterfield 16, 17
CIYMS 34, 35
Clare College, Cambridge 90
Clifton 16
Clontarf 33, 35
Collegians 34, 35
Combined Midlands & East Midlands 24
Combined Provinces 37
Combined Services (SA) 50
Combined Universities 37
Connacht 35
Corinthians 35
Cork Constitution 34, 35
Cornwall 14–16, 215
Counties 39, 41, 42
Coventry 13, 17, 18
Coventry Welsh 17
Crawley 17
Crawshay's 31
Crewe & Alsager College 21
Cross Keys 53, 55
Cumberland 14
Cumbria 16
Currie 44
Cwm 234
Cwmllynfell 55
Cyfarthfa 234

D
Dalziel HSFP 44
Defence 48
Derby 17
Derbyshire 16
Devizes 16
Devon 14–16
Devon & Cornwall Police 16
Dolphin 34, 35
Dorset & Wiltshire 16
Downing College, Cambridge 90
Dulwich College 85, 87–9, 91
Dungannon 34, 35
Durban Collegians 48
Durham 14–16
Durham University 21

E
East Grinstead 17
East Midlands 14–16, 24, 50
East Wales 57
Eastern Counties 14–16
Eastern Free State 48, 50
Eastern Province 48, 50
Eastern Transvaal 48, 50
Eastern Union (USA) 50
Ebbw Vale 53–5
Edinburgh 44
Edinburgh Wanderers 23
Emmanuel College, Cambridge 22, 91
England B 27, 38
England Under 23s 27
England XV 27
English Colleges 21
English Students 27
Esher 17

Essex 16
Exeter 13, 16
Exeter University (formerly St Luke's College) 16, 21, 215

F
Falmouth 16
Far North 47, 48
FC Lourdais 28
FC Lyon 28
Fettesian-Lorettonians 87
France B 31, 44, 57
French Army 31
French Barbarians 31
French Police 31
French Regional XVs 31
French Selection 31
Fullerians 16
Fylde 13

G
Gala 44
Galway Town 35
Galwegians 35
Garryowen 34, 35
Gazelles 50
Glamorgan 9
Glamorgan Wanderers 53, 55
Glasgow Academicals 44
Gloucester 13, 17, 18
Gloucestershire 14–16
Glyncorrwg 53
Glynneath 53
Gold Cup XV 36, 38
Gordon League 16
Gordonians 44
Gosforth 13, 17, 18, 24
Gowerton 55
Grangemouth 44
Greenock Wanderers 44
Griqualand West 47–50
Guildford & Godalming 17
Guy's Hospital 13, 21
Gwent 57

H
Haddington 44
Halifax 13
Hampshire 14–16
Hanan Shield Districts 42
Harlequins 13, 17, 18, 22–4
Harrogate 13, 17
Hartlepool Rovers 13, 16
Havant 16
Haverfordwest 55
Hawick 23, 44
Hawke's Bay 41, 42
Headingley 13, 17
Hedl-y-Cyw 53
Henley 17
Heriot's FP 22, 44
Hertford 16
Hertfordshire 16
High Wycombe 16
Highfield 34
Hillhead GSFP 101
Hinckley 17
Huddersfield 13
Hull & East Riding 13

I
Instonians 34, 35
International Sportswriters 55
Ipswich 16
Ireland B 27, 38
Italian Under 23s 27
Italy B 27

J
Japan B 27
Jesus College, Cambridge 90
Johannesburg Reef & Country 50
Johannesburg Wanderers 235
Jordanhill College 21
Jourdain, L'Isle 230
Junior Springboks 50

K
Kansai Provinces 27
KCS Old Boys 17
Kelso 44
Kent 14, 16
Kettering 16
Keynsham 17
Kilmarnock 44
King Country-Wanganui 42
King's College Hospital 21
King's College, Cambridge 90, 91
Knock 34
Kyushu Provinces 27

L
La Tablada 234
La Voulte 28
Lampeter 55
Lancashire 14–16
Lancashire & Cheshire 24
Langholm 44
Lansdowne 32–5
Launceston 16
Leeds Polytechnic 21
Leicester 13, 18, 55
Leicestershire 14, 17
Leicestershire & East Midlands 24
Leinster 35, 42
Lenzie 44
Lewes 17
Lezignan 28
Lichfield 17
Limerick Bohemians 34, 35
Lincoln 17
Lincolnshire 17
Linlithgow 44
Lisburn 34, 35
L'Isle Jourdain 230
Lismore 44
Liverpool 13, 16, 89
Llandovery 55
Llanelli 42, 53–5, 57, 58, 230, 231
Llantrisant 53
Llanybydder 55
London Counties 24, 50
London Irish 13, 17, 18
London Scottish 13, 17, 18, 22–4
London Welsh 13, 18, 22–4, 53
Loughborough Colleges 22–4
Loughborough Students 17
Loughborough University 21
Lydney 16
Lyon OU 28

M
Machen 234
Madeley College 21
Maesteg 42, 53, 55, 58
Maesycwmmer 234
Maidenhead 16
Malone 34, 35
Manawatu 11, 39, 42, 50
Manchester 13
Maoris 10, 42, 50, 57, 58
Marlborough 39, 42
Marlborough-Buller-Nelson-West Coast XV 42
Marlow 16
Matson 16
Mazamet 28
Melrose 44
Metropolitan Police 13, 17, 22
Mid-Canterbury 42
Mid-Western (USA) 50
Middlesbrough 13
Middlesex 14, 15, 17
Middlesex Hospital 21, 22
Midland Counties 25
Midland Counties West 25
Midland Division 25, 27
Midlands 14
Millfield School 24
Moderns 17
Monkstown 33, 35
Monmouthshire 42, 58
Mont de Marsan 28
Montauban 28
Montchanin 29
Morley 13, 42
Moseley 13, 17, 18
Mountain Ash 54
Munster 35, 37
Musselburgh 44

N
Nantyglo 53
Narberth 55
Natal 49, 50, 235
Neath 53–5
Nelson Bays 50
Nelson-West Coast-Buller-Golden Bay XV 42
New Brighton 13, 16
New South Wales 9, 10, 11, 12, 26, 50

New Zealand Universities 27, 43
Newark 17
Newbold on Avon 17
Newbridge 53, 55
Newbury 16
Newcastle Emlyn 55
Newport 50, 53–5, 57, 233, 234
Newquay Hotel 55
Nice 28
NIFC 34, 35
Norfolk 17
North & West Transvaal 50
North Auckland 39, 41, 42, 50
North East Counties 25, 215
North Eastern Cape 48, 49
North Island 39
North Midlands 14, 15, 17
North Otago 43
North West Counties 25
North Western 48
North Western Cape 49
Northampton 13, 23
Northern 13, 17
Northern Counties 25
Northern Division 25, 27
Northern Free State 48, 50
Northern New South Wales 41
Northern Provinces 50
Northern Transvaal 47, 48, 51
Northern Universities 51
Northumberland 14, 15, 17
Norwich 16, 17
Nottingham 13, 17, 18, 22
Nottinghamshire 17
Notts, Lincs & Derbyshire 17
Nuneaton 13

O

OCTU Sandhurst 22
Old Alleynians 87, 88
Old Baileans 17
Old Belvedere 33, 35
Old Merchant Taylors 22
Old Millhillians 55
Old Wesley 33, 35
Oloron 31
Orange Free State 47, 48, 51
Orange Free State Country 51
Orrell 13, 16
Otago 41, 43, 50, 56
Oxford 17
Oxford University 13, 19, 20, 25, 50, 85, 91, 96, 98
Oxfordshire 17

P

Palmerston 35
Paris Olympique 28
Pau 28
Paviors 17
Pembroke College, Cambridge 88–91
Penarth 53–5
Penryn 16
Penzance & Newlyn 16
Peterborough 16
Plymouth Albion 13, 16
Polytechnic of Wales 21
Pontypool 53–5, 57
Pontypool United 53
Pontypool, Newbridge & Cross Keys 57
Pontypridd 53, 55
Portobello 44
Poverty Bay 50
President's Trophy XV 38
Pretoria 51
Pretoria Harlequins 48, 235
Pretoria University 48
Public School Wanderers 23, 24, 55

Q

Queen's College 34
Queen's College Galway 35
Queen's University Belfast 34, 35
Queensland 9, 10, 11, 49

R

Racing Club de France 28, 29
RAF 22, 24, 100
RAF Jurby 22
Randwick 9
RC Narbonne 28, 29
RC Toulon 28
RCMS Shrivenham 16
Reading 16
Redruth 16
REME Arborfield 16
Rhydyfelin 53
Rhymney **228–35**
Richmond 13, 22–4, 87
Rosslyn Park 13, 17, 22–4, 87, 100
Roundhay 13, 17
Royal HSFP 44
Royal Navy 24
Rugby 13
Rumney 53

S

St Bartholomew's Hospital 21, 22
St George's Hospital 21
St Ives 13, 16
St Luke's College 16, 22
St Mary's College 231
St Mary's College (Ire) 33–5
St Mary's Hospital 21, 22
St Mary's Liverpool 24
St Medard 29
St Paul's College 21
St Paul's School 87
St Thomas's Hospital 21, 22
Sale 13, 16, 22
Salisbury 16
Saracens 13, 17, 22
Scotland B 31, 45
Scottish Colleges 21
SCUF 28
Scunthorpe 17
Seddon Shield Districts 43
Selkirk 44
Shannon 35
Sheffield 13
Shelford 16
Slava Moscow 229, 231, 235
Slava Prague 235
Sligo Town 35
Solarians 55
Solihull 17
Somerset 14, 17
South & South West Counties 25, 27
South Africa Country XV 38
South African Country XV 51
South African Gazelles 38
South African Invitation XV 51
South African Mining XV 38
South African President's XV 36
South Australia 10, 41
South Canterbury 41, 43, 50
South Canterbury-North Otago 43
South District (Scot) 44
South East Transvaal 48
South Glamorgan Institute 21, 53, 55
South Island 39
South of Scotland 42
South Wales Police 53
South West Africa 48
South West Counties 25
South West Districts 30
South West France 31, 50
South Western Districts (SA) 48
Southend 16
Southland 41, 43, 50
Spain B 42
Spain Under 23s 58
Stade Bordelais 28
Stade Francais 28
Stade Tarbais 28
Stade Toulousain 28
Staffordshire 15, 17
Stamford 17
Steepholme 55
Stellaland 49
Stellenbosch University 48
Stewart's College FP 23
Stewart's-Melville FP 23, 24
Stirling County 44
Stoke Old Boys 17
Stourbridge 17
Streatham-Croydon 17
Stroud 16
Sudbury 17
Suffolk 17
Sunday's Well 34, 35
Surrey 14, 15, 17, 215
Sussex 17
Swansea 42, 53–5, 57, 58, 233
Sydney 10, 11
Sydney University 9

T

Tabard 16
Tablada, La 234
Taranaki 9, 11, 39, 43, 50
Tenby 55
Terenure College 33, 35
Thames Valley 43
The Army 24
The London Hospital 21, 22
Thurrock 16
Tondu 53
Torquay Athletic 16
Transvaal 47, 48, 51
Tredegar 53, 55
Tregaron 55
Trimsaran 55
Trinity College Dublin 33, 35
Trinity Hall, Cambridge 91

U

Uddingston 44
Ulster 35, 42
University College Cork 34, 35
University College Dublin 33, 35
University College Galway 35
University College Hospital 21
University College Swansea 53
US Agen 28
US Dax 28
US Perpignan 28
US Portsmouth 16
US Quillan 28
UWIST 21

V

Valencia Select XV 58
Victoria (Aus) 10, 36
Villagers 48
Vipers 17
Voyagers 55

W

Waikato 39, 41, 43, 50
Wairarapa 9
Wairarapa-Bush 43
Wakefield 13, 17
Wales B 31, 57
Wales XV 58
Walsall 17
Wanderers 33–5
Wanganui 43, 50
Waratahs 57
Warwickshire 14, 15, 17
Wasps 13, 17, 22
Waterloo 13, 16, 18
Wellington 39, 41–3, 50
Wellington (S Afr) 235
Wellington-Wairarapa-Horowhena 43
Welsh Academicals 55
Welsh Colleges 21
Welsh Guards 22
West Coast-Buller 43
West France 50
West Hartlepool 13, 16, 18
West Midlands 25
West of Scotland 101
Western Australia 10, 25, 26
Western Counties 25
Western Districts 10
Western Prov. Juniors 48
Western Prov. Town & Country 51
Western Prov. Universities 51
Western Prov., SW Dist & Boland 51
Western Province 51
Western Province Country 51
Western Province Town 51
Western Transvaal 30, 47, 51
Westleigh 17
Westminster Hospital 21, 22
Weston-super-Mare 17
Widnes 16
Wigston 17
Wigton 16
Williston 48
Wilmslow 13
Wimborne 16
Winchester 16
Witwatersrand 51
Woodford 16
Worthing 17

Y

Yorkshire 14, 15, 17
Young Munster 34
Ystralyfera 54

COMPETITIONS

A

Aberaeron Sevens **55**
All India Tournament 240
Asian Championships **185**
Australian State Championship 9

B

Bledisloe Cup 9
Brisbane Grand Final 9
British Colleges Cup **21**
British Polytechnics Cup **21**

C

Calcutta Cup 238
Caribbean Tournament **183**
Chilean Club Championship 242
Connacht Senior Cup **35**
County Championship **14–16**, 239
County Cup winners **16–17**
Currie Cup **47–8**

E

European Cup 243

F

FIRA Championships **182–3**
French Club Championship **28–9**

G

Gold Cup **48**
Grand Slam, The 85
Gulf League 104, 182

H

Hong Kong Sevens 42, 116, 143, 144, 178, **184–5**
Hospitals' Cup **21–2**, 238

I

Inter-Services Championship **24**
International Championship, The 29, 30, 36–8, 44, 46, 56, **82–3**, 85, 238, 243
Irish Provincial Championship **35**

J

John Player Cup **17–18**

L

Leinster Senior Cup **33–4**

M

Madras Gymkhana Cup 239
Middlesex Sevens **22–4**
Monmouthshire League 234
Munster Senior Cup **34–5**

N

NZ National Championship **39**
NZ National Sevens **39**

P

Pacific Tournament **185**
Pan Pacific Tournament 244
President's Cup **48**

R

Ranfurly Shield **39**, 189
Rosslyn Park Schools Sevens **24**

S

Schweppes Welsh Cup **53–4**
Scottish Border League **44**
Scottish Club Championship **44**
Scottish Inter-District **44**
Snelling Sevens **54–5**
South Africa Club Championship **48**
South American Championships **183–4**, 243
South Pacific Games 243
Soviet Union Championship 241
Sport Pienaar Trophy **48**
Sydney Premiership 9

T

Thailand Championship 243
Trans Tasman Cup 11

U

UAU **21**
Ulster Senior Cup **34**

University Match, The 18, **19–20**, 85, 86, 237

W
Welsh Brewers Cup **53**
Welsh Club champions **55**
Welsh Counties Cup **53**
Welsh National Sevens **53**

VENUES

A
Aberavon 53, 57
Adelaide 10
Agen 32
Aguila 32
Albany 50
Albi 32
Angouleme 31, 32
Annaheim 12
Aquila 12
Auckland 11, 41, 42, 50
Aurillac 31

B
Ba (Fiji) 238
Bangkok 46
Barbados 243
Barcelona 32, 42
Barna 32
Bath 14, 25
Bayonne 31, 32
Beeshoek 48
Belfast 37
Berlin 32
Besancon 32
Bethlehem 50
Beziers 32
Bilbao 58
Birkenhead 189
Birkenhead Park 14, 15
Birmingham 14
Blackheath 14, 19, 188, 238
Blaydon 14
Bloemfontein 50
Blundellsands 14, 15, 24, 25
Boerbok Park 48
Bombay 240
Bordeaux 31, 32
Boscombe 14
Bourg-en-Bresse 31, 32, 57
Bradford 14, 239
Breschia 32
Bridgwater 14
Brisbane 12, 49
Bristol 14, 15, 25
Bucharest 32
Buenos Aires 12, 27, 31, 37, 42, 57, 237
Bully 32
Burnaby 42
Burton-on-Trent 15

C
Calcutta 238
Calgary 31
Camborne 25
Cambridge 14, 19, 20, 24
Cambridge, Mass. 237
Cape Town 38, 237
Carcassonne 32
Cardiff 57, 238
Cardiff Arms Park 29, 53, 59–81
Carlisle 14
Casablanca 32
Catonia 32
Centaurs RFC 21
Chambery 32
Cheltenham 21
Chicago 32
Christchurch 11, 41, 50
Clermont-Ferrand 31
Colombes, Stade 239, 240
Colombo 27
Constanta 32
Cork 37, 238
Coventry 14, 15, 25
Cradock 49
Czestochova 32

D
Dax 31
Devonport 14
Dubbo 10
Dublin 100
Dundee 31, 45
Dunedin 11, 41, 42, 50
Durban 38, 49
Durham 15

E
East London 38, 49

G
Galashiels 42
Geneva 239
Gijon 58
Gisborne 50
Glasgow 237
Glenville 50
Gloucester 14, 15
Gosforth 14, 25
Grenoble 31, 32

H
Hagondage 32
Hague, The 241
Hamilton 11, 41
Headingley 14
Heidelberg 32
Hendaye 32
Hilversum 32, 46
Hong Kong 27, 46, 58
Honor Oak Park 241

I
Invercargill 11, 41, 50
Inverleith 240

J
Johannesburg 10, 47

K
Kidwelly 53
Kimberley 49

L
La Rochelle 31, 32
Lansdowne Road 29, 32, 33, 37, 38, 42, 59–81
Leeds 42
Leicester 14, 24, 25, 191, 240
Liberec 31
Lichtenburg 49
Lille 32
Limerick 37
Limoges 31, 32
Llanelli 57
Lodz 32
Long Beach, Cal. 57
Lourdes 57
Lyon 31, 32

M
Madrid 32, 42, 58, 241
Manchester 238
Mantua 27
Marmande 32
Marsiglia 32
Masterton 9
Mauleon 32
Melbourne 10, 12
Melrose 238
Menton 237
Merignac 32
Milan 12, 32
Montauban 32
Montevideo 49
Moscow 31, 32, 231
Moseley 15, 25
Murrayfield 44, 46, 48, 59–81, 240

N
Nairobi 57, 242
Nantes 32, 57
Napier 11, 41, 50
Naples 32
Narbonne 31
Neath 9, 57, 238
Nelson 50, 237
New Plymouth 11, 41, 50
Newcastle 14, 25
Newcastle (SA) 49
Newport 58
Neyland 53
Nice 32
Northampton 14
Nuku' Alofa 27

O
Odsal Stadium 241
Oloron 32
Osaka 27, 58
Otley 25
Oudtshoorn 38
Oval, The 19, 87, 238
Oxford 19, 20, 25

P
Padua 27, 32
Palmerston North 11, 41, 50
Parc des Princes 29, 59–81, 239, 240
Paris 31, 32, 57
Parks, The 237
Parma 32
Pau 32
Perpignan 31
Perth 10
Plymouth 15
Pontypool 31, 57
Port Elizabeth 49, 51, 239
Potchefstroom 38, 49
Prague 31, 32, 239
Pretoria 38, 47–50
Pukekohe 11, 41

Q
Queen's Club 19

R
Racine 50
Raeburn Place 237, 238
Ravenhill 27, 38, 42
Redruth 14, 15
Richardson's Field, Blackheath 238
Richmond 14, 15
Richmond Green 237
Rome 32, 42
Rotorua 11, 41, 50
Rouen 57
Rovigo 32
Rugby School 238

S
San Francisco 42
Sarafend 242
Singapore 27
Split 32
Stockholm 242
Strasbourg 31
Suva 12, 27, 32, 37, 42, 57, 240, 243
Sydney 9, 10, 11, 12

T
Tarbres 31, 32
Timaru 11, 41, 50
Tokyo 27, 32, 46, 58
Toronto 57, 237
Toulon 32
Toulouse 31, 32, 57
Treviso 27, 32
Twickenham 13–15, 19, 20, 24–7, 46, 59–81, 86, 92, 239–44

U
Upington 49

V
Vale of Lune 15
Valence 31
Valencia 32, 58
Valladolid 58
Vancouver 27, 57

W
Wanganui 50
Warsaw 32
Welkom 50
Wellington 11, 38, 41, 42, 50
Wembley Stadium 188
West Hartlepool 14
Weston-super-Mare 14
Westport 11, 41
Whangarei 11, 41, 50
Workington 25

GENERAL

A
Alcock, C W (editor) 237
American Football 238
Association Football 85
Attendances 9, 18, 29
Australia v England **59**
Australia v France **59**
Australia v Ireland **59–60**
Australia v New Zealand **60–1**
Australia v Scotland **61**
Australia v South Africa **61–2**
Australia v Wales **62**

B
BBC (publishers) 236
Blues 238
Broken Time Dispute 239
Bystander, The 98

C
Cambridge Rules, The 236
Centenaries 9, 228–35
Chronology **236–44**
Coaches, coaching 26, 47, 52

D
Daily Express 88
Daily Mail 101
Daily Telegraph, The 98, 100, 101
Devon Referees Society 215
Diffley, Sean (author) 237
Dublin Daily Express 237

E
England v France **63**
England v Ireland **64–5**
England v New Zealand **65**
England v Scotland **66–7**
England v South Africa **67**
England v Wales **68–9**
Expenses, match 238

F
First World War 86
Floodlights 238
Football Association, The 236
France v Ireland **69–70**
France v New Zealand **70–1**
France v Scotland **71–2**
France v South Africa **72**
France v Wales **72–3**

G
Grand Slam 82

H
History of Scottish Rugby, The 237
Honours, Awards 15, 241
Hughes, Thomas (author) 236

I
International Board 238
International Board Matches **81–3**
Ireland v New Zealand **73–4**
Ireland v Scotland **74–5**
Ireland v South Africa **75–6**
Ireland v Wales **76–7**

J
James, Carwyn (author) 236
Jersey numbering 239

L
Laws, The, Rules etc 236–8
Leading Cap Winners **59–77**
Lillywhite's Football Annual 237
London Gazette 99
London Opinion 93

M
Men in Green, The 237
Morning Post, The 87, 89, 91

N
New Zealand v Scotland **77–8**
New Zealand v South Africa **78**
New Zealand v Wales **78–9**
North Midlands Referees Soc 215
Northern Union 239

P
Pall Mall Gazette 96
Player of the Year 52
Points scoring, values 238
Professionalism 239

R
RAF 86
Records 209–14

Red Arrows, The 86
Referees 47, 215, 238, 244
Replacements 243
Royal Flying Corps 86
Rugby League, The 239
Rugby School 236

S

Scotland v South Africa **79**
Scotland v Wales **79–81**
Seasons, close 238
Sin bins 244
South Africa v Wales **81**
Sportsman, The 89
Springbok Head **50**
Star, The 87

T

Tag Rugby 186
Television 13, 44
The Times 87, 91, 96, 100
Tom Brown's Schooldays 236
Tours 9, 11, 12, 24–7, 31, 36–8, 41–3, 46, 48, 49, 56–8, **216–27**
Triple Crown 82

W

Welsh Rugby Writers Club 52
Women's Ruby 192
World of Rugby, The 236